Soviet Trade Unions and Labor Relations

Soviet Trade Unions and Labor Relations

Emily Clark Brown

Emily Clark Brown is Professor Emeritus of
Economics, Vassar College.

HARVARD UNIVERSITY PRESS
Cambridge, Massachusetts
1966

TO THE MEMORY OF

H.A.M.

Preface

MY curiosity about labor relations in the Soviet Union came out of long study of American trade unions, labor relations, and national labor policy, and the teaching of courses on labor and comparative economic systems. In 1954 several experts on Soviet labor encouraged my idea of seeking an on-the-spot investigation. Effort to obtain a Soviet visa led finally, after the Geneva conference of 1955, to a five-week trip. In 1959 it was possible to visit the Soviet Union for ten weeks, and in 1962 for six weeks.

I am grateful to Vassar College for the Faculty Fellowship that made possible the 1955 trip; to the Social Science Research Council for a grant, supplemented by one from the Inter-University Study of Labor Problems in Economic Development, which financed the 1959 trip, and to the American Council of Learned Societies for a grant for the 1962 trip. My debts to other workers in the field are great: especially to Professor Abram Bergson of Harvard University, the late Professor Alexander Baykov and Mr. G. R. Barker of the University of Birmingham, and the late Jerzy Gliksman of the RAND Corporation, all of whom encouraged me at the start; to Dr. Solomon M. Schwarz, who has given me the benefit of his long experience in the field; and to two fellow workers on Soviet labor, Professors Warren W. Eason of Syracuse University and Edwin B. Morrell of Brigham Young University, both of whom have been generous with ideas and materials. Thanks are due also Professors Frederick H. Harbison of Princeton University, Charles

A. Myers of Massachusetts Institute of Technology, and John T. Dunlop of Harvard University, from the Inter-University Study of Labor Problems in Economic Development, and Professors Walter Galenson of the University of California and M. Gardner Clark of Cornell University, for helpful criticisms and suggestions.

Many Soviet citizens helped to make my visits fruitful—among them economists, labor law experts, officers and workers of the unions at national and regional levels, and administrators and union leaders in many plants. The Society for Cultural Relations with Foreign Countries arranged many contacts in 1955 and 1959, and their affiliate, the Institute of Soviet-American Relations, was helpful in 1962. Several efficient and interested Intourist guides and interpreters contributed substantially to the pleasure and value of the trips.

This book draws on earlier published articles. I am grateful to the editors for permission to use material from *Industrial and Labor Relations Review*: "The Soviet Labor Market," January 1957; "Labor Relations in Soviet Factories," January 1958; "The Local Union in Soviet Industry," January 1960; and "The Interests and Rights of Soviet Workers and the Resolution of Conflicts," January 1963; and from *Soviet Studies*, "A Note on Employment and Unemployment in the Soviet Union in the Light of Technical Progress," January 1961. Parts of Chapter II were published in Marshall Goldman, *Comparative Economic Systems* (Random House, New York, 1964), and are used with permission; Chapter II appears also in Morris Bornstein and Daniel R. Fusfeld, *The Soviet Economy: A Book of Readings* (Richard D. Irwin, Inc., Homewood, Illinois, 1966).

My sister, Helen A. Brown, has helped greatly in improving the form and readability of the text.

For all the help I have had I am grateful, but I alone must bear the responsibility for any errors in fact or interpretation.

Emily Clark Brown

Minneapolis, Minnesota
December 1965

Contents

Soviet Trade Unions
and Labor Relations

BPA	*Bibliotechka profsoyuznovo aktivista* (Little Library of the Trade Union Activist), Moscow, Central Council of Trade Unions.
CCTU	VTsSPS, All-Union Central Council of Trade Unions.
CDSP	*Current Digest of the Soviet Press,* New York, Joint Committee on Slavic Studies.
CPSU	Communist Party of the Soviet Union.
Gosplan	State Planning Committee.
Izvestia	(News), Moscow, newspaper of the government.
Komsomol	Young Communist League.
Orgnabor	Administration for the Organized Recruitment of Workers.
Pravda	(Truth), Moscow, newspaper of the CPSU.
RSFSR	Russian Soviet Federated Socialist Republic.
SGP	*Sovetskoe Gosudarstvo i Pravo* (Soviet State and Law), Moscow, Institute of State and Law.
Sovnarkhoz	Regional Economic Council.
Sovprof	Regional Trade Union Council.
SP	*Sovetskie Profsoyuzy* (Soviet Trade Unions), Moscow, Central Council of Trade Unions.
ST	*Sotsialisticheskii Trud* (Socialist Labor), Moscow, State Committee of the Council of Ministers on Questions of Labor and Wages.
Trud	(Labor), Moscow, daily newspaper of Central Council of Trade Unions.
TZP	*Trud i Zarabotnaya Plata* (Labor and Wages), Moscow, State Committee on Questions of Labor and Wages.
USSR	Union of Soviet Socialist Republics.
VE	*Voprosy Ekonomiki* (Questions of Economics), Moscow, Institute of Economics.

CHAPTER I

The Political
and Economic Setting

IN the West it is believed by many that Soviet trade unions have so little in common with traditional trade unions that they should not be given the name. The Soviet view is seen in Premier Khrushchev's statement in 1957, "Not a single event of any importance in the life of our country takes place without their active participation."[1] His successors continued to assert "the great role" of the unions. In 1963 the unions claimed a membership of 68 million, including 94 per cent of all wage and salary workers.[2]

What, then, is the nature of this huge union structure and what is its role? Is it a facade for control over the workers? Is it an agent to carry out policies of the Communist Party and the government? Does it represent workers and protect their interests and rights? Are these unions in any sense "real trade unions" according to the classic definition, "a continuous association of wage earners for the purpose of maintaining and improving the conditions of their working lives"?[3]

An intelligent young woman, chairman of a shop committee in a big textile plant, voiced the skepticism shown by many Soviet citizens toward the foreign economist who was venturing to write about their unions. "It would take more than one book to describe the activities of our unions," she said, "And will you be able to describe our work accurately and honestly?"

Another industrial worker, met over dinner in a hotel, asked, "Will you write honestly? American writers have misrepresented us and our unions."

The aim of this book is to describe and appraise Soviet unions and industrial relations in their own political and economic setting, with emphasis on developments in industry since Stalin's death. The analysis is not concerned with the desirability of one or another social system, or with what "real trade unions" are or ought to be. It does not assume that human dignity, individual freedom, and equality of opportunity are, inevitably, the monopoly of any one system.

Several essentials in the political and economic setting are basic to the nature of Soviet unions and labor relations. First is the fact of domination by the Communist Party. All major trade union, as well as all governmental policies, are determined by the party, and especially by the small group of its leaders in the presidium or executive committee of its central committee. Key figures in industrial administration and in the unions, as in all aspects of Soviet society, are communists. Party members in 1963 numbered more than ten million; or (in 1961) about seven per cent of all adults aged twenty years and over.[4] Their influence extends into every corner of Soviet life.

Second is the centrally planned and controlled economy, which conditions all labor relations. Since the start of the five-year plans late in the 1920's, national economic plans have been adopted by the USSR Council of Ministers (earlier called the Council of People's Commissars) and the Supreme Soviet, the elected legislative body, after being worked out by Gosplan, the State Planning Committee.[5] These plans, determining the direction of industrial development and the distribution of resources among all needs, are carried out through the state agencies that manage government-owned enterprises and regulate and administer other wide-ranging activities from the level of the local soviets to that of the republic and national governments. Other laws and regulations control most aspects of industrial life, including labor relations. Economic plans for the enterprise have the force of law, after being negotiated and adjusted up and down the line from the enterprise to regional, republic, and national authorities, and finally approved.[6]

Many changes in the balance between centralized control and decentralized decisions in the management of industry have affected labor relations. In 1957, in a shift from control by central industrial ministries, the government set up some one hundred regional economic councils, the *sovnarkhozy*, to administer industry, as the main link between the enterprise and the government in most industries. In the republics, planning agencies and the councils of ministers also received increased powers. In 1962-1963 came a turn toward more centralization; small economic regions were combined and the number of sovnarkhozy reduced to less than fifty, to increase efficiency in planning and administration; for a number of major industries central state committees were established, attached to Gosplan or to the Council of Ministers. In 1964-1965, after several years of public discussion over widening the scope of decisions by enterprises and improving incentives for management, radical changes in methods of planning and administration were forecast.[7]

A third influence on Soviet labor relations is the rapid rate of industrial growth. The drive for industrialization transformed an agricultural country into the second industrial power in the world. By 1962 more than half of the population was urban and 42 per cent of the labor force worked in manufacturing, mining, construction, transportation, and communication. Women were 48 per cent of all wage-earners, 46 per cent of those in the industrial branches.[8] Western scholars, reworking Soviet data, reach differing estimates of the rates of growth, but there is no doubt that the achievement is substantial. Rates of growth have declined since 1958, as greater difficulties were met in the planning and centralized direction of the increasingly complex economy.[9] The drive to maintain high rates of growth continues to color all aspects of life and labor relations.

Consumers have not gained proportionately with the growth of production and national income, for priority has been given to heavy industry. Real wages declined during the rapid industrialization of the 1930's and further during the war. Despite rapid gains in the postwar decade, and in the later 1950's and the 1960's, real incomes are still relatively low. The Soviet claim is that real incomes of working people per capita increased twenty per cent from 1959 through 1963. Gains were slowed, however, in 1962 and 1963 when difficulties in agriculture led to increases in food prices and to delay in promised gains for certain groups. According to an American estimate in 1963, the real income of Soviet citizens averaged only one-fourth to one-third that of Americans.[10]

Soviet doctrine holds that the USSR has built a socialist society, that it has replaced private ownership of the basic means of production by public, and that it has built a strong industrial base and created a trained and experienced working class who work under the incentives of both moral influences and differences in pay, according to the classic formula for this stage of development toward communism, "From each according to his capacity, to each according to his work." Under the program of the Communist Party adopted in 1961 at the Twenty-Second Congress, the USSR claims to be building "the material and moral base for communism," and to be moving toward the goal of a classless society in which distribution will be according to need.[11]

One other significant factor has been a growing emphasis, since the Twentieth Congress of the Communist Party in 1956, on "socialist legality" and "socialist democracy." New civil and criminal codes stress protection of the rights of citizens as well as the interests of society. Counter to this trend are the "anti-parasite" laws and the reintroduction of the death penalty for "economic crimes." "Socialist democracy" is said to be shown in broad participation of the people in discussing policies and proposed legislation and in taking part in "administering the affairs of society."[12] The role of the trade unions and of other "public organizations" has grown. A gradual transfer of government functions to public organizations is said to be taking place. While such trends do not in any way limit the basic control by the Communist Party, they have brought protection from some of the coercions and injustices of the past, and they give a basis for rising expectations among the people for more protection of rights and more opportunity to influence what happens.

Nevertheless, the long history of regimentation of labor, coercion, terror, the secret police, the labor camps, under Stalin, still leaves its mark on industrial relations. Many people in responsible positions had years of experience under those conditions and show in their behavior the results of what the Soviets call "the cult of personality." Many workers remember the years in which the unions did little to protect people. Many citizens, speaking of the terrible times under Stalin, say "We never think of it," and "Those conditions can't return, the people wouldn't let it happen." Still, the fear is not entirely gone, and it casts shadows over the landscape, in spite of the generally brighter light.

In this environment, Soviet trade unions now have a double role. Operating always under the leadership of the Communist Party, they help to carry out policies of the party and the state. They also have the more traditional function of representing and protecting the interests of workers—a role that has grown continuously since Stalin's time. These unions are

peculiarly Soviet institutions, with functions important both
for the state and for their members. As they have developed
in the decade since Stalin's death, they are not merely tools
of the party and the government. They are not "company
unions"—at least when they use their real powers vis-à-vis
managers. While they do not, like traditional unions, work
primarily for the direct interests of their members, still,
workers exert pressure through local union elections, through
criticisms and appeals, and through their volunteer local union
activities. To some extent these pressures bring greater efforts
to protect the interests of workers. As an increasingly educated
working class listens to statements of party policy on the rights
of workers and of unions, the influence of the unions will undoubtedly grow. An amplification of this view will appear in
the analysis that follows.

A NOTE ON METHOD OF INVESTIGATION AND SOURCES

Sources for the study are found in the recently increased
volume of official and semi-official Soviet documents, in studies
and discussions by Soviet economists and other experts on
labor law and labor problems, in publications of the trade
unions, and in extensive news reports and propaganda in the
press.[13]

These materials have been supplemented by observation and
interviews during trips to the Soviet Union in 1955, 1959, and
1962. The author was able to meet with industrial and trade
union leaders and with economists and experts in labor law
in ten cities: Leningrad, Moscow, and Ivanovo, Kharkov, Rostov, Kiev; Tbilisi in the South; Alma Ata, Tashkent, and
Samarkand in Middle Asia. While her ability to speak Russian
is limited, it was enough, especially in the later trips, to help
in the interviews, and to make possible conversations with
other Soviet citizens. In thirty days in 1955 she visited four

cities and five factories and had interviews at the All-Union Council of Trade Unions and the Leningrad Council of Trade Unions and with a number of experts in the labor field. In ten weeks in 1959 it was possible to visit nine cities and seventeen plants. Interviews were held at the headquarters of several regional economic councils and regional trade union councils, the Central Council of Trade Unions, and the Central Committee of the Union of Textile and Light Industry Workers, and with economists and labor law experts. In a six-week visit in the fall of 1962 the hoped-for intensive study of one or two plants did not materialize, but there were lengthy talks with union leaders in Leningrad and visits to four plants. In one of them, attendance at a factory committee meeting gave opportunity to see a trade union at work. In other plants there were talks with directors, chief engineers, and union officers, and with representatives on production conferences and labor disputes commissions. The twenty-four plants visited in the three trips included four machine tool and heavy machinery plants, nine textile factories, two tea-packing and two champagne plants, and one each in the shoe, clothing, food, tobacco, printing, tractor, and construction materials industries.

These factory visits provided information on policy and descriptions of activities, and permitted impressions of attitudes and interests of the people involved. It was possible to observe workers and their attitudes toward union and management representatives who acted as guides, and to see the propaganda notices, banners, slogans, bulletin boards, wall newspapers, and "Red Corners"—all prominent aspects of the working environment. Talks with individual workers in the plants and elsewhere were illuminating. Conversations with many other Soviet citizens provided some check on what was said in the interviews. Discussions with economists and labor law

experts in scientific institutes and universities and in trade
union central offices clarified policies and methods of administration, and indicated problems of concern to them.

Official documents give the text of major laws, decrees, policy statements of the Communist Party, regulations and instructions issued by government organs and by the Central
Council of Trade Unions, though access to needed information may still be limited by an old practice of sometimes distributing important laws or regulations to responsible parties
without publishing them. Speeches of leaders and reports of
congresses and sessions of the party, the government, and the
trade unions are published though these are carefully edited
and do not give full reports of any discussion. Annual statistical handbooks of the Central Statistical Administration
since 1956 make available useful official data, but unfortunately
not (as of 1965) any comprehensive publication of wage or
income statistics. All Soviet statistical reports must be used
with caution, but since the present study is not primarily
quantitative, it is not markedly hampered by the inadequacy
of official statistics.

Many professional publications are available. Textbooks on
economics, labor economics, and labor law give useful ex-
positions of policy although as descriptions of society they
are more in the realm of what should be than of what is. On
the other hand, there are many books as well as articles
in professional journals which combine theory with realistic
analysis and discussion. A mine of information is found in
journal articles and monographs by experts in government
agencies, scientific institutes, and universities, who are working on labor problems. Chief among the research institutions
are the Scientific-Investigation Institute of Labor of the State
Committee of the USSR Council of Ministers on Questions of
Labor and Wages, and the Institute of Economics and the

Institute of State and Law of the Academy of Sciences. Regional institutes also are engaged in studies in the labor field.

The publishing house of the Central Council of Trade Unions issues books by professional experts and also popular books and pamphlets directed to trade union workers and members at the local level. Many answer questions and give detailed explanations of laws and regulations and of methods of union work. Frequently these are written by local leaders, who describe successful operation of their union committees. Although colored by a desire to show how good a job was done, these descriptions help to fill the gap left by inability to do more personal investigation in the field. The union daily newspaper *Trud* (Labor) and the twice-a-month magazine *Sovetskie Profsoyuzy* (Soviet Trade Unions) also include detailed accounts of life in the trade unions and factories, in addition to the discussions of policy and the ever-present propaganda.

Soviet daily newspapers are an invaluable although limited selective source owing to the central control and careful selection of news and comment. As a rule priority is given to those issues that the party is concerned with at the time. The press publishes speeches and reports of leaders, policy decisions of the party and government, and often the texts of resolutions and decrees; it also reports extensively on industrial matters. Especially important in this area are the detailed accounts of incidents occurring in individual plants and regions, despite the failure to mention any strikes, which Western correspondents occasionally report to their papers. Stories from the plants are found in *Pravda* (Truth), the party newspaper, and in *Izvestia* (News), organ of the central government, as well as in trade union papers. Large numbers of worker correspondents keep the papers informed of local developments and problems.

Letters from individuals and groups to the press and to public agencies are a traditional and much-used method of seeking redress of wrongs, although such "criticism and self-criticism" is limited to specific sore spots and never questions established policies on income distribution, wage levels, trade union issues, or other major matters affecting workers' welfare. While there is recurring criticism of delays in handling the complaints on details, many of them get publicity, often with a follow-up statement by the editors as to whether the difficulty has been resolved. Despite the uncertainty as to how much weight to give these reports, they do provide a wealth of information on sore spots in industrial relations and on efforts to eliminate them.

Knowledge of Soviet labor relations and the trade unions is more complete with respect to the structure of the system, policy issues and activities as described for the benefit of the outsider than it is on actual operations. Yet, as indicated, there is still much concrete evidence which, if carefully used, weighed, and appraised, justifies an attempt at analysis. Future intensive field studies can, it is hoped, throw further light on some of the unanswered questions as to the part played by unions and their developing role in Soviet society.

CHAPTER II

The Labor Market

ALTHOUGH the concept of the labor market[1] is foreign to their philosophy of planning, Soviet planners have long dealt with the theoretical and practical problems of labor force distribution and remuneration. Various combinations of planning and reliance on market forces have been used, including central and decentralized planning, planned training and recruitment, direction of labor and control over turnover, and voluntary self-direction under the influence of wage and other incentives, social pressure, advertisements, and local and country-wide methods of recruitment. After Stalin, changes in manpower policies gave workers increased freedom to respond to market forces.

Following the Twentieth Congress of the Communist Party in 1956, study of these problems increased. Economists and labor law experts in the institutes, universities, and state planning agencies spoke frequently of "deficiencies in labor resources in some areas" and "surplus" or "overplan" workers in others, and of "the need for redistribution of workers freed from some enterprises." Beginning in 1959, annual conferences on labor resources brought together representatives from all parts of the country.[2] It was recognized that the economic plans called for labor forces beyond the expected population growth and that wartime losses would still be felt. Although the situation improved after 1961, shortages in certain areas continued to pose difficulties.[3] The eastern and central parts of the country, where intensive development was planned, were rich in natural resources, but they were underpopulated. The rapidly developing oil and chemical industries needed labor. More workers were needed also in the service occupations. It was expected that in spite of growth in productivity, "the demand of all branches of the national economy for labor will grow faster than the number of able-bodied population of working age."[4]

At the same time, mechanization and automation were decreasing the need for unskilled hand labor and displacing workers from old skilled occupations.[5] In some areas the demand for labor was reduced by changing industrial structure. Surpluses of skilled workers were foreseen especially in old enterprises in heavy industry centers and in small cities where it was not expedient to build up new large industry.[6]

The demand for labor in the growing fields and regions was expected to be met in part by released industrial workers and by large numbers not needed in agriculture because of mechanization and improved organization. Another source was the small part of the "able-bodied population" of working age (men 16–59, women 16–54) not working or studying—a little more than 10 per cent, according to the 1959 census of population. Most of these were women occupied at home in household work and caring for children. There were also members of the families of peasants or workers engaged in private subsidiary farming—7.7 per cent of the labor force.[7] It was hoped to draw many from these groups into employment in the public economy. It was argued also that new enterprises should be located with more attention to availability of labor.[8]

Differences among regions were reported in 1962 by one expert. Labor resources were found insufficient in the Northwest, Siberia, the Far East, and Kazakhstan, but generally adequate in the Urals, the Volga region, and part of the Baltic area; there were surplus labor reserves in a majority of the

regions of the European part of the country, and in republics
of Middle Asia, especially Uzbekistan.[9] Another expert complained, however, that current statistical reports on labor resources failed to show how many of those not employed in the
public economy were actually engaged in household work,
how many could be brought into jobs, or how many were "in
need of placement"[10]—the Soviet euphemism for "unemployed."

Soviet theory holds that distribution of manpower is "by
planned recruitment, preparation and distribution of the labor
force," in contrast to a market economy where labor is "a
commodity, bought and sold in the market." Nevertheless,
market influences are admitted, since wages are said to be
"one of the economic instruments of the planned distribution
and redistribution of labor forces."[11] Thus the labor market
depends on planned economic and legal measures and on individual choices in response to them.

The legal setting is the citizen's constitutional duty to work
and guaranteed right to work. The duty to work means his
obligation to engage in "socially useful labor" and neither to
live on "unearned income" from private profit or speculation
nor to be idle. Only for women with young children is it
generally approved for people of working age not to participate
in the labor force; and it is considered preferable if facilities
provided for the care of children are enough that these mothers
can work. Laws against "persons who avoid socially useful
labor and lead a parasitic way of life," adopted in most of the
republics from 1957 to 1961, permit exile of "parasites" for
stated periods and oblige them to work; or they may be sent to
work in their own locality.[12]

As to the right to work, Soviet spokesmen insist that in their
system "there is not and cannot be unemployment." Experts
argue that the socialist economic system ensures full employment by so organizing the distribution of labor "that each

citizen has the possibility to work at his speciality and qualifications and in accordance with social needs."[13] Under conditions of technological displacement and shifts of industry, increased attention turned to the need for "insuring full and rational employment of the able-bodied population in all regions."[14] Solution of the problem is recognized as requiring carefully planned action.

It is apparent that at times Soviet workers do experience problems in finding work. References to "unoccupied people" (*nezanyati*) and to citizens needing "labor placement" (*trudoustroistvo*) appear frequently, although these people are not called unemployed. The concept of frictional or seasonal unemployment is not explicitly recognized. Only rarely does the Soviet press mention difficulties in getting jobs. The most numerous reports, in 1956-1958, concerned young persons, especially minors leaving school after seven or ten years. Occasionally other reports of "being out of work" have appeared, especially concerning persons unable to find jobs for some months after being illegally discharged and before being reinstated.

Soviet authorities are concerned over loss of time between jobs, whether the turnover is voluntary or involuntary, but they consider the problem one of instability of labor forces or defects in the organized distribution of manpower. Failure to employ seasonal workers throughout the year is discussed as a problem of waste of labor. Shortage of workers is felt to be the main problem. If a man is out of work, an economist insisted, "approximately suitable jobs are available, even if not exactly what the worker thinks he should have."

Displacement by technological or other changes in industry, rather than causing an unemployment problem, is relied on as a major source of workers for expanding fields. One Soviet expert, writing in 1959, held that in most cases a decrease of workers in one department was compensated for by expansion in others. He also considered redistribution of workers between enterprises "a healthy process" which should be more used, since "overplan numbers of workers" in many enterprises adversely affected productivity.[15] Under the Labor Code of 1922 and later regulations,[16] when reducing its staff an enterprise is obligated to shift workers with their consent to other suitable work in the plant or related plants. A labor economist, who said flatly that management is required to find jobs for workers displaced by mechanization, emphasized the "moral principle that people need to have work, not only for the money involved," and so "it is not easy to fire people," even if they are not needed. A management official in the Bashkir autonomous republic wrote, "Is it thinkable that under our conditions party and trade union organizations would agree to discharges of thousands of people, as a result of automation, without finding jobs for them? Of course not."[17]

A new term, trudoustroistvo, or labor-placement, which appeared with increasing frequency in Soviet publications after 1959, was defined as "assistance of government and public organs to different categories of citizens in receiving suitable work in the shortest time and without delay; one of the additional guarantees of the right to work."[18] In several instances the government specifically required local authorities to find jobs for groups who were being displaced.[19] It is said also that administrative agencies are obligated to arrange transfers from enterprises with overplan numbers on their staffs to other enterprises where workers are needed. However, as one expert points out, there is no general governmental system to ensure that the shifts of people displaced are entirely painless. Even when retraining is at government expense, as when railroads shifted to electric operation, pay during training may be less than previous wages, and difficulties may be even greater when people shift by their own decisions.[20]

Freedom of citizens to choose fields for training and the place and type of their work is a major Soviet principle.[21] On the whole, workers could select their work and move by their own choice during most of the Soviet period up to World War II; yet there were many exceptions. In 1919-1920 conscription was used extensively, and again during and after the war. Starting in 1928 young graduates of higher education and later of trade schools were directed to jobs. Efforts to curb wasteful mobility culminated in 1938 in the system of permanent labor books, giving the worker's employment record, without which he could not be hired. A month's notice was then required for leaving jobs.[22] Youths were drafted for industrial training in Labor Reserve Schools from 1940. Finally, in 1940, harsh legislation prohibited workers from leaving jobs without permission of the director and permitted compulsory transfer of skilled workers and experts, with severe criminal penalties for "truancy." Use of coercion declined in the early 1950's, until, with the complete repeal of the 1940 laws on April 25, 1956, freedom of choice of jobs again came to the fore. Workers could then leave jobs on two weeks' notice.[23]

This change of policy is held to have reestablished voluntary labor contracts as the chief way of entering jobs, on "the principle of genuine freedom of contract"—meaning "strict voluntarism in entrance on work, freedom to shift to other work and freedom to remain at work by choice of the worker . . . , permitting transfer to other permanent work only with the agreement of the worker."[24] The aim is said to be to combine protection of the interests of the individual and of society and to assure both satisfaction in work and high productivity.[25] Wage differentials and a variety of other incentives are used to influence workers to go to jobs and to stay as stable members of the labor force where needed. In addition, constant propaganda seeks to educate workers as to the needs of the state and to enlist their cooperation.

PLANNING FOR LABOR RESOURCES

Central planning determines the nature and location of jobs, and seeks to provide the needed labor. Annual production plans include "limits" on the number of workers to be employed, the wage fund, average wages, and expected increases in labor productivity. Data from analyses at lower levels make possible nation-wide planning for needed training and shifting of workers. Each area is responsible for estimating its labor resources and demand.[26] Planning starts in the enterprise, which is expected to study its own labor, the expected demand, and sources for new workers. Then the *sovnarkhoz*—the regional economic council—works out the balance for meeting the needs of its plants for all types of labor; and administrative and government agencies work out the combined balance for the cities, regions, and republics. Each industry needs attention, and also various groups of workers—women, youths, and specialists of all levels of training.[27] Thus, the experts claim, the national economic plan provides for the mobile labor resources needed for fulfilling plans and for full employment.[28]

Many regions, however, are said to be lax in their analysis, especially in planning for the full use of available labor.[29] There is particular concern with the questions of surplus labor that should be shifted, of seasonal workers not utilized the year around, and of women who could be drawn into employment.

Labor surpluses result when population growth supplies more new workers in a locality than needed, when the chief industry provides jobs mainly for one sex—women in textiles, men in heavy industry, and when an industry or big enterprise shuts down or there is large scale automation. Local authorities are often remiss in planning for needed shifts of labor to other areas or for the development of new industry. When coal mines closed in an area 1500 miles from Moscow, because of a change-

over to gas in Moscow and other cities, it is said that new
factories were brought in, some miners were retrained for the
new industries, and some moved to other coal fields.[30] But
when a somewhat similar problem arose from automation in the
Bashkir oil industry, an administrative worker complained
that no plan had been made for released personnel and that
other types of industry were lacking; as a result, large numbers
of unneeded workers were kept on the payrolls.[31]

Individual plants often have unnecessary workers. This sometimes arises from poor organization and lack of mechanization,
especially in materials and product handling.[32] On the other
hand, surpluses result when mechanization has not been accompanied by adequate shifting and retraining of workers.[33] Economists insist there is no real difficulty in the transfer of young
workers, since other jobs are available locally or in other areas,
and there are facilities for retraining. Older people, however,
are more likely to be kept on though not needed and though
productivity is adversely affected. Experts complain, also, of a
tendency to underestimate the difficulties of providing employment for released workers; a time lag in the expansion of other
job opportunities and lack of adequate organization to facilitate
placement often lead to maintaining surplus staffs.[34]

Planning for full use of seasonal workers is another problem.
Many are said to be "temporarily not working" in off-seasons;
they are not called unemployed, as it is assumed that, typically,
seasonal work is well paid and other off-season work at lower
pay is available. The American social security delegation in its
1958 examination of pension records, however, found numerous
instances of seasonal unemployment, with extended periods of
low or no earnings.[35] It has been recognized that there is underutilization of such workers and therefore high turnover, in
areas where the general supply of labor is inadequate. Regional
authorities are urged to develop supplementary industries to

provide off-season jobs for workers in fishing, mining, prospecting, agriculture, food processing, and other industries.[36]

Underutilization of the potential labor of women continues. Employment of women varies greatly in different regions. In 1962 they were 51 per cent of all employed persons in Russia, but 40 per cent or less in most of the republics of the East.[37] It was not known how many women were not working simply because of lack of job openings or lack of facilities for child care. Sample studies in Novosibirsk, Kemerovo, and Krasnoyarsk found thousands of women, many with vocational training and experience, who would take jobs in industry if available and if their family duties were lightened by provision of more kindergartens and nurseries, if improvements were made in housing, public catering, and other consumers' services, or if they could work part-time. In many areas of heavy industry there was a lack of light industry that could offer jobs to women and help to meet the need for better supplies for consumers.[38]

The effectiveness of manpower planning is deeply affected by decisions on distribution of resources, location of industry, and provision for satisfaction of workers' needs. Complaints continue of labor shortages on the one hand, of surpluses of labor on the other, of wasteful turnover, and other problems. Although there is no large-scale unemployment, full and productive employment of the entire potential labor force has not yet been achieved.[39]

PLANNED TRAINING

A major means of providing industry with manpower is planned education and the job placement of workers on completion of their courses. The educational system was reorganized under the 1958 law "on strengthening the relations of schools with life."[40] Final decisions on numbers of students and on educational facilities are made by Gosplan and the USSR Council of Ministers. Plans for fields requiring training in specialized technical schools, institutes, and universities are under the Ministry of Higher and Specialized Secondary Education. A State Committee on Vocational-Technical Training assists the republics in planning and organizing vocational training and job placement of youths. Educational and planning authorities at the local level work with enterprises and other agencies to relate education to the needs of the local economy.[41]

The 1958 school law provided for free education at all levels, compulsory through the eighth grade, with secondary and higher education combined for the most part with "socially useful labor." Secondary "polytechnical"[42] schools give general education through the eleventh grade, and training for selected occupations. Their graduates could continue education or more usually went directly to work, preferably in the place of their practical training. Children finishing eighth grade had the right to enter one of these schools or go to work; or they could attend one of the vocational schools, with terms of one to three years, that replaced all former trade schools.[43] Some were admitted to specialized secondary schools for semi-professional training. Admission to higher education was competitive, based on entrance examinations and recommendations from the lower schools and from the place of work, with preference in most fields given to those who had worked two years in production jobs.

It was thought desirable that a substantial part of education beyond the eighth grade should be in evening and correspondence courses carried on while working. Facilities for full-time study were limited—young workers were needed, and the combination of study with work was considered educationally sound. Most eighth-grade graduates, it was expected, would go directly to work, but according to scattered reports they have not done so, although graduates of secondary schools go to work in relatively large numbers.[44] In 1963, of all in specialized secondary and higher education, 55 per cent were studying while working.[45] Young workers who study in evening and correspondence courses have shorter hours, additional vacations, and paid leaves for final projects and examinations. Students who are getting part of their training in industry are paid, under government regulations, for work done. Full-time students in specialized middle schools and higher education, who also have periods of production work, receive state stipends, varying with the fields of study, provided their work is satisfactory.[46]

Problems developed in this ambitious effort to tailor education to the needs of the planned economy.[47] Most secondary schools were poorly equipped for production training, and practice in the plants was poorly organized. Good teachers were scarce. Frequently there was preparation only for traditional skills, and too few pupils could get training for the new and growing occupations. Many children were dissatisfied with their practice work. There were also too few vocational schools, especially in the East. Educational plans for regions and republics were said to be insufficiently related to the needs of the area. Young workers often had to be retrained or shifted to other industries or regions.

In practice, the right of young citizens to choose their fields of study and work was limited by the availability of educational facilities. Youngsters finishing eighth grade were helped in considering opportunities and were urged to choose carefully, but severe competition for some schools limited choices. Often fields of training were restricted to the needs of a nearby plant or farm. School officers insist, however, that a child is not bound by his secondary school training, and that there is ample chance for any able and energetic young person to shift fields later.[48] Many young people have had to begin in evening and correspondence courses, since the number of openings for full-time study in the specialized and higher educational institutions, though growing, was limited. Preference for these courses was given to young workers chosen by enterprises. On the recommendation of their enterprise, they could transfer to full-time study for the later stages of their education.[49]

Many difficulties were found in the combination of work and study. Managements did not always provide the necessary conditions, and in spite of the generally strong drive to get education, not all workers were interested. There was concern also that the combination of general education with production training was weakening preparation for advanced study. By 1964 dissatisfaction had led to extensive discussion, and changes began to be made in the 1958 law. Secondary schools were reduced to a basic ten-year program, with less time for production training. Increased numbers of the most able were permitted to enter higher education directly from secondary school without two-years' prior work.[50] Educational policy was to continue as a key part in planning for the manpower needs of the economy.

Training on the job by enterprises themselves is still the predominant means of preparing skilled workers. Among applicants for apprenticeship training, ordinarily for six months, preference is given youths who have completed eight-year or eleven-year schools, although included also are recruits from collective farms, women without experience in industry, people sent by local soviet executive committees, and workers wanting to learn a second trade. Short-term courses provide retraining to meet the needs of changing technology. Contracts with educational authorities provide for training for students.[51] Training by the enterprises is thought useful for its close relation to current needs, but is criticized as tending to be too narrow. There is hope that in the future increased numbers will be prepared in the vocational and higher schools, especially for the more complex jobs in automated industry.

Progress in developing manpower resources appears in the rising level of education reported. According to the Central Statistical Administration, people with seven or eight years of education increased from 83 per thousand inhabitants in 1939 to 281 in 1959 and 308 in 1963. Among wage-earners, 44 per cent had at least this level of education in 1963. The number with secondary specialized education who were working in the national economy rose from 1.5 million in 1941 to 6.3 million in 1963. Those with higher education increased from under one million to 4.3 million.[52] The average level of general education of industrial workers increased from 3.5 years in 1929 to 5.9 years in 1959, and according to a preliminary estimate would reach 7.5 years in 1965.[53] Broader educational facilities, free education, stipends, and the drive for education to promote both individual and social interests, all contributed to this upsurge. Financial inability does not prevent able young people from getting the education they want, although low family incomes as well as limited opportunities for study in their localities sometimes result in youngsters going directly to work rather than to full-time education. Local unions encourage the young to study, and their officers sometimes boast that every third worker is engaged in advancing his general or specialized education.

JOB CHOICE AND PLANNED PLACEMENT

Measures designed to direct or influence job choices and placement vary for different groups. The extent of these groups was shown in a report on expected sources of additional workers in 1962 in the industries of eleven sovnarkhozy. Only 15 per cent were to come from vocational and other schools, and twice as many from people hired and trained by enterprises

themselves. More than half were to be people shifting from
other plants, including a small group trained in other enterprises. Only 2 per cent were to come through organized recruitment systems.[54]

In general the needs of enterprises for young workers and
specialists are expected to be met by local and regional educational systems. When the numbers of youth exceed the local
need for additional labor, shifts of young people for work or
training in other areas are possible through coordination at the
republic level. Even secondary school graduates can be sent,
with their consent, to other districts within the republic, or,
with permission of the USSR Council of Ministers, to other
regions of the East or North where they are needed.

For young people finishing or leaving school, job placement
is not left to chance. The state seeks to guarantee jobs for
graduates of general education or for school leavers, with
opportunity for further training. Difficulties have arisen when
managements prefer not to hire such youths because of shorter
hours and other privileges required. Children of fifteen can be
hired, but only with the consent of the union committee and
for four hours work daily. Sixteen- and seventeen-year-olds are
permitted to work only six hours but are paid for a full day,
and there are other regulations on conditions of work and
provisions for study. School directors are obligated to know
whether their graduates and others who left are working or
studying, or both. Most children find their own jobs. If not, the
child is referred to the executive committee of the local soviet,
which has responsibility for placing young workers or assigning
them to vocational schools.

District soviets in the cities have commissions on labor placement (*trudoustroistvo*) or on the affairs of minors, whose function it is to see that jobs are available for youths, with opportunity to continue study. Since 1957 they have had the obligation
to assign to enterprises quotas of the number of youths to be

The Labor Market

hired. Under 1962 and 1963 decrees of the Council of Ministers, such quotas were to amount to 3 to 5 per cent of the enterprises' workers, in order to assure jobs in accordance with the youths' training, for all leaving the eight- and eleven-year schools and vocational schools. An enterprise may not legally refuse to hire the boy or girl sent with the commission's order of placement. On the other hand, it is not compulsory for the young person to take the job.[55]

Difficulties of these young, partially trained, new workers in finding jobs were not entirely solved by the 1958 school reorganization and the assignment of quotas for their hiring. Mistakes were made in planning types of training, but the cost to the enterprise in hiring and training such youngsters was also a factor. There were reports in 1964 of refusals to hire boys and girls sent with placement orders from the commissions. Not over 15 per cent of secondary school graduates are said to begin work in the fields for which they were trained. Local agencies were urged to see that all who finished school could get jobs according to their abilities.[56]

Graduates of vocational schools are distributed to jobs by the schools, under plans approved by the republic councils of ministers. Graduates of specialized secondary and higher education are directed to jobs by state commissions including representatives of the schools and their social organizations and of the economic administrations concerned, under plans approved by the USSR Council of Ministers and Gosplan. In general, graduates of specialized and higher education have an obligation to work for three years where placed. Managers are forbidden to hire one of these graduates without a certificate directing him to the job, unless he has received formal permission to find his own work. Thus the state seeks both to assure jobs to all the young people according to their choice of fields and training and to see that they are used where most needed.[57]

Planned placement of new entrants is one of the major methods of achieving the desired distribution of the labor force. Soviet spokesmen insist that the temporary limitation on free choice for "young specialists" does not mean compulsion, and that there are no penalties for refusal to take jobs assigned. Many young people tell how they declined jobs offered and found preferred work or opportunity to continue study. Yet there seems to be a strong sense of moral obligation to work where needed, after education at the government's expense, and this is heightened by social pressure from youth organizations and the public. The student can present objections to the proposed assignment, and often is given a choice or may be permitted to find his own job. The commissions consider the student's wishes and health and family circumstances. Regulations issued by the Ministry of Higher and Specialized Secondary Education put specific obligations on authorities carrying out the distribution and on the employing agencies, but they lay down only general obligations on the graduates to take the assignments and work for the stated term. If a graduate does not take the job assigned or leaves it ahead of schedule, he is expected to repay any sums given him for his journey to the place of employment; leaving the job without an acceptable excuse breaks his record of continuous work, which affects rights to certain social insurance payments and other benefits.

Many criticisms are made of the way this placement system operates. There is concern over the number of young specialists who refuse to go where assigned and over those who do not continue in the occupation for which they were trained, or who exercise their right to return home after the required period. Enterprises are criticized for failing to use graduates according to their training and for not providing proper living and working conditions; when conditions do not meet required standards the young specialists have the right to refuse the work. Efforts were made in 1963 to improve the distribution and use of these specialists, and to put pressure on them to fulfill their obligations. Jobs were to be assigned a year in advance and, when possible, practice work was to be carried out in the enterprise of future work. Only temporary certificates were to be given on graduation from higher and specialized education; diplomas were to be issued after one year's work.[58]

The problem of finding jobs arises also for adults, especially peasants who leave for industry, women who wish to enter or return to the labor market, people whose construction jobs or other temporary work have terminated, and workers released by technological change or other causes of staff reduction. Others who need to find work include any who have been discharged for disciplinary reasons, or have left jobs by their own choice, or who for family or other personal reasons have come to the locality; also demobilized soldiers and persons released by an amnesty or after serving a sentence, or any brought into the labor market by warnings under the "anti-parasite laws."

Local employment exchanges went out of existence early in the 1930's, as there was said to be no longer any unemployment.[59] When economists were asked in 1959 why there was no coordinated local organization for recruiting and placing workers, their answer was in effect, "There is no need. There is no unemployment. It is a question of choosing jobs, not finding jobs." The enterprises themselves have the largest role in local recruiting. Methods used include "open door days" for youths finishing general education schools, group and individual talks with workers about to be released from other enterprises or with demobilized soldiers, and different forms of publicity.[60] People generally find jobs for themselves through notices at factory gates, newspaper and radio advertisements, and street bulletin boards, and through the spread of job information by friends and fellow workers. In many cities in 1955, 1959, and 1962 large bulletin boards on the streets showed numerous unfilled demands for all types of workers.

Although there are no coordinated job information and placement services, regional economic councils are expected to
arrange placement of workers released from other jobs. In the
larger cities, commissions on labor placement of the district
soviet executive committees may aid any who come to them for
help, but these are seldom mentioned except for their responsibilities for youths and demobilized service personnel. Their
work is said generally not to be based on the labor balance of
the area, nor to have enough contact with enterprises.[61] Moscow has a Department of Resettlement and Organized Recruitment and an Information Bureau with street kiosks. All of these
may supply information on job openings. City party committees
were reported in 1959 to have lists of people not employed,
whom they tried to place. Trade unions may help to find jobs
for their members. A complaint appearing in 1957, however,
probably continued to be typical:

In a city, job placement is handled to some extent by everyone—
special committees of local soviets, officials of various public organizations and militia departments. This results in an immense waste
of time, and unnecessary phone calls and paper work. This lack of
coordination does not help those who honestly want to work but for
some reason have not been able to find a job.[62]

A growing body of expert opinion has called for improved
placement machinery, in order to avoid the wastes of lack of
full information among plant managers on the availability of
workers, and among workers on openings in their fields. Some
have argued also for strengthened obligations to find jobs for
workers displaced and to prevent individual hardship.[63] No
unanimity developed on these questions by 1964-1965. Many
believed that no further machinery was needed, or feared
bureaucratic interference with local management of labor
placement. Development of a well-coordinated system of employment exchanges, to meet the needs of the dynamic econ-

omy, appears to have been hindered by the official dogma that there is no unemployment.

In a 1965 book, however, a leading authority of the Institute of Economics, M. Ya. Sonin, argued that good organization of the process of distribution of labor resources was not so simple as thought by some who "master only that truth" that under socialism there was no objective basis for unemployment. He insisted that it was wrong "to hide behind our advantages" and to decline active organized work on this "great and complicated business" which to this time proceeds "with great costs for society." He proposed a system of organs from the national to regional and local levels, relating the work of authorities in technical-vocational education, organized recruitment, and planning. Their duties would be to study labor resources and work out proposals for their use, to provide for meeting the needs of enterprises for workers and of youths and others for job placement, to help enterprises and administrations in the retraining and placement of workers displaced by mechanization, and to provide information on opportunities and conditions in other areas and arrange for recruitment.[64] Similar opinions were expressed by a number of leading economists later in 1965.

ORGANIZED RECRUITMENT

Only for major recruitment needs for distant areas has there been a coordinated system—the Administration for Organized Recruitment of Workers, or Orgnabor, supplemented after 1953 by mass appeals and recruitment by the Komsomol, the Young Communist League, for work in the East. Orgnabor originated in 1931. The great flow of labor from the villages to industry was handled through Orgnabor contracts made by enterprises with collective farms and individual peasants, under governmental regulation. Quotas for the number of peasants to be released for industry were established by the planning authorities. From 2½ to 3 million came to industry each year from 1932 to 1940 through this chief form of recruitment for the major branches of industry.[65]

After 1947, to avoid competition between industries in the same village, the Central Administration for Organized Recruitment made contracts with ministries for leading industries to recruit planned numbers of workers. Later, responsibility was given to the councils of ministers of the republics. Plans for interrepublic shifts of labor must be approved by Gosplan and the USSR Council of Ministers.[66]

The role and significance of Orgnabor changed after the war. It became chiefly an agency for planned redistribution of labor between branches of industry and regions. By 1956 two-thirds of the recruits came from the cities. Recruitment for the old industrial centers fell sharply, though it increased for the North and East. The average annual number signed up for permanent work through Orgnabor fell to little over 500,000 for 1956-1958; seasonal workers signed up were about 200,000 each year. For the country as a whole, Orgnabor in 1958 supplied only 5.8 per cent of those hired in manufacturing, compared with 13 per cent in 1950; for construction, only 9.3 per cent as against 29.8 per cent in 1950. It continued to have an important role in supplying forces for developing industries and big construction projects in the East and North.[67] Orgnabor also handled resettlement of whole families, especially collective farmers, for permanent residence and work on the new farms in the sparsely settled areas of the East. Some returned home, dissatisfied with conditions; others left the farms for industry, helping to fill the need for industrial labor.[68] Beginning in 1958 it also recruited skilled workers and engineers on requests from sovnarkhozy.[69]

Local Orgnabor offices, under republic Administrations for Organized Recruitment and Resettlement, conduct information programs, check on requests for labor, and sign up workers for jobs in other areas. Contracts are made in the name of enterprises for short period seasonal work, or for one- to three-year terms, or more recently, for permanent work. Cost of transfer is paid, suitable housing and training when needed are guaranteed, and additional lump-sum benefits are given for work in distant areas. On completion of the term, cost of the return journey is paid. The worker may also sign for a further term, or, in many cases, he may stay for permanent work.

Some economists believe that Orgnabor has outlived its usefulness. As it concentrated on short-term contracts, most of those recruited ultimately returned home. It was criticized for not adjusting to changes in the character of the labor force and the needs of industry. Complaints were made of poor selection, of sending "floaters" or "undisciplined workers." Skilled recruits were often sent to jobs without regard for previous training and experience. Since Orgnabor usually recruited for one enterprise in only one or two districts, it had limited ability to find the skills needed by industry and to offer workers a choice of openings in their present fields. The result was loss of skills and need for retraining. Recruitment was often carried out in disregard of available local resources. Enterprises often failed to use recruits according to their qualifications and to provide proper housing and working conditions, knowing that Orgnabor would supply more workers on request.

It is generally thought that while improvements in its methods are needed, Orgnabor still has a place, especially in supplying workers for big construction projects and in facilitating shifts of workers released by technological change. If wasteful mobility is to be avoided, however, there is need for increased local responsibility for full use of labor resources and more attention given to providing suitable living conditions and consumers' services in the areas to which people are sent.[70]

Starting in 1954, Orgnabor was overshadowed by the mass appeal, "public call-up," carried out by the party and especially

the Komsomol for work in distant areas. The huge drives for
agriculture in the "new lands" of Kazakhstan and for construction and industry in the East and North were conducted
on the whole by such mass appeals to young men and women.
Meetings were held in plants, newspapers were filled with reports and appeals, and the Komsomol took special responsibility for encouraging volunteering, clearing applications and
arranging for placement and transfer of those chosen. Party
discipline could require volunteering if necessary and at times
the pressure of "public opinion," with the possibility of reprisals against "slackers," amounted to coercion to "volunteer."
There was also the appeal of adventure, of pioneering, and of
patriotism. Young people signing up received benefits similar
to those under Orgnabor.[71]

Hundreds of thousands responded. The number of volunteers was said to be always larger than the number sent. In
1959 the secretary of the Komsomol reported that over one
million had gone to work in agriculture and on new construction projects in the East—hydroelectric stations, steel plants,
and others. Hardships were often severe when housing and
other facilities were not ready or when farms and enterprises
did not provide the promised training or use the recruits
effectively. Retraining was often required when there were
unnecessary shifts of occupation. In spite of the high morale
with which many volunteers came, many left. It is said, nevertheless, that no other method of recruiting could in so short
a time have met the needs for huge numbers of new workers
in these areas; and that these recruits proved much more
stable, as permanent members of work forces, than those sent
by Orgnabor.[72]

During the Seven Year Plan this method of mass appeals continued to have an important role in providing workers for
developing areas. Efforts were made to improve its effective-

ness by setting up special recruiting commissions with members from the party, the Komsomol, local soviets, and representatives of the sovnarkhozy and enterprises wanting workers, and by recruiting at enterprises and organizations with workers above the planned numbers. Administrative organizations were enjoined to do more to provide proper living conditions, cultural facilities, training, and other needs.

Thus the Soviet system, with its ideology of the right to work and the duty to work, its planning, and its propaganda, developed characteristic forms of recruitment and placement that met, at least to a degree, the basic requirements of the developing industries and areas. The need continued for better methods of assuring the voluntary and prompt shift of people to enterprises and areas where needed, and inducements for them to remain there on a stable basis.

UNPLANNED MOBILITY AND THE PROBLEM OF TURNOVER

Excessive turnover of industrial labor was a problem during the period of rapid industrialization.[73] Under conditions of great labor shortages, with an inexperienced labor force and inadequate working and housing conditions, efforts of workers to better themselves by shifting jobs could not entirely be suppressed, even if this had been desired. Measures to promote stability included incentives, penalties, compulsion, and attempts to develop "self-discipline and responsibility." The problem came to the fore again after the 1956 repeal of the 1940 law prohibiting any leaving of jobs without permission.

At the party congress in 1961 concern was expressed over the costs of unnecessary turnover, and the problem continues to receive attention. No comprehensive turnover statistics are published currently, but rates seem not to have been excessively high in general, and to have decreased from prewar rates. After 1957, turnover is said to have decreased under the influence of reduced hours, improved housing and living conditions, and changes in wage systems.[74] The per cent leaving jobs in industrial enterprises by choice or on disciplinary discharge is reported to have fallen by 1956 to one-fourth that of 1932, and by 1960 to one-half the 1956 figure.[75] A Western scholar estimated in 1961 that average rates of turnover per month had ranged recently between 3 and 4 per cent in most regions and industries—rates not far from those in the United States and the United Kingdom.[76] The Institute of Labor of the State Committee on Labor and Wages reported in 1963, on the basis of an extensive study of turnover, that currently in the majority of enterprises 85-90 per cent of the labor force was stable, but that monthly turnover in some amounted to 1.5–2 per cent of the average force. This meant a substantial loss to the state, since the time between jobs for many workers amounted to 10-15 days or more. Workdays lost by newly hired workers had varied from about fifteen days in Moscow up to over thirty in several of the more distant regions where interregional migration was a major influence. An average loss of time of thirty days is frequently mentioned. Unnecessary turnover results not only in loss of worktime, but also in lower initial productivity on new jobs and in costs of retraining the many who change occupations when they shift jobs. For all industry and construction the annual loss from turnover is estimated as almost three billion rubles.[77]

The extent of turnover varies between regions, with disastrously high rates in construction and in other industries in the East and North. A Siberian study found that while 700,000 persons came to Siberia from 1956 to 1960 through organized recruitment programs and a still larger number came independently, more left than came in. Three cities of the Krasnoyarsk area lost within three years about half of those arriving from 1956 to 1960. A construction trust in Kemerovo in 1962 hired 13,000 and lost 8,500 workers.[78] Such reports are numerous.

Much of the turnover is caused by workers shifting to enterprises, industries, and areas where they are needed, or leaving for study. This is recognized as coinciding with social interests. But when workers move to better themselves, it is said that the individual movements "far from always answer the interests of society."[79]

The Central Statistical Administration includes in its figures of "instability of personnel" (*tekuchest kadrov*) all who leave by choice or on disciplinary discharge; this is criticized by Institute of Labor experts, who consider that many who leave by their own choice really belong with the group of "organized" shifts, and that accordingly current figures of instability should be reduced by about one-third to indicate the extent of harmful turnover.[80]

Ways to decrease the wasteful shifts have been sought through a number of studies of the causes of turnover. The most extensive, by the Institute of Labor, covered 70,000 workers from 670 enterprises in a wide range of industries and regions.[81] One by the Siberian division of the Academy of Sciences covered 4,700 workers who left 60 enterprises in Krasnoyarsk.[82] Another by the Leningrad Public Institute of Social Research studied almost 11,000 newly hired workers in 25 enterprises of 12 major industries, who had shifted jobs.[83] The Institute of Labor found that about 17 per cent of all shifts were through organized channels—Orgnabor, recruitment by public organizations, distribution of young specialists, and contracts with sovnarkhozy. Of the rest, the "unorganized shifts," the great majority were influenced directly or indirectly by state plans, especially investments in industrial, housing, and other construction, education, and planned wage differentials. Significant numbers went independently to work in

the developing industries of the East and North, sometimes
because there were overplan numbers in their own enterprises.
Many young people shifted to be nearer educational institutions where they were studying. The Leningrad study found
that a significant part of the movement was related to training
and to social changes and shifts in industrial structure.

Separations by the worker's own choice were about 60 per
cent of all, according to the Institute of Labor's extensive study.
Of these leavers, the great majority were young workers, 50
per cent of them under 25 years and 85 per cent under 35. Most
of them were unskilled—22 per cent were in common labor
jobs. Most had worked not over 3 years, and almost a third
of these had shifted twice or more during that time. In the
Institute's sample, and also in the Leningrad and Krasnoyarsk
studies, dissatisfaction with wages was not the main reason
for quitting, though it was important in the low-paid groups.
Dissatisfaction with the work and working or living conditions
was of far greater importance. The character of housing and
its distance from the job, and lack of places for children in
kindergartens and nurseries, ranked high in the reasons for
quitting, especially in some localities. The Institute of Labor
and Krasnoyarsk studies, which included all leavers rather
than only those newly hired as in the Leningrad study, showed
very large groups leaving the area or stopping for education,
pensions, or health or other temporary reasons. The Leningrad
study of newly hired workers who had shifted jobs showed
a large group of shifts related to study or to placement after
graduation; it also showed disciplinary discharges, but these
were relatively few. Although no complete analyses are available and the categories lack uniformity, a summary is given
below, from the three studies, of causes of turnover in areas
with differing conditions. (The Leningrad column totals more
than 100 per cent because the "education or placement" cate-
gory overlaps others.)

Reasons for leaving jobs	Institute of Labor	Krasnoyarsk	Leningrad
Wages	13.8%	17.5%	23.5%
Work and working conditions	17.4	13.9	37.4
Living conditions	15.9	19.4	29.9
Leaving the city or region	25.4	18.1	—
Stopping work for education, pensions, et al.	18.3	14.4	—
Education or placement after graduation	—	—	25.0
Disciplinary discharge	—	—	1.4
Other	9.2	16.7	7.8

It is clear from these and other reports that reduction of unwanted turnover requires more attention to working and living conditions. Some of the deficiencies can be removed only by added assignment of resources for improvements; some can be done by enterprises themselves. It is also clear that in many plants workers leave because of heavy, unmechanized labor, irregular work, inequalities between enterprises in pay for equal work, lack of opportunities to improve skills, and because of arbitrary managements, inadequacies in the introduction of new workers to their jobs, and failure to provide young workers with proper living conditions and opportunity to study. Mistakes in distribution of housing, especially lack of housing near the place of work, cause many shifts. Managements and unions, planning and educational organs, Orgnabor and other recruitment systems, all are urged to work on these problems. The Leningrad study, which gave detailed reasons for quitting in different industries and occupations, and for groups of young workers and women, was able to direct attention especially to improvements that should be made by plant managements in the interest of stabilizing their labor forces.

To a degree, job shifting is inhibited by indirect influences. The requirement of a passport, registered with the police and presented to the new employer along with the labor book, may prevent unauthorized movement to the old centers, although this requirement is not always successfully enforced, at least in Moscow.[84] Difficulty in finding housing is a major check on mobility. The control by enterprises over allotments of land for gardens and the possibility of their loss may hinder movement. In some of the older centers, increased difficulty in finding other jobs may make work forces more stable.

Direct inducements to promote job stability include shorter hours and longer vacations for work performed under potentially harmful conditions, additional vacations for long service in major industries, preference in housing, and variations in disability benefits and pensions related to length of continuous service. New wage systems introduced from 1956 on, however, reduced the former supplements to wages for long, uninterrupted service in major industries as not decisive in holding workers and as interfering with the other aim of tying earnings to "the quantity and quality of labor." Wage benefits for long service were maintained primarily only for workers in a number of branches of heavy industry and especially for underground workers.[85]

Since the repeal of the 1940 restrictions on changing jobs, only two weeks' notice of intention to leave is required, and the record of uninterrupted work is preserved for those leaving by choice if a new job is taken within thirty days; it is preserved also for any period if the worker leaves for education or other approved reason. At first, with some exceptions, persons leaving by choice lost the right to temporary disability pay until they had worked six months on a new job, but this limitation was dropped on January 25, 1960.[86]

These varied influences and inducements have more impact on older, established workers, than on the young. It is not surprising that the larger part of the job shifts are among younger workers who have not yet settled down to the rather permanent attachment to an enterprise that is characteristic. Efforts to promote stability, accordingly, are directed especially toward young workers, as well as toward those who are considered "flitters and self seekers," putting their own interests above those of society.

Continuous efforts are made through the press, the unions, the party, and older workers in the plants, to promote habits of stability and to censure those who move irresponsibly. From 1962 to 1964 there was much talk about possibilities of reducing turnover by further rewards for long service and penalties for shifting jobs without adequate reason. Delay in adopting any such proposals suggests that authorities were concerned with the reaction of workers to any limitation of their freedom to change jobs.[87] The fact that, as one union leader said, "The workers would not like it," probably held back changes in the laws. Also, the investigations were making clear that basic reasons for turnover were to be found in working and living conditions.

Union committees in many plants sought to reduce turnover by giving more attention to the conditions of young workers and to removing causes of dissatisfaction. Some of them arranged to talk with every worker who applied to leave. Often they could learn the sources of discontent and eliminate them, so that the worker was willing to stay. This form of social pressure seems to have brought constructive results in improving conditions and stabilizing work forces.[88]

WAGES AND THE DISTRIBUTION OF MANPOWER

Wage differentials based on the principles of "the material self-interest of workers in the results of their work" and "pay according to the quantity and quality of labor" are an important means of influencing workers' decisions in choosing fields and jobs, and managers' decisions in hiring and utilizing workers. The structure of differentials is designed to compensate for differences in training, skill, and effort, and for difficulties or dangers in working or living conditions. In addition, differentials are used to promote employment in occupations, industries, and regions of special national significance.[89] A major incentive for the Soviet worker to work where and as the government wants is his opportunity in this way to increase his earnings and thus acquire a claim to a larger share of the still scarce consumers' goods.

Since wages are too important to be left for determination by market forces and private decisions, wage standards are centrally established. Before 1957, with administration of wages mainly in the hands of central industrial ministries, there were great variations and inequalities among industries. Reorganization of industrial administration put wage planning and administering largely under regional economic councils. At the same time, standards for differentials of all types came under strong central control. In 1955 a State Committee of the Council of Ministers on Questions of Labor and Wages was set up to strengthen state control and insure uniformity in regulating wages.[90] The entire wage structure was revised gradually in a nation-wide wage reform that was completed for industry by 1962.[91]

The structure of wage rates consists of the base rates (*stavka*) for the lowest wage grade and the schedules (*setka*) of percentage increases for the higher grades, for each occupation. These are determined by the government—the Council of Ministers in key cases and in others by the State Committee on Labor and Wages in agreement with the Central Council of Trade Unions. Job evaluation handbooks approved by the State Committee and the CCTU set rules for allocation of jobs and workers by wage grades. Earnings are determined by wage rates and incentive systems. Wage systems, production standards, and details of premium systems established in the plants are expected to conform to central standards.

Wage differentials are intended to be large enough to induce entrance into more difficult and needed occupations and to provide incentives to increase skills. Differentials for skill became very large under the pressure of great scarcity of workers as industrialization proceeded.[92] Before the wage reform, base rates for the top grade in many schedules ranged from 1.8 to 4 times the rate for the lowest grade. In order to attract and hold workers, managers also established low production standards and piece rates that permitted high earnings. Actual earnings of skilled workers were sometimes 4 to 8 times the base rates for the unskilled. Such extreme differentiation became unnecessary as levels of education and skill increased and as mechanization reduced the differences in skill required. Minimum wages were raised and base rates were adjusted to give substantial increases in the lower grades. In most branches of industry the new schedules adopted after 1956 provided a range of rates giving the most skilled group only 1.8 or 2 times the lowest rate. Special higher rates are provided in crucial cases and for work under hot, arduous, or harmful conditions.[93] While no comprehensive wage statistics are available, a 1961 study reported that differentials in earnings have been decreasing since the early 1950's, especially since the wage reform.[94] It was expected that differentials for the most skilled could be reduced in the future to 80 per cent or even 60 per cent above the lowest rates and still give incentives for doing more complex work.[95]

Industrial and regional differentials also are used to attract workers. During the early 1920's, consumers' goods industries led in earnings, but the drive for industrialization brought greater increases in heavy industries. Even before the war, wage levels in the coal, iron and steel, oil, and machinery industries were brought to the top. In these and others important for war production, and in regions where climatic and living conditions created hardships, further increases were given during and after the war. Differences in average wages between branches of industry increased during the 1950's. In 1960 the ranking of a group of 17 industries by average wages showed coal at the top, then iron ore, iron and steel, oil, paper and pulp, chemical, machinery, and electric power production. Further down were textiles, woodworking, printing, footwear, and at the bottom, food processing and garment manufacture.[96] Levels of average earnings reported for eleven industries in 1959 (all industry = 100), ranged from 182.7 for the coal industry, to 65.8 for the sewing industries. The gap between industries was said to be narrowing as the reform increased wages for the lower-paid workers.[97]

Under the post-1955 central regulation of wages, attempts are being made to develop scientific criteria for determining wage levels for different jobs and industries. Differentials are said to take account of difficulties in working conditions, complexity of the work and the skill required, territorial distribution, and national economic significance of the industry. Studies in the Institute of Labor have tried to estimate the relative effect of these factors on wage levels, but it is not clear to what extent the actual planning of wage changes has been based on such considerations.[98] Differentials between industries are expected to decline further under the policy of raising low wages, the decreasing necessity for extreme differentials for skill, and improving conditions. In addition, the industries of national economic significance are no longer under so much pressure of labor shortages. It is said that labor supply is now basically a regional, not branch, problem.[99]

Regional differentiation continues to be emphasized to stimulate shifts of workers to the rapidly growing areas, by compensating for differences in living conditions, prices, and availability of consumers' goods and public services. A great variety of practices had grown up under regulation by the industrial ministries, each with its own wage zones and wage and non-wage supplements for work in difficult regions. The result was a hodge-podge, with inequities between industries and between workers of similar skills in the same regions. In 1956, a start was made toward a more uniform system. Regional co-efficients were approved, providing additions to the base rates in coal and other industries as their new wage systems were established. The coefficients ranged from 1:00 in the central, south and western European parts of the Soviet Union, to 1:10-1:20 in the Urals, southwest Siberia, Kazakhstan and Middle Asia; more for other remote regions and up to 1:50-1:70 for the Far North. The highest coefficient, for the Far North, was said to represent about 10 points for differences in the arduousness of work, 40 points for differences in living conditions, including higher prices, and 10 points for the relatively smaller supplements to wages from government services.[100]

For personnel in the Far North, further incentives are given, under a law of February 10, 1960, which replaced the earlier variety of benefits. On top of the regular zone coefficients, workers receive supplements to monthly pay depending on length of service—in addition to extra vacations and increased disability pay. Special benefits are provided for those transferring on Orgnabor contracts for five years, or other similar transfers. One year of work in these regions from 1945 to 1960 is counted as two years, and from March 1960 as a year and a half, for the record of service that determines pension rights.[101]

Except for the Far North, not all workers and industries are covered by the new zonal wage system. Inequities, not yet entirely eliminated, still limit the effectiveness of regional differentials as a means of assuring stable work forces. In addition, higher wages and money benefits are not enough to hold workers in the East and North when normal living conditions are lacking. An expert from the State Committee on Labor and Wages suggested that major differences in conditions in some regions should be compensated for by additional expenditures from public funds on housing and communal and cultural services. Regional additions to wages could then be reduced, except in the Far North, although some differentials would continue to be needed because of variations in prices and climatic conditions, and temporarily for rapidly growing industries in these areas.[102]

The Soviet planned wage system is not entirely different in its operation from that of a free labor market. It has necessarily responded to changing conditions of demand and supply, although both were influenced by planning. When unskilled labor was abundant, wages for the less skilled were very low. During the rapid growth of industry, wage differentials played a role in attracting labor. As education and experience increased the relative amount of skilled labor, and decreased that of unskilled, large differentials were less needed, earnings at the lower levels increased, and enterprises tended to avoid classifying workers in the lowest wage grades. General increases were made later in minimum wages and in rates for the lower wage grades. Higher wages continued to be paid in occupations and regions with labor shortages. Earnings thus responded to changes in the demand and supply of labor and to the rise in productivity. Groups strategically placed in relation to demands obtained higher earnings, in part according to plan and in part because of manipulations in the incentive systems. However, when unjustified differentials resulted in unwanted mobility, rigidities in the centrally determined standards limited the freedom of managers to adjust earnings. Soviet experts hope that scientific bases for all differentials will make these "levers" more effective in the future for the planned distribution and redistribution of the labor force.

ACHIEVEMENTS AND PROBLEMS

Over the years, for training and distributing its labor force the USSR developed methods and institutions on the whole fitting the needs of the centrally planned economy with its principles of the duty of citizens to work and their right to work. Growth of the economy and of modern industry was accompanied by the development of an increasingly educated, skilled, and experienced working class. Harsh controls over labor were modified to allow more freedom of job choice. A combination of planning with a degree of freedom to respond to market forces served, to a workable extent, the interests of both the state and individuals.

Many unsolved problems continue, and are under study. Among the difficulties of planning for a huge country and an increasingly complex economy are those of forecasting needs for labor and of long-range planning for training in a time of dynamic changes in technology. Deficiencies in analysis and planning in the regions limit the success of efforts to achieve full and productive use of labor. Continuing inadequacy of resources to meet all needs has had adverse effects on manpower problems. Inefficient managements have failed to provide the conditions under which workers settle down as stable members of the work force. There are wastes when huge numbers move to and from new areas and enterprises; also when needed shifts are not adequately planned and facilitated. The efficiency and economy of job finding and recruiting appears still to be limited by lack of local employment centers and a good system of clearance between areas.

The claim of the Soviet Union to have no unemployment rests in part on terminology. By definitions used elsewhere

there is evidence both of unemployment and underemployment. Seasonal lack of work, frictional loss of time between
jobs, and lost time in the plants are recognized problems.
Technological unemployment is probably felt temporarily in
some cases, or it takes the form of underutilization of workers
no longer needed. There is underutilization of labor resources
also when women are unable to work because of the structure of local industry or inadequate provision of services.

Large scale unemployment is avoided by the continuing
growth of the economy and by planned training and retraining, placement and recruitment; by reluctance to displace
workers; and by underemployment of workers inefficiently
and unproductively employed on farms, in factories, in street
work, public housekeeping, and other fields. Soviet workers
do not suffer from mass unemployment, and the Soviet state
avoids the waste and tragedy of such failure to use its human
resources. Yet the cost of failure to use the whole labor force
fully and effectively is spread over the entire population in
the form of lower incomes resulting from the low level of
productivity. This may be called the "Soviet equivalent of
unemployment."[103] And any who are involuntarily out of work
for a time are without unemployment insurance protection.

Freedom of citizens to choose their fields of training and
their jobs is enough on the whole to serve the interests of individuals and of the state. Educational opportunities have
greatly expanded, though they are still not enough to meet
the demands of Soviet youth, and political and other forms
of discrimination are possible. The ideal of equality of opportunity has a wide enough effect in practice to open the
door both for individuals to develop their capacities and for
the economy to develop its human resources and the needed
skills. Public interest in the distribution of labor and individual
interests in finding satisfactory work are both served in the
long run by freedom to choose jobs and to change jobs under

the influence of planned incentives and political and economic conditions. Although turnover is a problem in many fields, and a source of loss to the state, it also serves a social purpose. By changing jobs, workers express dissatisfaction and direct attention of authorities to unsolved problems. The party and the state have continued to emphasize incentives for steady work and the development of responsible attitudes.

The Soviet labor market is not and could not be a free market. The planned elements are large and facilitate adjustment to change. At the same time workers are able to promote their own interests. Although official dogmas at times make realistic analysis more difficult, serious study of practical problems can be expected to lead toward pragmatic solutions in the interest both of the state and of individual workers.

CHAPTER III

Trade Unions: Development, Principles, and Structure

Growth of the unions is to be seen in the membership reported at the date of each trade union congress.[1]

1918	2.6 million	1926	9.2 million
1919	4.2 million	1928	11.5 million
1920	4.2 million	1932	17.5 million
1921	8.5 million	1949	28.5 million
1922	4.5 million	1954	40.4 million
1924	6.4 million	1959	52.8 million
		1963	68.0 million

The 1963 statute or constitution of the Soviet trade unions[2] gives an indication of the position of the unions in Soviet society and the contradictions in their role. The unions are defined as voluntary "mass public non-party organizations," uniting wage earners and salaried employees of all occupations and "carrying on all their work under the leadership of the Communist Party"—with a continuously growing "role and significance as the Leninist school of communism." Their central task is said to be "the mobilization of the masses for . . . creation of the material-technical base of communism, struggle for the further strengthening of the economic power and defensive might of the Soviet state, the steady growth of the material welfare and culture of the working people." In addition, they have a duty to "defend the interests of the workers."

These unions, inevitably differing in many respects from unions in Western societies, have been conditioned by the vicissitudes of a revolutionary society. Firm control by the Communist Party over union activity and policy followed open controversy in the first decade as to the role of the unions. Political and economic necessity, as the party saw it, brought emphasis now on one and now on another of the stated union functions. Throughout the history of these unions an issue has been whether they could be independent representatives of their members, or were essentially arms of the party and the state; and whether they were to promote and protect the interests of workers, or were chiefly to serve the production needs of the state as the basis for long-run gains. Policies have been influenced by the development of the working class itself, as workers became more experienced and better educated, and more ready to express their own wants. The party in recent years has shown recognition of the need for active cooperation of workers in an increasingly technological society.

THE FIRST DECADE

In the first months of the revolution the trade unions, which had been largely destroyed by czarist repression from 1905 to 1912, were outshadowed by factory committees that sprang up to control enterprises.[3] But freedom to organize led to rapid growth, and as the attempt at direct control by workers gave way to more centralized control, the factory committees were absorbed into local trade unions. A movement for cooperation between unions resulted by early 1918 in twenty-three all-Russian industrial unions, with many regional union committees and inter-union councils. The Central Council of Trade Unions was set up in June 1917.

In the chaotic years of revolution, international intervention, and civil war, the unions carried major responsibilities.[4] They chose the Commissar of Labor and had representatives in all key governmental agencies, local and national. They helped to reorganize industry and to recruit, educate, and discipline workers, and they shared with the party and with plant directors the management of industry. Union membership was obligatory. Leaders were more often appointed than elected. The unions accepted the necessity for compulsion and supported conscription and militarization of labor. They issued "rules of internal labor order" in the plants and organized "comradely courts" to enforce discipline. They did what they could to protect workers by safety regulations and other attempts to improve working conditions. The eight-hour day, introduced by agreement in big enterprises, was made general by governmental decree.

For a time, wages in money and kind were determined chiefly by collective agreements worked out by local unions and approved by the Commissariat of Labor. As nationalization spread and the problem of inflation arose, central regulation of wages took the place of collective bargaining, but the unions still participated in working out national wage schedules and in applying them in the plants. In an effort to increase productivity, the unions helped to introduce incentive pay systems and cooperated in establishing output standards and revising piece rates. Unions were also active locally in collecting and distributing food supplies and other necessities in a time of great scarcity.

While the unions were playing an important role in the administration of the economy, uncertainty as to their functions and their relation to the state led to open debate in party and trade union congresses. At the first all-Russian congress of trade unions in 1918, opinions ranged from those favoring independence and emphasis on protecting the inter-

ests of workers, to those viewing the unions as part of the
state. It was assumed, nevertheless, that with the spread of
nationalization the unions would become organs of the socialist state. Controversy continued until 1921, when, after spirited
debate, the party congress finally adopted the policy favored
by Lenin, and the trade union congress followed suit. Unions
were to be voluntary non-governmental organizations, led and
controlled by the Communist Party. They were neither to administer industry nor to interfere in management. Rather, they
were to lead and educate the masses. Lenin called the unions,
in the phrases still quoted, "school of administration, school
of management, school of communism." They were to be
concerned with the broad production interests of society as
a whole as well as with protection of workers. Party groups
in the unions and the power of the party to control appointments to union positions would assure that party policy was
followed. The Russian labor code adopted the next year—
still, with modifications, the basic regulation of labor conditions in the entire country—gave unions the right to appear
before governmental bodies in the name of workers on all
matters relating to work and life. In the plants they were to
represent workers and safeguard their economic and legal
interests. These general principles did not settle all questions,
however, and the years were to see many shifts in the role
of the unions.

With the adoption of the New Economic Policy in 1921, in
an effort to get the economy on its feet by permitting revival
of private trade and industry, the unions lost much of their
former authority and became more like unions in capitalist
industry. Membership and dues again became voluntary. The
Central Council of Trade Unions was subordinated to the
Commissariat of Labor, which gained authority for regulation of labor conditions. Unions were still represented in the
economic agencies and were supposed to be consulted on

labor legislation and planning. In the plants, "one-man manage-ment" came to be accepted in the interest of efficiency. For a time, protection of interests of members came to the fore as the chief function of the unions, but key officers were al-ways party members and dominance of the party was assured. Collective contracts, both local and general, regulated wages within limits set by governmentally established minimum standards and "wage funds." The CCTU recommended stan-dard wage schedules providing differentials for skill. As piece work came into extensive use, the unions were expected to cooperate in establishing production standards. The decade saw growing emphasis on the unions' responsibility to help in maintaining labor discipline and increasing production. At the same time unions carried on educational and welfare work, setting up workers' clubs, libraries, cultural and educa-tional programs, nurseries and kindergartens for workers' chil-dren, summer camps and rest houses, all of which continue to figure largely in the work of local unions.

Production conferences began in big enterprises of several cities in 1922, and by 1924 the party was emphasizing them as an important means of interesting workers in improving production. A series of decisions by the party and the CCTU in the next two years tried to broaden this movement, bring in larger numbers of workers and engineers, and see that management paid attention to criticisms and suggestions. The role of the conferences was unclear, however; managements were often uninterested, and in spite of some successes workers showed only limited interest and there was much dissatis-faction with results.[5]

Contradictions in the role of the unions were obvious. Unions came to serve chiefly as agents of the party and the govern-ment in promoting discipline and production, often in disre-gard of the opinion of workers. Discontent led to many unau-thorized stoppages. Strikes were not banned by law, either at this time or later, but they were frowned on as unnecessary and harmful. Disputes were expected to be settled by elaborate systems of conciliation and arbitration. In 1925 managements as well as unions received the right to appeal for binding arbitration. Criticisms were voiced even at party and trade union congresses that often union leaders formed a bloc with management and the party and disregarded workers' interests. The dilemma was shown in the trade union congress in 1926 where it was said that some unions and their officers were concerned only with protecting their members' interests while others neglected this function and unconditionally supported management, even when collective contracts, labor legislation, and the needs of workers were disregarded.[6]

Toward the end of the 1920's there was talk again of trade union democracy. Election methods were changed to allow members to vote on their local officers individually, instead of being given a list to approve. Membership continued to grow, helped by advantages in jobs, in social insurance benefits, and in preference for passes to rest houses and other facilities. By 1928 national industrial unions included eleven million members or some 90 per cent of all manual and non-manual workers.

THE FIVE-YEAR PLANS

A turning point came in 1928-1929 with the adoption of the policy of rapid industrialization. Open discussion of controversies came to an end. On orders of the party the trade unions removed leaders who had stood for relative independence and for emphasis on defending the interests of workers; chief among them was the right-wing communist leader Tomsky, CCTU chairman, who later committed suicide. It was assumed that "the victory of socialism" made the defense function obsolete and that the unions should "face towards production." Their main job was to be educating workers and cooperating in every way in the interest of fulfilling the five-year plans.[7]

In the planned economy wages inevitably became a matter for high policy decisions. New wage policies aimed at widening individual incentives by greatly increasing differentials and by using piece rates that rose progressively as output went up. The trade union tendency to favor equalization of wages was derided as harmful "trade unionism." The national unions were involved in discussions with economic administrations before wage decrees were issued, but local unions lost any right to bargain on wages and could only protest management decisions through the grievance machinery. If workers tried to obtain higher wages, or supported efforts of managers to increase pay as a means of getting more labor, they were harshly criticized by authorities. Unions were expected to back the tightening of production standards and to explain the necessity for it to workers.

Union cooperation in production took many forms. Most important in the prewar period was "socialist competition," in which "shock workers" and "shock brigades" pledged to overfulfill production plans. Soon nation-wide competitions between enterprises were widely publicized. By 1933 more than 70 per cent of all industrial workers were said to be involved. From 1935 on, competition took the form of the Stakhanovite movement, which spread rapidly. This was named for a coal miner who undertook to greatly increase his output through better organization of work.[8] Improved methods and better utilization of skilled workers resulted in higher productivity and earnings and other benefits for the Stakhanovites. Many workers, especially among the young, joined enthusiastically in these movements, but many others resented the pressures, the tightening up of production standards, and speedups. The role of the unions was to help organize competition, stimulate the interest of workers, and try to see that improved methods were widely introduced. Production conferences and general meetings of workers in the shops were increasingly used. The conferences and workers' meetings were active in establishing the rules for socialist competition, checking the results, and trying to improve conditions that affected production.

Efforts were made to tighten labor discipline and to decrease excessive turnover. The development of industry ended the serious unemployment of the 1920's and brought from the villages a great influx of new inexperienced workers, unaccustomed to factory discipline. The unions took major responsibility for training and indoctrinating new workers, especially youths, and organized social pressure in the shops against slack workers. People were dismissed or expelled from the unions for absence or other violations of discipline. Finally, in 1938, the Central Council of Trade Unions joined with the party and the government in a decree that set severe penalties, up to dismissal, for lateness or absence without excuse, and made social security benefits dependent on length of service. Notice required for leaving jobs was increased from seven days to one month. In addition, the system of individual labor books was instituted.[9]

Other functions of the unions suffered. Numerous complaints appeared in the press on lack of attention to workers' needs. Collective contracts were no longer free to establish any better conditions than those provided by law and became primarily statements of obligations of workers and management on production. Finally they were dropped completely, not to be reinstated until 1947. Protection of health and safety at work suffered, although on paper the functions of the Central Council of Trade Unions in this area were increased in 1933 by abolition of the Commissariat of Labor and transfer of its functions to the CCTU. The unions were to administer social insurance benefits and work on "protection of labor." They issued safety regulations and provided inspectors, and volunteer safety inspectors were elected in the plants. However, when necessary support from higher authorities was lacking, these protections proved ineffective. In 1935, when the CCTU tried to remedy bad conditions in a big plant, the party censured the unions and their newspapers for supporting "opportunists" among the workers and their "anti-state" aims.[10] The production drive came first, above the interests of safety or enforcement of labor laws.

During the 1930's the unions reached their low ebb. In 1930, in an effort to bring them into closer touch with the workers, the basic unit had been made the small "trade union group," which elected its group organizer. Shop committees also were to be elected as a link between the worker and the factory committee. But for long periods no elections were held in the plants or for higher union bodies, and officers were appointed from above. Union democracy went by the board in spite of official statements and complaints in the press. On decision of the party national unions were split along narrower industrial lines, so that their central committees could more easily keep contact with the industrial ministries or administrations. Inter-union councils at the republic and regional levels were abolished in 1937, since the main emphasis was then on the industrial unions. The number of union members rose as industry expanded and in 1932 reached 17.5 millions, but this was only 75 per cent of all wage and salary workers, in spite of the advantages of membership.

At the end of the 1930's the unions in the plants were chiefly occupied with propaganda and efforts to increase production. They shared in settling grievances, administered disability benefits and other welfare services, and carried on cultural and educational activities; but there was widespread feeling among workers that the unions were chiefly agencies of management and the party, not able or willing to do much for their members. At the national level the unions, led by prominent communists, shared in the regulation of labor conditions, functioning more like a governmental department of labor than an agency of the workers. Significantly, after the 1932 Congress of Trade Unions, no further sessions were called until 1949, a period of seventeen years. Union leaders and ordinary workers suffered in the terror of the thirties, and many of them joined the millions in the forced-labor camps.[11]

In 1940, by the decree said to have been recommended by the Central Council of Trade Unions, workers were frozen to their jobs; they could leave only with permission of the manager, and harsh penalties were imposed for absence or tardiness without acceptable excuse. Unions cooperated in reorganizing production as plants were evacuated and set up in the East, and in training and disciplining the new workers, largely women and youths, who were recruited or drafted to replace those mobilized. Control of wages, hours, and other conditions was strictly centralized in the militarized economy. Unions helped promote wage-incentive systems, and joint wage commissions were set up in the plants to solve local problems. Socialist competition, organized by the unions, continued to provide a stimulus to effort.

Under the stress of the war, unions could do little about working conditions. Hours were long and safety was often disregarded. However, as welfare agencies serving the daily needs of workers and their families, the unions were able to help on the difficult problems of food, housing, and other necessities. They arranged for vegetable gardens to supplement food supplies. They worked on problems of supplying clothing, medical services, and care of children. Officers and committees were appointed or co-opted, and hundreds of thousands of workers were drawn into participation in these activities.[12]

At the end of the war, with the need for reconstruction of

industry and of the devastated areas, the unions' job was still mainly to promote the needs of industry. But a start was made toward increasing the role of the unions as representatives of workers, especially at the local level. In 1945 the CCTU demanded that more attention be given to living conditions and to health and safety at work and the enforcement of labor legislation, especially for the protection of women and young workers. Local unions were instructed to call regular meetings of workers in the shops. In 1947 the CCTU issued detailed instructions for elections, from the local unions up to the central committees of the national unions.[13] Inter-union councils, republic and regional, were reestablished in 1948, on orders of the party, to better coordinate the work of the local unions and provide closer relations with local party organs and the new regional economic councils. The number of national unions was reduced to sixty-six.

In 1947 the Council of Ministers, "on recommendation of the CCTU," directed that collective contracts again be negotiated in enterprises. The main function of these new agreements was to mobilize the workers for fulfillment of the five-year plans. For ten years the contracts largely followed models sent out by the central committees of the unions. Yet there was room for improvements wanted in working conditions and for decisions on the use of funds for housing and other services. Frequently, however, no real consideration of local needs was reflected in the contracts, and managements and unions failed to take them seriously.

A report published later on textile unionism spoke of the weakness of the unions at this time and of managers' violations of labor legislation and the collective contracts. It complained that many managers continued to use wartime methods of administration, and that union officers often limited their protests to complaints to higher union organs, or, "not wishing to dispute with management," they tolerated violations of labor legislation and did not seek punishment of those guilty. Finally, in a typical post-Stalin touch, the activity of the unions was said to have been adversely affected by "the cult of personality of Stalin."[14]

When the Tenth Congress of Trade Unions met in 1949, after seventeen years, it heard much criticism of lack of democracy in the unions. Membership had increased to 28.4 million, or 87 per cent of all workers. The number of "actives" in all aspects of union work was said to have grown from 3 million in 1932 to 9.3 million in 1949. But in many unions there had been no elections for years. Officers were appointed, sometimes from outside the plant, and frequent turnover in leadership resulted in poor work. Among delegates to the congress, only 23.5 per cent were workers directly engaged in production. The greatest representation was from full-time officials of the national unions. Communist party members or candidates were 72 per cent of all delegates.[15] In the congress, the main interest of the unions was in socialist competition and other activities to increase production although some attention was given to strengthening compliance with labor legislation and to improving living conditions and services. Increased attention was given also to training for trade union work.

A new union statute was adopted that provided for democratic practices in all union elections, but it was frank in its acceptance of party leadership. Significantly, its statement of functions emphasized first the responsibility towards production, then educational and cultural work, and last, the work on problems of safety, labor legislation, and improving working and living conditions. Only at the end did it repeat the 1922 legislative provision of the union's right to appear in the name of workers before government bodies. Another revision of the statute in 1954 implied some increase in the role of the local unions. It included among their functions that of checking on the revision of production standards and the proper application of the wage system.[16] Further expansion of union rights had to await the Twentieth Congress of the Communist Party in 1956 and the policy changes that followed the reaction from Stalinism.

At the Eleventh Congress of Trade Unions in 1954, union membership was reported to have increased to 40 million, or 90 per cent of all employed. Among the delegates, the number of workers had increased to 30.9 per cent; party members, as before, were the large majority. The party's message to the congress emphasized the role of the unions as a "school of communism" and a promoter of production. But it also said that concern for the welfare of workers was a primary task, and it called for increasing the role of the unions in public life and improving their ties with the people.[17]

POLICY AFTER THE TWENTIETH CONGRESS OF THE COMMUNIST PARTY

The stage for a greater role and increased activity of the trade unions was set by the Twentieth Congress in 1956, with its denunciation of Stalinist methods and call for "collective leadership," "socialist democracy," and "socialist legality." This followed signs in 1954 and 1955 of the larger role that the party was preparing to give the unions. Severe criticisms of trade union work by the Central Committee of the party led to detailed self–criticism at plenary sessions of the CCTU, and instructions were issued to all levels of the unions to improve their work, both on production and on activities related to the workers' interests. A CCTU decision of March 17, 1956, acknowledged the party's criticism "that the level of work of the trade unions obviously lags behind the demands of life, of the tasks set by the party. The chief thing lacked by the trade union organs, including the CCTU, is militance, creative fire, keenness, action on principle, and initiative in posing fundamental questions, important for life—whether one speaks of means for raising the productivity of labor or of questions of wages, construction of housing, satisfying the living needs of workers."[18] The CCTU admitted the justice of the indictment, gave detailed evidence of lacks in union work, and went on to propose methods to eliminate them. But it said nothing of why the unions had been so slack.

The authoritative statement of the new role of the trade unions came in a lengthy resolution of the Central Committee of the party on December 17, 1957, which was to serve as a guide to party and government leaders and industrial administrators, and for the unions themselves.[19] The "central task" of the unions was still declared to be "the mobilization of the masses" for the progress of the economy. The role of the unions in "economic construction" was to increase. Planning organs at all levels were obligated to consider the opinion of union organizations. Regional economic councils and local soviet organs were to review all questions affecting labor together with union representatives, after discussion at workers' meetings. "The greatest task" of the unions was said to be to improve conditions for workers. Unions should use fully their right to check on observance of labor legislation and to make demands on administrators. They should participate in improving wage systems and in preparing for the shift to shorter hours of work. They should check on progress in construction of housing and on the work of trade and other agencies. They should also raise the level of intra-union life. The functions of the factory, plant, and local union committees should be substantially increased. Finally, party members were instructed to take more responsibility for work in the unions at all levels.

This policy of increasing the role of the unions, especially at regional and local levels, was related to decisions that to a degree decentralized economic planning and administration and increased the scope for local action. After the regional economic councils, the *sovnarkhozy*, were set up in 1957, the CCTU gave the regional trade union councils, the *sovprofs*, substantial authority in direct leadership of local unions and in working with the sovnarkhozy on all questions related to planning, production, and the lives of workers.[20] In one of several governmental decrees, a new system for handling grievances emphasized more prompt settlement on the spot, by increasing the powers of the factory committees and providing for appeal to local courts.[21] In the summer of 1958 the rights of factory, plant, and local union committees were defined and extended.[22] The same month a regulation on production conferences was approved, designed to increase their effectiveness.[23]

Greater union activity resulting from these increases in union powers was expected to provide an extra check on managements, and also to stimulate the "creative initiative" of workers in solving production problems. As always, the basic decisions on these policies were made in high circles of the party, although the national trade union centers, led by important communists, had an active part in working out many of the measures. The workers themselves and their local unions stood to gain substantially, though they had nothing to do with making the decisions.

The Twenty-Second Congress of the Communist Party in 1961 reaffirmed the increased role and significance of the unions. It declared that "the rights and functions of the trade unions in the decision of all questions touching the living interests of the working people had significantly widened," and would continue to grow as Soviet society moved toward communism and new problems were included in the sphere of union activity.[24]

Other laws in the labor field reflected trends toward liberalization after the Twentieth Congress, among them the April 1956 repeal of restrictions on changing jobs, and, that same year, the increase in minimum wages. In succeeding years, changes in wage standards raised the earnings of most lower-paid and middle-paid workers. Pension and disability benefits were substantially improved. The basic workday, still with the six-day week, was reduced from eight to seven hours—six in some cases—beginning with coal and heavy industry, and by 1960 covering workers in all industries.

TRADE UNION PRINCIPLES

Soviet trade unions are governed by principles established by the party and reaffirmed in party and trade union documents, especially the union statute. Fundamentally, these are the principles of the compromise proposed by Lenin and adopted in 1921, but far from always observed in the later years. As formulated after 1956, they gave the unions the two-sided function of "participating in economic construction" and also serving the needs of the working people and defending their interests. A CCTU booklet boasts, "For the first time in the history of mankind, trade unions are not limited only to defense of the rights of the working people, but effectively participate in the administration of production and in all affairs of society."[25]

The most basic principle is that the unions carry on all their work under the leadership of the party. Initiative for major developments in union work comes from party directives. Soviet spokesmen insist that the party does not interfere in the work of the trade unions, and that there is no "party group" or caucus in local unions. There are party groups, however, in shops and enterprises, and the party bureau often has its office conveniently near the offices of the director of the enterprise and of the union committee. The influence of the party is supposed to come through its members who are members of the trade unions, by persuasion and education. Communists in the trade unions are enjoined to be active in nominating and training trade union leaders. Party groups are established in the trade union congresses and conferences and in the elected organs of these sessions, according to the party statute, with the duty to promote party policies and on all questions to be "strongly and steadfastly led by decisions of the leading party organs."[26]

"Democratic centralism" is the basic organizational principle. This means, according to the trade union statute, that all union organs from top to bottom are elected by the members and report to them, that union organizations decide all questions in accordance with the union statutes and decisions of higher trade union organs, that decisions are made by majority vote, and that lower organs are subordinate to the higher.[27] It includes the concept of collective leadership and of democratic elections with the secret ballot, with some exceptions, after open criticism and discussion of past work and open nomination and discussion of candidates. It involves also the idea of wide participation of the rank and file in trade union work. The ideal is *samodeyatelnost*, a word difficult to define, literally "self-activity," or "spontaneous activity"—yet the wanted initiative and independence are to be disciplined, within the limits of approved policy. As explained by an authority:

Every trade union organization can and should display its own initiative, employing forms and methods of work most suitable in given concrete circumstances, most helpful for success in the work, in the decision of tasks before the collective. However, trade unions united in a community of aims and tasks could not act in one direction if . . . there were not in effect uniform rules on the chief questions of trade union life.[28]

A "production principle" governs union structure. Each national union has jurisdiction over all who work in one industry or a group of related industries. The number and jurisdictions of these unions have been changed many times, to fit changes in administrative structure in industry, since the unions work closely with management at higher levels as well as in the plants. The inter-union regional trade union councils became key links in the structure when the center of administration for most industry was shifted from national ministries to the regional economic councils.

The principle that the unions have an important function in furthering workers' interests came to the fore only after this was authorized by the party. This right was specified in the 1922 Labor Code,[29] but subsequently the defense function came to be replaced by emphasis on production, and the term, defense (*zashchita*), dropped out of use. That the unions are representatives of the workers and defenders of their interests was only slowly and cautiously reinstated in official statements. Changes in terminology appear to reflect real shifts in party policy, and acceptance of the need for advocates for labor with effective means for protecting the workers' interests.

The 1949 and 1954 union statutes declared that the state, not the unions, defended the rights of workers; but that the unions could "appear in the name of workers before state and public organs on questions of labor, life and culture"; also that the members could "turn to the unions for defense and support of their rights" in case of violations by managements.[30] A CCTU resolution on August 20, 1957, promised increased union efforts toward defending the workers' interests, "following the instructions of the Communist Party."[31] By 1959, in the list of union functions, the statute gave first place to the right to appear in the name of workers before government and public organs; and added a clear statement that the union committees "effect representation in the name of the workers" on all questions of labor and life.[32] The new party program in 1961 emphasized the unions' duty "to protect the material interests and rights of working people."[33] Finally, the 1963 union statute added the unequivocal statement, "Trade unions defend the interests of workers and employees." It went on to say that unions "have the right of legislative initiative, participate in planning the national economy, protect the material interests and rights of the working people."[34] The extent to which these increased powers are used by the unions, and are supported by higher union, administrative, party and government organs, must be analyzed.

A final principle is that the unions are "schools of communism." Efforts for the communist education of the workers are expected to permeate every activity, from those on production and protection of workers' interests, through all the educational, cultural, recreational, and welfare programs.

These principles and policies result in a wide range of activities. How this work is carried on will be explained in the discussion concerning the different levels of the union organizations. It will be seen that the duty of the unions to represent their members does not always combine easily with that of following the leadership and dictates of the party.

TRADE UNION STRUCTURE

The sixty-eight million members of the Soviet unions in 1963 were said to include 94 per cent of all employed in industry, state farms, trade, education, medical services, governmental, and other organizations. Only collective farmers as a group are not covered.[35] Union organization,[36] as shown in the diagram (page 67), starts with the small trade union group of fellow workers and reaches up to the national congress of trade unions, which is supposed to meet once in four years to elect the All-Union Central Council of Trade Unions. The CCTU is the authoritative spokesman for the unions and directs all union activities between congresses. It holds plenary sessions not less than once in six months, and its work is carried on regularly by the elected presidium and secretariat.

National industrial unions are headed by their central committees, elected once in two years at congresses of elected delegates. They also have lower level elected organs such as

TRADE UNION STRUCTURE

Meetings, Conferences and Congresses	Elected Union Organs	
	National Industrial or Branch Unions	Inter-Union Councils

All-Union Congress of
Trade Unions *elects* .... All-Union Central
Council of Trade
Unions (CCTU)

Congress of National
Union *elects* .... Central Committee of
National Union

Republic Inter-Union
Congress *elects* .... Republic Inter-Union
Trade Union Council
(Sovprof)

Regional Inter-Union
Conference *elects* .... Regional Inter-Union
Trade Union Council
(Sovprof)

Regional Conference of
Industrial or Branch
Union *elects* .... Regional Committee

Plant Meeting or Plant
Delegate Conference
elects .... Factory, Plant, or
Local Committee

Shop Meeting *elects* .... Shop Committee

Trade Union Group of
Union Members *elects* .. Trade Union Group
Organizers

Note: Authority of the union organs runs from the top down, as shown
by the arrows, and from the inter-union CCTU and sovprofs to the branch
unions with their central, regional, and local units. Responsibility of the
elected organs to the membership is supposed to be provided by their
election by the conferences and congresses composed of delegates elected
from below, and by the general membership meetings in the trade union
groups, shops, and plants. The all-pervasive influence of the Communist
Party cannot be shown in such a diagram.

republic, regional, and city committees. The number of these branch unions is determined by the Central Council of Trade Unions. The twenty-three unions of the first decade were split up into forty-five, and then during the industrialization drive of the 1930's, to 168, and during the war to 192. After the war, consolidations reduced the number to forty-three. Finally, with the reorganization of industrial administration and the increased importance of the regional trade union councils, another consolidation established twenty-two large industrial unions. The fields, as listed in 1960, were the following.[37]

Agriculture and state purchasing
Aircraft and defense industry
Aviation
Coal mining
Communications and road transport
Construction and building materials
Cooperative and state trade
Cultural workers
Education and scientific institutions
Food industry
Geological prospecting
Government
Health workers
Local industry and communal economy
Machine building
Metallurgy
Oil and chemical industry
Power and electrical industry
Railroad transport
Sea and river fleet
Textile and light industries
Timber, paper and woodworking

Inter-union republic councils of trade unions have many of the same functions that the All-Union CCTU performs for the country as a whole and for the Russian republic. They are elected at congresses of the trade unions of the republics. Since 1957, trade union councils, or sovprofs, covering regions (*oblasts*) or territories (*krai*) or small republics, have been the most important organs for direct day-to-day leadership of the local unions. These are elected by delegate conferences of the unions of their areas. In 1961 there were 14 republic councils,

7 territorial and 127 regional trade union councils.[38] In 1963 in 75 territories and regions where both industry and agriculture were important, the sovprofs were divided into separate sovprofs for industry and agriculture. This followed decisions of the Communist Party to reduce the number of regional economic councils and to set up separate party and soviet organs for work in industries and cities, and in agriculture and rural areas. This division, which was said to have created many difficulties, was ended late in 1964 when the party reversed the policy after the removal of Khrushchev.[39]

The primary unit is the organization at the work place, where workers elect their factory, plant or local union committees, or in very small enterprises a trade union organizer. In 1963 there were 470,000 local units; 120,000, with forty million members, were in industry, construction and transportation; 33,000, with ten million members, were in agriculture. The rest of the units with their eighteen million members were in trade, services, and governmental, cultural, and educational institutions.[40] In large enterprises there are also shop committees. General meetings of the membership, or conferences of elected delegates from shops in the larger plants, are the supreme local authority to which the elected union committees are responsible. At the bottom is the trade union group, of members of a brigade or section, who elect their group organizer and other representatives.

In 1962, according to the CCTU, there were three million members of factory, plant, local, and shop committees, over ten million members of their commissions, and 1.5 million group organizers. A total of twenty-three million, about one-third of all union members, were said to be actively engaged in union work.[41]

Membership is voluntary and open to all manual and non-manual hired workers, including the highest governmental administrators, professional personnel, and managers of enterprises, and the newest worker. It is also open to students in higher education and in vocational-technical schools. Admission is through the trade union group. The extent of coverage differs considerably by regions, industries, and individual plants—possibly reflecting variations in attitudes of workers towards the union, or in the diligence of the union in enlisting membership, or the rate of turnover in the enterprise.

The large coverage of union membership is accounted for in part by the value of the local union as a vehicle for expressing the desires of workers and serving their needs. Union membership also gives advantages, especially preference in some of the social insurance benefits. Non-members receive only one-half of the regular rates for non-occupational sickness benefits, and maternity benefits are lower for non-members. Union members have preference in obtaining passes to rest houses and sanitariums and in getting places for their children in nurseries, kindergartens, and summer camps. Free legal aid is provided by the unions, and there are possibilities of financial assistance from union funds in case of emergency.[42] These specific advantages in membership are sufficient to keep most working people enrolled. People who do not join are said to be mostly young workers who do not yet feel themselves permanent members of the staff or others who have not got around to joining, or in a few cases, individualists who as a matter of inclination stay outside.

Union dues are in general at the rate of one per cent of wages and salaries, with lower rates for those earning under seventy rubles a month.[43] The greatest part of the dues, 70 per cent or more, remains with the primary organizations. In addition, the local units have funds from the enterprises and from economic administrations for clubhouses and other educational, cultural, and sports facilities and activities, and from dues from the voluntary sports societies and other organizations. In 1963 it was reported that only 13.5 per cent of all union funds went for administrative staff and organizational purposes, and 86.5 per cent for educational, cultural, physical culture and sports activities, and for other services to members.[44] Efforts were made to reduce paid staffs and to have the greatest part of the work carried on by members in their free time.

The rights of union members were somewhat more strongly spelled out in the 1963 union statute than earlier, and the statement on members' obligations was considerably amplified.[45] The democratic rights of members include participation in elections and in discussion at union meetings, with the right to criticize and raise questions in union organs on the work of unions and administrations, and to bring in any proposals. Members are entitled to be present at any union meeting where their own activity is being discussed; and they may join the union's bureau of mutual aid.

The list of obligations sets high standards of economic, political, and cultural behavior, as well as such duties as attending meetings, fulfilling public assignments from union organs, and paying dues properly. Members should work "honestly and voluntarily," increase the productivity of labor, promote economies in production and support the progress of science and culture and the fulfillment of production plans, and participate in socialist competition. They should work for strict observance of labor discipline and the full use of work time. They should increase their own political understanding and general education, their skill, and "cultural-technical level." They are under obligation to oppose any "anti-social manifestations" and to observe the rules of the socialist community.

These formally stated rights and obligations are far from always observed. Nevertheless their spirit is often to be felt in the work and attitudes of individual workers and their local unions.

CHAPTER IV

The Trade Union Centers

AT the apex of the huge Soviet trade union structure is the All-Union Central Council of Trade Unions, located in Moscow, and deriving its authority, according to the union statute,[1] from the All-Union Congress of Trade Unions. Also located in Moscow and near CCTU headquarters are the central committees of the national industrial unions. These union centers have close contacts with government and administrative agencies and with the party. They have extensive powers over the lower union organizations and they influence all labor relations in the localities.

The All-Union Congress of Trade Unions is supposed to meet once in four years, with delegates elected from the national industrial unions and the republic and regional interunion congresses and conferences. It hears and approves the reports of the Central Council of Trade Unions, approves the trade union statute, elects the CCTU, and plans the current programs, in line with instructions from the Communist Party. It is entitled to hear reports from planning and administrative organs and is expected to provide for union participation in efforts to fulfill economic plans and to promote the welfare of workers.

The congress is not an independent decision-making body representing the membership.[2] Sessions are thoroughly organized and controlled, and are dominated by party policy. Decisions made by the leadership or by working commissions are unanimously approved. Top leaders of the party and the government take part in the meetings. Each congress opens with greetings from the Central Committee of the Communist Party. In both 1959 and 1963 these greetings spoke of the growing role of the unions and urged them to participate more effectively in all planning and production activities. They also urged them to show initiative and persistence in improving working and living conditions and in protecting workers' rights. The duty to educate workers in the spirit of communism was emphasized and the unions were told to increase democracy, initiative, and spontaneous activity in trade union life, with criticism and self-criticism at all levels. Chairman V. V. Grishin of the CCTU made clear the dependence of the unions on the party and gave assurance of loyalty to its purposes.[3]

The elected delegates are widely representative of the unions in all industries and all parts of the country. Reports of the credentials commissions give details, though more in 1959 than in 1963. In 1959 there were 1,322 delegates, 404 elected by congresses of the national industrial unions, the rest by inter-union congresses and conferences in republics and regions. Delegates who worked in manufacturing and extraction industries, construction, transportation, and agriculture numbered 676, of whom 468 or more than one-third of all delegates were wage earners, the rest being engineers, office workers, or administrative officers. Full-time union officers and staff members were 481 of the total. Active union members working on production jobs numbered 568; among these were 100 members of the central committees of their national unions, or of inter-union councils, 89 from the branch union committees in their areas, 218 from shop, plant or local committees, 92 trade union group organizers, and 69 members of commissions of the plant and local committees. Ties with governmental organs were shown by the inclusion of 158 deputies to the Supreme Soviet of the USSR or of the republics, and 335 to local soviets. There were representatives from 47 nationalities. Women were 38.5 per cent of all delegates. More than 40 per cent of all were under 40 years of age. The number of party members was not reported, but they must have been in the majority, as in 1954.[4]

At the 1963 congress the number of delegates, 4,001, had more than tripled. The CCTU had increased the number to be elected, based on membership, in the name of greater democracy. As a result, to a larger extent even than in 1959 the congress became a mass meeting for purposes of information, propaganda and morale-building, rather than a working session to decide policy. Representation from people working in production increased; over half of the delegates were wage earners, compared with 35 per cent in 1959. There was no report on the number or positions of the union officials. Deputies to Soviet organs, as in 1959, were about one-third of all delegates. Women had increased to 41.7 per cent of all; the number of delegates under 40 years also increased, to 63 per cent compared with 40 per cent in 1959. Sixty nationalities were represented. Communist party members and candidates were 60 per cent of all delegates.[5] The make-up of the congress reflected the policies of bringing larger numbers into active work in the unions, especially bringing younger people into the committees and councils, and reducing paid staffs. For these new people, election as delegates to the congress was an honor, a reward for service. Attendance was expected to educate them and stimulate them for effective activity on their home grounds.

The Twelfth Congress, in 1959, lasted five days, and the Thirteenth, in 1963, six days, both sessions shorter than the eight-day congresses of 1949 and 1954. At each congress the long CCTU report, read by Chairman Grishin, the auditing commission report, and the report on changes in the union statute were followed by speeches from officers of major

unions and a few workers. Finally the chairman gave his
concluding speech. The reports were adopted, a resolution on
the work of the CCTU was accepted, the changes in the statute
were voted, the election was held, and a message to the Central Committee of the Communist Party was adopted. For
the most part, delegates who spoke reported on progress on
production in their areas and how the unions had helped.
Some spoke of their educational work and their efforts to improve working and living conditions. Some brought out criticisms of higher union bodies, of government agencies, and of
enterprise managements. A few, especially workers and other
local representatives, spoke of the need to improve working
and living conditions and enforcement of labor laws. But, so far
as is shown in the brief published reports, there was no effort
to pose and discuss major problems facing the unions, and
no controversies were threshed out on the floor.

The list of speakers shows how the sessions were dominated
by the officialdom. In summarizing the 1963 session Chairman
Grishin said that forty-two delegates had spoken. The press
reports show that eleven of these were from republic union
councils and six from regional councils; four were from central
committees of the industrial unions and one from a regional
committee. From the plant and local committees there were
eleven speakers, nine of them workers and two chairmen of
committees. Others included a plant director, a captain of a
trawler, a teacher, a Komsomol officer, an artist, representatives
from the society of inventors and rationalizers and from the
Academy of Sciences, and two astronauts. In addition there
were speeches by seven ministers or chairmen of state committees of the USSR or the Russian republic. Also, at both
sessions, time was taken by representatives of foreign labor
movements; eighty were introduced at the 1963 congress and
forty-five of them spoke. Time was not allowed for any thorough discussion of problems by delegates.

At both the 1959 and the 1963 sessions the long reports by Chairman Grishin on the work of the CCTU since the last congress followed the same general pattern.[6] In the press coverage of the 1963 report, covering five pages of the union newspaper, more than a third of the space was given to production problems, said to have been the area of the unions' chief activity. The next section, on "care of workers—the high duty and obligation of the trade unions," took about a fifth of the report. The reduction of hours, increases in wages, and other gains, were discussed. But while there was talk of the need for improvements in wage systems and incentives, to help production and make gains in living levels, the problem of low wages was not specifically mentioned. Pointed statements were made on the need for improving working and living conditions and observance of safety standards and other labor laws. Shorter sections followed on educational and cultural work, with attention to discipline and to organization questions—elections, the development of volunteer activity, and the choice and training of union officers. A final section dealt with the international trade union movement.

In essence the resolutions adopted at the end of the sessions only repeated the points made in the reports, and showed no decisions on policy, nor any demands on the party and the government in behalf of workers. Support was pledged for the programs of fulfilling the seven-year plans and for construction of communism. In summarizing the discussions Chairman Grishin mentioned that many good suggestions had been made for improving work, and surprisingly he acknowledged that some delegates had spoken of the need for improvements in pay. He admitted that there were still serious deficiencies in the organization of wages, which the CCTU should seek to remove. He promised that the new CCTU would study these and other questions and make the necessary decisions.[7] But no real discussions of any such issues were published.

One subject on which there was a limited amount of debate in 1959 was that of the new statute. A commission to revise the document had been set up by the CCTU in 1958. It had thirty-nine members, most of them from officers and staff of the CCTU, central committees, and republic councils, a few from regional councils and unions in the plants, and the editor of the union newspaper *Trud*.[8] Their report proposed changes to bring the statute into line with the December 1957 party decisions and the 1958 law on the rights of factory, plant, and local union committees. Changes were needed in the statements on functions of central committees and inter-union regional councils; also, additions to the section on the primary units. Proposals to lengthen the term of office for factory and local committees to two years, and for central committees and republic councils to four years, and to change from secret ballot to open vote in the election of local committees, were rejected. The aim should be, it was held, to increase union democracy rather than limit it, and to strengthen relations with the masses and draw them into active participation by regular and frequent meetings, reports, and elections.[9] In discussion that followed the report, the changes in functions of the different levels of the unions were approved as in line with current practices. Some delegates, however, still argued for lengthened terms for committees, so they could know their work better; others considered the short terms with the secret ballot essential for democratic functioning. A number of other suggestions were made for revisions. The next day the commission reported again, making some minor changes, and the statute was unanimously adopted.[10]

In 1963, to bring the statute into line with other changes already in effect on party instructions and with the stated objectives of the new party program, it was necessary to provide for separate regional trade union councils for industry and for agriculture, and for rotation in the make-up of elected bodies and the leadership. Volunteer activity was to be emphasized in place of paid staffs, and statements of the functions of the unions at all levels were to be strengthened. A draft drawn up by the CCTU had apparently been made available to the delegates. The report on changes, by Secretary Bulgakov of the CCTU, was followed by speeches by seven delegates, all approving the draft. A member of a commission elected by the congress to review the draft reported that all changes proposed by his commission had been incorporated. No details were given, however. The congress then approved those changes, and unanimously adopted the proposed statute.[11] There had been no open discussion of issues involved in the new statements on rights of the unions and their members.

The new statute reaffirmed union dependence on the leadership of the Communist Party and its program. Detail was added as to participation in government and administrative affairs, with a clear statement on the function of defending workers' interests. The right of the CCTU and the republic councils to propose labor legislation was specified—a highly significant right because of the important role of legislation in determining wages and other labor conditions. The right of union members to criticize was strengthened—"to criticize at union meetings, conferences, congresses and in the press the activity of trade union, administrative organs, soviet institutions and their workers, regardless of their positions." Secretary Bulgakov in his report had implied lacks in the past when he said, "Trade union organizations are obligated to establish such conditions that every working person can boldly, openly criticize any trade union and administrative workers."[12] New provisions were added for the recall of officers.

In the 1963 congress an elected committee reported on the election by secret ballot of the Central Council of Trade Unions, but there was no indication of how the nominations had been drawn up. (The list could have come from the CCTU presidium or secretariat, or from a party caucus.) The ballot offered no choices, apparently, for Chairman Grishin told the delegates that "the unanimous vote . . . was an evidence of the high level and orderliness (organizovannosti) of the congress."[13] In 1959 the council elected had 197 members and 69 alternates. It included, among those identifiable, representatives of many central committees and of all republic and several regional councils, several chairmen of regional branch committees and of plant and local committees, a plant director, local party workers, the editor of *Trud,* and of course Chairman Grishin, who is a candidate member of the presidium of the Central Committee of the party, and all the CCTU secretaries. Party representation was strong. The list included 21 who were delegates to the Twenty-First Congress of the Communist Party later in 1959, and 5 members and 3 candidate members of the Central Committee of the party.

The CCTU elected in 1963 was increased to 279 members, with 93 alternates, in line with the effort to bring more people into active work. Most of the members were newly elected; less than 50 were carried over from the 1959 list of members and alternates, but these included the CCTU officers and the leaders of major councils and central committees of the industrial unions. How many were communists is not known, but in all probability they were in the majority. The Central Committee of the party was represented by Chairman Grishin, one council secretary, one member of the presidium and three others; another secretary and four others were candidate members of the Central Committee of the party. Several others of the secretariat and presidium have been delegates to party congresses.[14]

The most important function of the congresses has been to provide for spreading information, exchanging experience, and promoting a feeling of unity and a consciousness of duties and opportunities. Nevertheless, both the 1959 and 1963 sessions allowed for expression of opinion, criticism of higher and lower bodies in the unions, government agencies, and managements, and for the stating of felt needs. The range of matters covered reflects the increased role of the unions and their growing capacities for improving workers' conditions, though always within the limits of policies decided elsewhere. While the public reports have given only little indication of the feelings of the mass of members, upward communication took place to some degree. Communication from the top down was expected as delegates returned home, reported to workers' meetings, explained the decisions of the congress, and tried to improve the effectiveness of the work locally.

THE ALL-UNION CENTRAL COUNCIL OF TRADE UNIONS

As leader of the mass organization of Soviet workers, the CCTU has a responsible position in Soviet society. Although led by directives of the Communist Party and headed by prominent party members, it also speaks for workers at high levels of the party and government when policies are being considered. It issues authoritative instructions to all union organizations. It joins government agencies in issuing decrees and regulations.

Major functions of the CCTU, as defined in the 1963 statute, include the control, direction and leadership of all the unions, and, on the other hand, relations with government and public affairs. On intra-union matters the CCTU determines the structure and staffs of all union organizations and approves their budgets, checks on their work and gives them instructions. It establishes trade union schools and publishes books and periodicals at its own press. In the public sphere, the CCTU is entitled to participate in working out the national economic plan and to receive reports from all government and administrative agencies. It has the right to take part in the preparation and consideration of all governmental decisions affecting labor, and has responsibilities in the administration and enforcement of labor laws.[15]

Plenary sessions of the CCTU, according to the union statute, meet not less than once in six months; twelve such sessions were held between the 1959 and 1963 congresses. The first plenum elects by open vote the chairman and seven secretaries and the presidium of fifteen members. The presidium is scheduled to meet twice a month. Day-to-day work is directed by the secretariat, which makes many decisions subject to approval of the presidium, of which they are members. Sessions of the council serve to spread information and instructions, and formally, at least, check on the work of the presidium and secretariat, and make decisions on policy.

Staff departments in the CCTU deal with labor and wages, protection of labor, social insurance, organizational-instruction work, housing and living conditions, physical culture and sports, international relations, finance, and administration. They make studies and carry on the detailed activities involved in directing the huge union structure and in relations with governmental decision-making bodies. The program of increasing volunteer activities in the unions, after the Twenty-Second Congress of the party, led to setting up six widely representative public commissions in the CCTU. These studied and prepared proposals on major questions of the economy, labor and wages, social insurance, improvement of living conditions, and legal questions. In 1964 a public commission on cultural work was reported.[16]

Little evidence is available on the work of the CCTU in connection with the state's long range and current economic planning. The unions from the enterprises up to the top are entitled to be consulted. Officers of the CCTU are in position to speak with Gosplan and the Council of Ministers for the needs of workers, but we know little of these operations. As described by responsible staff members and other high union officials, each year when Gosplan prepares its proposals for the Council of Ministers, the CCTU takes part in the preliminary work. It sends its own statement to the government and may propose changes. The 1963 draft plan, sent to the CCTU by Gosplan for consideration, was discussed at a meeting with chairmen of the central committees of the branch unions, and comments and suggestions for changes were given to Gosplan.[17] According to a union leader, himself a member of the CCTU presidium, "The unions considered that the most important thing for workers was to increase wages of the lower paid. The leaders know, and they hear constantly from workers, of increases needed for medical workers, teachers, workers in trade and other fields. But what is possible will be determined by those who know more of the whole situation." Allocation of resources for housing and other consumers' needs is another point on which the unions put forward their case, at top levels and in the localities. As this spokesman described it, "There is a struggle over the plan, beginning in the enterprises." At a discussion of the 1965 draft plan with the vice-chairman of Gosplan, changes aimed at improving workers' conditions were proposed by the CCTU presidium and representatives of central committees and republic trade union councils. Central committees and sovprofs are said to be actively involved in the working out of annual and long-range plans.[18]

Major labor legislation is drafted directly by the CCTU or with its participation. The 1957 decree on the settlement of labor disputes and that of 1958 on the rights of factory committees were worked out by the CCTU and approved by the Presidium of the Supreme Soviet. In some cases the Council of Ministers issued a decree jointly with the CCTU, as on "permanently functioning production conferences," in 1958, and on improving safety protection in enterprises, in January 1962. Important decrees are sometimes issued jointly in the name of the Central Committee of the Communist Party, the USSR Council of Ministers, and the Central Council of Trade Unions —for example the minimum wage law of 1956 and the decree on the shift to the shorter day and revision of wages in heavy industry in 1958. In other cases decisions are made by government agencies after consultation with the CCTU.[19]

Especially important are the relations with the State Committee of the Council of Ministers of the USSR on Questions of Labor and Wages, although evidence is lacking on how this work is carried on or the nature of the discussions that result in decisions. A crucial question is whether the CCTU has full access to the unpublished data on wages in the hands of the Central Statistical Administration and the State Committee— the basic information needed by workers and their representatives for full protection of their interests still being limited in 1965 by lack of any general publication of wage statistics. All major decisions of the State Committee, however, are issued jointly with the CCTU.[20]

The program of the Communist Party adopted in 1961[21] declared that the unions should be given the "right of legislative initiative, that is the right to introduce draft laws," and this was included in the union statute in 1963. The unions appeared to have this right without further legislation, but experts on labor law argued that the rights of the middle and higher levels of the unions needed to be defined as specifically as was done for the plant and local committees in 1958. They also wanted more exact definition of questions on which government and administrative agencies must consult the unions or make decisions jointly with them.[22] A number of republics, including the Russian, had legislation obligating all government agencies to work with the unions on all questions affecting workers' interests.[23]

For some years a proposed basic code on labor was under consideration, to replace the 1922 Russian labor code on which, with many modifications, regulation of labor in the entire country was still based. The draft was worked out by the CCTU on instructions from the party. During a nation-wide discussion of the published draft in 1959 and 1960, the CCTU collected suggestions for changes and additions for use by the legislative commission of the Supreme Soviet. Published discussions showed wide support for liberalizing the code.[24] Surprisingly, action was delayed, following adoption of the new party program, and was said to wait on decisions as to a new USSR constitution, which would include a labor section. Reportedly, CCTU Chairman Grishin was a member of the Constitutional Commission, and an expert of the CCTU legal staff was in the working group for the section on trade unions. Differences of opinion had developed between those who wanted further definition and liberalization of rights and others concerned with problems of discipline and excessive turnover. In all probability the difficulties that slowed the rates of economic growth also made authorities reluctant to grant further improvements in basic labor conditions, and they may have thought it better to have no new code, rather than to adopt one that would disappoint workers and the labor law experts.

The CCTU also has the right to issue explanations of labor laws and further regulations, especially those relating to safety and to social insurance. By government authorization the CCTU establishes rules for the safety inspection carried out by regional and local unions. The major responsibility for issuing safety codes, in agreement with administrative agencies, was given to the central committees of the national industrial unions.[25] The CCTU has six scientific institutes on protection of labor, located in big industrial centers. These institutes study questions of safety, industrial lighting and ventilation, hygiene, work clothing and similar matters. They offer consultation services, provide educational material, and give courses for workers in the field.[26]

Social insurance for temporary disability benefits is administered by the unions.[27] The CCTU issued detailed rules on February 5, 1955, following a decree of the Council of Ministers. The CCTU works out the social insurance budget, included in the state budget, and determines rates of contribution for social insurance by enterprises in different fields. It issues regulations for administering the extensive systems of rest houses and sanitariums that were turned over to the unions in 1960.

Published collections of decisions of the CCTU presidium and secretariat include many explanations of legislation and further regulations and instructions, some issued by the council alone, some jointly with a state agency. Examples from 1960 to 1962 involved incentives for the introduction of new technology, improving the quality of work clothing, allocations to the "enterprise fund"[28] and its use, and union responsibility in improving production training of secondary school pupils. A decision of June 16, 1961, on medical services in the Russian Republic and ways to decrease illness among workers, included an agreement with the republic Ministry of Health for improvements in services. On January 5, 1962, new regulations were approved for administration of social insurance benefits—regulations on the local unions' commissions for administering temporary disability and maternity benefits, on their commissions on pension questions, and on their insurance delegates.[29]

Closeness of the CCTU to government is evident in all these activities. The council functions like a governmental department of labor in studying labor problems and drafting legislation. It supplements the work of state administrative and judicial agencies by its responsibilities in administering a number of state programs and in inspection and checking on the observance of labor legislation. Soviet theorists hold, nevertheless, that the unions are non-governmental organizations, even when governmental functions have been transferred to them.

Unions issue regulations with the force of law only when specifically authorized, or with the later approval of state agencies, or jointly with government bodies. From the highest level down to the plant committee, the unions supervise and control by a combination of state authority and "public influence." As one authority says, in the decision of an elected union body such as a trade union council on protection of labor at a given plant, management may be given "a proposal arising from the governmental competence of this union organ, and recommendations without legal sanction, but based on the authority of the union organization."[30]

Checking on observance of labor legislation, both through the state function of inspection and through education, persuasion, and public influence, is largely carried on by the unions in the plants and the regional union committees and councils. Much of the work is done by millions of workers, engineers, and others, enlisted for "public work in their free time" on special commissions and assignments as "public inspectors." Over the years complaints of extensive violations of safety regulations and other legislation have continued. Chairman Grishin spoke in 1963 of gains achieved during the four years since the last congress, but he complained that many managers did not give enough attention to providing safe conditions and that some trade unions went along with this. In many cases plans for new enterprises still failed to provide proper working conditions. The CCTU had discussed these questions many times, he said, and on demand of the unions managers had been punished or removed for violating labor legislation. He insisted that the unions strengthen their control over observance of the laws and show more principle and persistence in their fight against violators.[31]

In spite of many such statements from the CCTU, it can be questioned how persistently the top leadership of the unions and the party seek full enforcement of labor standards when the interests of production seem to be at stake. In recent years, as earlier, regional union councils have often failed to support complaints against managements on these questions. An additional check could be made, however, through union representatives on the recently established committees of party-state control, if more effective observance of standards for workers' protection were desired.

THE CCTU AND UNION DEMOCRACY

A major part of CCTU work concerns activity within the unions. The council splits or combines national unions and shifts groups from one union to another. It approves the trade union budget, from the local units up to the national level. It issues instructions on elections and regulations for socialist competition, sets the dates and gives instructions for working out collective contracts in all enterprises. It instructs the unions on their duty to explain to workers important current decisions of the party and the government. It constantly holds before the unions their obligations as the "school of communism."[32]

The CCTU frequently hears reports from a central committee of one of the national unions, a regional trade union council, or a factory or shop committee of an important enterprise. Or it conducts an on-the-spot investigation of their work. This is often followed by a published decision. Occasionally the work is complimented and held up as an example to other unions. Most typically a statement on good work is followed by criticisms of "deficiencies." Sometimes individuals or union committees are named as guilty of slack work or compromising attitudes toward violations of workers' rights and are instructed what to do to correct their work. Frequently, an individual letter of complaint to the CCTU or to *Trud* leads to pressure on a regional union council to see that a violation of rights is rectified. Especially since 1957, CCTU decisions show an increasing effort to teach workers and the local unions their rights and obligations and to induce the unions to use their powers.

Both the CCTU and the party are interested in how posts of responsibility at all union levels are filled. The December 1957 resolution of the Central Committee of the party held that union councils and committees should be strengthened with "workers with experience and initiative" and that "fresh forces" should be brought in from workers, including women and youths. Party committees were instructed "to recommend for responsible posts in trade union organs the best, well-prepared workers displaying organizational capacity and respected among communists and non-party people."[33] In 1961 the resolutions of the Twenty-Second Congress and the new party program laid down the principle that approximately half the membership of committees and councils be replaced at each election and that in general the leaders be elected for not more than two consecutive terms, in the interest of "the proper combination of old experienced workers and young energetic people." Paid staffs also were to be reduced and as much as possible of the work put on a volunteer basis.[34]

The CCTU had frequently directed the union councils and committees to work more carefully with the plant unions in selecting and training union officers and workers. CCTU spokesmen, in discussing the 1961 instructions from the party, admitted defects in some of the old leadership, qualities that in fact accounted for many of the well-known weaknesses in union work. They spoke of "people who are inclined not to consider the opinion and will of the collective and the masses, who lose the feeling of responsibility towards workers," and of leadership that was not changed for long periods. "Some leaders stayed too long, got used to deficiencies and stopped growing, poorly coped with their obligations." Now conditions were to be established "to open the door for capable leadership

in the unions."[35] The CCTU plenary session instructed the
unions to be led strictly by the new demands of the party and
to make appropriate changes in the general union statute and
those of the industrial unions.

Results were reported to the 1963 congress. In the last elections the membership of the plant committees and of central
committees had been "renewed" by two-thirds, that of district
and city committees and of regional and republic committees
by over 70 per cent. New chairmen had been elected in 64.5
per cent of the plant and local committees, and "in significant
numbers" new people were elected officers of inter-union
councils and central committees of the national unions.[36] To
what extent this meant simply bringing more of the younger
members into active work is not known, or whether to any
important degree there was displacement of inefficient or old
style leaders with Stalinist tendencies, or possibly of local
leaders who were too aggressive and troublesome.[37] But probably the direction was toward more democratic and effective
leadership.

Elections are governed by the union statute and by detailed
instructions that emphasize "trade union democracy."[38] Yet
party and higher union organs are expected to make recommendations and to exert influence on the choice of leaders.
Election of all committees and councils and of delegates to the
inter-plant conferences and councils that elect these bodies is
by secret ballot, after open nomination and discussion of
candidates. On the other hand, officers of these organs are
elected by open vote, although this is no longer specified in
the union statute. The 1964 instructions, as before, provided
for open voting for trade union group organizers, delegates to
shop and plant conferences, and officers of all union committees
and councils from the shop committees up to the regional and
national organs.

Elections begin in the small trade union groups, which

choose their leaders by open vote after discussing past work and nominating and discussing candidates. Next come general meetings in the shops and plants, or, in big enterprises, conferences of delegates elected from the shops, which nominate, discuss, and by secret ballot elect their committees and their delegates to inter-plant conferences. These inter-plant conferences similarly choose their local and regional committees and councils by secret ballot. At the first meeting of each of these organs, from the shop and plant committees up, which is called and chaired by a representative of the next higher union body, and typically attended by a higher representative of the party, candidates for officers are nominated and discussed, and the election is by voice vote by a simple majority. Election for a second term running must be by three-fourths of the votes.[39]

Only scattered evidence is available on how this works in practice. Violations of democracy and abuses by officers of higher committees and councils and the party in making recommendations are sometimes aired in the press or in statements from the CCTU. The leadership always urges that union elections be approached with great responsibility and complete observance of "the norms of trade union democracy."[40]

Choice of union officers is influenced also by the fact that election to certain union posts has been subject to confirmation. These so-called "nomenklatura" employments, such as officers of union committees and councils and important staff members, are "confirmed" or "released from work" by decisions of higher trade union organs.[41] Little has been published about the nomenklatura system of the unions, but a decision of the CCTU presidium on August 3, 1955 gave instructions for the questionnaire to be filled out by workers "confirmed or named to nomenklatura employments" for the register of personnel by central committees and union councils. In May 1961 the CCTU secretariat criticized certain trade union councils for violating a regulation of June 5, 1959 and ". . . freeing from work and nominating to posts of chairman and secretary of republic, territory and regional committees . . . without preliminary agreement with the appropriate central committee . . . ;" and criticized some that "without consent of the CCTU and central committees without basis co-opted chairmen and secretaries of union committees, a gross violation of the principles of trade union democracy."[42]

The nomenklatura system has been documented and described for the Communist Party.[43] Lists of jobs over which the party apparatus has control of appointments are given to the various levels, from the Central Committee down to district committees, and all such organs keep personnel files of people in these positions or available. The coverage is very wide, from important positions in the economy and government, to posts in educational institutions and all other major aspects of Soviet life. For the unions less is known but it is clear that the CCTU itself has the right to confirm officers of central committees and republic and regional councils, while nomenklatura over lower posts, down to those of chairmen of factory, plant, and local committees, is in the hands of the regional councils or the committees of the branch unions.[44] Coordination with party organs assures decisive party influence in key cases.

Evidence is contradictory as to whether in practice the union organs now confirm or may refuse to confirm or may remove officers properly elected in the lower union committees or councils. There were reports earlier of the removal of newly elected officers; in other cases the higher body only questioned the lower as to whether a certain officer should be continued in his post. One CCTU staff expert, interviewed in 1962, insisted that the CCTU itself could not remove the chairman of a central committee, but could only raise the question with the committee. A CCTU statement in 1961, however, had said that there were cases "when higher union organs . . . decide the question of removal from the post of chairman of the committee of a primary organization of a comrade who does not cope with obligations he is charged with, or has compromised himself in something. The leading trade union organ has this right, and its decision . . . is obligatory . . . . Then the factory or shop committee elects from its membership the new chairman."[45] In an authoritative editorial in 1964, on the other hand, the union journal insisted that only the local committee itself, not a higher union body, had the right to choose or remove its chairman.[46]

Influence over the selection of personnel for union posts is exerted by regional councils and committees in making recommendations at "report and election" meetings. Workers may find it difficult to oppose nominations from above in open voting for officers, but in the secret balloting for committees and councils they can easily oppose any such nominations.[47] Since nominees must get the majority of the votes, people recommended by the party and higher union organs need to be recognized by the workers as capable and deserving of respect, but sometimes are not. An officer of a republic trade union council complained that some people were still sent to union posts by "the system of job placement," though they lacked the respect of the people.[48] And the textbook on organizational work criticized bureaucratic practices and nominations on the basis of formal documents rather than actual work, or for reasons of birth or friendship. However, it justified the concern of the party and higher union bodies with the choice of union leaders, holding that personnel should be chosen first for their political reliability, second for their capability for the particular job; the requirement of sensitiveness to the needs and requests of the workers was mentioned only later.[49]

A responsible and effective union officer, with a background of both party and administrative experience, explained the concern for choice of officers in this way:

Union work is too important to leave to chance. People come to a meeting and have not thought who should be elected. To head a factory committee in a big plant or a regional trade union council is a very difficult and important job. Not all good workers are competent to lead a big organization. So it is impossible to allow events to flow without control. This does not mean that recommendations from the party or higher union bodies always win. Sometimes the recommendation is rejected. There has to be support of the majority. Mistakes are sometimes made. The secret ballot is dangerous, but the members themselves make the decision. It is democracy, but there is also leadership and discipline.

As to whether the elected officers are usually communist, he answered that the party requires at least 40 per cent of union officers to be non-party. However, a party worker pointed out that many leaders are nominated for trade union posts from responsible party work.[50]

In 1963 the union statute incorporated a democratic procedure for removing officers or members of union committees who lost the confidence of the members, "abuse their trust, conduct themselves bureaucratically toward their obligation, violate norms of communist morality."[51] Such a person could be removed from a committee or council at a session of the organization by vote of two-thirds of the members on a secret ballot. In the primary organizations a member of the trade union committee could be removed at a general meeting of the workers by open vote, by two-thirds majority; or, in large enterprises where the committee was elected at a delegate conference, by two-thirds vote on a secret ballot of the committee itself.

It can be assumed that the higher they are in the trade union structure, the more likelihood that officers are in effect chosen by the party, even though the forms of democratic election are carefully followed. By long history the chairman of the CCTU is a trusted communist, high in the ruling circles of the party. It is known that in 1953 a "recommendation" for a new chair-

man of the CCTU was made by the Central Committee of the
Communist Party, the Council of Ministers, and the presidium
of the Supreme Soviet, and Mr. N. M. Shvernik was thereupon
elected, and reelected in 1954. He had been chairman from
1930, after Tomsky's removal, until 1946, when he left to become chairman of the presidium of the Supreme Soviet, and
returned to the union post in 1953. The 1953 procedure was
criticized by the Committee on Freedom of Association of the
International Labor Office as "inconsistent with the principle
of the freedom of organizations to elect their representatives in
full freedom," but the committee noted that the present chairman "was elected in accordance with the statutes of the trade
unions."[52] However, Mr. V. V. Grishin, who was elected in
1956, and again in 1959 and 1963, came to this post from party
work and had not been a member of the CCTU before his
election. From 1961 he was a candidate member of the presidium of the Central Committee of the party.[53] A communist
chairman of an important regional sovprof is known to have
been recommended by the party, and this must be true for
many leaders of central committees and sovprofs, and for important lower posts.

Because of the need for training union personnel, the CCTU
established two Higher Schools of the Trade Union Movement.
The one in Moscow emphasizes labor economics, while the
Leningrad school prepares personnel for educational, cultural,
and art activities in the trade union clubs. The CCTU stresses
the obligation of regional councils to plan the training of newly
elected local officers. The educational work is furthered also
by publication in large editions of union newspapers, magazines, books, and pamphlets.[54]

In the main, the work of the Central Council of Trade Unions
is that of the secretariat and presidium. The plenary sessions
of the full council are held twice a year and are attended by
members and candidate members of the council—also, depend-

ing on the agenda, by leaders in the party, government, and industrial administrations, by union staff and officers, and by prominent workers from the plants. Usually the first point on the agenda is an important decision of the party or the government and the resulting "tasks" of the unions. These sessions as reported in *Trud* reflect the dominating concern for economic progress and fulfillment of party programs. Lengthy reports by the CCTU chairman and secretaries on the work and on plans and problems are followed by talks by representatives of major union central committees and republic and regional councils, and sometimes by factory committee representatives and workers from important plants. Successes are reported and frequently there are criticisms of the work of enterprises and unions on production and on working conditions, safety, and services for workers. The long resolutions adopted at the end of the sessions summarize accomplishments and criticisms, and instruct the unions to improve their work—all in the familiar terms that had been included again and again over the years in speeches and resolutions.

With broad participation from different areas, industries, and unions, and with wide publicity, these meetings serve to disseminate news on policy and developments, to criticize laggards, and to whip up interest in solving problems. If there are debates on policy, this is not reported; rather the session approves decisions already prepared by the secretariat. Any criticism of the CCTU and of unions in general is likely to come from the party or from officers of the CCTU who speak in the name of the party, but many criticisms of particular national and local unions are expressed by others.

Following party instructions to widen their relations with the masses, the CCTU sends its officers to report on its work at meetings in big enterprises or at city-wide meetings of active union workers. Chairman Grishin reported that in four years since the last congress there had been about three hundred such meetings. Reports have been published on some of these meetings. At one in Moscow, after Grishin's detailed accounting of progress and problems, there were questions and comments from the floor with suggestions for improvements in union and administrative work.[55]

The All-Union Central Council of Trade Unions is characterized chiefly by its two-sided responsibilities and functions. While its first duty is to the Communist Party and the state, it also has the obligation to speak in the name of its members and to protect their interests. Its functions having to do with production, protection, and education of workers are all closely connected, and all serve party policies. It does not get binding instructions from below, but information as to what workers are thinking and asking reaches it constantly through organizational channels and from letters and requests to its offices and to the union press. It considers opinion from below when it makes its requests to the government and presses its views, though always within the limits that seem possible in the light of high policy as well as of the state of the economy. Significantly, its increased emphasis on protection of workers' interests came only after the party decided that this was in order. But evidence was abundant that the morale of workers demanded better satisfaction of their needs and better protection of their rights and interests. Decisions at the top must in part have reflected this unorganized pressure from below, which was growing with the increasing education and sophistication among workers. Specific interests of workers are far more explicitly recognized than before Stalin's death. In guiding the work of the unions the CCTU has at least moved toward a long-lacking balance between its dual roles.

CENTRAL COMMITTEES OF THE INDUSTRIAL UNIONS

These governing bodies of the national unions are accountable both to the Central Council of Trade Unions, to which they are directly subordinate, and to the members who elect them at biennial congresses. Union structure, being determined by the CCTU, is remarkably uniform, although the differences between such fields as transportation, trade, and other services, compared with manufacturing, are reflected in their internal union structures. Staffs of the central committees are in general not large, usually not over twenty-five to thirty-five people.[56]

National congresses of all the branch unions met in April 1962 and all adopted revised statutes. As described by a spokesman of the CCTU organizational-instruction department,[57] the new statutes changed election policies and procedures in accordance with party and CCTU instructions. These changes were designed, it was said, to draw into union work "people with initiative, able to ensure further improvement in the activity of the union organizations." All this implied considerable lack of success in the past. The changes would possibly result in better guidance and in more opportunity for members to elect officers who would represent them effectively. The policy of "renewal" of the makeup of union committees was quickly put into effect; 68.6 per cent of the members of the central committees were reported to be newly elected. Chairmen of the central committees, on the other hand, were in most cases re-elected. Of 20 congresses of the branch unions in April 1962 reported in *Trud,* only 4 elected new chairmen. Similarly at the congresses in the fall of 1963, the central committees elected had 66 per cent new members; but the reports included only 2 mentions of new chairmen.[58]

Three main fields of activity, on which the central committees ordinarily set up departments at their headquarters, are labor and wages, safety and protection of labor, and international relations.[59] After control over the day-to-day work of local unions was shifted to the regional union councils in 1957, the central committees were to deal chiefly with basic questions significant for their branch of industry. They participate in planning, both for the industry and for construction of housing and cultural and service facilities. They organize socialist competitions and are responsible for disseminating and popularizing new methods and promoting the introduction of new technology. They share in working out laws on labor conditions and new wage systems, and establish safety rules. They hear reports of administrative agencies. They study the work of their union committees and publicize good experience. And they develop relations with the unions of other countries.

An important area of their work is the analysis of wage questions, as a basis for decisions of the Central Council of Trade Unions. The latter, not the central committee, has the right to share in decisions of the State Committee on Labor and Wages. The central committees work closely with the State Committee, its research Institute of Labor, and research institutes of their industries on proposals for changes in the wage structure for the industry. They assist in working out job evaluation handbooks, for final issuance by the State Committee in agreement with the CCTU. For example, the central committee of the oil and chemical workers reported that jointly with the State Committee and the CCTU they had worked out 35 such handbooks for chemical enterprises.[60] On production standards the central committees work with the Institute of Labor and research organizations in developing basic standards of time and output for different processes and jobs. The committees were deeply involved in the analyses in their industries that preceded the reduction of hours and the introduction of new wage systems from 1956 to 1962. New wage systems and production standards are finally put into effect in the plants under the guidance of the regional or city committees and instructions from the central committees of the unions.

The central committees have major responsibilities also for safety and health in their industries. They work with scientific institutes and the Ministry of Health and organize conferences of local people on these problems. They may make demands on administrative agencies for improvements in planning related to the health and welfare of workers. By government authorization they issue binding regulations for safety and sanitation in their industries, in agreement with state committees or regional economic councils, or other government agencies. Safety inspections are carried out by the regional and local unions, under supervision of the central committees. However, the lack of over-all control results in duplications and overlapping jurisdictions that lead to confusion and even conflicting rulings, since there are a number of special state inspections—sanitation, mine inspection, and others. In 1963 the CCTU reported that in four years the central committees and the CCTU had developed about 500 new branch rules for safety.[61] The committees work with the State Committee on Labor and Wages in determining lists of difficult, dangerous, or harmful occupations in which workers are entitled to special work clothing or protective foods, shorter hours, or additional vacations. They also work out special rules for the protection of women and young workers in the industry.[62]

It is said that after the central committees turned more to questions of significance for the whole industry, they began to "listen more to the voice of the lower organizations, more boldly to raise and decide the most important questions affecting the interests of workers."[63] The chairman of the metallurgical workers reported to the Twelfth Congress that his union was working with scientific institutes to have more attention given to safety in planning new enterprises and new processes; he had urged that two local CCTU institutes on the protection of labor be placed under the authority of his union. The chairman of the coal miners' union complained in *Trud* about "management leaders and trade union workers who do not concern themselves with providing miners good sanitary, hygienic, and safe conditions at work." He said that in one mine where there were gross violations of labor legislation "the central committee was obliged to release from his post [the chairman of the mine committee] as not justifying the trust of the collective, and to demand from the administration . . . to remove from work the manager of the mine."[64] This union was demanding improved safety equipment from the technical institutes and urging government agencies to give more attention to conditions for safe work.

The central committees are frequently criticized in the union press, at congresses of the national unions, and by the CCTU. At the Thirteenth Congress in 1963 Chairman Grishin urged them to make better use of their opportunities to influence decisions in their industries, to strengthen their relations with state agencies and local unions, and to show more initiative.[65]

On occasion the CCTU presidium studies the work of a central committee and issues a report with instructions and demands for improvements in its activities. There were several such published reports in 1961 and 1962.[66] The food workers' committee, though complimented for its work on the new wage system and on new safety rules, was told to improve its work on production and in helping local unions eliminate difficulties in the wage system, to be more demanding with regard to safety, mechanization of heavy labor, and working conditions. It was also told to improve its work with local unions, especially as to the choice and training of leaders, and to do better in reviewing letters and complaints from workers. The construction workers' committee was told that on planning, increasing productivity, and safety, it had failed to analyze problems adequately, and that it should use its influence to remedy deficiencies.

The central committee of the oil and chemical workers was criticized in *Trud* in September 1962. It was said to rely on paper work and on repeated discussions without following up its decisions effectively. For years it had failed to revise old safety rules in many branches of production. Members were said to be asking why the committee did not show persistence and demand respect from the State Committee on Chemistry for decisions of the union. "Why do they not argue a little? Sometimes this is necessary for the good of the cause. Why do they not seek fulfillment of proper demands, dictated by the interests of the government?" The central committee was urged to replace paper work and their "fuss over meetings" by well-organized activity. A year later at the congress of the union it was said that the work had improved, but that there still was not enough persistence in improving protection and safety and in checking on the work of design and research organizations.[67] Despite the criticisms, the chairman of the central committee was re-elected both in 1962 and 1963.

Congresses of the national unions in April 1962 and in the fall of 1963 were reported in the union newspaper in summaries covering up to half a page. Whether the reports give a balanced account of the discussions is not known, but in many of them enough detail is included to reflect voices from the local unions and workers. Usually a CCTU officer took part; sometimes the presence of a high party officer was mentioned. The major emphasis was on production and the duties arising from directives of the party and the CCTU. Socialist competition and the "movement for communist labor" and other work in the interests of production were discussed. Planning and administrative agencies and unions were criticized for failing to solve problems related to the growth of the industry. Often there were complaints of delays in mechanization and in introduction of new technology.

A second major theme in most of the news reports was the demand from members and local officers for more attention by central committees and local organizations, managements and planning authorities, to questions of safety and working conditions, quality of work clothes, and provision of housing, everyday services, kindergartens and nurseries, and recreational and cultural facilities for workers and their families. Lacks in these areas in several industries were said to be reflected in unstable work forces. Officers of many central committees were criticized for not enough persistence in making demands and following them up. Such criticisms were reported of the central committees of railroad workers, chemical and oil workers, and in construction, coal mining, trade and local industry, lumber and woodworking, electric power stations, and others.

Of the construction workers' union committee it was said that only "timid remonstrances and requests" were made to state agencies, and that the newly elected committee needed "to be more sharp, militant, persistent." At the textile congress it was said that in spite of strengthened control over safety and observance of labor legislation, there were still many enterprises with serious lacks in working conditions, and that unions should use their rights more vigorously. This congress, according to the report, "requested the leaders of Gosplan USSR, the State Committee on Light Industry . . . the Administration for light industry of the USSR Sovnarkhoz, to review the proposals and suggestions directed to administrative organizations, and to report on measures taken." At the timber and woodworking congress the new central committee was told "more decisively to put before leading administrative and planning organs questions of improving protection of labor and mechanization of hand work."[68]

Discussion of wage issues was only rarely mentioned. At the congress of trade workers, however, delegates were said to have "directed many reproaches" to the central committee and state authorities for not showing persistence in deciding important questions. They complained especially of slow introduction of mechanization, with the result of much unproductive hand labor; and that "questions of the reform of wages are decided slowly."[69]

A different sort of complaint, rare in the press, was raised at the 1962 congress of workers of electric stations and the electrical industry. The ministry of construction of electric power stations was criticized for lack of concern for retaining staffs after completion of a station; "in order to retain cadres of electric builders, it is necessary that every collective know that upon completion of work in one place it will be utilized on a new project."[70]

These 1962 and 1963 congresses of the national unions, even though incompletely reported, reflected several dominating characteristics of Soviet trade unions at this time. Control of basic policy by the party and the CCTU was seen in the prompt change of union statutes on orders from above. Former officers were in most cases re-elected, despite the new policies on elections and often severe criticisms by delegates. The unions were deeply involved in carrying out the economic and social plans of the party. At the same time there was concern for workers' welfare, as shown by criticisms of government agencies, managements, and union officers and organs, and demands for improvements in working conditions and services. How often issues of wage levels were raised is not known. But more persistence and militance in general by central and local officers in protecting the workers' interests were demanded.

Lines of communication are open from the shops and other work places up to the top officers of these national unions. Through the conferences and congresses as well as through day-to-day contacts, conditions that affect the morale and stability of work forces can be brought to the attention not only of union officers but of authorities in the planning, administrative, and policy-making bodies. The national unions lack power to bargain, and they are not independent organs in developing programs. Yet the evidence available suggests that workers have become more articulate in expressing dissatisfactions and in pushing their national union bodies to greater activity and persistence. Occasionally old officers, holdovers

from Stalinist days, have been replaced by younger leaders—
though more likely on decision from above than on pressure
from the members. However, the rank and file are less distant
from their central committees than from top CCTU officials, so
it is possible that pressures from below account, more than a
little, for the signs of greater activity by the central committees
in speaking for their members' interests.

CHAPTER V

Regional Trade Union Councils

INTER-UNION councils, the *sovprofs,* have wide responsibilities and authority, both in supervising the unions of their areas and in relations with governmental and administrative agencies.[1] In the administrative regions (*oblasts*), regional union councils parallel and work closely with regional economic councils, the *sovnarkhozy*. In small republics, which are without regional sovprofs, the republic sovprofs supervise the unions of their territories. All republic sovprofs work with governmental authorities on planning and labor legislation for their republics.

The structure and activities of the regional trade union councils as described here are those characteristic after the 1957 reorganization when the sovnarkhozy were established and the sovprofs given increased authority—and before the late 1965 reorganization which returned parts of the sovprofs' responsibilities to the central committees. The sovprofs supervise the regional committees of the national industrial unions as well as the unions in the plants. They represent the unions before soviet and administrative organs, and have the right to receive reports from administrative agencies and to seek improvements. Regional committees of the industrial unions operate like industrial sections of the sovprof and work closely with the industrial administrations of the sovnarkhoz, in addition to acting under the direction of their central committees on questions of wages and standards for health and safety.

The functioning of these regional union bodies affects all the work of the local unions and the interests of the workers as well as those of the party and the state. For the unions, good leadership and support from the sovprofs, though not always forthcoming, are important; and the sovprof's relations with soviet and administrative agencies have significance both for the local unions and for the lives of workers. The chairman of the Leningrad sovprof, sitting at his desk in his big office, pulled out a decree signed jointly by himself and the chairman of the local soviet on a question of improving medical services, and said, "No one can do anything without me."

The Leningrad sovprof, which is recognized as one of the more successful,[2] provides an example of effective leadership. In this city, with its educational and cultural background, the unions may work better than in some areas, especially in less developed sections without a strong union tradition, but much the same sort of activity under devoted leadership is found in many union committees and councils. This was seen in cities in the West and as far East as Middle Asia.

The trade union council for the Leningrad administrative region, with its population of 4.8 million in 1963—3.5 million in the city itself[3]—and 2.6 million union members, covered 22 regional committees of the industrial unions and 11,000 factory, plant, and local union committees. The council and the regional committees are housed in the handsome old Palace of Labor— once the Institute of Noble Maidens—which was given to the trade unions in 1917. It has a great staircase, rising through a white-columned hall to the third floor, with a statue of Lenin against a red background at the top. In the Palace of Labor there are concert and lecture halls, conference rooms, large and small offices, a library and a bookshop. A rank and file worker, driver of a car, said with satisfaction, "Every worker is represented there."

In 1962, the Leningrad sovprof consisted of 140 members

elected at a regional inter-union conference. The sovprof elected a presidium of 11 and the officers, had 8 departments and, in 1959, a staff of 57. These were assisted by volunteer public councils and commissions and instructors. In the entire region about 600,000 union members were said to be active, as members of shop, factory, and local committees, as trade union group organizers, social insurance delegates, and public inspectors, and as members of the numerous commissions of shop and factory committees. The regional committees of the national unions all had paid officers and staffs, but only those factory committees representing memberships of more than 700 had full-time officers.

Regional sovprofs, and the sovprofs of the smaller republics, are elected every two years at inter-union conferences and congresses with from 120 to 600 delegates, varying with the number of union members according to standards set by the CCTU.[4] In the Ukraine, Belorussia, Kazakhstan, and Uzbekistan, large republics which have a number of regional sovprofs, congresses for election of republic sovprofs since 1963 are held only once in four years, like the all-union congress of trade unions. Regional committees for each industrial union are elected at biennial conferences of delegates from their local and plant unions. Representatives from higher union bodies and the party take part in all conferences and congresses. The first session of the newly elected inter-union council or union committee elects its officers and presidium by open vote.

An officer of a regional union committee in Leningrad described the election at their last conference, attended by 250 delegates from local unions with 40,000 members. A candidate for the committee of 45 was nominated by each union from its membership; all of them were then elected on the secret ballot. At the first meeting of the new committee the members divided into 9 groups, each of which agreed on its candidate for the presidium. As each candidate was nominated, he was discussed and then voted on openly, and all were elected.

Reports of union congresses in all republics in September and October 1963 were published in *Trud*. Always there were accounts of progress in production and of socialist competition and voluntary activities to promote fulfillment of plans. In most cases there was talk by delegates of problems, safety violations, and poor working conditions, inadequate provision for the care of children and for everyday services and housing. In many of the congresses delegates demanded more persistence from the sovprofs in taking up such questions with administrative agencies. But no mention was made of how many new representatives were elected to the councils. The former chairmen were re-elected in all but two cases.

While the sovprofs get instructions from higher union bodies and from the party, all their work is supposedly under democratic control of the membership, as represented at conferences and congresses and on the councils. It is said that at their sessions there should be well-prepared reports and practical discussion. The trade union press carries many reports of constructive criticism at these meetings. A Moscow regional conference in April 1963 was described as a good businesslike session, in which delegates discussed achievements in production and in working and living conditions, and also demanded improvements where conditions were poor, safety or other standards were disregarded, or the rights of the unions violated.[5]

Conferences and plenary sessions of the Leningrad sovprof are said to be well-organized, with fruitful discussion and self-criticism.[6] Reports of the 1962 conferences spoke of discussions on production progress and problems, socialist competition, and efforts to expand use of volunteers. Some administrations were criticized for using overtime as a means of fulfilling plans, or otherwise violating labor legislation. Local unions that went along with such conditions also were criticized. Unions were urged to get more deeply into problems of production and to stop violations of safety rules. They were also urged to work on violations of discipline, especially tardiness and "thoughtless" absence and quitting of jobs.[7]

Plenary sessions of the sovprofs are expected to meet regularly, at least once in four months. Between sessions the elected presidium supervises the work of the staff departments and special commissions and groups of instructors and inspectors, with their many volunteers from the membership. While small councils may have only groups of instructors for major activities, large sovprofs ordinarily have departments for organizational-mass work, labor and wages, protection and safety, social insurance, housing and living conditions, cultural work and physical education, and finance.[8]

A textbook of the Moscow Higher School of the Trade Union Movement criticized many of the sovprof conferences and sessions.[9] It said that sometimes there was "a false tone" and a practice of "excessive praise of people"; any "business-like criticism" was directed chiefly toward lower union organizations and administrations. At the sessions of the councils not enough initiative was shown in posing new questions for discussion; some leaders brought in only questions recommended by higher union organizations or "related to the conducting of the immediate economic-political campaign." Increasing the collective responsibility of these sessions was urged, in order to improve the work of the unions in the regions.

Many, if not all, of the chairmen of the sovprofs are communists. Of 20 sovprof chairmen on the 1959 Council of Trade Unions who can be identified, half were delegates to the party congress in that year.[10] Undoubtedly many others were active in the party in their areas. Sovprof officers interviewed in several cities showed their devotion to union work and the interests of the workers, yet it was clear that the party and its program, which they considered basic for the welfare of the people, came first. Most of these leaders had been workers who had obtained higher or secondary specialized education. Many had had experience in party or administrative posts, or came up through trade union work.

In 1962 a taxi driver in Leningrad said of the chairman of his sovprof, "He is a good man; he came from the workers." A turner by trade, the chairman had worked in industry after graduating as a mechanical engineer, and became director of a plant. He had posts in the district party and soviet committees. In 1957 when he was recommended by the party for the sovprof chairmanship, one worker at the regional conference asked him, "Why should you be chairman of the sovprof?" The answer given was that he was a man of wide experience. In the election of the council, only sixteen of two hundred crossed out his name on the secret ballot. In 1962 the chairman was a member of the executive committee of the city soviet and of the technical-economic council of the sovnarkhoz, and a deputy to the Supreme Soviet of the Russian Republic, as well as being a member of the presidium of the Central Council of Trade Unions.

In Ivanovo, a textile center, the chairman, a graduate of a party institute, had for many years been regional party secretary. The secretary, a textile worker and graduate engineer, had been in party work as well as an officer of the regional textile workers' union. In Rostov-on-Don, a center of heavy industry and agriculture, the chairman was a graduate safety engineer who had worked in the big agricultural machinery plant and later as chief of the administration for machine building in the sovnarkhoz. The secretary had been a state farm worker who moved up from the chairmanship of the local union committee to the regional committee, and then to the sovprof. In Kiev the chairman had been a railroad worker who had studied at night and by correspondence, became chief of a railroad station, then a member of the regional committee of the railroad workers' union, and finally of the sovprof. The secretary had been a sugar worker, a graduate engineer, safety inspector for the unions, and chairman of the regional committee of the union of textile and light industry workers. In contrast, in 1959 the chairman of the regional committee of this union was a teacher without experience in industry.

ORGANIZATIONAL WORK

The sovprof in supervising the unions of the area approves the staffs and budgets of the regional union committees and of the factory and local committees. It is expected to see that local leaders and active members know the laws and regulations and insist on their observance, and to give them aid and support. The sovprof can change any decisions of the lower organizations if contrary to law or to instructions of the CCTU or the central committees. It supervises the conclusion of collective contracts and it joins the regional economic council in registering the contracts and settling any disputes. It is responsible for seeing that the annual "report and election meetings" are properly held, and for influencing the selection of officers. Representatives of the sovprof and the regional committees often suggest candidates. Cases are reported also where sovprofs have removed officers of a lower union for cause.

Expansion of the rights of local unions after 1958 brought increased need for strengthening union work at the enterprise level. Urged by the CCTU, many sovprofs ran seminars and special courses for new local officers and the growing numbers of workers active on particular problems. Some sovprofs organized courses and lectures in "people's universities." In 1962, according to a CCTU report, eight million local union leaders

and active members were trained through educational programs of the sovprofs and the regional committees. But many
councils were criticized for neglecting this work.[11]

The long-standing policy of bringing large numbers into
active union work on "public assignments" (*obshchestvennye
porucheniia*) received an impetus from the party's instructions
in 1961 to put more and more of the work of social organizations on a "public basis" (*obshchestvennye nachala*) and to
reduce paid staffs. In April 1961 the CCTU presidium reported
with approval the experience of the Minsk sovprof with non-
staff instructors. In July it noted an experiment in Volgograd,
where a regional committee of the machine-building workers
was set up on a non-staff, public basis, with officers and active
workers who held production jobs. A year later the plenary
session of the CCTU instructed all levels of the unions to increase the use of volunteers.[12]

By 1962 there were 23 regional sovprofs and industrial
union committees operating without paid staffs. In 1963 Chairman Grishin reported that sovprofs and regional committees
had 8,000 non-staff departments, over 25,000 public councils
and commissions, almost 100,000 non-staff instructors and 23,-
000 public technical inspectors. From the district organizations up, 850,000 members were said to be engaged in active
union work. At the lower level, 95 per cent of all factory,
plant, and local committees and district and city committees
worked without paid staffs.[13]

The union press, following instructions from the CCTU to
publicize this movement, carried many enthusiastic reports.
A few came from regional committees working without paid
staffs; others from councils and committees making wide use
of non-staff departments and public instructors and commissions. The chairman of the textile workers' regional committee
in Tambov, where there was formerly a small paid staff, reported that now all officers worked on jobs in industry and

that with increased numbers of active workers the union was functioning better than before. He said that four departments were organized with groups of "actives," that the union office was kept open all day and into the evening so members working on any shift could come in for help, and because the industry operated three shifts, members of the committee and its departments could visit plants at times when not working on their own jobs. The Poltau machine workers' committee, which covered 24 plant committees with 39,000 members, reported seven non-staff departments, with 135 public instructors, including workers, engineers, and others, representing most of the plants and functioning basically on non-working time. The question was raised, nevertheless, by both of these committees, as to whether a minimum of released time might not be needed in order to cope with all problems. The Crimea regional committee of food workers, which was operating in 1963 with sixty volunteer instructors in five non-staff departments, reported closer relationships with local unions and more possibilities for effective communication, instruction, and exchange of experience.[14]

The Leningrad sovprof in 1962 had 500 public instructors, 12 public councils, and 103 public commissions, while the industrial committees had over 200 departments and commissions, more than half of them working without a chairman from the staff, with nearly 3,500 volunteer members. Though this widened base permitted study of many more questions, an instructor warned that this could turn into a business of meetings and resolutions, rather than of concrete work. He scoffed at the frequent boast that every third or fourth union member was active; some of the assignments, he said, were only on paper, and some of the people carried too many jobs for effective work. He urged that a wider group of active members be enlisted.[15]

This highly propagandized movement brought millions, including many pensioners, into active union work, but resistance of sovprofs and regional committees to further reduction of staffs reflected not only a distaste for change but also the difficulties in operating with people who had their own regular work. There were the problems in training volunteers and organizing their activities, and the danger of too many meetings. The most active officers and workers tended to be overloaded, and assignments were sometimes made without considering the capabilities and the wishes of the individuals. Union activities were sometimes carried on during working time. One of the complaints appearing in the press was that many union committee officers spent full-time at union work, although carried on the payroll of the enterprise as workers. The CCTU charged the sovprofs and committees to prevent such illegal "distortions."[16] In total, however, the movement strengthened democratic tendencies by widening the base of union work. It brought further protection of workers' interests and gave the unions more influence in the areas both of production and of community life.

There were special difficulties in guiding union activity in fields where the work groups and local unions were small. In 1962 it was reported that for the entire country about one-third of the more than 20,000 enterprises under the regional economic councils had 100 employees or less, and that in local industry under the soviets there was a similar problem.[17] In the Leningrad region, the committee of workers in local industry and communal economy covered 1,732 widely scattered units. The committee sought to solve the problem of contact by monthly meetings of chairmen of the factory and local and group committees. At these sessions information was given on recent decisions of the CCTU, the sovprof, and the regional committee itself, and important problems in the work of the unions were considered. The staff was available after the meetings for consultation with individual representatives.

The committee had 200 volunteer instructors who visited locals and offered help. It maintained close relations with city and district soviets; 120 of its members worked on permanent commissions of the soviets. In 14 districts where it had arranged meetings of local people with enterprises supplying services, it reported that some services had been improved and their prices reduced.[18]

PLANNING, PRODUCTION, AND WAGES

The regional union councils are entitled to be consulted and, at many points, to share in joint decisions with the sovnarkhoz and with the local soviet executive committee. They are expected to check the economic plans of enterprises after these have been discussed with the union committee on the spot and before the sovnarkhoz accepts them. The sovprofs and union committees were told to take an active part in working out the draft Five Year Plan for 1966-1970, and to join the sovnarkhozy in reviewing proposed plans for their areas.[19]

The sovprofs are especially concerned with decisions on the use of funds for plant building and rebuilding and improvements in working conditions and amenities for workers; also for house building, nurseries and kindergartens, medical facilities and cultural and recreational institutions. In a number of regions formal collective contracts have been signed between the sovprofs and the sovnarkhozy, with commitments on amounts to be spent on such projects.[20] Another area of concern is that of trade and public catering and other facilities for everyday services. Reports of pressure on planners and administrators for improvements in this area, as well as complaints of lags in house building and faults in distribution of housing, appear frequently in the trade union press.

A major obligation of the sovprof and the regional committees is to promote the production work of the enterprises, and this interest pervades all aspects of their work. The chairman of the Leningrad sovprof saw no contradiction between promoting production and defending the interests of workers. "To live well, it is necessary to work well," he said. Representatives of the sovprofs are members of the technical-economic councils of the sovnarkhozy. Sovprofs and regional union committees check on the work of enterprises and draw workers into efforts to improve results. They review the work of production conferences and push managements to put recommendations into effect. A staff member of the Leningrad sovprof told how three managers were called to a meeting to report on their use of proposals made by their production conferences, and how, when one manager sent only his deputy, he was ordered to come himself, and the next day was summoned to appear before the presidium of the sovprof to explain his behavior. The staff member said, "He will never do that again." On occasion, a production conference chairman appeals to the sovprof for help in getting proposals used. The unions are entitled also to be consulted on appointments of management personnel, and the sovprof can demand removal of any who systematically violate their obligations.

The sovprofs organize socialist competition between enterprises as a method of stimulating workers and administrations to improve production records. Results are appraised quarterly by the sovprof and the sovnarkhoz and awards of "traveling red banners" and money premiums are made to winning enterprises. There is also competition for the honorary title of shock worker, brigade, department, or enterprise of "Communist Labor," won for exceptionally high standards in production and in educational and cultural progress, labor discipline, and morale. Decisions on awarding the title to enterprises are made by the sovprof and sovnarkhoz, in agreement with party and Komsomol committees. In Leningrad, the first step toward this honor was the award of the title of "Enterprise of High Culture of Production," which had been won in 1962 by forty enterprises. When sovprofs and union committees review the results of socialist competition, they are expected to analyze the reasons for successes and failures, organize the dissemination of good experience, and help lagging enterprises improve. Frequent complaints are still made against sovprofs and committees that fail to follow up the results of competition and to promote adoption of the best methods.[21]

While unions at regional and local levels are increasingly involved with planning and administrative organs, dissatisfaction continues with the ineffective nature of the relationship in many cases. In 1959 CCTU Chairman Grishin complained that some officials in planning agencies and regional economic councils still under-emphasized the role of the unions and that many union organizations lacked initiative and persistence in making demands on administrative organs. Four years later he criticized many sovprofs and committees for lack of sufficient concern with questions of production and planning, and called for increased responsibility of administrators for putting into effect proposals made by the unions. He urged the sovprofs to be "concrete and purposeful," to maintain close relations with administrative, soviet, and planning organs and to put before them "questions of fulfillment of state plans, growth of productivity of labor, improvement of the conditions of work and life of workers."[22] In trade union sessions reported in the press, demands were increasingly heard for more activity and for increased pressures from the sovprofs on the sovnarkhozy.

Regional union councils share responsibility with the sovnarkhozy for seeing that the application of established wage systems and the setting of production standards are properly done in the plants. The regional committees work with the unions in the plants, under directions from their central committees, to make sure that jobs and workers are classified in accordance with the job evaluation handbooks, that the proper rates and wage schedules are used, and that output norms are revised as methods improve. Many regional councils and committees shared in developing the new wage systems, introduced from 1957 to 1962 along with the reduction in hours. They worked with the Institute of Labor and the State Committee on Labor and Wages and with the central committees of the national unions, and checked proposed new systems in practice before these were finally approved by the State Committee and the CCTU. They were involved in the preparations in the plants for the shift to the new systems—shifts that were put into effect only after the sovprof and the sovnarkhoz agreed.

Changes in mechanization and in the organization of production continued to bring new problems as to wages and hours. In the sovprof and the sovnarkhoz, departments on labor and wages supervise any revisions, in line with nationally set standards. If a rate or differential seems wrong to them, they can apply to the State Committee and the CCTU for a change, but they cannot themselves alter the standards. Numerous other issues involving the application of general standards can be decided jointly in the region by the union and the administrative agencies—issues such as determining the groups entitled to special rates, or additional vacations, free work clothes or protective foods, and details of the premium systems.[23] Disputes between factory committees and enterprise managements over any matters affecting compensation come to the sovprof and the sovnarkhoz for settlement by their joint decision.

The CCTU frequently reviews the work on wages in different regions and points out mistakes, especially in the setting of production standards. It has directed the sovprofs to help the unions in the plants, to provide instruction in norm setting, and to see that this is properly done and that working conditions are such that reasonable norms can be fulfilled.[24]

SAFETY AND PROTECTION OF WORKERS

Enforcement of safety regulations and other labor legislation is a major responsibility of the regional trade union councils, and the administrative agencies are obligated to support their efforts. The technical inspectors, paid by the state, were shifted from the union central committees to the sovprofs in 1957 and are usually assigned to the regional committees for work in particular industries. They are aided by "public inspectors" elected in the shops, and by commissions on the protection of labor, appointed by the shop and plant committees. In the enterprises, staff safety engineers and departments are expected to cooperate with the union officials. Technical inspectors are authorized to demand changes in safety and health provisions, to fine violators of standards, and to stop work on dangerous equipment. They can bring to the sovprofs, for final decision by them, the question of shutting down whole departments or plants that violate the demands of safety or hygiene. The inspectors and the sovprofs can bring issues of personal responsibility for violations of labor laws to the administrations and the courts. The criminal code of the RSFSR provides for fine, discharge, or imprisonment for such violations.[25]

Complaints as to enforcement of standards have been among the most frequent criticisms of the unions, as seen in continuing stories in the press, reports of union conferences, and statements of union leaders and experts. Chairman Grishin told the Supreme Soviet in 1960 that in some regions "not enough attention is being paid to . . . labor protection, and the rate of accidents on the job continues high." He demanded that administrative agencies and the unions show more persistence in securing observance of the rules. In 1961, at a meeting of trade union workers in Moscow, he criticized union councils and committees for not always utilizing their rights and for "insufficient demandingness" on protection of labor. In 1963 he reported that while in four years the rate of industrial accidents had decreased by 25 per cent, in some branches the rate still remained high, and he blamed the unions as well as managements for permitting failure to provide safe working conditions.[26]

One difficulty was inadequate support for the technical inspectors. Sometimes their demands were disregarded and their appeals to regional union committees, sovprofs, and sovnarkhozy brought no action against violators. In 1962 one non-staff inspector of the Leningrad sovprof protested in the press that he did not get enough support from the council, and that fines were not effective in stopping violations of labor legislation when "it seems that for administrative leaders and trade union workers there is one task, to fulfill the state plan." The editor urged the sovprof to take action against any administrators who put obstacles in the way of the inspectors.[27]

There was also a lack of sufficiently clear authority. New shops or installations were sometimes accepted for work by official commissions in spite of opposition of technical inspectors. An additional problem was lack of authority to require changes at the planning stage for new enterprises.[28] In 1960 Gosplan and the state committee on automation and machine building strengthened the union central committees and the sovprofs by specifying their right to share in early decisions as well as when units were accepted for operation, and the CCTU obligated the unions to take part in these early decisions. In case of disagreement later, a technical inspector's refusal to accept a new installation could be appealed to the presidium of the sovprof or to the central committee.[29]

Nevertheless, reports continued of new plants and units put into operation without the required provisions for health and safety and without approval of the safety inspector. This happened in the case of a Stavropol steam power plant, a

Kuibyshev oil refinery, and the first turbine aggregate of a great hydroelectric project. An editorial in *Trud* protested vigorously, but the Kuibyshev sovnarkhoz chairman and others argued that putting these installations to work ahead of time, with some imperfections, was a "production necessity" and in accord with government interests. In several such cases, however, the CCTU raised the question of removing those responsible and censured sovprofs for not preventing illegal actions. "Law is law and to violate it is not permitted to anyone," said the trade union paper.[30] In 1963 Chairman Grishin reported that some management, design, and construction organizations still failed to see to the provision of proper working conditions, and he insisted that the unions give more attention to conditions in new plants.[31]

Efforts to make the protections effective have been reported in many cases. Directors, chief engineers and others have been reprimanded or discharged for systematic violations of safety rules and other labor legislation. Union chairmen have been removed by higher union organs for "unprincipled and irresponsible actions" in regard to such violations. Early in 1964 *Trud* reported that when a number of new plants under the Krasnoyarsk sovnarkhoz were put to work despite objections of the technical inspector, this led finally to sovprof action, warning the sovnarkhoz and enterprise managers against further violations and declaring that they would be held accountable for failure to follow the decree issued by the Council of Ministers and the CCTU on January 23, 1962, on proper conditions in new enterprises.[32]

This important decree[33] on improving protection of labor gave the unions the right of advance inspection of plans for machines and enterprises and stated that special attention was to be paid to conditions in new enterprises before they were accepted for operation. The decree authorized the state committees on industries and the councils of ministers of the republics to work with the unions' central committees and the organs of state inspection in developing rules of safety on basic types of machinery and equipment. It proposed to the republic councils of ministers and the sovnarkhozy that jointly with the sovprofs they work out plans for improving working conditions in every enterprise. They were to study conditions at each plant and arrange for discussion at workers' meetings on proposed measures, which, when approved, would be included in the collective contracts. The councils of ministers were obligated to see that necessary resources for improvements were provided in the annual plans. They were instructed to take effective measures for enforcing protective legislation and for holding those guilty of violations personally responsible.

A CCTU report on improvements in the work of the Kuibyshev sovprof was distributed to all regional councils in April 1962. That council had appointed 435 volunteer technical inspectors, who were assigned to enterprises to check on observance of safety and other regulations and to work for improvement of conditions. The result was said to have been a 20 per cent reduction in two years in the number of injuries and an accident rate 40 per cent under the average for the country as a whole.[34]

Many sovprofs appointed groups of legal inspectors to supplement the work of technical inspectors, as recommended by the CCTU, since the check on observance of labor legislation covers not only safety and other working conditions, but also such laws as those on the work of women and youths, use of overtime only under strictly limited conditions and with the consent of the factory committee, and discharge only on bases set by law and with union consent. On all such matters factory committees and their commissions and public inspectors were in need of help from the regional committees and the sovprof. The Chelyabinsk sovprof in 1963 had thirty-seven volunteer legal consultants, who checked on observance of labor legislation at ninety-two enterprises and offered legal assistance directly in the plants. In the Donetz sovprof where seven legal inspectors checked two hundred and fifty enterprises in 1963 and gave obligatory orders to directors to remedy violations, more than eighty illegally discharged workers were restored to their jobs. In these and many other regions legal inspection was found fruitful in lessening violations of law and complaints of violations of rights.[35]

The CCTU recommended to others the initiative of the Zaporozhe sovprof, which, in 1960, joined with the sovnarkhoz in setting up a "public university" on the protection of labor, with a two-year course. Workers, foremen, shop chiefs, and safety workers numbering 392 enrolled in the courses. In 1962 many of these were elected public inspectors and members of the commissions of their local unions; a number became members of the sovprof and of regional committees.[36]

Some of the problems of enforcement were illustrated in a sharp criticism of the Ivanovo sovprof by a local correspondent in *Trud*. When shops and enterprises were put to work without normal conditions for safety and health, and violations of legislation were permitted, the union leaders "decided not to dispute with the sovnarkhoz" or "spoil relations." The sovprof tended to request, not demand. "The style of work was as of a suppliant." Workers were saying that they had elected the officers to protect their interests, not to "keep silent about important questions." At a session of the sovprof, accusations of compromising with the sovnarkhoz were made. The chairman of the sovprof, admitting the charges, promised that "principled and uncompromising action" would be taken.[37]

In 1962 the Leningrad sovprof's department on protection of labor had a staff of five. There were seventy-six technical inspectors in addition to nine others assigned to railroads or other fields, all paid by the state and working with the union committees in particular industries. Cooperating with the public inspectors and the commissions on protection of labor in the plants, they worked mainly on safety engineering and sanitation, but also checked on observance of other labor legislation. Violations of standards were said to come in some cases from the director's lack of attention or from ignorance of the law, for instance as to types of work forbidden to youths 16-18 years of age. In other cases managers were so intent on fulfilling production plans that they illegally required overtime or work on free days, but the chief of the sovprof department insisted that "production necessity" was never accepted as an excuse.

The work of the Leningrad technical inspectors was primarily educational and prophylactic; often a warning was enough to stop violations. When necessary, the technical inspectors imposed fines for systematic violations or even stopped the work. Questions of violations were discussed at workers' meetings in the shops, by the regional committees, and when necessary, by the sovprof and the sovnarkhoz. The aim was to increase knowledge of law on the part of workers and managements and to lead to better observance of standards. Use of criminal sanctions was rare. Attention to safety had increased in the past two or three years, according to a sovprof spokesman, largely because at last the material means were available to overcome lacks, and workers were becoming more demanding. If conditions were now substandard, this was considered the result of management's carelessness, which could be overcome by pressure from the workers and the unions.

The secretary of the Leningrad regional committee of metallurgical workers told of their drive for observance of labor legislation, staged two years earlier on CCTU orders. Some forty persons, engineers and others from the plants, took part in a two-month survey. Many violations were found—illegal overtime, violation of safety requirements and of those on the work of women and youths, and illegal discharges. All were discussed by the committee and orders were issued to stop the violations. The secretary said the union had continued after this to be more active on these questions.

The Leningrad sovprof also had eight legal inspectors, assisted by volunteer instructors. Their first function was legal consultation; about 150,000 persons a year came in to ask about their rights. The instructors also held meetings in plants and consulted with managements and the union committees. They had the right to issue orders to management to remedy violations and could bring systematic violators up for administrative pressure.

On occasion, even the Leningrad sovprof has been prodded by the union press and the CCTU to improve work on protecting labor in some plants and to give more support to the volunteer inspectors. In other regions, numerous criticisms of regional union bodies and administrations show that violations still occur. But there is evidence of increasing activity by the unions and administrative agencies in improving conditions of work. The vice-chairman of the Moscow regional sovnarkhoz, in a statement on the work of that agency and the unions, emphasized the responsibilities both of managements and of the unions for safe and healthful conditions of work.[38]

SOCIAL INSURANCE AND LIVING CONDITIONS

The sovprofs are responsible for the social insurance budgets for their areas, covering pensions, temporary disability and pregnancy benefits, temporary assistance to union members, and some other expenses, and for checking on all work of local unions in administering the programs. They work with health agencies, executive committees of local soviets, and the sovnarkhozy in planning for facilities, and check on work in the health field. They have representatives on pension committees of district soviets, which determine pensions due and arrange for payments. They are represented on district "doctor-labor-expert committees," which determine a disabled worker's degree of disability. They provide instructions for local union workers engaged in social insurance administration in their enterprises and in checking on the work of welfare institutions and medical services. They organize public councils of active union members to assist and check on all medical institutions. Staffs of physicians directly under the sovprof supervise health services and insurance administration, study causes of illness in enterprises and plan preventive measures, and work with health and administrative agencies on plans to improve conditions and medical facilities. They also aid local unions.[39] In Leningrad in 1962, the sovprof's department of social insurance had 6 staff members, each assisted by several volunteer workers, and 25 staff doctors who worked in different branches of industry. They had a public commission of 19 people, including scientists, doctors, and active workers, to review the budget and work on various problems.

This far-flung system of social insurance and health and welfare services operates under centralized governmental policies and budgetary control, but with administration through the unions at all levels, republic ministries of health, and local governmental authorities, with extensive use of volunteer workers and councils. The unions hope that the administration of the pension system will be transferred to them, as has been done for temporary disability and maternity benefits and the sanitariums and rest houses. The CCTU, in supervising the work of the unions, is concerned with the proper administration of receipts and benefits, and also with improvements in health facilities and working conditions, as a means both for increasing welfare and for cutting down losses of time that hurt production.

The CCTU has criticized some sovprofs for inadequate control over budgets and over the financial work of the unions in the plants. Some were said to be slack in collecting the required contributions from the enterprises and in making the necessary transfer of funds to the CCTU. Some permitted "over-expenditure of the funds for disability payments." Some failed to insist that the local unions, in accordance with the law, require enterprises to reimburse the social insurance funds for disability payments resulting from injury or illness for which the enterprise was at fault.[40]

It was apparent that over-expenditure of funds could result either from high rates of injuries or illness, or from lax administration. The CCTU pointed out that high rates of sickness or accidents in some regions and plants had not been investigated sufficiently, nor had the sovprofs made enough demands for improvements in working conditions or medical or other services in the plants, in order to reduce losses of work time. Obligatory reports on accidents were not always made. Occasionally, laxness had been found in issuance of sickness certificates by the doctors; medical authorities were warned of their responsibility to promote labor discipline and to prevent unnecessary absence from work. The recommended public councils had not been set up in all medical institutions and health resorts. Some local unions had failed to set up social insurance commissions, or to elect insurance delegates in all trade union groups. In several areas abuses had been found in the issuing of passes to sanitariums and rest houses; too few passes went to workers, and some factory committee chairmen gave out passes to favorites without consulting the committee. Several sovprofs were guilty of inexcusable slackness and delay in considering and acting on complaints from individual workers. In discussing the social insurance budgets for 1961 and 1962, the CCTU warned several sovprof chairmen to tighten their control over expenditures for temporary disability. All councils were instructed to tighten supervision and to make more demands on enterprises and agencies for improving conditions and services.[41]

The sovprofs and the local unions also have substantial responsibilities related to the provision of housing, kindergartens and nurseries, dining facilities, and the network of shops and consumers' services.[42] They exert pressure on administrative and local governmental authorities to make adequate funds available and to use them where most needed. Annual instructions from the CCTU for the conclusion of collective contracts tell the unions to include provisions for improving housing and cultural and living conditions and services. The unions are supposed to check on the fulfillment of plans, the progress of construction, and the quality of services for meeting everyday needs. They participate in deciding the distribution of apartments. This work is done with the aid of many thousands of volunteers.

In Leningrad, the sovprof's department of housing and living conditions in 1962 had a staff of four, including its chief, a woman engineer. One staff member dealt with housing, another with trade and public catering, and a third with communal services, community gardens, and workers' dormitories. A "public council on housing" was made up of thirty-two members, seven of them pensioners and twenty of them party members. It included construction engineers, people in important posts in city planning and administration, in the sovnarkhoz, and in construction enterprises, officers of regional union committees, and several skilled workers. They worked without pay on questions of planning construction and organizing a check-up in each district on building progress.

Recommendations from the council were sent to soviet and administrative agencies, or sometimes to the regional party committee. When a house was completed it could not be used until both the state inspector and union members assigned from the district agreed that it was ready for service.

In view of the continuing shortage of housing despite the huge amount of new construction, distribution of apartments is under strict rules set by the government and the CCTU which provide for union participation in all decisions. Preference is required for workers, engineers, technical workers, and office employees needing housing and with long service records, for young specialists, demobilized soldiers, war invalids, and families of war casualties. The needs of pensioners and of women who are not heads of families also must be considered.[43] The lists assigning priorities for housing are supposed to be made public, with provision for appeal to higher union and administrative agencies. Most building is now done by the local soviets; in Leningrad in 1962 only twenty enterprises were building housing from their own funds. Any housing at the disposal of an enterprise is distributed by joint decision of the management and the factory committee. Housing built by the city or district soviets is distributed by agreement of the sovprof and the city soviet's executive committee. In each district people sent by the sovprof work with representatives of the soviet, in close contact with local factory committees, in preparing the list, or "queue," and revising it each year.

In this field where private interests are so deeply involved, favoritism occurs and there are violations of the rights of union committees to share in the distribution of apartments, and of workers to have their needs impartially weighed. Apartments are sometimes assigned by directors without consulting the unions, or by union committee chairmen without full discussion and publicity and proper consideration of the greatest needs. The CCTU criticizes sovprofs that fail to influence planning and construction and the proper distribution of quarters. Many directors and union officers have been reprimanded or removed for mishandling questions of housing.[44]

The sovprofs also organize commissions for public control over urban transport, trade, and service enterprises such as those providing shoe repair, clothes cleaning, watch repair, and the like. Volunteer public inspectors assigned to trade organizations take up individual complaints and try to help in improving consumer services.[45]

Under supervision of the Leningrad sovprof a system of collective gardens was organized. Any plant may get an assignment of land from the district soviet executive committee. Workers are assigned plots and as a group they reclaim land and build roads, water systems, and communal buildings, while individuals build their own summer houses. Enterprises may supply materials and transportation. The group organizes under a model statute for such collectives. In 1962, Leningrad enterprises had 458 gardens with more than 38,000 members. They raised flowers, fruits, and vegetables and gave large amounts to hospitals and children's institutions; part was sold to the state and in farm markets. Some workers, especially women, take the entire summer off from their jobs to work in these gardens. After cultivating the land for five years a member has the right to continue to use it on changing jobs or retiring. In the four gardens of one big plant, 400 workers had plots. A big textile mill had two settlements where all who wanted had plots and summer houses. On a fall weekend, buses and electric trains were seen full of workers' families returning from the country, loaded down with flowers, fruits and vegetables, products of their summer activity.

RECREATION, EDUCATION, AND CULTURE

Programs of sports, recreation, and cultural and educational activities, carried on by the sovprofs and by local unions in every center, reflect the interlocking aims of the party for increasing health and morale, group loyalty, understanding of the aims of the party, and for raising the level of education and culture of workers and their families.

The thoroughly organized "voluntary sports societies" and other physical training, sports, and recreation programs are the responsibility of the unions. The sports societies, operating under statutes recommended by the CCTU, start with local organizations in big enterprises or other groups, join in district, regional, and republic societies, and are headed by a national council. Stadiums, halls, grounds, and equipment are provided for free use, largely by the enterprises, with contributions from union budgets.[46] In Leningrad, in 1962, half a million persons were enrolled in over two thousand sports groups. Most big enterprises had their own stadium and sports grounds. The Kirov House of Culture had eleven clubs, including those for underwater swimming, hunting and fishing, motor cycling, cars, gymnastics, health for elders, and tourism. Many shops in big plants had their own sports group. Non-staff volunteer instructors played an increasingly important role. A movement for "production gymnastics"—five minute intervals twice a day in the workshops—began in the old shoe factory Skorokhod after the war and was in use in 1962 in one hundred plants in Leningrad. The CCTU urged all sovprofs and sports societies to introduce the program wherever possible.[47]

Tourism on a large scale is organized under the auspices of the sovprofs. Summer or year-round camps are increasingly provided, and children's summer camps—the pioneer camps—are sometimes used for winter sports for workers. The sov-

profs are responsible for seeing that union committees and
enterprise managements make the necessary preparations for
children's summer vacations. For 1962 they were instructed
to prepare for over four million children in the camps, and
to see that sports and recreation facilities were provided for
children who remained in the city.[48]

Workers' club houses, "houses of culture" and "palaces of
culture" play a large role in leisure-time activities for workers
and their families. Big enterprises usually have their own
club. Sometimes one building serves several plants or a particular group of workers or a district of a city. All are under general supervision of the sovprof but are managed by the union
committee of an enterprise or an industry, with financial support from enterprises and the social insurance budget. The
CCTU reported in 1963 that the unions had over 18,000 clubs
and houses of culture, 167,000 "Red Corners" in plants, 33,000
big libraries, and 25,000 motion picture facilities.[49] The unions
make demands for additional resources for these purposes to
be included in annual economic plans and collective contracts.
When provisions are lacking or inadequate, especially in newly
developing areas, complaints are bitter.

Programs of these clubs and houses of culture include lectures, discussions, exhibits, and courses on technical subjects,
on trade union work, and on political and ideological themes.
Motion pictures are offered frequently. Varied interests are
met by the large numbers of clubs for children and adults.
Many workers, reportedly seven million in 1963, took part
in dramatic groups, choruses, orchestras, opera and dance
groups, and in classes for painting, sculpture, and other arts.
Concerts and performances by these groups and by profes-
sionals are popular. The honorary title of "People's Theatre"
is given to the best of the permanent groups, in recognition
of high level achievements in drama, opera, or ballet; by
1961, 184 of them had received the title.[50]

A development since 1958 has been the establishment by unions of People's Universities of Culture in clubs and palaces of culture. By 1963 there were over 4,300 such programs in which more than a million workers were said to be studying. Courses are taught on a volunteer basis by professors, other experts, musicians and other artists. Programs sometimes are limited to a single field, sometimes range from technical subjects to science, economics, literature, languages, and music and the other arts.[51]

Leningrad, with its long cultural tradition, may have a more highly developed program than many cities, but their program is repeated more or less in most industrial centers. The Leningrad sovprof has a department on cultural-mass-work, which supervises the activities of factory committees and the 396 union clubs, houses and palaces of culture, 818 libraries, and 500 motion picture facilities. Clubs, seminars, and special lectures and discussions on technical problems and trade union work are set up by the sovprof and regional or plant committees. In 1962 Leningrad had about 8,000 amateur art groups with 160,000 members. Most of these were small music, drama, or dance groups in enterprises, but there were also 9 large, well-established groups that had received recognition as People's Theaters. Among them were the Theater of Opera and Ballet of the Kirov Palace of Culture, with 350 members; the Ballet Theater in the Gorki Palace of Culture, with 500 participants; the Musical Comedy Theater in the Palace of Culture of the First Five Year Plan; and the Dramatic Theaters at the House of Culture named Ilyich, belonging to a big electrical equipment plant, and at the House of Culture of a sewing factory. There were 4 big symphony orchestras. The actors, dancers, and musicians were manual and non-manual workers, some of them with long training and experience in their arts. They were helped by professional actors and musicians from the Leningrad theaters, opera houses, and conservatories. Training for staffs and volunteer workers is provided by the Leningrad Higher School of the Trade Union Movement. There are also a trade union conservatory, a theatrical school, and a ballet school in one of the palaces of culture, all with volunteer teachers from professional schools.

The chief of the Leningrad sovprof's department on cultural work claimed that the great majority of workers participate in one way or another in these activities, in attendance at lectures and performances, or as readers in the libraries. It was hoped to double the number in the amateur art groups in the next few years. He said that ordinary workers are becoming more and more interested and are "thinking people," and that barriers between workers and intellectuals are decreasing. The department also promoted general education, and had one instructor who worked with local unions on this, urging all young workers to continue their education.

Visits to several Leningrad houses of culture showed evidence of all this activity. In spite of the large number of clubs and houses of culture, however, the Leningrad sovprof considered facilities in the city inadequate, and in November 1962 it decided to open its own center, the Palace of Labor, to all workers of the area for concerts, lectures, and other activities. A public council of the Palace of Labor was organized to plan for mass political and cultural programs, especially for the youth. Shortly it was reported that hundreds came on evenings and free days for the programs, and that there was "new life in the old halls."[52]

An example of union initiative in public work and aid to other groups was the organization by the Leningrad sovprof of patronage by local unions over state and collective farms in the region. Working with clubs and houses of culture and educational institutions, libraries, and cultural organizations, they arranged to send the villages hundreds of volunteers, experts on technical questions, accounting, trade union methods, sports, and the arts. They organized courses and seminars for the rural people; they helped them build clubs, arrange for traveling libraries and exhibitions, set up amateur arts groups, and plan concerts, dances, and dramatic performances. The CCTU recommended this initiative to all councils and committees.[53]

A careful check on educational, cultural, and recreational activities is kept by the CCTU. It has investigated the work of particular sovprofs and the unions under them, and has conducted nation-wide inspections and competitions, with awards for the best clubs and "Red Corners." In many regions sovprofs were criticized for giving too little attention to this work and for permitting clubs to be led by people with little education. Councils were told to seek wider participation and especially to insure the proper ideological emphasis. The sovprofs were instructed to pay more attention to anti-religious propaganda, which was considered an essential part of this effort.[54] After a meeting of the Central Committee of the Communist Party in June 1963, on ideological work, the CCTU gave new instructions to all unions to strengthen their "upbringing and cultural work with the masses," to develop in people "creative activeness" and "love and respect for socially useful labor."[55] The role of the unions as the "school of communism," it was insisted, must continue to be central in all union programs.

CRITICISMS OF THE REGIONAL TRADE UNION COUNCILS

In reporting at party and union sessions and in the press, the sovprof leaders inevitably emphasize successes, but many criticisms by the CCTU and by workers and press correspondents have also been published. It is clear that despite centralized policies and controls there are many differences in the effectiveness of the more than 100 sovprofs. This was apparent in visits and interviews in a number of cities.

The CCTU devoted much energy after 1958 to teaching local

and regional organizations to use their increased rights. It issued detailed reports, including sharp criticisms, on the work of more than forty sovprofs from 1960 through 1962.[56] In addition, the union press ran many critical stories and told of complaints made at union conferences and congresses. These published criticisms were designed to prod the union organs and to teach administrations, unions, and the workers themselves their obligations and rights.

While individual sovprofs were cited for weaknesses in regard to planning and production, housing, and social insurance administration, and for inadequate attention to choosing, training, and helping local officers and active members, the most numerous and the sharpest criticisms, both from the CCTU and in the press, were of failure to prevent violations of safety rules and other labor laws, of permitting illegal overtime and discharges, and of failure to support claims of union committees for their rights. A recurring theme was "a poor style of work," lack of "demandingness," and lack of energy and persistence in seeking better protection of workers and the punishment of violators.

In one story a CCTU inspector recounted difficulty after difficulty that a "principled and energetic" woman chairman in a Bukhara cotton plant had with a new director who disregarded the union and violated labor laws. She appealed to the regional union council but was told only to "find a common language with the director." She appealed to the Uzbek republic sovprof but got no help. Only when she wrote to the CCTU and they intervened, did the regional sovprof act. They "put to the regional economic council the question of removing the director from his post," and this was done.[57]

In Lvov, the chairman of the regional sovprof was removed after the CCTU ordered the republic union council to call a meeting of the regional sovprof to consider taking this step. The CCTU had investigated a number of complaints, and it criticized the regional sovprof for its "unprincipled position" in allowing several enterprises for some time to violate labor laws and the rights of the unions. The sovprof chairman, "not wishing to spoil relations with administrative leaders—frequently came to their defense—" and meanwhile the republic union council failed to intervene. The CCTU also raised the question with the republic council of ministers of removing the chairman of the food industry administration, and with the sovnarkhoz of removing a plant director.[58] It brought a number of violations of law to the attention of the legal authorities. This extreme case of intervention by the CCTU served as a warning to union organs and managements in other areas.

In Kemerovo, also, it was only after sharp criticisms from the CCTU that a plenary session of the sovprof released its chairman and elected a new one, formerly chairman of a big plant committee.[59] While cases have been reported in which, after complaints from workers or the press, sovprofs have removed officers of factory or local or regional committees, many problems remain unresolved until workers complain to the CCTU or their central committees. The union journal asked "why so many councils and committees as a rule effectively and attentively review signals from Moscow, but often pay little attention to the same letters, if they receive them directly from the working people. Is there really need every time for a 'pusher'?"[60] Reports continue to be published of failure of some sovprofs to respond effectively when workers complain of violations of their rights.

At the regional level especially, contradictions occur between the demands of production and those of protection of workers' interests. The sovprof works in close and frequently harmonious relationship with the sovnarkhoz and local soviet authorities. It shares responsibility for fulfilling the production demands of the party and the state. Many of the sovprof leaders, like those in the administrative agencies, are communists, and they all

speak a common language. Their dislike of "spoiling relations"
is mentioned in many complaints. Some union leaders have
been quoted as saying that "since with us the interests of
administrators and trade unions, as of the whole people, are
one, how can there be disputes and cleavages with a director?
It is necessary always to find a common language with him."
But legal experts, commenting on this opinion, pointed out
that the functions of unions are different from those of government and include representing and protecting the interests of
workers, and that cooperation does not eliminate the need to
fight against violators of rights.[61]

Effectiveness of the regional trade union councils and committees is limited by hangovers in leadership and in attitudes
from the Stalinist time when the drive for production overrode
the interest in protecting workers, and unions could do relatively little against this pressure. Some party committees still
disregard violations of the rights of workers and of unions, and
protect party members and other administrators for personal
reasons or in the supposed interest of production. The tide
seems to have turned against such leadership, nevertheless,
under policies of the party and the government since 1957, and
the resulting pressures from the CCTU. The call of the party
for "new forces" and for removing old leaders with outmoded
attitudes may in time affect the work of the regional union
councils and committees. The workers themselves, with their
increasing knowledge of their rights and their increasing volunteer activity in regional union bodies, exert a strong influence
for change. Administrators also are becoming more accustomed
to the demands of labor legislation and are recognizing more
than before the need and value of cooperating with the unions.
As a result, the regional trade union councils are tending, with
many variations among them, to become more representative
of workers and more active in promoting their interests, along
with their loyal support of the programs of the party and the
government.

CHAPTER VI

Local Unions
and Their Members

W HEN a Soviet worker is asked about the unions, he is likely to say something about his local organization. This is understandable. The worker knows that many aspects of his life are influenced by his local union, by the officers he helps to elect, and by the work of the union committees. Very possibly the worker himself takes an important part in union activities. The factory, plant, and local unions, as they are termed, play a decisive role in trade union work under present policies.[1]

In its December 1957 decision on the trade unions, the Central Committee of the Communist Party declared that under the new conditions of industrial management the rights and powers of the unions should be extended, especially at local levels. In due course came appropriate proposals from the Central Council of Trade Unions, and these were formally adopted in the July 15, 1958 decree of the Presidium of the Supreme Soviet of the USSR on the rights of factory, plant, and local committees of the trade unions.[2] The rights defined in this important decree were by no means all new. Some derived from the 1922 Labor Code and had been expressed in the union statute, or had been a practice in well-run plants. Codification, with extension at some points, made the rights more explicit and increased the obligations of managements. Also because of the weight of the authority back of it, this decree gave the union in the enterprise more status. Managers and union leaders in plants visited showed their awareness of the increased powers of the union committees.

In addition to the basic right of the committees to represent manual workers and salaried employees "on all questions of labor, living conditions and culture," specific rights relating to the major functions of the local unions were spelled out. First, the union committees have the right to participate in the enterprise's planning for production and for construction, whether in the plant or of housing, cultural, and service facilities. They are responsible for conducting workers' meetings and for leading production conferences, and, jointly with management, for organizing socialist competition. They are entitled to have their opinion considered in appointment of management personnel.

In rule-making and the application of rules affecting workers, the union committees have authority that sharply limits the manager's right of unilateral decision. On many points his decisions must be made jointly with the factory committee, and on others the managers issue orders in accordance with general regulations, but only after agreement with the union. A joint commission on labor disputes settles grievances, with appeal to the factory committee, subject to further appeal to the local People's Court.

Wide "control" functions, or the right to supervise,[3] are given the union committees in the plants. They have the right to check on observance of labor laws and the collective contract, on the progress of construction, and on the provision of services. They are entitled to have reports from management and to demand that deficiencies be eliminated. They can take suggestions for improving the work of the enterprise to higher organs, which are obligated to consider their proposals and inform the factory committee of their conclusions. The committees can raise with higher union and administrative bodies the question of punishing or removing administrators who do not fulfill obligations under the collective contract, or who "display bureaucratic attitudes, permit red tape, violate labor legislation."

The decree reflects in part the wide functions of the factory committees in services to members. The committees take part in the administration of the social insurance system, provide passes to rest houses and vacation resorts, and check on the provision of medical services. They organize programs and administer the facilities, paid for by the enterprises, for the work of the union and for cultural, educational, health-building, and sports activities.

Finally, the decree protects the jobs of union officers. Anyone released from work in the enterprise, on election to a full-time, paid post as a member of the factory committee, is entitled to return to his former job on completion of his term, or to other work not less well paid in the same enterprise. Other members of the committee may not be discharged or given administrative penalties without the committee's consent.

This 1958 legal definition and extension of union rights in the plants reflected the stated aim of the party to broaden economic democracy by bringing the people into more active participation in economic and social life, and to reduce the top-heavy bureaucracy by shifting functions to the localities. Another purpose was to make unions more responsible to their membership and more effective in protecting workers' rights, than they had been for long years. The party apparently felt that the time had come for more activity and greater answerability of union officers to their members. The increase was expected to lessen abuses and to give the rank and file more confidence in the unions. It was also designed, as was the increase in the supervisory role of local party committees, to provide a further check on management under the new system of somewhat decentralized administration. Many of the points in the decree were repeated in the union statute, along with emphasis on the development of "criticism and self-criticism, the upbringing of members of the trade union in the spirit of intolerance toward deficiencies."[4]

The highest authority in the local union is the general meeting of the members. When necessary, shift meetings take the place of a single meeting, and in large enterprises elected delegate conferences are used. Meetings are usually held directly after work, and to be authoritative they must have the attendance of two-thirds of the members. Practically all who work in the enterprise, from top management officials down, belong to the union.

The factory or plant committee is the "organ of collective leadership" for the local union. Its size, depending on the number of union members, ranges up to 25 in the larger plants. According to standards set by the Central Council of Trade Unions, it may have one paid worker in enterprises with 500 to 2,000 members, and up to 10 in those with over 35,000.[5] In 1963, 95 per cent of the factory, plant, and local committees were reported to have no paid officers.[6] In small enterprises with less than 15 members (25 before 1963), only a trade union organizer is elected. The first meeting of a factory committee elects a chairman and secretary and sets up permanent commissions responsible for major parts of the work. These usually include commissions for "production-mass-work," wages, protection of labor, social insurance, housing and living conditions, cultural work, and sometimes others. The factory committee has its representatives on the labor disputes commission. Large numbers of union members are brought into the work of the commissions, which are usually headed by members of the factory committee.

Big plants have shop committees, also, which choose their officers and organize permanent commissions like those of the factory committees. Numerous questions are settled in the shops, as many of the plant committees' powers are extended to shop committees. These organizations work closely with the shop administrations, under the guidance of the plant committee.

At the base of the union structure is the trade union group, made up of twenty or more fellow workers in a brigade or section. Here the worker has his closest connection with his union. The group annually elects a trade union group organizer and, depending on local conditions, an organizer of production-mass-work, an insurance delegate, a cultural organizer, a public inspector on the protection of labor, a physical culture organizer, and perhaps others. The importance of the trade union group was emphasized by a special regulation adopted by the CCTU in 1960.[7] The group organizer brings new workers into membership, collects union dues, and has responsibilities for production, protection of workers' rights, and educational and cultural activities. He may not be discharged or shifted to other work without agreement of the shop or factory committee.

In the plant too small to have a factory committee, the position of the trade union organizer is not defined by law, or clearly established. A member of the CCTU legal staff holds that in general the organizer has the same rights in relation to management as does the union committee in larger plants, but another legal commentator thinks that their lack of legal authority may be a reason for the numerous violations of law in small enterprises.[8] Organizers in these plants work under the direction of district, city, or regional committees of their national union, or under the regional trade union council.

ELECTIONS

According to procedures prescribed in the union statute and in CCTU directives, a member has the right freely to nominate, support, or oppose candidates and to elect his plant and shop committees by secret ballot, or, in a big plant, through an elected delegate conference, and to elect his group organizer by open vote in his trade union group. This right is exercised under the supervision of regional union committees and councils and "the leadership of the party," and it may also be influenced by management. Elections are valid only when participated in by two-thirds of the members working on that day, or by two-thirds of the delegates to the conference.

An election meeting begins with a report from the officers on the past year's work, followed by open discussion. This is sometimes perfunctory, but often there are detailed discussions and sharp criticisms by the members, according to frequent reports in the union press and accounts of officers and directors interviewed. The meeting votes whether the past year's work is considered satisfactory or unsatisfactory. Then comes nomination of members for the new committee. Each candidate proposed is discussed and, if there is objection to him, the question of keeping his name on the list is decided by majority voice vote. An elected committee then prepares the secret ballot, often running it off on the mimeograph while the meeting stops for entertainment. Members or delegates vote by crossing off names of those not wanted, or they may write in other names. The first meeting of the new factory committee is called and chaired by a representative of the regional committee; the shop committee is convened by the factory committee. At these meetings officers are elected by open vote, after nomination and discussion of candidates.

Each year the CCTU sends out instructions setting the dates for all elections from the trade union groups up to the regional councils and central committees. For 1963 it stressed the party's directive to bring new members into the committees and, as a rule, not to elect members or officers more than twice in succession; exceptions could be made only by a three-fourths vote.

As in earlier years, the instructions provided that candidates could be nominated at preliminary meetings of union representatives—those so nominated to be discussed at the regular meeting, along with any others nominated, before the voting.[9] This was an apparent attempt to get more reliable and effective candidates.

In most of the more than twenty plants visited, elections appeared to follow the democratic rules and local officers seemed to consider themselves responsible to the members who elected them. In seventeen plants where details of the last elections were obtained, the final list of nominees on the secret ballot was larger than the number to be elected. Sometimes names proposed had been dropped but the ballots still had from two or three up to sixteen more names than places to be filled. In one large textile combine, on the contrary, the chairman expressed surprise when told that many plants had ballots providing for choices; at his plant conference in 1959 the number of nominees was reduced to twenty-five, the number to be elected, and members voted on the list as a whole, though they could cross out names and write in others. This restricted system was considered outmoded and wrong by officers interviewed in other plants and union organs. They said there was strong interest in the elections and often a real contest. In a machine-tool plant some candidates were elected with as many as eighty votes against them, out of six hundred, and a number of shop chiefs and foremen were defeated, although the chairman, a worker who had been promoted to be a shop chief, was re-elected with only thirteen adverse votes.

Numerous detailed stories in the press give a similar impression of active interest and often of democratic processes. Accounts of good election meetings and sometimes amusing, sometimes grim, accounts of others where things went badly, are published in an apparent effort to promote local democracy and the election of honest and effective local officers. As a rule

eighty-five to ninety per cent of all members are said to attend
the annual meetings, and large numbers to take part in the
discussions. In large plants where the election is by a delegate
conference, preliminary meetings are often held in shops and
for shifts. The work of committees or of their chairmen was
often sharply criticized. Occasionally officers or members were
said to have been "blackballed" when they had lost the members' confidence. For example, in Tambov one-fifth of the factory
committee chairmen were not re-elected one year because of
"unsatisfactory work." The chairman in a Tbilisi plant, who
"did not know enough . . . ran to the administration on everything and decided nothing for himself," was defeated. A
woman chairman in Pskov was replaced, though she had been
supported by the administration and the sovprof; "She was too
yielding a character, she did everything the director wanted,
though he had often acted improperly," and the members
elected a new committee, "strong characters, they will not let
us down."[10] While such press reports were clearly selected or
even written to influence attitudes and behavior, there are too
many of them with circumstantial detail to be disregarded. In
many cases workers were finally able to elect local leaders they
wanted.

The instructions to bring new people into leadership in the
unions resulted in large turnover in the membership of the
factory committees and in their chairmen. In the 1963-1964 elections two-thirds of the committee members were newly elected,
and nearly two-thirds of the committee chairmen. Good results were expected from this influx of new blood into local
union leadership. In the formal votes in 1963-1964, it was
reported, the work of only 0.7 per cent of the committees
was held to have been "unsatisfactory"; but this can hardly
have indicated the extent of the criticisms.[11]

Violations of "trade union democracy" in election meetings
occurred frequently enough to be of concern to the leader-

ship. The union press for the period 1959-1964 carried on a campaign, criticizing particular instances and admonishing regional leaders to see that elections were conducted properly. The most frequent criticism was of meetings poorly prepared for, with dull reports that had little effect in arousing the interest and participation of members. Also, delegate conferences were held when general meetings of all workers were easily possible. Sometimes there were no shift or shop meetings to discuss reports. Some shop committees were elected by open vote. Sometimes elections were held without the required quorum. In certain large plants, delegates to election conferences were appointed by the plant committee or the administration. Sometimes, in flagrant violation of the rights of members, the leaders presented a list of candidates prepared in advance, rather than relying on nominations in open meeting. Occasionally such a list had been drawn up by the plant manager. Sometimes "unworthy people" had been recommended.[12]

The plant director and representatives of the regional union organizations are expected to take part in the report and election meetings—the director to hear and respond to criticisms, and the regional union officers to influence the choice of leaders. Abuses sometimes result. Cases are reported where directors persecuted critics and tried, sometimes successfully, sometimes not, to get their own candidates elected. In a small printing plant in Gorki, the director as secretary of the meeting refused to put a certain name on the list for the secret ballot, but thirty of the forty-five voters wrote in this name, and the man they wanted was later elected chairman. In Kalinin one director, by special privileges to some and persecution and demotion for others, filled the union committee year after year with people satisfactory to himself. The chairman of the regional committee also "connived with him." Only after workers wrote a strong letter to *Trud* was the situation remedied by action of the party and the sovprof. In 1963 in a plant of the Tambov region, the director's candidate for chairman, elected, though with many votes against him, was removed after five months for violations of labor discipline. The next chairman also lacked independence in the face of violations of workers' rights, and the sovprof was urged to intervene.[13] The danger of abuses by management was discounted, nevertheless, by a regional union officer who had himself been a director; he held that it was proper and helpful for a director to advise the union as to candidates capable of coping with the job of running the union in a big plant.

Regional union committees and the sovprofs are expected to influence the conduct of elections and the choice of chairmen of the plant committees, under the *nomenklatura* system.[14] They sometimes set aside an improperly conducted election, or require a new election for other reasons. Since they call and preside over the first meeting of newly elected committees, they are in a position to influence the election of chairmen. Many stories in the press mention recommendations by regional committees or councils for these positions. Sometimes there was pressure from above for candidates unknown to the local union members and from outside the plant. In some instances the recommendation apparently was of a person who for one reason or another was out of work and dropped in at the regional office, needing to be taken care of. Committee members have sometimes refused to go along with recommendations from above, though this may be difficult. Cases have been reported where the sovprof refused to confirm an election.

Attempts by higher union authorities to dictate choice of local officers sometimes lead to conflicts with local unions. In 1963 *Trud* published a complaint from five delegates to a conference of state trade workers in Baku held to elect a "united committee" covering a number of local committees.

At the conference, the woman chairman of the Azerbaidzhan republic committee of the union had declared that the former chairman could not be re-elected; she urged the election of an outsider, unknown to the workers, and did not answer questions as to his experience and qualifications. The delegates defeated her candidate overwhelmingly on the secret ballot. The next day she called another meeting, saying the election had been illegal as there was less than a quorum—of seventy-six elected delegates only fifty-seven were present and only forty-seven voted. In the new election the same committee members were elected, her candidate getting only five votes. Despite her objections, at the first meeting of the committee the former chairman was re-elected. Her answer, three weeks later, was a decision by the presidium of the republic committee to abolish the "united committee." The *Trud* correspondent confirmed the story, and reported that the chairman worked "not by the method of persuasion, but by the method of an administrator, not characteristic of union workers," that she had no moral right to recommend a man who had been dropped from many posts in union work, and that the sudden decision to abolish the united committee was "bewildering." The paper suggested that the republic council of trade unions should put her straight.[15]

Higher trade union authorities are concerned over the sending of poorly qualified people to posts by some union organs, even persons who had failed as chairmen in other unions. The CCTU sharply criticized the Uzbek sovprof for a perfunctory approach to the choice of personnel and for recommending "unworthy people."[16] The Ukraine sovprof criticized the Vinnitsa regional sovprof because the chairman of a regional committee of communication and auto transport workers had written to directors asking them to select candidates for the posts of local committee chairmen—"a scandalous fact possible only because the sovprof poorly organized the upbringing and teaching of personnel"; the republic sovprof reported, however, that work with cadres had improved in all regions.[17] The CCTU campaign for better selection of union personnel shows its recognition that good leaders at the local level are important. It shows also that there are difficulties in trying to combine local democracy with strong centralized leadership from the unions and the party.

Local union elections, like all aspects of life in an enterprise, come under the all-pervasive influence of the Communist Party, but little detailed evidence is available on how this works. In a group interview, a Soviet economist remarked in an aside and with surprising frankness, "Sometimes to us as economists it is hard to understand." A young party worker with whom there was talk on a train declared, "The party does not command." In an informal conversation one member of a group interested in industrial relations, including a communist, exclaimed, "You have no idea how strong the party is in the plant." Party members are often described as the "leading core" of the trade union and other organizations, and the party as serving as "the helmsman." A Soviet legal expert, himself a communist, described the relationship in these terms. "It is simple. The party people in the union are the most active and progressive people, the most understanding. They are leaders among the active group. They are not an organized ruling group, but the most active and most respected nucleus in the trade union."

The party structure in big plants reaches down to the party organizations in separate shops and even to "party groups" in brigades and departments. There is said to be no "party group" in the union itself, but communists, subject to party discipline, are present as union members. The chairman of the Ukraine sovprof spoke of "remarkable people" elected to leadership in one plant—communists for whom "work in the trade union became their chief party assignment, and they fulfill it with great willingness."[18] The party secretary in the plant is supposed to carry on political education and promote production plans, but without interfering with the manager's right to manage or with the "broad democracy" of the trade union. The party committee, it is always said, does not interfere with day-to-day union work. In one plant visited, the chairman of the party committee was present at the interview and made the trip through the plant, along with the vice-chairman of the factory committee and the chief engineer. The easy friendly relationship between them was evident. In this plant the trade union chairman was a member of the party committee, the vice-chairman was not. In another plant, in an interview with the chief engineer and the competent trade union chairman, the latter, a skilled worker with strong ideas about trade union democracy, was asked about the relationship of party and government to the union. The answer came from the engineer, but only indirectly, in a general statement of the common interest and goal of all, "gathered together in love of their country."

It is not difficult to see how a nucleus of well-informed and trained communists working in the ranks can influence workers to accept the policies of the party and the government and to cooperate in putting them into practice. Party members have every chance during nomination and open discussion of candidates to see that effective criticisms are made against undesirable candidates and that approved workers are nominated and strongly supported. In all likelihood the party bureau considers such questions earlier, perhaps in consultation with the director and with higher union officers who are communists. Nevertheless, workers can vote down even a communist, if he is not liked and respected, and in some cases have done so.

Party members, plus members of the Komsomol, are a minority of the personnel, but since they may include many

of the most active, skilled, and respected people in the plant,
their influence is large. In 1963 one in every nine workers was
said to be a party member.[19] According to the report of the
International Labor Office in 1960, 10 per cent of the workers
in the plants visited by their delegation were communists, and
a somewhat larger number Komsomols. They were told that
only 28.6 per cent on all factory, plant, and local union committees were party members, but that 48.6 per cent of the
chairmen were communists.[20]

All available evidence shows great diversity among local
unions in Soviet industry, as in other countries. Some function
democratically, under the control of their members and effectively representing them, though within the limits set by party
and state policy; others do not. Under present circumstances,
Soviet workers are not helpless if their right to a democratic
and effective factory committee is violated. Their main re-
course is in their own elections, through which they can if
they will, and in many cases do, defeat weak or unprincipled
leaders and elect those they prefer. While they do not always
get help from higher union and party bodies, an appeal to
these organs sometimes brings relief from abuses. Rather frequently a letter to *Trud* or other newspapers has led to enough
pressure to get results. Some groups, through fear or apathy or
lack of knowledge of what is now possible, fail to assert their
rights in spite of strong statements from the highest party and
trade union leadership that they should do so. Under pressure
from above and from below, however, the trend since 1957
has been toward better functioning of the local unions.

THE LOCAL LEADERS

Since the union includes all kinds of workers—among them
administrative and office workers and engineers—it is not surprising that some of these, as well as production workers, are

elected to the factory and shop committees. For the country as a whole it was reported in 1964 that in the factory, plant, and local union committees, 32.6 per cent were workers, 31.8 per cent engineers and technical employees. Non-party people were 73.2 per cent of the total.[21] In manufacturing plants the proportion of manual workers was undoubtedly larger. In a machine-tool plant visited, only four of the fifteen members of the union committee were administrative workers or engineers. In an electrical machinery plant, of twenty-five committee members, fourteen were workers, nine, office employees and two, engineers. In a big textile mill, nineteen of the twenty-one committee members were workers, as were nine of the eleven members in a building materials plant. In other plants visited the majority were rank and file workers. Surprisingly, in two plants the director was a member of the committee and in two others the chief engineer was included. The committee chairman in one explained, "The director was a worker for many years. He is very close to the workers and they elect him to the committee." The other case of election of the director was in a plant where no choices were provided on the ballot. Sometimes when the question was raised whether it was proper for directors and chief engineers to be elected to union committees, the answer was, "Why not? He is a member of the collective, and the workers may elect him if they choose. They could defeat him if they wished." More often union officers and directors felt that the man whose work was to be checked by the trade union should not be on the committee, though he should have close relations with it; in any event, he was too busy to put time into union work and it was better for another worker to have the experience.

Although the union committee is an organ of "collective leadership," the key figure is the chairman; much of the success of the local union depends on his qualities of leadership,

skill, energy, and even courage. These elected chairmen are
above average in education. In 1964 the CCTU reported with
satisfaction that 74.5 per cent of chairmen of the plant and
local committees had secondary or higher education.[22] A considerable sample of local leaders, most of them full-time paid
officers, was obtained in visits to plants. Often the committee
chairman was present during the interview with the director
or chief engineer and accompanied the group through the
plant. Most of these union officers appeared to be respected
and able, and to be dealing with the administration on a basis
of equality, sharing responsibility for the success of operations and at the same time feeling accountable to their members. These union leaders seen in relatively large plants were
probably above the average in intelligence and capacity for
leadership.

In light industry employing many women, factory committee chairmen are often women. In three clothing, tobacco,
and tea packing plants visited, women had served long terms
as chairmen, up to seventeen and eighteen years. Of one the
director said that she was due to retire, "but the workers
won't let her."

In all plants visited, the union chairmen were, or had been,
workers in this plant. A composite picture of these chairmen
would be something like this: He or she had worked in the
plant many years; probably began as an unskilled worker,
studied at night and worked up as a skilled worker; was
elected first to a shop committee, perhaps becoming its chairman, and then to the factory committee, and five or six years
ago was elected its chairman. The chances were even or better
that he was a party member. Perhaps he was studying to become an engineer. In a rare case he had been promoted to
foreman, or even chief of a shop, but still continued to be
elected to the committee and to its chairmanship. In a heavy

industry plant the chairman was a skilled worker when elected to the committee and later to the chairmanship; sometime later he was promoted to be chief of a shop, but continued to be overwhelmingly elected. His co-workers said, "He is very diligent in protecting the rights of the workers." In a big electrical equipment plant the chairman had been a fitter, became a foreman, then a superintendent, and was in administrative work when first elected to the committee. He had been re-elected several times, and was said to be a good organizer, respected and popular. In five of fourteen plants the chairman had been most recently in administrative or lower management posts. In other plants the chairmen were spinners, knitters, machinists, a printing pressman, or other skilled workers, and in one case a bookkeeper who had been a textile worker.

A group of shop chairmen in a big textile plant that was visited in Leningrad in 1962 included an older woman—a skilled worker, warm and sympathetic—who had been chairman in a big shop for ten years; and a young woman, also a skilled worker, who was now an assistant foreman, intelligent, efficient, probably a party member, sure of herself and the union. Both women were proud of the wide activity of their organizations and were outraged at a comment quoted to them from one worker who claimed that the unions did not do much, and only what the higher levels of the unions let them do. "He is illiterate," they said, "Workers have the right to elect the leaders they want. Some people are dissatisfied when a question is settled not in their favor, but the unions try to consider the interests of the state as well as of the workers. Someone should explain this to him." They spoke with feeling of the great increase in recent years in the interest, understanding, and activity of workers, and of how the workers love the factory and speak of it as "ours."

In a group interview in Kiev in 1959, five chairmen of

factory committees described their jobs and finally gave a joint answer to the question, "What is a good factory committee chairman?"

He works a long time and the people like him and vote for him. He is very active and is elected for many years. He is very close to the workers and their aims. He is honest and strict and fair in all decisions, whether the worker is right or wrong. If workers don't like him, they will speak up at union meetings, or speak to members of the factory committee. He cooperates with all members of the committee and does not make decisions alone. He is responsible to the whole collective, the general meeting, and also to the regional committee. To some extent the party bureau checks his work.

When asked whether there might not be conflicts between these responsibilities, they laughed, as though admitting there might be, but answered firmly:

The first responsibility is to the people who elected him. This is democratic centralism, with responsibility to the higher trade union organization, which also is elected by the people, and to the membership. He is responsible also to the party, which helps, shows the way to the unions, and listens to their work. It has its regulations and its field, and the trade union its own. But the chief authority for the factory committee chairman, the highest point in the plant, is the general meeting of the people.

In another interview an officer of a regional sovprof described a woman chairman in a local tobacco plant:

She is a fine person and a good chairman. She knows production thoroughly. She knows people, she is a good comrade to all, helps and advises them, and the workers love her. She is a good organizer, able to organize the activity of the workers in union work. She teaches people on production and in committee work. And so at the Fiftieth Anniversary of the trade unions she was awarded the Order of Lenin as "the best factory committee chairman."

One chairman, the only full-time union officer in a shoe plant employing many women, described his work in some detail. First was the necessary aid to commissions, helping them plan, and checking on their work and that of the shop committees. In the morning he usually spent several hours in the shops, meeting workers, discussing any questions they had, checking on safety and on work of the shop as a whole, working on questions of organizing competition between shops and with other plants. Then before and during lunch he talked with any workers who came to his office with problems. Often from 4 to 6 P.M. there was a meeting (factory committee, shop committee, wage or labor disputes or other commission). If not, he visited the kindergarten or nursery, or schools in the plant, or worked on the question of building a children's camp, or on housing, the dining room, or other problems. He listed typical matters that workers brought to him: One worker thought too much tax was deducted from his wages. The union checked and settled the matter. A dispute over a worker's classification was referred to the classification commission and settled. A worker needed sanitarium care, and another wanted help on vacation plans for his family. An old worker was retiring—the union needed to check the books and documents and help him get his state pension. As usual, on retirement, presents were given him. Workers needed special food or clothing and the union made arrangements. Someone wanted a new apartment and the union looked into what could be done. A worker had a good idea for production and didn't wait for the shop meeting or production conference but came in to discuss it. A group had an idea for a sports program and asked money for a team or a competition; workers owning motor boats on the river wanted an organized competition under union auspices. When other workers wanted the union to organize a cultural program, a theater party, a holiday program, an excursion, or a conference on a book, a planning committee was set up.[23]

In the plants visited in 1959 and 1962 there were clear indications that typically the local union officers were representing their constituents on a democratic basis; their strong feeling of common interest with management in fulfilling their duty to the party and the state was also apparent. No conflict between these duties and interests was ever admitted. Yet as late as 1964-1965, cases have been reported of administrative officers serving as unpaid factory committee chairmen and defending the management point of view in disputes. A CCTU spokesman insisted that a member of management should not be elected as union chairman since he could not properly fulfill his union obligations—most chairmen appropriately were workers—but that a full-time paid union officer who had formerly been in management could function without conflict of interests.[24]

"COMMUNIST UPBRINGING"

The trade union groups especially are expected to be active in developing the understanding, morale, discipline, and cultural level of their members. The group organizer, with the help of the cultural organizer, has the duty to bring all workers into union membership and to develop group feeling, love of the enterprise, and understanding of the aims and programs of the party and the state. They are supposed to encourage workers to raise their educational and technical level and to use the opportunities for growth in their capacities and interests. Leisure time should be well used, it is thought, for developing the cultured, well-qualified, and public-spirited Soviet citizen who is promised an increasing share in all affairs of society. The aim is well-organized work, recreation, educational and cultural activities, all conforming to the spirit of the communist moral code. The trade union group organizer and cultural organizer are helped by the commissions on cultural work of the shop and factory committees and by the party and Komsomol organizations.

Varying with the interest and energy of the leaders, this

work takes many forms. Group meetings are held during lunch breaks and after work. These and the shop meetings provide opportunity for reports and discussions on party and governmental decisions and programs, production plans, and problems in the life of the union and the work group. Sometimes there are cultural activities—reading, entertainment by the plant's amateur art groups or by professional artists—or plans are made for group excursions to museums, theaters, or concerts, a special evening at the club, or other activities. The group organizers are expected to work with young workers, encourage them to complete their general education and help them enroll in courses for technical training. Some of them work with the plant library, or arrange for traveling collections of books from local libraries, and try to get non-readers into the reading habit. They try to make inviting places of the "Red Corners," small club rooms or spots in the shops themselves, with union and other literature and facilities for reading and recreation, and bulletin boards with notices, reports of honors, and statements on socialist obligations and their fulfillment. Wall newspapers are frequently to be seen, with accounts of developments, notices of coming events, cartoons and other satirical comments on the life of the "collective." Banners, posters, and slogans proclaim communist aims and the purposes of the section or department, and remind people of their past successes and of future goals. The organizers encourage all workers to participate in programs at the clubs and houses of culture. Factory committees are supposed to teach the group organizers and help them carry on these programs, always with attention centered on raising the workers' "political level," and often they are criticized when they fail to do so.[25]

Promotion of discipline is a special responsibility of the trade union group and the shop and plant committees. Discipline is strict, but workers are protected by detailed regulation of the penalties permissible and the conditions under which they may be applied. Using model rules approved by the State Committee on Labor and Wages and the CCTU in 1957 as a basis, management and the union committee agree on "rules of internal labor order."[26] These include details on procedures in hiring and firing, obligations of management and workers, the time schedule, incentives, and penalties. The permissible penalties include warning, reprimand, severe reprimand, and transfer to a lower-paid job for a period up to three months. In addition, for cases of truancy—absence for a whole day without excuse or coming to work drunk—the worker may lose, for as long as three months, any addition to wages for long service, or up to 25 per cent of a one-time award for long service; or he may be discharged. Or the manager may send the worker to the comradely court. Only one penalty can be imposed for any one violation. Penalties must be imposed promptly, and only after the worker has been heard. Dismissal for truancy or other violations of discipline may be imposed only for systematic violations.

The unions are expected to use "social influence" in support of discipline, and thus to reduce the need for administrative penalties.[27] In their "upbringing of workers" the unions show a paternal feeling and also attitudes of cooperation and mutual aid. If a worker does not cope adequately with his job, fails to fulfill his production standard, or turns out inferior products, he may need help in mastering his job. This should be forthcoming from fellow workers or he should be helped to get further training. If he is simply indifferent, lazy, or antagonistic, comes to work late or stays away without excuse, or violates rules, perhaps his fellow workers can help to straighten out a problem; if it is simply a matter of attitudes, a talk with an older worker may set him straight. If this is not enough, his behavior may be discussed by the whole group in open meeting. Frequently there are caricatures of such

workers in wall newspapers or in the enterprise paper. Many
stories appear in the press and in union pamphlets, telling
how the truant or drunkard or careless worker promises to
reform, and, with the help of his comrades, is on his way to
becoming a skilled and responsible member of the group. It
is claimed that all this is highly effective. When management
proposes to discharge a worker for violation of labor discipline,
the shop committee or factory committee may discuss the matter and refuse agreement. Sometimes they say, "He has to
work somewhere. We know him better and can do more to
reform him than others can." In many plants discharges are
said to be rare, and social pressure by the workers' organizations is the main reliance for labor discipline.

The CCTU continues to express concern over turnover,
truancy, and violations of discipline in some enterprises and
industries. It urges local unions to study the causes, increase
efforts to improve working and living conditions, and
strengthen their educational efforts, especially with young
workers. Chairman Grishin in his report to the Thirteenth
Congress said, "Not one case of violation of discipline and
social order should remain without attention of the trade
union organization, of the workers' collective."[28]

In some enterprises special efforts to prevent irresponsible
shifting of jobs have begun to be made by talking with workers
who give notice to quit, finding out the reasons, and if possible
eliminating the cause and inducing them to stay. In Leningrad, Chelyabinsk, and other centers a number of big plants
have set up "public personnel bureaus" of volunteers who
work with newly hired workers to see that they get a good
start in the plant, and also work with any who propose to
leave, or whom management wishes to discharge. It is said
that as a result attitudes have improved and there has been
a substantial decrease in voluntary quitting. From the Donbas
have come reports that union committees have set up "councils

of workers' honor" of members who work to increase labor discipline and reduce turnover.[29]

"Comradely courts" have an important role as "the extreme measure of social influence against violators of labor discipline," although more frequently the cases are simply discussed in the shops and in the union committees. These comradely courts are set up in shops and plants by election, or sometimes they are appointed by union committees. They hold open hearings on cases sent by the administration, or, under a 1961 regulation, by the union committee or other organizations. The case is discussed by the workers, and the decision of the court expresses group opinion. Often there is only a warning or a public reprimand, but there may be a recommendation to management for a reprimand, temporary shift to lower-paid work, or even discharge. To workers, this public discussion of their behavior is said to be the worst possible punishment. It is considered extremely effective, both in the individual case and for the general education of workers.[30] The CCTU urged the unions to make more use of this method for improving discipline.

In Leningrad in 1962 there were 3,772 such comradely courts. In a big electrical equipment plant the court was made up of 11 people, 8 of them workers. According to the chairman of the union committee, ordinarily from 25 to 300 workers attended a hearing, half a dozen or so spoke, and in the majority of cases, there were good results. The number of truancy cases was significantly decreased. In most plants visited, comradely courts were only rarely used, but they were always a possibility and were considered valuable. In a big textile mill with 10,000 workers, about 20 cases had been brought before comradely courts in 10 months. Of three cases of unexcused absences reported in an issue of the enterprise newspaper, the paper held that two deserved strong censure by the comradely court. In one of these, a girl took a month's vacation in September although she knew that the shop's schedule provided for her to be away in November; the paper thought "this indicated that K. did not take account of the plan or the collective, did not respect her comrades." In the second case the worker was guilty of systematic truancy, which hurt the shop in competition for the title of "Communist Labor." In the third, a three-day absence might have been excused, but the young woman had not consulted her shop chief and made the decision herself. A group of shop chairmen in this plant were astonished when asked whether workers did not resent such pressure from fellow workers. "No, they all work collectively, and the worker understands. Before, many were discharged. Now, usually there is only a reprimand. The factory committee won't let him be discharged, but tries to reform him." They said that discussion at group or shop meetings was effective, and the number of disciplinary cases had decreased.

SOCIAL INSURANCE AND HOUSING

Among the most important and popular union activities are the administration of benefits under the social insurance program and the efforts to improve medical services and working conditions. These activities serve both the welfare of workers and the state's interest in reducing absenteeism and improving discipline. About 1.6 million rank and file union members are said to be involved as insurance delegates and members of the social insurance commissions of the factory and shop committees. Insurance delegates are elected in the trade union groups. The commissions, appointed by factory and shop committees from volunteers who are interested and qualified, include insurance delegates, medical workers, production workers, engineers, and technicians, and are headed by the shop and factory committee chairmen. In small enterprises this work may be carried directly by the factory committee or by district committees.[31]

Insurance delegates have the duty to visit the sick, or workers absent for unexplained reasons, and to see that medical service is provided, check the medical certificates, and offer any help needed such as getting food or medicines, providing for the care of children, or arranging for supplementary aid. They are expected to be on guard against malingering and truancy, and also against abuses in the issuance of medical certificates, and to check whether the sick worker is following doctor's orders. They help in arranging places for children in nurseries and kindergartens, and in plans for sending them to summer camps. On questions of safety and health and plans for improving working conditions, they are expected to cooperate with their group's safety inspector, the technical inspector from the regional trade union council, and the commission on protection of labor.[32]

The unions' commissions on social insurance determine eligibility and the amount of benefits due in each case for temporary disability payments, maternity leave benefits, burial benefits, and other special allowances. The commissions check the medical documents and the reports from the enterprise on the worker's average wages—also his record of uninterrupted service when this is pertinent to the amount of benefit. They are responsible for seeing that the enterprise makes the required payments, from the fund built up by its contributions for social insurance. The commissions make the decisions on distributing passes to rest houses and sanitariums, and on sending children to nurseries and kindergartens and to vacation camps. They decide on special assistance needed in emergencies, paid from the social insurance fund. They study records of illness and accidents and help to work out measures to improve working conditions and safety and also medical services, both in the plant's dispensary or polyclinic and in local medical institutions. It is their duty to see that medical certificates are properly issued. They are expected to arrange for training the insurance delegates and the special groups that assist the commissions. Permanent groups of active members are often set up for different parts of the work, headed by members of the commission. Under the factory committee a special commission on pension questions helps retiring workers get the documents needed for receiving their state pensions from the social security authorities. The factory committee itself is held responsible for seeing that all this work is done properly.[33]

When an injury or case of occupational disease is determined to have been at the fault of the enterprise, the plant must reimburse the social insurance fund for the disability payments. It is the duty of the factory committee to order this reimbursement, upon its approval of a recommendation from the social insurance commission that investigated the cause of the disability. Factory committees are sometimes criticized for lack of attention to this requirement, which is meant to influence enterprises in observing the rules of safety and of healthful working conditions.[34]

For distribution of passes to sanitariums and rest houses, under CCTU regulations, quotas of places available come to the factory committee from the sovprof, and passes are distributed by decision of the commissions on social insurance, subject to approval by the factory committees. The decision is a group responsibility, which is supposed to be exercised with full publicity. Cases of favoritism or of decision by individual union leaders or management officials are denounced. It is expected that places be given workers according to their physical needs, but also as reward for good work, with priority to workers and others directly involved in production. Ten per cent of the passes to rest houses and 20 per cent of those for sanitariums are free, at the expense of the social insurance budget; for the rest, individuals pay only 30 per cent of the cost.[35]

All these activities engage the energies of large numbers of union members. Frequently when workers talk about what the unions do, they mention first the sick benefits, the free or low-cost vacations, and similar services received through the union. The unions gain in popular esteem from their share in the administration of the social insurance systems, which have improved markedly since 1956.

Union committees are concerned also with questions of housing, trade, and the supply of consumers' goods, public dining facilities, and other services to consumers. Factory committees work with management on plans for any new housing to be built by the enterprise and for repair and improvement of old housing, and for aid to individual and cooperative house building. The commissions on housing and living conditions set up control groups to check on the progress of new building and to work with the building unions for quality and fulfillment of plans. For distributing housing at the disposal of the enterprise, either its own houses or any given it by the local soviet, priority lists of those needing housing are set up by agreement of the manager and the union committees. Applications for housing are investigated by the housing commissions, which consider present living conditions and needs, and the claims of special groups and of good workers with long service records. All these conflicting claims are considered by the shop committees and administration. A list is drawn up and made public before final approval by the factory committee and the director. Any disagreements may be threshed out at an open meeting of the shop committee or at a shop meeting. One chairman described hot disputes in his factory committee as they voted on each name in order on the proposed list for available apartments; the director usually agreed to the factory committee's list, since he knew they were aware of the needs. Any final disagreement between the director and the union committee would go for decision to higher union and administrative agencies, usually the sovprof and the sovnarkhoz.[36] Factory committees share also in determining the lists for distribution of housing by city and district soviets, through representatives on the soviet housing committees.

Factory committees are said to have become more active since 1958 in protecting the interests of members in the equitable distribution of housing. Perhaps typical was a story from Pskov in 1959 of an engineer, worried that he might not get an apartment now that "the factory committee has to know everything," and he could no longer simply go to the director. He hoped that in the coming election they might be able to elect "more obliging people" to the union committee. In response to this a union leader commented, "Nothing will come of it, times have changed, workers know their rights and ask more from the committee."[37] On the other hand, complaints continued of managers who distribute housing without the agreement of the union, and of unions that fail to see to proper distribution. Publicity on such cases, including the removal of directors or union officers as a result of complaints, aimed to promote the just operation of the system. In May 1962 the CCTU instructed all unions to note serious violations of rules in some regions and republics and to see that this important business was properly handled.[38]

Problems in the upkeep and management of houses belonging to the enterprise are also of concern to the union committees. House committees are elected in the buildings, to check on repairs and services, to arrange for cooperative work in planting trees and gardens and in maintaining and beautifying the grounds, and to organize cultural and educational activities. Efforts are made also to improve trade and other services. Union commissions on public control or groups of volunteer controllers are organized in big enterprises to check on services in the enterprise and on dining rooms, stores, and other service agencies. They take up complaints and propose improvements. Many thousands of union members, including pensioners, share in this work. Other volunteer groups help in services to workers' families. For example, in some enterprises councils of pensioners help in the kindergartens and nurseries and in preparation of children's camps for the summer.

ATTITUDES OF WORKERS TOWARD THEIR LOCAL UNIONS

The local unions in Soviet industry after 1957 gained in the respect and confidence of their members. They have been able to enlist millions of workers in trade union functions serving both the workers and the state. This conclusion is warranted by much evidence from Soviet publications, including the daily press, and from talks with workers, managers, trade union officers, and other Soviet citizens. This awakening of union activity did not arise independently from workers and their demands, but came only when the Communist Party opened the door to greater union effectiveness by its 1957 decision. Summoned by the party and instructed and urged by the CCTU and by constant propaganda in the press, working people increasingly used the opportunity to choose officers whom they could trust. Industrial workers are no longer raw and poorly educated as were the recruits from the villages in the early years. Their increasing education and experience profoundly influenced the ability of the unions to function effectively. Local unions, like the higher union levels, work within the limits of policies decided elsewhere, yet their field for maneuver is considerable and workers are learning to use it for protection of their rights and interests.

Many stories in the press make it clear that far from all local union officers, even after 1958, used the increased powers of the local unions honestly and effectively; these complaints will be analyzed further. Nevertheless, the sample from the plants visited can probably be assumed a fair representation of typical labor-management relations in the bigger and better-run enterprises. Expressions of confidence in the unions were heard in 1959 and 1962 from many local union officers, management officials, experts in institutes and universities, workers, and other Soviet citizens met by chance in trains, planes and buses, theaters, dining rooms and cafes, as well as drivers of Intourist cars and ordinary taxi drivers who were sometimes as talkative and informative as their New York counterparts. By and large, the comments could be summed up in the statement, "People are more interested in the unions now and like them better because they do more, they have more power."

A retired coal miner, met in a village, said, "Some local unions are good, some not. If they pick good leaders, it goes well. It is hard to say which is more common." But he believed that in his industry most were good unions. A textile mill director insisted that most union committees in that industry in her city worked effectively. A woman engineer from a building materials plant and a director from a big plant in Kazakhstan both spoke of the increased role and importance of their plant unions and of the activity and interest of the workers. Several other engineers and research people expressed the opinion that most unions worked well and that, in general, workers trust the unions. One said, "If not, it is some exceptional situation. Experiences differ, but it is rare that a worker is seriously dissatisfied."

In a big machine plant in Middle Asia the director declared, "Workers are happier now that they feel they have some power of their own," and one of the shop chairmen, met in his shop, said, "Workers are more interested in the union than before, because the union defends their rights, helps them, and they know that someone will support their demands when they are reasonable." A director of a big textile mill said, "Workers demand more from the unions now, they are more interested, and the authority of the union is higher. Not all unions are equally active; some leaders are more literate, matured, 'conscious'; some are not. It is important how good the chairman is, how energetic—there are differences as in other fields. It depends on people. Members of our committee now are more educated, and their rights and obligations grow. Responsibility is the best teacher, and with increased responsibility they work better. It is hard to say why some union committees are inactive, but nearly all in textiles in this city are very active and honest. Bad ones are criticized in *Trud*, with the aim of improving them. The party wants them to be strong. Many good young people are coming into union work."

Two prominent union officers who were interviewed admitted much dissatisfaction of workers with unions in the past "when the style of work was worse." But now, they insisted, the work was better, workers' activity had increased, and workers have more confidence in the unions. One officer said, "Now they criticize union bosses and won't stand a leader who doesn't satisfy them." The other held that bad cases are rare, and insisted, "Unions are very popular with the workers now." He said, "They are the only organization where any worker can go with his problems. The work of the committee depends on the man. It is partly the fault of the workers, if they elect the wrong man. But as a rule the committees are working better; if they have a poor chairman, next year they will elect a better one." He added, "Workers know they don't have to kneel to anyone, they speak up, criticize their leaders, say what they want."

Several taxi and Intourist drivers spoke with enthusiasm of the work of their own local unions, of how the workers vote and decide questions, cross off the name of bad leaders, straighten out the manager if he is wrong, and protect workers. One laughed at mention of criticisms of the unions, and said they are not general. "The unions are fine (*khorosho*), they work for the workers." One admitted that some workers are not interested, but "if they are interested in the unions, they are for them."

The comments quoted above represent only a very small sample of opinion, obviously, but the near unanimity of such expressed attitudes, including many from private and casual conversations, carries considerable weight. It was perhaps not by chance that the only worker met in 1959 or 1962 who seemed disgruntled with the unions was a young skilled worker in a small clothing plant with no union committee, only a trade union organizer. This worker felt that the union could do only what higher union organizations permitted.

In general, and not surprisingly, the unions may function better in larger plants where they can more successfully organize the range of activities they are expected to cover. A report from the regional committee of construction workers in the Donbas region held that most of the labor law violations are in small enterprises, but it went on to say that "the overwhelming majority of union organizations, including those in small enterprises, . . . take an implacable position . . . toward violations."[39] While unions are affected by differences in the officers elected and in the leadership from the regional unions and the party, workers learn from experience. One regional officer said, "It is not tragic if a mistake is made. Next year they can correct it." Even when higher union bodies or party committees supported weak or unprincipled leaders, this was remedied eventually in many cases by elections or by intervention from higher union authorities. Although news stories continue to appear about bad cases, where local officers fail to support the rights of members, much evidence indicates that workers increasingly know their rights and exercise them in order to have local unions that effectively represent them and protect their interests. Significantly, early in 1965 the union journal gave prominent place to a letter from a shop chairman asking discussion of what the qualities of a union leader should be, and the editors invited readers to respond.[40]

A surprising phenomenon in Soviet plants is the widespread participation by both ordinary and skilled workers and by professional personnel in activities organized by the unions. Through these activities many of them get an education in problems of industry and the community and have a feeling that they are of service. In many accounts of the work of a volunteer inspector or instructor, or a member of a union commission, these active participants show satisfaction in giving public service. These reports, despite their obvious propaganda purpose, often seem to be expressing a genuine feeling.

Why do millions of union members spend so many out-of-work hours in these unpaid activities? Often they are party members and fulfilling their obligations by this work, perhaps on assignment from the party committee. It is unknown how much pressure is put on non-party people to get them to accept these assignments. The frequent emphasis on the voluntary character of this work suggests some tendencies to co-opt people rather than waiting for volunteers; but union spokesmen deny compulsion. An officer in a textile plant said, "We have 100 public controllers because 100 volunteered." Often retired people find this a good way to keep contacts and also do useful service. Many others see these activities as valuable contributions and wish to participate. Along with work for the party and in the local soviets, here is an area for people with interest in public affairs and social welfare. Many, who in another society might be volunteers in social agencies and community organizations, in the Soviet Union find a field for their interests in the unions.

Not to be forgotten are the material as well as the non-material rewards. The CCTU gives honorary certificates and medals for many kinds of good work in the unions.[41] Local unions give bonuses to active workers. Participation in public work is considered in the distribution of passes to rest houses and resorts, and even of housing. "The material self-interest of the worker in the results of his work" is a strong all-pervasive principle. Trade union work shares with other aspects of life in the Soviet Union in being motivated by a variety of influences and pressures—material rewards, honors, enjoyment of the activity itself, patriotism and loyalty to the cause. A visitor in plants, talking with union officers, frequently meets the attitude that was expressed by a woman worker, a devoted union member, "The best thing in our society is the feeling of the collective."

CHAPTER VII

Labor-Management Relations and Protection of Workers

IN the Soviet industrial enterprise, as in plants in any society, the industrial system imposes its own discipline. Orders must be given and obeyed and workers must submit to the rigors of the factory regime. Yet this regime is influenced by the prevailing culture. A Soviet factory reflects attitudes inculcated by the years of experience, education, and propaganda under communist leadership, with the coercive pressures of earlier years not entirely forgotten. Relations between workers and management are influenced also by the fact of central control over many details, which narrows the area of possible local dispute. Since 1958 the local unions have taken an increasing part in decisions made in the plants. The traditional practice of "criticism and self-criticism" permits workers to influence production and the use of resources for improving working conditions and welfare. The quality of the relationships in any plant depends, in addition, on the character and attitudes of its management.

Evidence on a small sample of plant directors was obtained in visits in nineteen plants, most of them in light industry, but including large and important machinery plants as well as textile, food, and other enterprises. Five of the directors were women. At least fourteen of the nineteen had begun as workers, three of these in the plants they now directed. Four others had worked up in these plants from engineering or technical jobs; twelve were engineers and five had other higher or secondary technical education while two had no formal technical training. Rapid turnover among managers, of which there are many reports, was not evident in this group as a whole; twelve had directed their present plant for five years or more, six of these for over ten years. Most of them accordingly were in position to know their workers well.

In their family origins and in part of their work experience most of these directors and their chief engineers and other technical and administrative people had a common bond with workers and union officers. Large numbers of workers, also, were on their way up, studying at night and by correspondence. Many would become administrators. Consequently, it was insisted that there are no sharp lines between workers and supervisors and administration, and no change of attitude when a worker is promoted. The party membership of an active minority of workers as well as of large numbers of plant administrators also makes for a feeling of common bonds.

Although in many respects the job of the Soviet director is like that of the manager of a big American plant, his responsibility is to the state rather than to a board of directors. This difference appeared when several management people interviewed gave their concept of the qualities necessary for a good director. A textile mill director said,

What I strive for and what I believe all good managers must follow is this: All tasks set by the government must be fulfilled; and to fulfill them it is necessary to have "authority," respect, from those he works with. He must know those he works with, study the abilities of the people and his assistants. He must work to improve his qualifications and political knowledge, use foreign journals so that he can use the new processes in his practical work. This is the main task.

A director in a machine plant also described the requirements:

He must know the economics of the industry and the technology, and put all his life into education, mastering the knowledge of the industry. He must not be rude to subordinates, must be able to mix with them, know their life, their requests, their problems, think constantly of ways to improve their life. And he must never forget the state plan, not only for the year, but monthly, weekly. All this must be combined in one man.

A similar description was given when a group of factory committee chairmen expressed jointly a workers' view of a good director:

First, he must fulfill the plan. Second, he must work with the people, take their suggestions seriously, know the life of the people and their needs. He must create all good conditions for labor in the factory. Most directors were workers or came from poor workers' families, and it is rare if a director has not worked up. So a good director may be "chosen" by the people. There are no conflicts between a good director and the workers.

These comments from people in different areas, industries, and jobs showed basic agreement on the essentials of good management. Some of the directors and chief engineers seen in plants appeared much like any competent production manager in a big American plant; many others gave more of an impression of the "Soviet man." The general impression from this sample, however, was of a combination of technical competence and initiative, loyalty to the demands of the party and the state, and a strong feeling for "the collective"—and for the need to provide the conditions for the cooperative effort on which the welfare of the workers and ultimately of the whole people depends. The "human relations" aspect of the job of the Soviet manager, although the terminology is not theirs, seemed prominent in the thinking of this group of directors.

This sample, while limited to the relatively small number of good plants where visits were possible, is in all probability fairly typical of well-run enterprises. The press gives corroboration in many stories of successful plants. On the other hand, there are many complaints and criticisms from workers and trade union bodies. Numerous cases are reported where managers act like dictators, driving for production at all costs, violating labor laws, ignoring the opinion of workers and the unions, suppressing criticism, and violating workers' rights. These criticisms of managers and the occasional reports of penalties by administrative measures or even criminal sanctions are published to educate management, to increase observance of the standards set by the party and the government, and also to teach workers to demand their rights.

It is constantly held before the Soviet people that fulfilling production plans and increasing the productivity of labor is the necessary basis for gains in real incomes, and for the ultimate construction of communism, with all the benefits promised for the future. This is emphasized in statements of the Communist Party, and of party, government and union leaders, and in propaganda in the press. The people know that substantial gains in wages, housing, and the supply of consumers' goods accompanied the postwar increases in production. In addition, individual incomes rise as workers increase their skill, effort, and output. Success of shops and enterprises in meeting production plans brings bonuses. Socialist competition offers possibilities of premiums as well as honors for winning groups, their "best workers" and administrators. Tenure and advancement for management personnel are affected by the production records of the units for which they are responsible. Thus, all participants in the economy are caught up in the production drive, under a complex of patriotism and belief in communist aims, hopes for a general rise in standards of living and welfare, and immediate prospects for individual financial gains and honors.

It is not surprising that apparently many workers believe there is a basic common interest between them and their managements in promoting production. Regardless of whatever skepticism exists, workers are inevitably conditioned by the propaganda and by their experience. Soviet economists interviewed insisted that workers in general know that "they are the owners of industry" and that "working for themselves they also are working for society," and accordingly their attitudes are not antagonistic to management. In one plant a union chairman said firmly, "We speak a common language"; in another, "Only a foolish director disputes with the workers." The frequent talk of "the collective," the whole body of people engaged in an enterprise, implied some reality in the claim of a common interest and effort. Much evidence of such attitudes is to be seen in visits to plants, as well as in press stories and union publications.

Interests of workers and managers may diverge, nevertheless, and bring disputes that must be resolved. For a manager, the first duty is to fulfill production plans. In many instances an unscrupulous, "unconscious," incompetent, hard-driven, or short-sighted administrator tries to get out the production by requiring illegal overtime or work on free days, or with disregard of safety rules and other regulations. Workers, on the other hand, however great their interest in fulfilling plans, want protection of their rights. Differences of opinion occur over production standards. As an economist pointed out, there are contradictions between workers' interest in the highest possible pay and society's interest in equal pay for equal work and in control over the amounts of labor and of consumption.[1] The director represents the state and must protect state interests. In addition, his concerns may run counter to workers' desires as to the distribution of housing, of premiums, of passes to rest houses, and the use of funds for improving equipment or working conditions or facilities for the workers' welfare. Clashes may arise from favoritism, or the director's estimate of the interests of production, or differing judgments on priorities.

Soviet theory holds that in a system of public ownership of the means of production there are no contradictory class interests to cause labor conflicts. During an interview filled with propaganda, and in answer to a question about protection of workers against violation of their rights, an officer of long standing in one of the union central committees protested, "You always forget there is no one to be protected against." More realistic and serious discussions analyze the nature of disputes that arise in Soviet industry. Recognition of the problem appears in the increasingly clear statements, in the decade after Stalin's death, that the unions should protect the interests and rights of the working people. Attention to collective disputes and their settlement is growing, even though statements of basic policies on the use of resources and distribution of national income do not include explicit discussion, especially not in any context of labor conflict, of special interests of workers as a whole or in sections of the economy.

Government's dominating role in determining rules for labor-management relations[2] takes the form of central laws and decrees, with further elaboration by the republics; labor codes of the republics; regulations issued by the State Committee on Labor and Wages in agreement with the Central Council of Trade Unions; and regulations and safety codes issued by the latter or the central committees of branch unions, with governmental authority. These laws and regulations cover the rights of the union committees and the corresponding limits on the authority of managers; the right of workers to change jobs, and regulation of transfer, discipline, and discharge; the settlement of labor disputes; wage and salary standards and

general rules for premiums and incentive systems and for
the use of the enterprise fund; hours and overtime, holidays
and vacation rights; special regulations for working women,
youths, invalids, and students; lists of jobs with dangerous
or difficult working conditions that entitle workers to special
privileges; social security benefits; and other rules. In addition, the yearly finance and production plans assign resources
for construction and improvements that workers want.

Many local decisions are needed in applying this body of
central rules to the enterprise. Here the director of the plant
is the chief authority, but he works under strict control of
regulations and instructions from above.[3] Directors want wider
authority and they have received some increase in autonomy
in management decisions. The main changes after 1956, however, were in putting the superior administrative authority
nearer to them, in the regional economic councils, and in
limiting the decision-making powers of management by increasing the rights of union committees in the plants.

Under the decree of July 1958 on the rights of these primary
union committees,[4] their consent is required on many points
before the director can issue orders. The law is most explicit
that only with the factory committee's consent may a director
require overtime, discharge any worker, or discharge, transfer,
or give an administrative penalty to any member of a shop or
factory committee. Joint decision is required on distribution of
housing, on socialist competition, and on the budget for expenditure of the enterprise fund. Also subject to agreement are
vacation schedules and questions of hiring children fifteen or
sixteen years of age. All details of the wage system and production standards are determined by the director in accordance with general regulations, but only after agreement with
the union. Collective contracts include agreements on other
standards and improvements in conditions.

The differences in terminology in defining these rights indicate mainly different decision-making procedures, but in all cases an effective union committee can assert its right to prevent action it disagrees with or believes to be illegal. The committee has broad authorization, also, to check on the observance of labor legislation, safety regulations, and the collective contract, and to make demands on management for fulfilling its obligations. It is the final authority in the plant for settlement of individual labor disputes.

In a printing plant visited in 1959, two union officers showed their feeling of power to influence decisions in the plant. In an interview that included the director and that continued during the trip through the plant, the union men asked what the union does in an American printing plant, and finally said they thought American unions were less strong than theirs. (These Russian trade unionists did not appreciate the importance of wage bargaining.) Then they asked whether in an American plant there is a general meeting at which the manager reports to the workers, and were shocked at the negative answer. "How can it be," they said, "that the director does not have to answer to the workers for his work?"

In a heavy equipment plant the chairman of the union committee said, clenching his fist, "This union is strong and brave." He went on to say, "Whether there is a dispute depends on the director. A clever director never has a dispute with the workers. If he can convince us, the committee accepts his opinion. But this plant committee is able to settle questions itself; it has no need for outside help."

The increased rights of the union committees provided more effective means after 1958 for working out questions of common interests and for resolving conflicts, especially in negotiation of collective contracts, enforcement of central regulations, control over discharge, and in grievance settlement.

COLLECTIVE CONTRACTS

Collective contracts played an important role in regulating wages and other labor conditions in the first years of Soviet power and again under the New Economic Policy. As centralized control over the economy lessened scope for local decisions the contracts lost significance, and they were discontinued in the middle 1930's. In February 1947 the Council of Ministers decreed that the practice of concluding collective contracts should be resumed in all enterprises. The Central Council of Trade Unions was said to have proposed the new policy, though this must have been a party decision. Detailed instructions from the CCTU provided that the contracts were to be based on the approved state plans for production, wages, and construction, and the established wage standards. The central committees of the unions, jointly with the ministries, were to work out model agreements and directives to be followed in the enterprises. The contracts, with their joint obligations on production and labor conditions, and agreements for improvements in working and living conditions and in services, were to be drafted after discussion by workers in the shops and at general meetings, and finally registered with higher trade union and administrative authorities.

The aim of this postwar reintroduction of collective contracts was clearly stated. It was to "ensure the fulfillment and over-fulfillment of the production plans, the further growth of productivity of labor, and improvement of the organization of work; and also the increase of responsibility of administrative and trade union organizations for improving the material living conditions and cultural services of workers . . ."[5] Wide discussion of the contracts among the workers, it was apparently thought, would increase their understanding of the plans for production as well as of their rights. The contracts were expected to lead to better use of resources for improvements, better observance of existing standards, and more active interest and participation of workers in fulfilling production plans.

Each year the CCTU sent out instructions. In its letter on the contracts for 1952 it spoke of models worked out on the basis of experience of leading enterprises. An agreement for one machine-tool plant in Moscow was accepted as a model for that industry and as the basis for models for other industries.[6] Instructions frequently spoke of the need to conduct negotiations as a highly important campaign of political and economic education.

At the Twentieth Congress of the CPSU in 1956, dissatisfaction with the results under the collective contracts received official notice. Khrushchev called for more initiative and militance on the part of the unions, and added,

On every hand there is failure to carry out these contracts, and the trade unions keep quiet, as though everything were quite in order. In general, it must be said that the trade unions have stopped having disputes with the executives; peace and harmony between them reign supreme. But after all, when the interests of the cause are at stake one should not fear to spoil relations; sometimes it is even good to wrangle really hard.[7]

After discussion at a full meeting the CCTU adopted a scathing resolution.[8] It pointed out that many unions allowed violations of obligations, while many central committees and ministries failed to insist on fulfillment of the contracts. The collective contracts themselves were too general, not reflecting the special circumstances of the plants. The CCTU demanded more "principle and persistence" in negotiating contracts, and punishment of people guilty of violating them.

Reorganization of the administration of industry in 1957 gave opportunity to strengthen the collective contracts. Responsibility over them in most industries was transferred to the regional trade union and economic councils—the sovprofs and the sovnarkhozy—which were to issue instructions, settle

disputes, and register the contracts. No models were sent out
from that time, and on a large number of questions enterprises
were allowed more freedom to include decisions worked out
through discussion with workers.[9]

Instructions from the CCTU continued each year to give
dates for the conclusion and registration of the agreements, as
well as to set the tone of the "campaign." For 1962 a joint
directive letter from the CCTU and the All-Russian Council of
National Economy emphasized the significance of the contracts for carrying out the new party program and fulfilling
the economic plans; also for improving production processes
and workers' conditions. It recommended that special agreements be written on improvements in big shops. In 1963, instructions provided for the first time that two-year contracts
be concluded, and told the republic sovnarkhozy and sovprofs,
and the central ministries and central committees of the national unions, to issue further instructions. In 1965, however,
one-year contracts were again to be concluded for the next
year.[10]

Negotiation of the contracts gives workers an opportunity
to criticize the results of the previous year's contract and to
make new proposals.[11] As described in plants visited, and also
in the literature, detailed discussion takes place in the shops
and in the factory committee on how the old contract was
fulfilled, and management is sharply criticized for any failure
to complete the measures provided. Proposals for the new contract are collected and studied by special commissions and by
the factory committee itself. A draft contract worked out by
the factory committee and the administration goes to the shops
for discussion and further suggestions. Finally, the corrected
draft is considered with the director at a general meeting of
the workers, or in large enterprises at a delegate conference;
suggestions for changes may be made and accepted even at
this late stage. On the basis of decisions made then, the final

text is drawn up and signed by the director and the chairman of the union committee. Any points on which there is disagreement go to the sovprof and the sovnarkhoz for final decision before the contract is registered. Contracts are usually printed and given to all workers, or otherwise made available to them. The committee chairman in a big machine plant said, "Even if some workers don't like meetings, everybody comes to the ones about the contract, since the questions are very important for them." A chairman in a textile combine said that 75-80 per cent of all workers took part in the shop discussions, and that at the final delegate conference a number of points were changed before adoption of the new contract.

In a clothing plant visited, seventy-six proposals by workers were said to have been incorporated in the contract for 1963. The biggest issue was improvement in ventilation. The entire plant was to be air-conditioned over several years, but the money available made only part of the work possible at this time. The year earlier the workers had demanded construction of a new kindergarten. When the director said there was no money for it in the plan, the issue went to the regional union committee and the sovnarkhoz, which agreed with the director but said it should be included for 1963, and this was done. In a construction enterprise a dispute concerned one job the workers thought should be included in the list for additional vacations, although it was not explicitly in the standard list; when the regional committee agreed, it was included. In a big machinery plant there had been disputes over questions of expanding rest houses, facilities for winter vacations, and kindergartens; in each case the union won out. In a tobacco plant the workers wanted an improved dining room and extended medical services at the plant, and finally achieved both.

Disagreements over terms occur rather frequently. They may involve issues as to the proper application of central regulations and legislation; more often they involve demands for improvements in working conditions, safety and sanitation, or for increased mechanization in a difficult department, improvement of medical services, additional housing, or other amenities. The issue frequently hinges on the availability of financial or material resources and the sovnarkhoz may make them available. The right of the unions to participate in drawing up the draft plans for production, finance, and construction in the enterprise and the region gives them an additional chance to obtain resources for meeting such demands.

The contents of these collective contracts differ greatly from those familiar in the West. They start with general statements of aims, such as to draw the workers into active participation in efforts to fulfill production plans, and to increase responsibility of management and the union for improving workers' conditions. The commitments made by management are legally enforceable, but those of the union committee and the workers have only "a moral and political character," subject to "social influences."[12]

A group of 1954 and 1955 contracts for enterprises in different industries showed their common source in the models sent out from Moscow; there were standard patterns and numerous identical clauses, many of them repeating in general terms obligations under legislation and other regulations.[13] Details were added on the production plans of the enterprise, on improvements in conditions and services, and on training programs. On such points the agreements reflected local negotiations. However, a Soviet scholar who studied a group of 1957 contracts complained that they were loaded with material from general regulations and legislation and the shop rules, until they were more like handbooks on labor legislation than concrete agreements for improvements and guarantees going beyond the minimum established by law.[14] After 1958 the increased rights of local unions and increased scope for local decisions were reflected in the collective contracts. A group for 1958 and 1959 tended to be shorter, with relatively more space for local matters. Two that are available for 1961 and 1962 have eliminated most of the general language and are much shorter and more concrete than the earlier contracts, although they still show the influence of the former models in their structure and language.

The character of these contracts can be seen in a brief summary of those for 1961 or 1962 in a building materials plant and a big textile plant. The structure remains like that of the earlier documents. Obligations for fulfilling the state output plan and developing socialist competition are given in the first part, but in far less detail than in the 1955 contracts. Agreements are included on certain technical measures, such as reconstruction of a shop, improvements in conveyors, ventilation, and the like, or changes in the organization of brigades. In one plant the workers promise to work with high productivity, conserve materials, and lower costs; the administration agrees to prevent interruptions of work, provide good equipment, and not to permit surplus labor forces or machines; both agree to improve the work of production conferences and workers' meetings. Agreements are included on methods of conducting socialist competitions, with assurance that the necessary conditions are provided for fulfilling the obligations adopted. Goals are set for the introduction of proposals of "inventors and rationalizers."

For both plants, part two of the contract on wages and production standards refers to the wage and salary scales, job evaluation handbooks, and premium systems approved by the government, without giving actual rates, although some contracts include the centrally decided rates. Both agreements specify the duty of the administration continuously to review production standards and revise them, in agreement with the union committee, in case of technical and organizational changes. The general rule is included that new norms must be announced to workers two weeks before introduction, and that when a change of norms occurs as a result of a worker's suggestion, the author of the proposal keeps the old standard for six months. The textile management agrees to analyze reasons for nonfulfillment of norms by some workers and to take measures to help them. The construction agreement specifies that their wage systems are agreed on with the plant committee, on the basis of the model regulation; any change is made only with consent of the committee and two weeks' notice to workers. It also includes the rules as to the workers' wage-account booklets, their individual record of wages earned. The days for the twice-a-month wage payment are specified. In both agreements, also, the union committees agree to check on the proper application of existing wage systems. The construction contract specifies that any disputes arising over the application of standards are to be decided in the commission on labor disputes; more usually the collective contracts do not mention the system of settling grievances, which is established by law and presumably well known.

In part three both administrations state how many workers they will train, and agree to keep these workers at jobs related to their study and to use them later in accordance with their new skills. The construction agreement has a special provision for protecting young workers. The administration will use them strictly in accordance with their training at the construction school, and check regularly on the progress of their technical study and work, and on housing and living conditions. The union committee agrees to help the administration in organizing technical courses, setting up exhibits and arranging lectures, and will send a representative to a council on educational methods.

Part four typically covers "state and labor discipline," though the construction agreement includes this, logically, as a final clause in the section on production. In the textile contract both sides agree to try to reduce sharply the number of violations of labor discipline, by systematic explanation among workers, strengthening the comradely court, discussing all violations at workers' meetings, and exposing violators in the factory and wall newspapers. The construction agreement provides that the administration will post prominently the "rules of internal labor order" and promptly acquaint new workers with them. It will take the measures provided by law and the enterprise rules against violators of regulations, and will send persistent violators to the comradely court. The union committee agrees to carry on mass work in "upbringing of the working people in the spirit of communist relations to work," to check on observance of labor legislation and the enterprise rules, and to lead the work of the comradely court and publicize its decisions in the wall newspaper.

Protection of labor is the subject of the next section, one of the most important. The administrations agree on a substantial number of measures, detailed here or in an appendix, for improving equipment for safety, health and hygiene, and the organization of first aid and of safety education. The amount of money provided for each is specified, and the time by which the work is to be done; also, in one agreement, the person responsible for seeing to it that it is done. The construction agreement adds details on the administration's obligation to give safety instruction to all workers, provide the necessary safety equipment and clothing, according to established standards, and check on the knowledge of safety rules on the part of technical personnel and on observance of the rules. It agrees to provide medical examinations every six months for workers engaged in heavy or dangerous work. The textile union at this point states its obligation to check on the fulfillment of the agreement and of labor legislation, not to permit violations of the workday schedule, and to check on the work of the dispensary. Both agreements mention that all receive vacations according to the schedule agreed on by the union committee and the administration. The basic standard is two weeks' vacation, but additional days off are given workers in heavy or dangerous work and under special conditions. The appendix lists people with "non-standard work days" who are entitled to additional vacations of twelve or six days, including the director, the chief engineer, and other administrative and technical workers. The unions also specify the number of passes to rest houses and sanitariums they will provide for the year.

Housing and living conditions, which continue to be in part the responsibility of the enterprises, are covered by the next sections. In the textile plant, which has its own apartments, the administration will provide specified funds for repairs on apartments, for improving the grounds of a new settlement with the aid of the residents themselves, and for a kindergarten and children's camps. It guarantees improvements in the factory dining room. The union committee will organize a constant check on the progress of repairs and on the housing conditions, and on the work of the dining room and buffet. The union guarantees to provide six thousand rubles for aid to members of the union. The construction administration, a newer enterprise in the outskirts of a city, agrees to provide fuel at established prices to its workers living in houses of the construction trust, and to aid individual builders and gardeners in getting locations, bank loans, and construction materials. The union agrees to check on the progress of construction and of preparation for winter, and on the work of the food services. A commitment is made by the management, beyond existing legal requirements, that all expenditures from funds received in socialist competition and from the enterprise fund will be made in agreement with the union; housing space provided by the construction trust will be distributed jointly with the union.

The extensive role of large enterprises in providing facilities for workers' children and for cultural, educational and sports activities is reflected in a section on cultural services. The textile administration agrees on improvements for the children's institutions and the "Red Corners" in the plant, and, jointly with the union committee, sets the number of children, nearly two thousand, to be sent to summer camps. The union states how much it is assigning from its budget for cultural work and physical culture, and agrees to carry on systematic political, educational, and cultural work. The construction enterprise agrees on repairs and upkeep of the "Red Corners," and the provision of auto transport for summer trips outside the city. The union will send 175 children to summer camps, and assign substantial sums for cultural and sports activities. It will carry on political-educational work, technical propaganda, cultural and sports activities, and encourage young workers to continue their education.

Finally, the agreements include provisions for change in their terms after discussion at workers' meetings, for a regular check on fulfillment of all sections, and for action to eliminate any violations. An appendix in the textile contract lists occupations paid at higher rates for "hot, heavy work, and work with harmful conditions," and those with conditions that entitle the worker to free milk.

Disputes over observance of the contracts are reported more frequently than those arising during negotiations. Mass check-ups twice a year are recommended by the CCTU. Such a check-up was reported from a textile plant in Ivanovo. Surveys by eight commissions of the factory committee, involving 200 workers, found 183 out of some 190 points already fulfilled. On the contrary, the machine shop administration had failed to carry out agreed improvements of ventilation and of safety devices on circular saws. It was necessary to carry the question to the factory committee and the director before the demands were met.[15]

In 1962 after years of criticisms of administrations and union committees, the union newspaper still complained that some administrative leaders did not fulfill obligations under collective contracts and that trade union organizations went along with them; there are cases, it said, where "if the enterprise does not fulfill the plans, the director has to answer to the sovnarkhoz, but if he ignores the collective contract, as a rule he gets away with it."[16] Many examples are reported in the press of the same provisions being included year after year without being carried out. The unions, however, can raise the question "of bringing to responsibility" administrators who do not fulfill obligations. All depends, said the union paper, on "principledness, persistence, militance. And much depends on the regional committees and councils."

The need for giving support to factory committees and for putting pressure on managements to observe the terms of the contracts has led to a movement for general agreements between regional economic councils and trade union councils. The CCTU approved and recommended such agreements in all regions. Some sovprofs considered them unnecessary, but others expressed enthusiasm for their results. These agreements include joint plans for cooperation on production matters and on insuring the observance of labor legislation and of the terms of the contracts in enterprises. The sovnarkhozy also promised funds for improving safety and working conditions, and for housing, clubs, nurseries, kindergartens, health facilities, education, and sports. Good results were reported from Kharkov, Kursk, Latvia, and Estonia, where the agreements were said to have led to better acquaintance between administrative and union leaders, to support for factory committees in demanding unconditional fulfillment of terms of the contracts, to the finding of resources for meeting some of the demands, and to better protection of workers' rights. In 1964 at least one general agreement was signed by a new larger sovnarkhoz with a group of sovprofs in its region.[17]

The significance of collective contracts in Soviet enterprises differs basically from that in American industry, since the major protections of Soviet workers come from governmental central standards. Yet the contracts provide additional protections. The important place given to provisions for housing, social services, educational, cultural, and recreational programs reflects a work-centered economy of great scarcity, in which the enterprise has necessarily assumed a paternalistic care for the welfare of its workers, in cooperation with the union. The emphasis on joint responsibility for production is contrary to all but the rarest cases in Western labor relations. Primary in the significance of the Soviet collective contracts is their role in mobilizing workers to improve production. Goals set are sometimes above those in the state plan. The negotiation of contracts and the involvement of many workers in the check on their fulfillment serves an educational purpose, promoting the interests of the state and of the workers.

Inclusion in the contracts of some provisions of labor law is often criticized as unnecessary and ineffective, but it may help by informing workers of their rights.[18] The contracts also include actual standards worked out in local negotiations. General standards need to be applied in the plant, sometimes made more concrete with provisions for safety measures and other improvements to meet the requirement of "normal conditions." Decisions are made on the use of piece- and time-work, on lists of jobs entitled to special privileges, and on the methods of classifying work and workers and revising production standards. Broad legal obligations are made more specific, such as an agreement that all expenditures from the enterprise fund, not only the budget estimates, are to be decided jointly. Additional protections may be provided for nursing mothers or for young workers and students. Legal experts emphasize as an important development, which they expect to grow, the increased scope for local initiative in determining standards for the protection of workers.[19]

Collective contracts have significance both for furthering the

needs of the state and for participation of workers through
their union committees in many decisions affecting their welfare. The contracts serve the interests of workers to substantial
degrees where local unions use their rights fully, but there
are many failures to do so.

PROTECTION OF WORKERS

The Soviets use the term protection of labor (*okhrana
truda*) either narrowly to cover only issues of safe and healthful conditions at work, or more widely to cover all the protections provided by labor legislation and collective contracts.
Under both interpretations the first responsibility is that of
management. The chief engineer has the direct responsibility,
and in large plants safety engineers and departments on safety
work with shop heads. The role of the local union is to work
out agreements for further definition of standards and the
means to achieve them, to cooperate in promoting good conditions, and to check on the observance of all regulations and
contract terms. The factory committees are said to have the
largest role in ensuring the protection of workers, especially
since the extension of their rights in 1958. Much of the detailed work is done by the special commissions of the shop and
factory committees and by the trade union group organizers
and public inspectors.[20]

In the field of safety and working conditions, the union in
the plant shares both in decisions for improvements and in
the state function of inspection.[21] However, leading engineers
and other experts in 1963 and 1964 called for more attention to
safety matters in the training of technicians and engineers,
since the majority of accidents were thought to be due to poor
training of workers and lack of technical inspection. The
CCTU urged that the responsibility of managements be increased for conditions of safety and health, and for improving
the work of safety staffs in enterprises.[22] In the sample of

plants visited, it appeared that in general there had been considerable improvement between 1955 and 1962 in plant conditions and housekeeping, and in the provision of safety devices. Yet even in 1959 and 1962 many instances were seen of heavy loads being carried by women and young workers and of other unsafe conditions. Accident rates are not published but they are believed to be high.

The union commissions on protection of labor take part in the development of "complex plans for improvement of conditions," and plans for reconstruction of shops, with attention to light and ventilation, sanitary facilities, provision of drinking water, and safety requirements. They are expected to check on safety instruction and on the requirement that safety equipment be used, to study every case of accident or industrial disease, and to work with the shop administration in eliminating the causes.

Much responsibility is carried by the workers who are elected public inspectors in each trade union group. They check on observance by management of the safety regulations and on the state of safety instruction, and cooperate with the foreman and group leader in efforts to ensure safe and healthful work. In case of accident the inspector has a duty to see that necessary aid is given any injured worker and that the incident is discussed in the brigade or the shop, with the aim of educating workers and removing causes of accidents.

If violations of law or the collective contract are not remedied, the inspector and group organizer can turn to the shop commission on protection and the shop committee. Shop and factory committees can ask any representative of the management for reports; they can make recommendations and demand that management fulfill its obligations. Any workers who fail to observe the safety rules can be called before the committee or before general meetings of the workers, or, in extreme cases, can be sent to the comradely court. Negligent administrative personnel also can be sent to the comradely court, but this is rare. In one reported case of an injury to a worker on a press, both she and her foreman were brought before the court; the worker, who had not used the safety device, was warned, but the foreman was given a public reprimand for his failure to check sufficiently on the work of the operators.[23]

Legal powers of enforcement of safety rules and other legislation are in the hands of technical inspectors from the regional trade union council. Only with the agreement of the technical inspector can the public inspectors in the plant or the union committees give obligatory orders to the management. In case the legal demands of the union are refused, the factory committee can raise, with the director or higher administrative bodies, the question of punishment or removal of management personnel.

Public inspectors and shop and factory committees check also on observance of other requirements, such as the proper application of the wage system and the hours schedule, and provision of free work clothing, protective foods, and safety equipment. They are supposed to see that women and minors under 18 are not used on heavy or harmful work prohibited for them, and that the rights of women are observed for pregnancy leaves and for time off to nurse their infants in the plant's nurseries. Attention must be given to the protection of youngsters, who are to be assured proper job training and opportunity for further education, and be given special privileges, such as shorter hours, longer vacations—a full month and always in the summer—and time off in connection with their studies. Early in 1963 the CCTU called on the unions to strengthen their work with young workers and their check on full observance of all the requirements for their protection.[24]

Prevention of illegal overtime is one of the obligations of the factory committees. The reduction of the normal workday from eight to seven hours for five days, with six hours on Saturday, the sixth day of work, was a much appreciated gain. For leading occupations in underground work the standard became six hours; for other occupations with especially difficult conditions a six-hour day, or even one of four hours, was established.[25] The long-standing prohibition of overtime work or work on free days was continued, but complaints of violations are numerous. Overtime is legal only in emergency cases, such as public danger or emergency repairs to prevent damage or interruption of the work of considerable numbers, and then only with the consent of the factory committee. The amount of overtime that may be required of a worker is limited by law to four hours in two days and 120 hours in a year, with pay at the rate of time and a half for the first two hours, and double time for additional hours.

Use of overtime to make up for stoppages or lags in fulfilling production plans is strictly forbidden, according to Soviet authorities. An administrator is held responsible for illegally required overtime, even if this is permitted by the union.[26] The union committees are expected to check on any request for overtime and prevent its illegal use to make up for failures to get out the work on schedule; they are expected to use their influence to promote "rhythmical work" instead of the widespread practice of "storming" in the last ten days of the month to fulfill the month's plan. Protests of workers over illegal and sometimes unpaid overtime are nevertheless among the most common complaints in the union press. Union and party committees in the plant are as deeply interested as management in good production records, since these indicators of success affect their standing in socialist competition and the premiums that come with good results. Many times they shut their eyes to overtime or agree to its use without legal basis.[27] Party and government leaders are concerned over the amount of overtime in industry.

Factory committees also have a key role in enforcing the legal protections against discharge. The law strictly defines permissible bases for discharge by the administration and no discharge is allowable without agreement of the union committee; but there are many complaints of violations. According to the 1922 labor code, the chief bases for dismissal are liquidation of an enterprise or reduction of staff, incapacity to do the required work, systematic non-fulfillment of labor obligations or violations of discipline, or absence without acceptable excuse. An additional basis, used against administrators who violate their obligations, is discharge on the demand of a trade union.[28] Two weeks' notice or two weeks' pay is required in most cases of discharge not arising from the fault of the worker.

Any proposal for discharge is supposed to be considered carefully at a full meeting of the factory committee, which then decides whether it is justified under the law and whether it is necessary. The committee, whose decision is final, may refuse consent even when a legal basis is present. Well-functioning committees take seriously their responsibility to prevent arbitrary or unnecessary dismissals. As a disciplinary measure discharge is considered an extreme sanction, to be used only as a last resort. There are many reports of how union committees refuse to agree to discharges and instead try to reform the worker through social pressure in the shop. If a worker is considered incapable of doing the work, he may be helped to get further training. If management tries to get rid of a critic on the pretext of reducing the staff, this can be prevented.[29] On the other hand there are numerous cases where the right of the union committee to decide on any discharge is violated, and others where dismissals without legal grounds are agreed to.

Discharge in reduction of staff poses special problems, especially when mechanization and automation are increasing rapidly. Factory committees are expected to verify whether there are valid production reasons for a reduction of staff and whether, in the choice of those to be retained, the required priorities have been observed. Factory committees are evidently able sometimes, before they will sanction dismissals, to enforce a strict requirement that other jobs be found for such workers. This practice received support from a statement of the RSFSR Supreme Court in 1963 that the administration must take active measures for placement of a worker discharged in reduction of staff.[30]

Special protections are provided in case of illegal discharge. A worker discharged without the consent of the factory committee is entitled to immediate reinstatement, on appeal to the labor disputes commission or to the factory committee or directly to the People's Court. One who believes his discharge illegal, though the union committee consented, can appeal directly to the People's Court. Workers ordered reinstated by the labor disputes commission, the factory committee, or the court, are entitled to back pay for time lost up to twenty days. If the manager does not obey the order of prompt reinstatement, the worker is entitled to back pay for the full time lost from the date of the order. Such back pay is paid by the enterprise, but the person guilty of the violation may be assessed individually to compensate the enterprise, in an amount not more than three months' salary.[31]

When labor legislation or the terms of a collective contract are violated, the first remedy is expected to be through consultation of union representatives with management or through more formal demands from the shop or factory committee. The unions can call for help from regional union committees and the sovprof, both of which exert influence through their contacts with the sovnarkhozy. Individual workers whose grievances are not met through informal channels may appeal to the labor disputes commissions of their shop or plant, and if necessary to the factory committee and to the People's Court. Technical inspectors of the sovprofs can fine those guilty of violations, order changes in the shops for reason of safety, and stop work on dangerous machinery. The sovprof can close down a shop or enterprise that fails to meet the requirements for protection of workers. Management personnel may be reprimanded, warned, or removed on demand of the sovprof. Local party committees may take action against those who fail in their obligation to workers. Serious violations may be brought to court, where administrators carry criminal responsibility for violations of labor legislation, the collective contracts, or the rights of the trade unions.[32]

Managers and their administrative personnel are accordingly under a variety of pressures to live up to their obligations—pressure from the local unions and the regional union bodies and from party and higher administrative authorities, and there is the possibility of administrative punishment and of fines or criminal sanctions. Criticisms in the newspapers as a result of complaints from workers may bring sanctions into operation. The unions have a considerable battery of methods they can use for enforcing standards and protecting workers—wide publicity and criticism, the right to make enforceable decisions, appeal to higher union and administrative and party bodies for pressure on directors, and appeal to the courts. When the union is effectively led and diligent in utilizing its rights, it can do much in this area. Soviet authorities consider that the observance of labor legislation has been markedly improved by the increased powers of the local unions since 1958 and the strengthened position of the regional trade union councils. The number of labor cases in the courts decreased substantially. Yet complaints over violations of rights continue to appear frequently in the press, reach the courts in considerable numbers, and are a subject of concern to union leaders, the party and the government.

Before further consideration of how this works in practice and of what is done to enforce obligations upon managers, it is necessary to turn to the handling of individual grievances and the question of collective labor disputes and their settlement.

CHAPTER VIII

Labor Disputes

COLLECTIVE interests and rights are the main concern of the law on the factory, plant, and local union committees, of legislation and regulations for the protection of labor, and of collective contracts. Individual rights are involved in the application of these regulations. Disputes arise in both areas. Soviet theorists make a sharp distinction between disputes concerned with establishing new conditions and those over the application of law, regulations, or collective contracts.[1] The former, such as disputes over the terms of a new collective contract, are "non-actionable" (*neiskovye*), outside the general system for settling disputes; if not resolved by agreement in the plant, they can be appealed to higher union and management bodies for determination. Grievances over the application of established rights are "actionable" disputes, handled by the commissions on labor disputes.

The major issue of wage levels is outside the scope of labor-management decision in the Soviet system. In a planned economy, money wages are fixed by the planners as an important element in the total planning of costs, prices, and incomes, which must take account of the plans for consumers' goods and services. Real wages are determined by the output of goods and services as well as by the level of money incomes provided. How much influence the unions may have at the top levels on these vital plans is unknown. Wages are not involved in labor disputes, except for details in the application of central standards. Workers can express dissatisfaction with wage levels only by requesting that at higher levels the union raise the question with governmental authorities—or as individuals they can shift jobs.

For the most part, labor disputes, as discussed in the literature, are concerned with complaints against violations of rights.[2] Disputes are said to arise often from "survivals of the past in the consciousness of people," such as the wrongful "uncommunist" behavior of managers who neglect "the rights, needs, and requests" of workers. They are said to come also from workers' lack of discipline, from demands not justified by law or for which means are not available at the time, from misinterpretation of the law, or from new issues on which the law has not yet been determined. Economists recognize also that on wage questions conflicts are possible between individual and social interests. The dean of labor law experts, Professor N. G. Aleksandrov, suggested that the increasing "communist education" of the working people would tend to decrease the number of disputes, but that on the other hand, their growing "activeness" would decrease the possibility that they would not protest violation of their rights, and so might lead to more disputes.[3]

Sources of labor disputes can be summed up as abuses of workers' rights by managements; violations of discipline by workers, or workers' demands considered excessive; misunderstandings as to legal obligations and rights; difficulties in applying standards on wages, safety, and the like; unresolved questions of interests and rights; and the growing knowledge and demands of an increasingly educated working population.

A system for settling grievances has been in effect since 1922, with joint "rates and conflicts commissions" in the plants.[4] In 1957 a decree of the Presidium of the Supreme Soviet provided a new system, proposed by the Central Council of Trade Unions and the Council of Ministers.[5] It aimed to

increase the speed and effectiveness of settlement on the spot
by giving greater powers to the factory committees and providing prompt consideration in the local People's Courts on
appeal. This eliminated a source of great delays in the former
system—the appeals to higher trade union bodies all the way
up to the CCTU.

Three agencies are involved in the handling of grievances:
the joint commission on labor disputes in the enterprise, with
shop commissions in big shops; the factory committee itself;
and the People's Court. The commission on labor disputes is
made up of representatives chosen in equal numbers by the
factory committee from its membership and by the management. The commission chooses the chairman and secretary for
each session, alternating between the two sides. In small enterprises with no factory committee the labor disputes commission consists of the trade union organizer and the director.
Meetings are held on non-working time so that interested
workers can be present. The worker has the right to protest
any commission member he considers prejudiced; then the
question of whether to replace that member is decided either
by the factory committee or the director, depending on whose
representative is challenged. The commission decides grievances by agreement of the two sides. If there is disagreement
among the representatives of either side, the case is adjourned
for further consultations—union representatives with the factory committee or management representatives with the director—to decide the position to be taken. The decisions, which
are supposed to be based on full consideration of the facts and
on proper application of law and pertinent regulations or
agreements, are posted for all to see. Decisions of the shop
commissions can be appealed to the plant commission.

If the worker is dissatisfied, he may appeal to the union's
factory committee, which has power to make a binding deci-

sion, but the management may not appeal, since its representatives in the labor disputes commission agreed to the decision. The factory committee holds a hearing, invites management to present its opinion, and considers the evidence. It may maintain or change the decision of the labor disputes commission, or decide an issue on which the commission was unable to agree. Its decision has legal force, if made by majority vote at a meeting with two-thirds of the members present. There is no right of appeal to, or intervention by, higher union bodies, except in case of a decision without the required quorum. In small enterprises with no factory committee, appeals go directly to the People's Court.

A worker dissatisfied with the decision of the factory committee may appeal to the People's Court. Management has the right to appeal only if it considers the decision contrary to law. The courts, however, accept appeals by administrations, since any decision not based on the facts is clearly not legal, and consideration of the facts of the case is necessary for determining that question.[6] Court decisions may be appealed to higher courts. The procurator, a legal officer of the state, may intervene on his own initiative, protesting decisions at any stage from the commission on labor disputes up to the courts, when he considers this necessary to protect the rights of either a worker or the state. The union committee can send a representative to appear in court in the name of workers to assist in protecting their rights, although this is said to be done less often than is desirable.[7] The worker is entitled to legal assistance from his union and has no financial costs in connection with his appeal to the court.

Emphasis is on settlement promptly and as close as possible to the source of the dispute. The union committee does not accept a grievance for the commission on labor disputes until after the worker has tried to get satisfaction from management.

Often the chairman of the factory or shop committee discusses the matter with the foreman or other management person and settles the case informally. On receipt of a complaint the commission must act within five days. Appeal may be filed within ten days and the factory committee must act within seven days. Appeal may be made to the People's Court within ten days after the committee's decision, and the court is expected to act within five days (or up to ten in some republics). It is said that the great majority of decisions are accepted and put into effect without appeal, at each level, so that decreasing numbers reach the plant commissions on labor disputes, the factory committees, and the People's Courts.[8]

Decisions of the labor disputes commissions and of the factory committees must be carried out by management within ten days, if no other time limit is set, or there is no appeal. If management does not obey the order, the worker concerned may apply to the factory committee for a document having the effect of a writ of execution for enforcement of the decision, and on presentation to the court this will be enforced by an officer of the court.

Since this settlement system deals primarily with disputes of individuals with management over established rights, other types of disputes may not be accepted by the commission on labor disputes. Conflicts between union committees and the director are settled directly by agreement or by appeal to higher union and administrative agencies. A number of other types of issues are explicitly excluded, such as disciplinary penalties in fields covered by special transportation and communications codes, and complaints of directors or other chief staff members, which are handled directly by higher administrative authorities. Discharge on demand of a trade union can be protested only to these administrative bodies. Questions of a worker's work record for determining social insurance benefits are decided by special commissions. Many court cases and a complex body of court decisions interpreting the law arise from uncertainties as to whether particular cases should be taken by the labor disputes commissions, as well as over the proper application of the laws.

A broad range of questions remains for the commissions on labor disputes. Some are specified in the decree and many others are covered by the catch-all phrase of "disputes over the application of labor legislation, collective contracts, and the enterprise rules." Included are questions as to the application of the established systems of wages, production standards, and premiums; calculation of wages under circumstances such as stoppages, breakage, overtime, layoffs; transfers without the required consent of the worker; rights to vacations and free days; disciplinary penalties; discharge without the consent of the factory committee; and many others.

The nature of disputes mentioned in interviews in seventeen plants may indicate the typical distribution of the grievances that reach the commissions. Disputes related to wages were most frequently cited, most of them involving details of the calculation of wages. A few dealt with premiums, or the wage class of the work or worker, or protested production standards. Disputes over vacation schedules seemed especially prominent in Leningrad. There were complaints against disciplinary penalties, or in a few cases against discharge. Several disputes concerned job rights involved in transfers. A few examples follow.

A man complained that his pay was wrong. It developed that his wage class had been incorrectly entered on an order and the mistake was rectified.

A worker lost a bonus on the grounds of unexcused absence, when he skipped his own shift, but worked another. As no agreement was reached in the shop commission, the complaint went to the factory commission, which decided it was still a violation of rules.

A hosiery worker lost a premium because in inspecting and

sorting for quality she exceeded her allowance for error; since quality is very important, she lost her case.

When a worker had agreed to take his vacation in February, but after his marriage wanted to shift to a summer vacation with his wife, the shop commission made the shift. It is said that many such questions are settled by exchanges although in case of dispute the agreed-on schedule is usually upheld.

On a delivery at a clothing plant some material was missing. The management blamed the workers who handled the shipment and deducted one-third from their wages; they objected and won their case, this time on appeal to the factory committee.

In the same plant a hot dispute involved the report of a group of workers that one lot on which they worked was silk, which was entitled to a higher rate than cotton. The management checked, found the work was cotton, and paid at the lower rate. The workers were probably mistaken originally, but they held out. In the labor disputes commission the union representative insisted on payment in accordance with the workers' report, but management refused. When the issue went to the factory committee, they finally decided after getting legal advice that the workers were wrong and should be paid according to the work actually done.

In a textile plant seven workers on one operation objected to a new production standard. The labor disputes commission had the calculations re-checked, found them correct, and accordingly approved the norm. The workers were not happy about it, but a little later they were overfulfilling the norm by substantial amounts.

A foreman in a glass plant was advised to shift to other work, and when he refused he was shifted regardless. On his appeal to the disputes commission, they agreed he should be kept in his original job.

Another case in the same plant showed an ingenious use of

means available for settlement. A man complained that the
director had paid him too low a bonus; the labor disputes commission ordered a further payment, which the management
refused. The factory committee again ordered the payment
and again it was refused. The factory committee then went to
the state bank, which paid the worker directly from the funds
of the enterprise. Since redress had been achieved, the factory
committee did not feel it necessary to bring to higher authorities the question of punishing the director.

In the case of disputes over disciplinary penalties, workers
may protest on the ground of the facts, or the severity of the
penalty, or incorrect procedures. The commission on labor disputes can order a penalty removed, if they consider it improper on any of these grounds. A penalty recommended by
a comradely court also may be appealed, as this recommendation is without legal force and the administration must act
within the law. Discharge may be appealed to the commission,
the factory committee, or the court if the factory committee
had not given consent, or directly to the court if an agreed-on
discharge is thought to be illegal.

The new system of settling disputes seems to have widespread approval. A group of labor law experts held that the
basic success of the new law was generally known. "The
settlement of disputes was brought closer to production, simplified and speeded up, and the number of labor cases in the
courts was significantly reduced."[9] In Moscow courts from
1954 to 1959 the number of labor cases decreased by over 71
per cent; dismissal cases by 54 per cent, wage claims by 79
per cent, and all other labor cases by 90 per cent. In the
Donetz region, labor cases in the courts in 1962 were only
half the number in 1956.[10] An officer of the USSR Supreme
Court reported early in 1965 that for the entire country, in
comparison with 1956, the number of wage cases reviewed
in the courts had decreased by three-fourths, other labor dis-

putes by four-fifths, and discharge disputes by one-third. The workers' complaints had been satisfied in a large majority of the 1963 cases, in 53 per cent of the complaints of illegal discharges, 70 per cent of the wage cases, and 73 per cent in other cases.[11] Relatively few complaints on the work of the labor disputes commissions appear in the press, in contrast to many on illegal discharges and violations of safety and other regulations. The great majority of disputes that earlier had reached the courts are now settled in the plants. Nevertheless, one expert warned against underestimating the role of the courts, which remain "a dependable instrument for the protection of the labor rights of workers."[12]

Management and union officers in plants visited were unanimous in their support of the new disputes system. Most grievances, they said, were settled directly in the shops or in the shop commissions on labor disputes, with smaller numbers reaching the factory committees, and very few going to court. In a big electrical equipment plant and in a textile mill with 10,000 workers, most formal disputes were settled in the shop commissions. In 1961 only 20 cases reached the textile mill's plant commission on labor disputes, and in ten months of 1962 only 12; only 4 cases reached the factory committee in 1961, and a very few went to court, most of them involving disciplinary penalties against administrative workers. In a men's clothing plant only 12 cases were considered in the factory committee in 1961, and only 5 in ten months of 1962.

Generally there were said to be fewer formal cases than before. This was sometimes explained by better knowledge of the law on the part of the administrative staff and more attention by union officers to settling disputes in accordance with the law. Increased efforts had been made by factory committees and by regional union organizations to educate both workers and managements. It was said also that management usually preferred to settle a case in the disputes commission where it had a voice, rather than let it go to the factory committee. Managers were said to be reluctant to appeal decisions to the courts. One vigorous plant committee chairman claimed that "management usually gives up at the first step." It was frequently said that the workers win most of their cases. One chief engineer commented, "Speaking objectively— the factory committee takes the side of the worker. Even if the fault is obvious, the union tries to smooth it over, and this is natural, since the majority of the members of the committee are workers." But in another plant the woman director denied this, saying, "The union committee knows the law and its decisions are just." In her plant the majority of cases in the shop commissions were won by workers, as most disputes arose from mistakes of foremen, not from a dispute with management. Cases that reached the plant commissions or the factory committee were tougher ones, which the workers were more likely to lose.

A CCTU legal worker spoke of the misgivings of many directors when the new system was adopted; they thought it gave too much power to the union committee. But the system was working out satisfactorily. He spoke with admiration of how ordinary workers, as members of labor disputes commissions, worked to learn the law and apply it properly, becoming "lawyers without education." Cases reported in interviews and in the legal literature give the impression that workers' complaints are generally handled with care in the plants and in the courts.

In the first years there were complaints that the factory committees did not always train the disputes commissions adequately, and that sometimes they took cases without waiting for decisions by the commissions, or permitted violations of legislation through careless decisions that necessitated appeals to the courts.[13] The problem seems to have been alleviated by training given by regional union councils and the legal inspectors in some regions, by use of the union booklets, and by generally increased knowledge of the law. A report from Kaliningrad in 1961 said that work on labor disputes had improved in many enterprises, with the result that no cases went to court from those plants. Since in some enterprises violations of law were still permitted and there was "red tape" in settling disputes, the sovprof set up legal consultations in big enterprises and recommended seminars for administrators for the study of labor legislation.[14] In 1962 the CCTU reported that in Chelyabinsk a system of volunteer legal consultants had led to a significant decrease in the number of disputes and of cases reaching the People's Courts; complaints to the sovprof or sovnarkhoz of violations of labor legislation also had decreased.[15]

Criticisms published in 1962 and 1963 of the handling of disputes in three regions still showed deficiencies in the work of some local unions and labor disputes commissions. The CCTU criticized the Omsk sovprof and regional committees for not giving enough attention to the work of the commissions, to training, and to punishing those guilty of violations of rights. Some commissions took cases not within their competence. Some factory committees themselves heard cases that should have gone to the commissions. There were delays in decisions, exceeding the legal time limits, and other infringements of proper procedures. Violations of rights were sometimes permitted, decisions were left unfulfilled, causes of disputes were not investigated or their sources eliminated. The regional bodies were instructed to train and help the factory committees and the labor disputes commissions and to see that disputes were properly handled.[16] Similar criticisms were made of the Krasnodarsk regional sovprof and committees.[17]

The procurator in Irkutsk wrote that the unions had done much to strengthen the observance of labor laws, but he blamed the large number of labor cases still in the courts on union committees that lacked interest in settling disputes, permitted delays, and failed to insist that violations of laws be eliminated. In the last year there had been 277 cases of wage claims, more than half of which had been satisfied, and 566 cases of protested discharge, with 349 persons returned to their jobs by court order. He urged more effort to educate workers as to the rights of the unions and the methods of utilizing these rights.[18]

The current system for settling disputes over violations of workers' established rights protects only one section of their interests, yet the general effectiveness of this system helps to explain why many workers have an increased confidence in the unions. While problems remain in poorly led units, especially in small enterprises, and the most serious problem is the large number of illegal discharges, there is no evidence of such widespread difficulty in getting satisfaction as was found under the former system of handling grievances.[19]

When grievances are not resolved in the plants, the courts give a further important protection. Even in the earlier years Soviet courts had a good reputation for protecting the legal rights of workers in labor cases. Professor Berman has said, "There seems to be little doubt that the Soviet courts in general guard zealously the rights of workers in the labor cases which come before them." He pointed out that an émigré Soviet lawyer, who had represented management, felt that the courts "tended to lean over backwards to decide for the worker."[20] Supervision by the procurators, decisions of higher courts on appeal, and general instructions issued by the USSR Supreme Court all seek to promote prompt and just support by the courts of the labor rights of citizens.[21]

ILLEGAL DISCHARGE

Although the number of illegal dismissals was reported sharply reduced by control of factory committees over discharge,[22] complaints appear frequently in the trade union press, and the largest number of labor cases in the courts involve this issue.

Many published stories of illegal firings ask how union committees can fail so often to protect workers in this crucial aspect of their rights. Many directors discharged workers arbitrarily and for their own purposes, without regard to the law and often without consulting the union committees, and committees "went along." When workers were ordered reinstated, some directors failed to carry out the order, yet went unpunished. Some workers remained out of work for months, and when reinstated were only partially compensated for their "involuntary absence." Back pay, when ordered, was usually at the expense of the enterprise, not of those responsible. Regional union committees and sovprofs sometimes failed to protest known violations. Many victimized workers were eventually restored to their jobs, sometimes by party action, often as a result of pressure from editors, and often by the courts. But in some instances, at the time of the press reports, justice had still not been done.

Much evidence on this problem comes from officers of the courts, which were still receiving hundreds of cases of illegal discharges permitted by factory committees. In 1960 it was said in Kuibyshev, "A large role in this is played by the harmful but still active 'family relations' of trade union leaders, their unwillingness to complicate mutual relations with the administration."[23] The chairman of the Lugansk regional court wrote in January 1964 that in the region as a whole the number of discharge cases was increasing. Every second case in the courts resulted in reinstatement and repayment of wages lost, although 63 per cent of those reinstated had been discharged with the union's agreement.[24] In many reports, up to a third of the complaints involved discharge without the agreement of the factory committee—an illegal action whatever the claimed basis; in others the union committees had agreed to the dismissal though there was no legal basis. From many areas came reports that the courts ordered reinstatement and back pay in about half or more of the appeals brought by discharged workers.[25] Sometimes when workers were reinstated by the courts it was at the cost of long conflict for them and loss to the state. For one group of illegally discharged workers who were reinstated, the loss of time was more than 20 days each for 123 workers and over 50 days each for 41 workers.[26] Several reports of individual cases spoke of long periods out of work after an illegal discharge.

Reports published in 1963 and 1964 illustrate the continuing problem. A legal inspector of the Moscow city sovprof told about a director whose "malicious" violations of labor laws should have been stopped promptly by the union committee either by protesting strongly or by bringing the matter to the higher union organs. After the chief of a construction enterprise had illegally fired a woman, and she was put back to work by the union committee, he had continued to persecute her until she applied to leave and was released. The court ordered the director to reinstate her once more. An attempt to fire two others without union consent was thwarted, but the committee took no further action, even when the chief began to harass the committee chairman; word of all this reached the sovprof only from an ordinary worker. Finally, the construction workers' city committee demanded removal of the director, and he was fired and required to repay the enterprise for the back pay to the first worker.[27]

A case from a Vladimir railroad station led to three reports in *Trud*. After working there 19 years, a woman with three dependent children was discharged, allegedly in reduction of staff. The local union committee and the People's Court accepted the manager's statement although the worker believed she

was fired for criticizing the work of the station. Her fellow
workers and the local paper came to her defense, but the Vladimir regional court supported the decision of the lower court.
When the worker appealed to *Trud*, the editors sent her letter
to the railroad administration, which after long delay only
repeated the claim of "production necessity." The editors asked
the Vladimir procurator to investigate; the case was reopened
in the regional court, which reversed the lower court and reinstated the worker. *Trud* continued to press the issue of responsibility. Finally, the higher railroad union committee
removed the chairman of the local committee, criticized the
district committee, and prodded the railroad administration.
The latter reported that strong reprimands had been given the
chief of the station and the personnel officer. The Vladimir
court reprimanded the People's Court and members of the regional court, and instructed them to use more care in handling
discharge cases. An officer of the Supreme Court of the RSFSR
said that the case had been discussed in Moscow, and that
Trud had been right in raising questions with the courts in an
effort to prevent such mistakes. The woman had been out of
work for almost a year. Nothing was reported on back pay,
but assuming that she was reinstated promptly, this would
have been due for only twenty days, according to the usual
rule. How she lived during the long delay was not explained.[28]

Compensation for wages lost in illegal dismissals is designed
to protect the victims and to penalize those guilty of the illegal
acts by requiring them to repay the enterprises for amounts
paid out. Back pay in considerable sums is reported. In Moscow in 1960 it amounted to about 50,000 new rubles ($55,500),
but almost all at the expense of the state enterprises, rather
than of the administrators. In 185 other cases of reinstatement,
enterprises paid the victims 8,775 rubles, or an average of
about 48 rubles, but in only 16 cases was the back pay assessed
against the individual responsible. In cases studied in the

Ukraine in 1963, only 9 per cent of over 95,000 rubles in back pay was repaid by management officials; in 1964 the per cent increased somewhat but was still not high. Many legal experts have argued that courts should make more use of their power "to punish by the ruble" and to hold administrators to criminal responsibility, but these penalties have only rarely been applied. Experts have called also for further protection of workers by extending the period for which back pay may be ordered; 20 days are too few since 40 are more usually required in cases that go to court. Average amounts of back pay ordered by the courts in 1963 have been estimated as only 100 rubles.[29]

Sometimes a misinterpretation of the complicated regulations gives rise to illegal discharges; to prevent these honest mistakes more education of managements and of union committees is relied on. But the use of subterfuges by managers to get rid of critics or other unwanted workers is a serious problem. The claim of reduction of staff, which is often used, is one the union committees need to check with great care, as to its validity and as to the attention given both to the needs of production and to the work records and family circumstances of workers; the committees should remember also the manager's duty to find jobs for workers displaced.[30] In the case of disciplinary discharges, permitted for systematic violations, the unions are urged to try social pressure instead of sanctioning the dismissal; in any event they are expected to see that the rule of only one penalty for one offense is observed. Managers sometimes oust a worker also by inducing him to leave "by his own choice." Many union committees give only superficial attention to discharge requests by managers, or to the unwilling application of a worker to leave, and thus permit violations that lead to court cases.

A decree of the Council of Ministers and the CCTU in January 1962 insisted that regional union and economic councils act more vigorously against any such violations of law and punish those responsible.[31] In December 1962 a long "explanation" on application of the legal requirements for discharge was issued by the plenum of the RSFSR Supreme Court. Concern was shown especially with applications to leave, induced by managements contrary to the worker's wish, and the courts were instructed to verify the facts carefully. Warnings were given on the need for care in cases of discharge of pregnant women and women with children under one year, who are specially protected; of members of factory committees; also of discharge for "incapacity to do the work." Finally, the statement instructed the courts to make more use of their power to require reimbursement of enterprises for losses in back pay, and reminded them that disciplinary and criminal penalties were the most effective means of combatting labor law violations. It summarized the penalties available under the law; warning, reprimand, shift to a lower post for a term not more than one year, and discharge; and, under the criminal code of the RSFSR, imprisonment for up to one year and discharge. It pointed out that this explanation was meant to guide managers and union workers who deal with labor disputes, as well as the lower courts.[32]

The USSR Supreme Court noted discrepancies in the practices of courts in different republics on cases of discharge without union consent. On June 30, 1964, its plenum issued a decree intended to resolve uncertainties. In the interest of the quickest possible restoration to their jobs, workers discharged without the agreement of their factory committee could choose whether to turn to their labor disputes commission or their factory committee, or directly to the court, and were entitled to immediate reinstatement. The courts were expected also to take preventive measures. The decree specified that the courts had the obligation, depending on the circumstances, to consider requiring guilty administrators to repay the enterprise for the back pay, or bringing them into court on criminal charges.[33] Also, under the civil codes of the Russian and other republics, the enterprise is required to fulfill at once a court order of reinstatement and back pay, even if the decision was being appealed. It was hoped thus to prevent the delays that had sometimes lasted for months. An officer of the Supreme Court, discussing efforts for protection of workers' rights, gave several examples of administrators who were held responsible for their illegal actions; one had to repay 1,165 rubles to his enterprise for back pay, and another was sentenced to six months compulsory labor for "crude violations of labor legislation." The CCTU in January 1965 issued detailed instructions to the unions at all levels on their duty to prevent illegal discharges.[34]

Protections against discharge are effective when administrations and union committees know and observe the law, and avoid discharges except in the most extreme cases.[35] But even with more effective action by unions, the courts would still need to make more vigorous use of the sanctions available against violators. Many statements from high authority in the party, the government, and the unions indicate increasing efforts to extend the legal protections more widely in practice.

COLLECTIVE DISPUTES AND VIOLATIONS OF RIGHTS

Conflicts between workers and their managements are getting increased attention in Soviet discussions of labor law. Collective disputes arise over demands of workers for improved working and living conditions and services, and over the establishment of rules and standards sometimes going beyond the centrally determined protections. Disputes arise also over violations of the right of factory committees to share in many decisions and to have their opinion considered in others. Many conflicts involve violations of safety rules, other labor laws and regulations, or terms of collective contracts.

In the area of workers' interests in improvement of conditions, management is limited by the resources available under the production and finance plans and by laws and regulations. These issues are usually worked out by the union committee and the manager. One account of good relations in a machine plant spoke of several unresolved issues, but concluded confidently, "The dispute continues, . . . but it will be settled in the interest of affairs, in favor of the collective." Another, referring to a dispute that could not be settled at one meeting, said, "This dispute has to be settled by life itself."[36]

When a conflict concerns the terms of a collective contract, it goes for final settlement to the next higher administrative and union bodies, but no legislation provides a method of settlement if they disagree. In general, any disputes between local unions and managers go up in the same way—if necessary to the central committees of the branch unions or the CCTU for settlement with administrative and governmental bodies. Soviet experts often say that methods for settling these collective disputes should be specified in the new basic labor code or in the law on settlement of labor disputes. One even suggested arbitration in the interest of avoiding delay in final disposition,[37] but this opinion is not generally accepted.

No specific evidence is available on the extent to which disputes between directors and their factory committees are resolved satisfactorily at the regional level. A report from Kharkov indicated that disputes that in former years had to go up to the central committees and the ministries for settlement were now quickly and easily decided.[38] In the absence of legal definition of the rights of the regional sovprofs or other higher levels of the unions in settling collective disputes, administrative and governmental agencies inevitably have the final word, when agreement is not reached with the unions on issues coming from the enterprises. The strike weapon is not available as an accepted method of pressure for settling such disputes.

The most serious disputes between factory committees and managements, and between workers and managements, come from violations of the well-defined rights, both individual and collective. Procedures for settling these disputes are thoroughly established in law and practice. Issues may be settled through public criticism and discussion in workers' meetings and in factory committees, check-ups by the union's public inspectors and commissions, and appeals to the regional union committees and the sovprofs for help and pressure on the administrative agencies. Appeals may go to higher union officers in the central committees or the CCTU, and to party committees. Complaints to the newspapers often start investigations that lead to redress. Legal powers of enforcement are exercised by the technical inspectors of the sovprofs and by the sovprofs themselves, and by state legal officers, the procurators. Violations can be brought to the courts. Violators of law and the contracts may be punished administratively, on demand of the sovprofs, or by criminal sanctions in the courts. Yet violations of collective and individual rights continue.

Evidence is plentiful of factory committees' failings in the past, of their preoccupation with the interests of production and with good relations with directors, of laxity in insisting on observance of labor laws and in protecting workers' interests —all of which led to dissatisfaction of workers with the unions.[39] It is not possible to measure how this has been affected by changes in the rights of the local unions since 1958, by increased answerability of officers to their members and increased emphasis on observing labor laws. Chairman Grishin of the CCTU said in his long report to the Twelfth Congress that in spite of much good work, "some factory and local committees are not utilizing the great rights given them," and some had "an unprincipled attitude." Unfortunately, he said, such cases were not exceptional. He demanded that trade unions insist on strict observance of regulations and see that "malicious violators are held strictly accountable." He denounced directors and officials of planning and economic agencies who "still do not always estimate the role of the trade unions properly."[40]

Reports continued to be published of cases where laws were violated but "peace and harmony reigned" between factory committee and director, and sometimes appeals to regional trade union, administrative and party bodies brought no results. Evidently old habits persisted, but a continuing effort to eliminate them was indicated by the publishing of these stories. Soviet experts and union leaders insist that the violations are now the exception, and that the large number of published reports prove that workers increasingly protest any violations. In 1963 Chairman Grishin told the Central Committee of the Communist Party that there were still

many cases of illegal application of overtime work and other violations of the work schedules. . . . There are unbased discharges . . . Although the government directs large resources for further improvement of conditions of work, in a number of enterprises there are serious deficiencies in protection of labor. . . . All this hurts the development in people of love of their enterprise and negatively affects labor discipline, leads to great instability of personnel, especially the young.[41]

The trade union newspaper, concerned over complaints they sometimes received of unions that "decide not to spoil relations, timidly come to the defense of legal rights of the working man," said that these complaints were "a direct reproach to trade union committees that forget their responsibility for conditions of work and life of Soviet people."[42]

Again in 1964 Grishin pointed out defects in the unions when he harangued a CCTU session on the need to decisively eliminate "indifference, inactivity, complacency, or lack of principle"; he called on them for "tireless struggle against inertia, bureaucraticism, extravagance, parasitism, against violations of labor legislation, neglectful relations to the needs of Soviet people." He insisted it is necessary "that the wide masses see in the unions their own closest organization, able to express and champion the interests of the working people."[43] Clearly, a "poor style of union work" was still to be found in many enterprises and regions.

A cursory reading of the union newspaper *Trud* and magazine *Sovetskie Profsoyuzy* for four years, 1960 through 1963, produced impressive evidence that violations continued, but also that workers protested and sought redress. Many reports came from worker correspondents in the enterprises, or from individuals who felt themselves wronged. More than 300 news stories or mentions of cases included about 140 instances of violations of safety regulations, illegal overtime, or other violations of labor laws or of the collective contracts, over 90 of illegal discharge, 53 of violations of the rights of union committees, and 24 of suppression of criticism. The trend during these years seemed to be toward a relative decrease in cases reported involving violations of the rights of the union committees and also illegal discharges. This might have been expected from the managers' growing knowledge and acceptance of the rights of the unions and of workers, and from more effective work by many local unions. The relative increase in reports involving violation of safety and other protections or of collective contracts—from 38 per cent in the first two years to 50 per cent in the period 1962-1963—probably reflected a real increase in demands from workers and the union committees that enterprises comply fully with their obligations.

The continuing difficulties with recalcitrant managers and negligent union officers come out clearly in many of these reports. Old style, unreconstructed managers and superintendents thought the union committee tried to undermine their authority, and they did not consider it necessary to work with the union. Some thought that "labor legislation was not for them." Some said, "I am boss here." In some instances union officers ignored complaints of workers or did not want to "spoil relations." Sometimes regional union officers disregarded complaints or told the union in the plant only to "find a common language with management." Regional economic councils and party committees were sometimes lax in reacting to legitimate complaints and continued to support administrators who violated the laws.[44]

Conflicting demands of production and of the rights of workers seem the most common basis for these violations. Especially is this true in the frequent instances of illegal overtime, with or without the consent of the union committee. Factory committees sometimes agreed when management said, "Production demands it." A plant in Zaporozhe was criticized for many violations, including illegal overtime, but the sovprof was said to have reproved the manager only lightly; "The bigger the enterprise, the softer the voice of the sovprof chairman." A girl worker from a Karaganda confectionery plant wrote that she was being criticized for her fight against overtime, and she asked, "Is it normal when a union committee, called to build up and protect the legal rights of the working people, gives its blessing to unlawful acts of the administration?"[45]

Overtime has reportedly increased in recent years in the enterprises of the regional economic councils. The main reason for illegal overtime was said to be poor organization of work. Chairman Grishin pointed out that many plants with such violations had losses from idle time. Another analysis found overtime caused by the necessity for repairs, preparation of unusual pieces, and the replacement of workers absent on vacation or for other reasons, or sometimes by a scarcity of workers of needed skills. The CCTU insisted that the unions put a stop to violations of workers' right to their scheduled free hours. Some managers were penalized, but Chairman

Grishin admitted, "We still have not done everything to increase the responsibility of administrative leaders and trade union organizations for strict observance of labor legislation."[46]

Production needs are frequently cited also when shops, entire plants, or new equipment are put to work without adequate provisions for safe and normal working conditions. Sometimes there is difficulty in getting equipment or materials. In other cases the desire to start work on time or ahead of schedule overrides protests of the union technical inspectors. Absurdities sometimes result from the conflicting demands on administrators. At the same time that violations of rules are protested and even fines for violations are imposed by union inspectors, premiums are given for successful production or for getting capacity into operation ahead of time. In one case reported by *Trud* a shop chief was fined 100 old rubles for a violation of the workers' free day, but his director gave him a premium of 840 rubles for good work.[47]

With so much reliance on "public influence" and "control from below," preservation of the right of criticism is crucial. The long tradition of open criticism at workers' meetings, in trade union committees, and in letters to higher agencies and to the press is encouraged in the interest of improving the work of administrators and unions—probably also as a safety valve and morale builder. *Trud* reported that it received 313,556 letters in 1963, almost 5 thousand more than in 1962. Similarly large numbers are received by the general newspapers, and by union, governmental, and party agencies. In four years the CCTU received about 400,000 letters. The CCTU Auditing Commission reported to the union congress in 1963 that the CCTU had improved its follow-up work on letters, but still needed to increase the responsibility of its departments for quick action on all such signals from working people.[48] Letters discuss and express opinion on current questions and include complaints against administrators, union

officers and agencies, occasionally party committees, and even
procurators. Many letters criticize people in responsible positions who failed to follow up on charges and to support
workers' just complaints.

The extent to which these complaints lead to remedial action
is not known. Letters sometimes are only sent back to the
agency complained against. But in many reported cases they
are followed up by inquiries to other agencies, or a special
investigator is sent out by the CCTU or by the editor. Frequent news reports in *Trud* and other papers give the original
complaint and tell what followed. Often after some time a
short note under the heading *"Trud* Answers," or a similar note
in other papers, reports the action taken.

Among the most distressing of the cases are those where
critics were persecuted. Some directors harassed workers who
dared to criticize them in wall newspapers or in meetings or
elsewhere, found excuses to give them penalties, lowered their
wage grades or premiums, even discharged them, or made life
unbearable in the hope that they would leave. Directors sometimes interfered in union elections in order to get rid of non-
compliant officers. Local party officials sometimes failed to
protect critics, or themselves harassed critics as disorganizers.
Under pressure from directors, active workers have been expelled from the party on such pretexts. Undoubtedly in some
cases fear of reprisal holds back effective local protests against
violators of rights. In addition, the livelihood of local union
officers, after their terms of office, may be affected. A union
leader in a Leningrad plant raised what he called "a delicate
question" of what will happen to one who shows principle and
persistence, since his job in the future will be decided by the
director with whom he has sometimes fought. There is no
problem, he said, if the director is a man of principle, but if
not? He asked for more attention by union committees and the
higher union bodies to guarding active members and officers

from injustice.[49] Another hazard is that the making of false accusations is illegal, and critics have sometimes found themselves accused of slander.[50]

Some twenty cases of managers' arbitrary actions against honest critics were cited in the émigré *New Review*.[51] Most of the cases had been reported in *Pravda* or *Trud* in 1962. Even party members had been victimized for efforts to stand up against callous managers, without any decisive action being taken by higher union, administrative, party, or court officers. The article ended on a note of extreme pessimism over workers' lack of protection from such employers. However, as pointed out by Dr. Solomon Schwarz,[52] later reports in a number of these cases told how protests finally succeeded, how guilty directors were penalized, discharged, and given strong party penalties. Dr. Schwarz concluded that rather than a "hopeless impasse," these cases showed an awakening "feeling of independence and of readiness to protest openly against illegality."

These stories of violations and protests give glimpses into the difficulties met by many workers in trying to assert the rights promised them. To evaluate these stories it is necessary to see them in the perspective of a huge country with nearly half a million union committees serving almost 70 million members. It must also be remembered that sometimes only the first chapter is given, but often later reports indicate a satisfactory outcome. In more than half the reports of complaints collected over several years, a follow-up told of action taken to remedy the complaint and warn or punish the guilty. For example, a factory committee, long "under the rein of the director" and not wishing "to spoil relations," permitted the discharge of an active critic, and even recommended to a general meeting of the workers his expulsion from the settlement. After several letters to *Trud* and the resulting intervention of the sovprof, the director was fired and the illegal discharge and eviction were rescinded.[53] In many instances complaints were turned over to one or several local agencies for investigation—the sovprof, the sovnarkhoz, the party committees, or the procurator—and confirmation of the facts followed. In some serious cases discussion at a meeting of a party committee or of the sovprof led to action. Occasionally a union committee chairman was removed by the sovprof for failing to stand up to his obligations. Sometimes the CCTU demanded from the sovprof more effective work with local unions and more insistence that administrators observe the required standards.

The unions have a strong sanction in their right to demand penalties on administrators. Under the 1958 law, the factory committees can "raise question" with higher agencies about administrative personnel who fail to fulfill their obligations. Union organs from the district level up have long had the right to "demand" removal of such administrators. It is said that in recent years unions had begun to make more frequent use of this power.[54] This must have an influence on old style managers who have been slow to accept their obligations. Publicity as to responsibility under the criminal code also has its effect.

Reports collected from the union press from 1959 through 1963 on penalties resulting from violations of rights included discharge of directors in forty-eight cases and reprimands or warnings to fifty-three others; removal of thirteen other management personnel and reprimands or warnings to nineteen. In ten reported cases violators were brought to court in criminal actions; party penalties on directors or others were reported in twenty-eight instances. Union committee officers were removed by decisions of higher trade union bodies in fourteen cases and reprimands were given in another twenty-five; in some reported cases, also, union officers were not re-elected. Occasionally it was reported, however, that a director was removed, only to be given another similar post, or to be replaced by a director who was no better.

News stories occasionally refer openly to adverse effects on workers' attitudes from a union's failure to stand up against an arbitrary management. In one mine it was said, "The trade union members no longer see the union as protector of their legal rights. They see no difference between the chairman of the mine committee and the chief of the mine."[55] The danger to morale and then to productivity when workers' rights are violated is recognized by the party and the CCTU.

Increasingly strong official statements have been made on protecting the right of criticism in the interest of securing observance of labor laws. Union papers and legal journals in 1963 and 1964 continued to emphasize the need for union vigilance. An editorial in *Trud,* admitting that it took courage to fight violations, called on union leaders to stand up against violators of workers' rights.[56] This discussion as well as another report early in 1964 frankly used the term "conflict."

In spite of continuing reports of violations and of reprisals against critics, workers, with their increasing education and experience, show signs of more independence in their protests. When they persist they can elect local and regional officers who will function responsibly. And they have channels through which they can bring pressure on higher authorities to support their demands.

THE QUESTION OF STRIKES

It is frequently said in the West that Soviet workers and unions have no right to strike. Significantly, no mention of strikes as a means of settling disputes in Soviet society has been found in current Soviet discussions of labor law and labor disputes. In many discussions with Soviet citizens there was never any indication of concern with the issue. Little evidence is available on the extent to which strikes have in fact occurred in recent history.

An official statement of policy on strikes, given by the Soviet government in 1955 during an investigation by the Committee on Freedom of Association of the International Labor Office, only indirectly suggests the policy of the party and the government that strikes are not an acceptable method of settling disputes:

A collective stoppage of work is not, and never has been, regarded as absenteeism, and Soviet law does not provide, nor has it ever provided, for any penalties to be imposed for a collective stoppage of work, where called by workers in support of their demands.

There is no reason for surprise at the absence of strikes in the Soviet Union, because the workers have every possibility of obtaining satisfaction in other ways—through production meetings and through the governmental and legislative authorities whose membership consists of workers' representatives.[57]

In 1922, at the Eleventh Congress of the Communist Party, strikes were not banned, but unions were urged to exercise restraint in calling them, since "neither the Communist Party, nor the Soviet Government, nor the trade unions can forget and conceal from the workers . . . that strike action in a state with a proletarian government can be explained and justified exclusively by bureaucratic deformations of that state and by remnants of capitalism."[58]

Numerous strikes took place in the 1920's, as long as local unions shared in determining wages through collective bargaining, but most disputes were settled by conciliation and arbitration. Many of the stoppages were unauthorized, since union policy discouraged strikes.[59] The 1929 Smolensk archives studied by Professor Fainsod mentioned seven strikes. A secret directive from the central committee of the woodworkers' union gave an important indication of policy. It said:

A strike in a state enterprise, in whose successful work we are directly concerned, is an extreme measure only and can only be the result of a clearly bureaucratic approach on the part of the economic organ or of an unconscious attitude on the part of some groups of workers and trade unionists who have not fully realized that we must not do damage to the state economic organizations. Therefore, the most important task of the trade union organs is to take preparatory measures on time in order to prohibit a strike movement in state enterprises. In case of demands to call a strike in a state enterprise, regardless of the size of the enterprise and the number of workers in it, the strike must be sanctioned beforehand by the Central Committee of the Trade Union, without which the calling of a strike is categorically forbidden.[60]

Several strikes in protest over changes in production standards were reported. In one, the miners were ordered back to work, and the mine manager, the union committee and the party bureau were dismissed because "they were incapable of managing the leadership of the economic and trade union organizations." In another case, where the chairman of the trade union committee tried to get the miners to go back to work, the trouble was attributed to "insufficient explanatory work among the workers on the task facing the country" and to "the alienation of the party and trade union organizations from the mass of the workers."[61]

As central control over labor increased and labor discipline became more stringent, policy toward strikes must have stiffened, and there is no evidence of continued occurrence of strikes at that time. One observer reported that in the Russia of 1936-1937 that he knew, the reaction to a strike would have been the dismissal of the manager and arrest of the strike leaders for counter-revolutionary and subversive activity, but the conditions that brought on the strike would have been eased; the district union and party organs would have checked on their local units and have tried to increase propaganda for the aims of industrialization, along with efforts to satisfy the workers.[62] During the war and immediate postwar periods any strikes would in all probability have been treated with severity, even if attempts were made to remove the causes. Few workers would have risked stoppages, whatever the provocation, when the danger of arrest and forced labor was ever-present.

In post-Stalin years, despite the decrease of compulsion and of coercive measures by the secret police, a number of factors combined to reduce any likelihood of strikes. Among these were the workers' right to change jobs to better their conditions, general improvements in wages and standards of living, increased power of the unions to protect workers' interests and rights, and the improved system for handling grievances. At the same time, increasing independence of workers may have raised the chance that under extreme provocation protests might take the form of work stoppages.

When the question was put to administrative or union officials in plants, or to professional experts, or was raised in private conversations, whether there might not be cases where workers' interests were inadequately protected and where the strike weapon might be appropriate, there was unanimous denial of any need for such action. There are so many other channels, it was always said.

In 1959 a cotton mill director said he could not imagine dissatisfaction that would lead to a stoppage; in case of an unresolved violation of law, workers would call in their regional committee to help; a dispute over production standards would be discussed and agreement reached; and if any dispute was not resolved, the workers would call a meeting and "make the director do the right thing." Another informant knew of a case where new production standards were in dispute, the workers "called a meeting," and the norms were changed; but he did not consider this a strike. In 1959, after a formal conference, two young lawyers interested in labor relations came on their own request for a long discussion in a hotel room. They insisted that there is no need for strikes now; strikes are not prohibited and there are no penalties, but they are not approved of, "surely because there is no need." In any case of great dissatisfaction, a meeting would be called and "so great a fuss would be made" that something would be done to remedy the situation, and the manager would be "pushed down." If necessary there would be an open party meeting in the plant, and appeal might be made to higher party bodies. Or workers would write to the newspapers, or even to Khrushchev. "Collective pressure is very great," they said.

In 1962, in a big plant, a management representative on the labor disputes commission and the vice-chairman of the factory committee laughed at a question whether in some bad cases, where workers had been unable to get help from regional union bodies, a strike might not be useful. They insisted that difficulties were not general; there were only individual cases, which could be remedied by other means. A whole collective would have no reason for a strike. In any case of serious dissatisfaction, a letter to *Trud* or to *Izvestia* is a very effective way to change a bad situation; they said, "It is very hard on administrators who are criticized in the newspapers, as they are responsible for their actions before the whole people." If an administrator violates the law, he is criticized and demoted or discharged; people say to him, "Move over a little, make room for a better worker." They added, "Criticism is a moving force in our society, and this is a way of control for proper action."

An Intourist driver in Moscow, chairman of the union committee at his garage, talked of how they settled disputes with their manager, of how they understand that wages can't be higher now but will be later, and he insisted there is no need for strikes. "Ne nado, ne mozhno; it is not needed, it is not possible (or permitted?)."

A group of American unionists from the International Long-shoremen's and Warehousemen's Union pushed hard on this question in talking with Soviet longshore union men. They asked, "What would happen if all efforts by a group of workers of a local union to settle their problems still came to naught?" The president of the Soviet longshore union finally answered that in the unlikely event that workers did walk off a job under such circumstances, "they would not be penalized or hurt in any way. But the people who would lose out would be the trade union officials and management people who would be considered at fault, and derelict in their duties because of their failure to stay on top of problems and the grievances and to resolve them before any such outbreak occurred."[63]

The Soviet press never mentions such stoppages, but Western correspondents have reported a number. Although the reports are based on second-hand evidence and rumor, they are well-enough substantiated to deserve attention. One of these, in 1956, was apparently a real, two-day sit-down strike over norms and pay. As reported by an American, at that time a student in Moscow, it involved forge workers who considered themselves grossly underpaid, due to the dishonesty of the shop manager. They returned to work only after the manager was fired and they were given supplementary payments.[64] Other stoppages involved mainly complaints over shortages of consumers' goods, in newly developing areas in Siberia and Kazakhstan. A strike lasting several days was said to have taken place in 1959 at a steel plant under construction near Karaganda, and another at Kemerovo, and to have been followed by shake-ups in the union, party, and administrative leadership. Another case reported from London was of dockers in Odessa, when there was a local butter shortage, refusing to load butter for Cuba until officials ordered additional supplies brought to the city.[65] One Soviet publication addressed to American readers mentioned, as evidence of no prohibition of strikes, a refusal of longshoremen in Baltic ports and Odessa to load coal for France during a French miners' strike; but the article went on to say that in disputes over working conditions there was no need to strike.[66]

The reported strikes and riots in Novocherkassk, near Rostov, in 1962, are of a different order, as are other strikes, stoppages, and demonstrations said to have occurred in many widely scattered places in 1962 and in 1963.[67] The reports are based on evidence from correspondents and diplomatic sources, Western tourists, Soviet tourists and delegates abroad, and from indirect references in the Soviet press. The serious riots in Novocherkassk reportedly arose in protest against the 1962 increases in meat and butter prices, aggravated by unrest in big factories over a drive to increase production standards and reduce piece rates, which threatened to decrease earnings. There were also grievances over illegal overtime and disregard of union rights, and discontent among students and young workers living in dormitories. When the first disorders were mishandled by local authorities, serious rioting broke out; troops were called in and reportedly bloody clashes resulted in deaths estimated in the hundreds. In other cases trouble began with the food price increases, or over food scarcities and rumors following the bad harvest in 1963.

Various remedial actions are reported to have followed. In the Rostov region at least two top party officers were removed. Changes in regulations of the militia and military patrols appeared designed for better control of disorders. A campaign began against people who spread "anti-Soviet propaganda" and there were reports of prison sentences given persons who contributed to panic by spreading rumors.[68] Alleviating measures also were taken, especially to improve food supplies in sensitive areas. In some of the areas where strikes had been reported there were special drives against violations of labor laws. The press gave increased attention during these years to official demands for better protection of workers' rights, and this also may have been related to signs of growing open protests from workers.

There is enough evidence, however limited, to indicate that workers are more and more ready to express their dissatisfactions, even in some cases by demonstrations and strikes. Reasons for discontent are inherent in the economic difficulties that delayed promised gains in wages and further reductions or elimination of income taxes. Higher food prices caused fear and resentment, while shortages of housing and consumers' goods continued, especially in Siberia and other newly developing areas. There is resentment when violations of labor laws are still permitted. It is not surprising that workers react when rights promised by the 1958 law are violated. While in extreme cases force was reportedly used to put down disorders, and critics were warned not to go too far, open protests also led to action to relieve conditions, stop violations of rights, and ensure more attention to signals of discontent.

Failure to permit any publication of reports of strikes, either in the past or more recently, can be explained both by the political and economic conditions that reduce the likelihood of their occurrence and by psychological considerations. With wages and other labor conditions centrally determined, the most basic issues are not subject to open pressure from interest groups. The concern for production works against acceptance of stoppages. In addition, many other channels are available for settling disputes over details of local conditions. Finally, published reports might encourage other workers under extreme provocation to resort to the un-Soviet method of strike pressure. And especially, the admission that workers in a "workers' state" sometimes failed to get attention paid to their grievances and resorted to strikes would be a confession of failure and give a weapon to critics of the Soviet system.

The question remains whether there is a need and place for strikes in the Soviet planned economy, where wages are not subject to collective bargaining, and where the effort is made to convince every worker that success in the production drive is the basis for all the gains achieved and promised. The director of a food plant, puzzled at a description of how strikes are used to settle disputes in the United States, shook her head and said, "It certainly is a different system. Our workers are interested in production." Persistent use of the other channels for settling disputes frequently brings the wanted result. It is not surprising if Soviet workers generally seek other means than stoppages to promote their interests and protect their rights.

On the other hand, a strike might bring a remedy more promptly in the many instances of long delay before workers' legitimate demands are met, as on safety and improvements in working conditions, or for proper attention to the union committee's rights. Where abuses still exist and there is serious dissatisfaction, strikes and demonstrations could direct the attention of authorities to problems and lead to remedies. Experience elsewhere has shown that pressure from the interruption of production in strikes often induces the parties concerned to reach agreement. A stoppage would be likely to bring prompt pressure to remove causes of discontent and avoid conditions that led to the strike, as seems to have been done in some of the reported cases. Occasional use of the strike weapon might have a salutary influence on labor relations where the accepted procedures and cooperation are lacking. It might also serve as a useful safety valve, if the legality of such protests were established and openly admitted, as has not been done. The policy of never publishing reports of such protests encourages rumors and may increase existing tensions. There have been no indications from Soviet authorities, how-

ever, of willingness to accept the strike as a proper tool for
last resort use by workers and by trade unions—however constructive such an acceptance might prove to be.

In a surprising report from Yugoslavia early in 1964 on a
number of short strikes lasting only up to an hour in plants
there, however, it was said that communist leaders appeared
to be grudgingly appraising strikes as a form of collective bargaining in a socialist society. One of the leaders said, "The
awareness of the workers is so strong that they do not permit
their rights to be violated nor their interests to be double-
crossed." According to another, the party leadership considered that the stoppages had produced "a positive effect on the
interests of the whole working collective."[69]

It is to be doubted that any extensive use of strikes will
develop in the Soviet Union. Even in difficult circumstances,
workers and their union committees can ordinarily bring about
remedies by vigorous utilization of their rights and of the
available channels of publicity and protest. The failures reported often result from lack of vigor and principle on the
part of union officers in the plant and the region. This also
can be changed if workers show courage and persistence.
Nevertheless, in extreme cases stoppages as a last resort might
have useful results.

In appraising the relative lack of strikes in the Soviet Union
it is well to remember the tendency toward "the withering
away of the strike" in Western countries.[70] With variations in
different countries, the trend in modern labor relations seems
to be toward seeking other channels for the settlement of disputes. Increasingly, also, large-scale strikes in crucial industries come to be thought intolerable because of their effects
on the economy, and the government uses its influence in one
way or another to get a settlement without a stoppage. The
planned economy of the USSR is not alone in its desire to
maintain uninterrupted production and to promote the settlement of labor disputes by means other than strikes.

CHAPTER IX

Cooperation in Production

IN 1957 the Communist Party called on the unions to develop the "creative initiative" of the masses and to bring them widely into "the administration of production." Much evidence indicates that this resulted in growing individual and group initiative and cooperation. After a policy is announced and a campaign of indoctrination begins, loyal communists and trade unionists in large numbers—workers, engineers, and technicians—put their minds to implementing the policy. A sometimes bewildering variety of programs and organizations results.

There had been long experience with "socialist competition" and with production conferences in which workers had the right to criticize and make suggestions. Effectiveness of these earlier programs varied. The current movement aims to bring the mass of workers, not only key personnel, into participation in improving methods. Emphasis is on improving technology and organization, not on intensifying work. The feeling of common interests may be less general than claimed, but fertile ground for "creative initiative" is provided by greater human resources—wider education and increased skills of workers, and more active local unions—as well as by increased capital for mechanization.

"One-man management" continues, but management is obligated to listen to suggestions and to get the cooperation of workers in solving problems. Some managers still find this irksome, but if so, Soviet experts insist, "they do not last long as managers." Many directors interviewed expressed appreciation of the help they received. Trade union and economic literature is full of descriptions of successful collaboration. On the other hand, criticisms are made of delays and bureaucratic failures to put valuable recommendations into operation, and sometimes of resistance by foremen and others to the interference of eager innovators.

All the varied forms of participation and cooperation come under the influence of the party committee and the Komsomol, the Young Communists, who often initiate programs. Overall leadership is by the union's factory and shop committees and their "production-mass-work commissions." The group organizers and production-mass-work organizers of the trade union groups are responsible for efforts to enlist the interest of individual workers. Huge amounts of unpaid, out-of-hours activity are devoted to these programs, in addition to cooperative efforts during working hours.

Important work is done in big plants by local units of the Society of Inventors and Rationalizers and the Scientific-Technical Society.[1] The former, with nearly three million members from workers, engineers and technicians, promotes interest in solving particular technical problems and works to get approved ideas put into effect. Monetary rewards provided by law are based on a percentage of the estimated economy for one year resulting from the introduction of an invention or "rationalization"—an improvement in existing mechanization or methods. These rewards range from 13.75 per cent of the resulting saving, but not less than 10 rubles, up to as much as 20,000 rubles for important inventions, and are tax free up to 1,000 rubles. When the introduction of a proposal leads to a change in production standards and piece rates, the originator keeps the old rates for six months. Those who aid in introducing new methods also get premiums. Factory committees take up complaints of violations of inventors' rights or of failure of management to introduce approved innovations. Many millions of rubles in economies are said to result every year—1,645 million rubles in 1963, in spite of delays in introducing proposals approved. It is said that up to 20 per cent of these every year are not used, but that the number put in operation grows yearly; in 1963 it was three times that of 1959. More than four million proposals were received and considered in 1963.[2]

The Scientific-Technical Society, with two million members, is concerned with major technical problems. On the national scale its industrial branches work with scientific research institutions and the central committees of the unions. In big plants the local units, including scientists, engineers and technicians, and skilled workers, are concerned with improving technical processes, mechanizing hand labor, introducing new equipment, and aiding the initiative of workers.

In many plants there are volunteer bureaus for solving problems. Large numbers, from skilled workers to engineers and management personnel, take part. For some of the participants the work is closely related to their jobs; for many it means taking on additional obligations that can only be fulfilled in out-of-work time.[3] Public design bureaus originated in Sverdlovsk and by 1963 were reported in 15,000 enterprises. With 155,000 participants they helped work out designs for mechanization and automation and the introduction of new equipment, and aided inventors in developing their projects. Public bureaus and groups for economic analysis, also arising first in Sverdlovsk, were reportedly established in 6,000 enterprises and included leading workers as well as professional personnel. These groups analyzed costs, utilization of equipment and work time, and methods of planning and accounting, and sought ways to improve economic results. In some plants they included special groups on production standards; in others, separate norm-setting bureaus were organized. In some enterprises seminars and courses were set up on economic questions.[4]

Thousands of similar developments were reported. Moscow in 1963 reportedly had 960 public design and technological bureaus, 450 bureaus of economic analysis, 224 councils of innovators, 796 public norm-setting bureaus.[5] In an Omsk tire plant, a "public scientific-investigation institute" starting in 1960 with a group of 15 leading workers and 7 engineers and technicians, promoted investigations in the shops, aided workers, and provided technical information in after-work sessions. By 1962 there were said to be 900 such institutes in different branches of industry.[6] There were also many public bureaus of technical information in enterprises.

Another much publicized form of involving workers in the search for better methods is a public review (*smotr*), a short-period intensive mass inspection and collection of suggestions on some issue. Organized by factory committees and shop committees together with the administration, these reviews involve discussions at shop and brigade meetings and the collection and evaluation of proposals. Sometimes there is competition between shops, with awards of titles and premiums to winners. The public review is considered a highly effective device, giving good results if not used too frequently.[7]

Factory and shop committees and their commissions use many different ways to disseminate improved methods of work.[8] "Schools of advanced experience," organized jointly with the administration, often take the form of after-work demonstrations at the work places by skilled workers for groups of young and inexperienced workers. Meetings for particular crafts in a plant are used for films and demonstrations of new techniques. Inter-plant institutes and schools are organized and frequently there are excursions to other enterprises and to museums. Experienced workers sometimes become sponsors for individual young workers to help them master their jobs.

A Council of Innovators was organized by the Leningrad regional economic council, with the cooperation of the trade union council and regional union committees. Councils in districts of the city and branches of industry promoted exchange of experience. By 1963 there were 340 councils in enterprises and the example had been followed in other cities. Large numbers of recommendations were adopted, but the chairman of the Leningrad sovprof complained that many enterprises delayed in putting the new devices and methods to work.[9]

Many individual workers have been honored as innovators and users of "communist methods of mutual aid," and their methods held up as examples to be followed. One of the most famous is Valentina Gaganova, a spinner, leader of a good brigade, who voluntarily shifted to one poor brigade after another and helped them bring their work "up to the level of the best." She was honored by the Central Committee of the Communist Party with the title Hero of Socialist Labor. Her example was followed by thousands of others, according to frequent reports. Another Hero of Socialist Labor is Yu. M. Vecherova, a weaver, who proposed to reach by 1960 the productivity of labor planned for 1965. She worked out improved methods of operation on modernized high-speed equipment and taught them to her entire shift. Other workers were honored for inventions and improvements in methods. In a big machine plant, cutting-machine operator Loginov and fitter Zaichenko proposed that workers adopt at every workplace "a complex individual plan for increasing the productivity of labor, utilizing all available knowledge and experience." This started a movement in other enterprises around the country. Many such stories of individual initiative are published, followed by propaganda urging others to use their creativity similarly, and then by reports that many are doing so.[10]

This playing up of individual achievements seems reminiscent of the Stakhanovite movement with its emphasis on individuals with remarkable production records. But the new movement is concerned with bringing the improved methods into use by others, and helping lagging groups. It is supported by the current efforts to induce all workers to continue their general and technical education.

That fruitful activity of this type is found everywhere cannot be assumed. Top union leadership is critical of many unions for failing to bring workers into effective participation in management or to press for the introduction of new technology. Some of the new commissions and bureaus exist only on paper, or their decisions are not followed up vigorously. Adoption of advanced methods meets resistance. The Communist Party hoped that pressure from workers and engineers would weaken the reluctance of many managers to risk the introduction of new methods, but this hope has evidently been realized only in part.[11]

A different problem is proliferation of organizations and busyness without correlative results. There were increasing complaints about too many meetings and loss of work time because of "public activities" carried on during work hours. Chairman Grishin of the CCTU warned against "the improper practice of diverting workers from production in work time to different meetings and conferences"; and in February 1964 the Central Committee of the party issued strict instructions that meetings were to be held to a minimum and that "public work" should not interfere with regular work.[12]

Since 1961 increased efforts have been made to involve local unions in the planning process in their enterprises, to see that their recommendations are included in draft plans, and that administrative and planning agencies do not consider enterprise plans before these have been discussed at general workers' meetings or in production conferences. It was thought that possibilities of increasing production, found by workers themselves in their shops, would be disclosed through their participation in planning. This would also provide an additional check on efficiency of operations and accuracy of reports; perhaps especially it would counter any tendencies of managers to seek unduly low production plans in order to reduce risks.[13]

Approved planning methods were outlined in a pamphlet published for local unions by the CCTU.[14] The planning process in a big textile mill was described by the director and the chairman of the plant production conference, both women. Early in 1962 the director reported to the production conference on the results for 1961 and the plan for 1962, which had already been approved and sent down as orders from the state. Problems involved in fulfilling the plan were discussed by the union committees and the production conference. The draft plan for 1963, after being worked out by the administrative departments, with cooperation from the union and the workers, was discussed in detail in shop meetings and production conferences. A public inspection of the work of the plant was organized by the factory committee and the administration through special commissions in every shop, which considered all possible "reserves" for improving production. Shop meetings discussed problems and offered suggestions. After the commissions and shop committees reviewed proposals, those accepted were included in the plan for the next year. The draft plan was finally considered at a general meeting to which 400 or more workers came. The draft submitted to the regional economic council thus was based on the work of administrative planners and of large groups of workers, engineers and technicians.

After the plan was approved, the union continued to check. A controversy developed when the union charged delay in introducing certain promised mechanization. The director was doubtful because of the funds needed, but when the production conference insisted, the changes were made; the results were good, and according to the union representative, "All were happy." As union officers saw it, "The director was accustomed to such intervention by the union and could not get along without it." The director said that the active interest of the union and the workers "stimulated the creative work of people, brought good decisions and had constructive effects on the carrying out of plans." She said that workers had become more interested in all the work of the union and the plant than a few years earlier, since they were now "more literate, more cultured and conscious."[15]

In the same city, officers of the sovprof and of the metallurgical workers' regional committee, telling about the discussion of plans at workers' meetings, said that without this check by people who know production the sovnarkhoz could not be sure whether enterprise plans were sound and that there would be many mistakes. The committee was arranging to have the plans of each enterprise checked also by specialists from other plants. The realism of plans was thought to be promoted by such checks by workers and by the regional union organs.

Many changes in plans are reported to result from workers' suggestions. It is said that nearly 5 million people brought in suggestions for the seven-year plan as a whole and that unions were especially active in the working out of plans for 1964 and 1965. In the Leningrad region, proposals collected from workers' meetings and production conferences reportedly led to an increase in the planned growth of industrial production for 1964 from 5 per cent to 6.5 per cent. Discussion of plans for 1964-1965 during the summer of 1963 at thousands of workers' meetings and production conferences is said to have brought forth valuable proposals for improving mechanization and organization of work in many industries.[16]

Nevertheless, there are many published complaints of lack of attention by union committees and by administrative authorities to participation by workers. Directors' reports to union meetings, general workers' meetings, or production conferences are frequently superficial and lead to little or no discussion. Sometimes plans are adopted without any wide discussion or consideration of workers' proposals. Draft annual plans are sometimes discussed only with a narrow group, or are presented to the workers only when completed, or with too little time for any real consideration and little or no chance to make revisions. Some regional economic councils fail to insist that enterprise plans be thoroughly discussed at workers' meetings before being sent in. Unions fail in many cases to use their right to influence plans. The CCTU continues to urge the sovprofs to improve the work on planning by plant committees.[17]

The right of the union committees to have their opinion considered on appointments to administrative posts provides another means for affecting the work of enterprises.[18] It is not clear how much influence the unions exert, either in evaluating candidates proposed by management, or in making their own recommendations. Only rarely is there mention of this in the union literature. However, a director interviewed in 1959 said that as a rule directors and chief engineers are appointed only with the agreement of the regional union committee. In 1962 a regional union officer spoke of union committees advising on the promotion of leading personnel in the plants. Local union officers have occasionally reported, with satisfaction, that they were consulted on promotions. In Estonia a candidate for the post of director was personally introduced to the factory committee by a representative of the regional economic council, and the appointment was made only after the union agreed. In Tashkent, on the contrary, an officer of the sovprof complained in 1961 that "in reality this system does not prevail. . . . It will come into practice only if the administrative organs are deprived of the right to nominate and approve administrative workers without official decision by trade union organizations." In 1963 and 1964, administrative appointments were said often

to be made without consulting union committees. It has been
suggested that the law should be more specific as to union
rights in regard to appointments.[19] On the other hand, in many
cases the unions have successfully used their right to bring
about the removal of administrators who failed to live up to
their obligations to labor.

PRODUCTION CONFERENCES

After the war a number of CCTU decisions instructed local
and regional unions to call regular meetings of workers for
criticism of union work and that of their enterprises.[20] The
move apparently met resistance in both union and management circles. Shop meetings or conferences on production were
sometimes useful, but their criticisms could be embarrassing,
especially when the tone was political rather than primarily
technical.[21] One chief engineer interviewed in 1955 implied
that these meetings were an ordeal for management, though
they often gave good results. In the middle 1950's, in spite of
party and CCTU efforts to make the production conferences
more effective, many were criticized. In numerous plants the
conferences met seldom or there was little difference between
them and ordinary shop or brigade meetings; managers often
did not attend or did not pay attention to the recommendations. Many union committees did little to see that good proposals were put into effect. The work was often poorly
planned, with no discussion of major production problems.
Workers lost interest and failed to take part.[22]

The Central Committee of the Communist Party in its December 1957 resolution on the unions proposed to transform
the conferences into "permanently functioning production conferences" with elected members and officers. The new system,
worked out by the CCTU, was adopted in a joint decree of
the Council of Ministers and the CCTU on July 9, 1958.[23] It
provided for formally elected and organized production con-

ferences in all plants employing more than 100. Membership was to include representatives of the workers, the union committee, the party and Komsomol, the management, the Scientific-Technical Society, and the Society of Inventors and Rationalizers. Members would be elected by general meetings of the workers and by the other organizations, for the same term as that of the factory committee. The conferences were to choose executive committees to make plans, prepare agendas and arrange for studies, publicize meetings, and see that recommendations were carried out. Decisions were to be by majority vote, with a quorum of two-thirds of the membership. Management was required to assist, arrange for carrying out decisions, and report on what had been done. The regional economic councils were to aid in every way possible. The production conferences would be led by the factory and shop committees.

From the previously often casual, time-to-time production meetings, this was a drastic change, indicating that the party was concerned over difficulties in carrying out the grandiose seven-year plan. Productivity was low in most industries, wasteful use of hand labor was widespread, mechanization lagged, there were inefficient managements and many that resisted innovation. It was believed that organization and technology could be greatly improved through regular consultation with all levels of the work force. Participation by workers was expected to bring to light inefficiency or laxness in using capacity, and to push managements to increase their effectiveness. Workers would gain in technical knowledge and understanding of the needs of industry. The work of the conferences would be directed to major problems. The members elected from the shops would feel responsible to fellow workers for their work. They also would be able to get cooperation from them in making proposals and in seeing that recommendations were carried out.

The draft regulation on the "permanently functioning production conferences," worked out by the CCTU, was distributed in January 1958 and experimentation began at once.[24] By July, when the decree was adopted, production conferences of the new sort were already at work in most big enterprises. In the absence of detailed instructions or recommendations from the CCTU, methods of operation were developed by trial and error. For the sake of wide involvement it became the practice to include 10 per cent or more of the labor force in the conferences and to have the majority of the members from the workers. In some plants representatives were chosen by the union and party committees, other organizations, and the management—with direct representatives of workers elected in shop and plant meetings; sometimes the entire group was elected at general meetings. Sometimes the executive committee, elected by the conference itself, included mainly engineers and administrators; sometimes even the director or chief engineer was chairman. Generally, however, it was thought that the executive body and the chairman should come primarily from qualified workers.

The factory and shop committees proposed issues to be considered and approved the plans. Thus, any tendency of the production conferences to duplicate or replace the union committee and its commissions could be avoided. Approved practice was to propose a single concrete problem for a meeting, with careful preparation and advance study. Often temporary commissions studied a problem and prepared a draft decision for consideration. Open meetings, which were usual, were attended by large numbers of rank and file workers, in addition to the permanent members. Management was expected to issue orders to carry out decisions, since their representatives had taken part in making them. If the administration disagreed, it could take the dispute to the shop or factory committee, and, if necessary, to higher administrative and union bodies. Bulletin boards seen in the shops often listed measures decided on, with both the proposed and the actual dates when they were put into effect.

By 1963, the CCTU reported, the activity and influence of the production conferences had grown. They had been organized in 66,000 enterprises and construction projects and in 52,000 big shops, with 4.6 million elected members.[25] Successful production conferences studied and made decisions on a great range of questions affecting the work of their enterprises. Special commissions were set up to study such questions as the reorganization of a shop or a production line, mechanization of certain processes, modernization of equipment, improvements in services supplying materials and tools. Suggestions were collected. Plans worked out were discussed in detail by the conference, and decisions adopted were put into effect. Bottlenecks in production processes were studied and changes made. Plans were developed to promote steady work in place of "storming" at the end of the month to fulfill plans. Some production conferences made a serious study of directors' annual reports and of draft plans. Some studied reasons for nonfulfillment of production standards and adopted proposals to make better work possible.

Many reports give an impression of active collaboration between management and the conferences, with wide participation of rank and file workers and engineers. In successful cases, management promptly gave orders to carry out decisions and the union committees actively supported the program. Often the factory committees or the regional union organizations arranged seminars and meetings for members of production conferences to exchange experience on their work and on technical and organizational matters.[26]

Among economists and management and trade union people interviewed in 1959 and 1962, the opinion was general that many production conferences had become real forces in their enterprises. Most directors and chief engineers interviewed said that their work was substantially helped by this participation of workers in solving problems. An American management expert who interviewed a number of Soviet managers reports that many spoke of getting valuable suggestions from the production conferences, although there was some evidence of workers' suggestions being disregarded and a feeling that some of the meetings were a waste of time.[27]

In a textile mill with 10,000 workers, the production conferences were described by the director and by the chairman of the conference, an attractive and intelligent woman with secondary technical education, who had been re-elected to her post each year from the start in 1958. There were 200 members in the plant conference and from 60 to 100 in each of 9 shop conferences. About 70 per cent of all members were workers. The executive committee of the plant conference included 9 workers and 6 engineers or technicians. The last quarterly session had worked on the problem of quality, an issue of great importance for them. A special commission of workers and engineers studied the matter over several weeks, discussing it at shop meetings and with individual workers. The commission's report was considered by the officers, and recommendations agreed on. The conference discussed these recommendations and a report from the plant's department of control, and adopted the proposals after making some changes. Fifteen points were included, touching on materials, equipment, supplies, analysis of spoilage and its causes, and further checks on quality, for different shops. On each point, the date at which the change should be effected and the person responsible for implementing it, were specified. The director regarded the decisions of the conference obligatory and gave appropriate orders. Then the commission checked on the progress of the work and, when it was behind schedule, called

in shop chiefs or other persons responsible for it. A full report
was to be given at the next session.

The production conferences also played an important part
in working out the production plan. Production conferences in
the shops met monthly and worked on rationalization, new
techniques, discipline, quality, or whatever problems they
chose. Workers attended shop production conferences in especially large numbers. According to the director, the union and
the production conferences used their powers "strongly and
persistently" and the interest of the workers had grown substantially.

Similar testimony was given in many other plants. In a
house building plant producing prefabricated concrete panels,
the production conference was regarded as important in its
work on "tight questions of production"; for example, with the
help of the workers concerned it had solved a difficult problem
of what was wrong with one panel. In a men's clothing plant
employing chiefly young girls and women, the conference was
said to be active especially on questions of quality, new mechanization and automation, and on labor discipline.

At several interviews that proved especially illuminating,
both the director or chief engineer and the union chairman
were present. In a printing plant, a plant production conference of 52 members and shop conferences had worked on all
sorts of production questions. The director was amused at a
question of whether this helped or hurt management. He said
he was "not afraid of it"; that it gave him much help. "It
organized the whole collective and the workers helped to work
out new methods; their initiative increased. The workers not
only advised, but demanded changes, and their decisions were
obligatory for management." In a tobacco plant the production
conferences were said to give such positive results that the
shop conferences and the all-plant conference met monthly

with many workers attending and taking part. The director considered the decisions obligatory, "because the workers know the work better than the director and chief engineer can." He and the union chairman emphasized the common interest "to improve the life of the workers by increasing production." The director went on to say, "If the workers like the director and do not fear him, they want to help him. Then the director and the workers can get good results." In several textile mills, production conferences were working vigorously; the importance of constant check-up on the fulfillment of decisions was emphasized. In a tea packing plant the production conferences worked on such questions as reconstruction of shops and increasing automation. Results were said to have been good in increasing production and improving working conditions.

Many published reports of production conferences in big machine plants, steel mills, on the railroads, and elsewhere, add impressive evidence of collaboration by large numbers of workers, engineers, and management personnel in solving important problems. Such activity is widespread in well-run enterprises. Whether these good examples or their opposites are more typical of industry as a whole, it is impossible to know. Clearly there is disappointment over the ineffectiveness of production conferences in many areas and plants.

In 1961 the chairman of the Leningrad sovprof found it disappointing that some production conferences "still work weakly, meet irregularly, without adequate preparation. Some administrative leaders ignore valuable proposals of workers."[28] Two years later the CCTU reported that in that city many conferences were working effectively, but in some plants the unions were directed to improve their leadership. The CCTU and the union press continued to criticize shortcomings of many factory committees and of sovprofs and branch committees in this work.[29] In three smaller republics in 1962—Azerbaidzhan, Tadzhikstan, Turkmenia—the majority of production conferences were said to work poorly. In many enterprises over the country there were no permanently functioning production conferences, or they had become inactive after the first flurry in 1958. In some, few workers were elected. Some re-elected the same people year after year, so that they became "staff representatives," rather than representatives of the workers. Some limited themselves to minor questions, better discussed in workers' meetings in the shops. Often there was inadequate preparation of questions for consideration, and decisions "remained on paper." Some directors and factory committees underemphasized the role of the conferences. Many sovprofs failed to press directors to put decisions into effect. Some conferences became merely "consultative bodies, not decision-making bodies."

It was clear that in many cases the lacks resulted from failure of local unions to use their rights, or of regional officers to support this activity. Another factor was disinterest, or resistance, by managements. A growing body of opinion argued that there was need for clear definition by law of the right of production conferences to have their decisions put into effect, or to have disputed issues decided in the factory committees or by appeal to higher bodies. The CCTU was instructed by the 1963 trade union congress to work out proposals to improve the effectiveness of the conferences.[30]

It is difficult to assess the overall impact of this attempt to bring workers more widely into major production decisions. There is little doubt of the good results in many cases. Yet always present is the danger of overlapping functions of union committees, production conferences, and the numerous other organizations that develop in the plants. In other plants, inertia, fear of change, or desire for "the quiet life," often keeps

the leadership on either side from making full use of the possibilities. Results depend most of all on the initiative and imagi-
nation of union, party, and administrative personnel.

SOCIALIST COMPETITION

Many of the cooperative programs draw in chiefly the most
skilled, energetic, enterprising, and devoted people in the
party and the unions, as well as careerists interested primarily
in their own advancement. But few workers, whatever their
feelings, can remain outside the scope of socialist competition.
In 1963 it was claimed that 85 per cent of all wage earners and
salaried workers were participating.[31]

"Socialist competition" is a term meaning that individuals,
brigades, shops, and entire plants adopt "socialist obligations"
to fulfill or overfulfill production plans in definite respects and
compete with others for good records. Success brings honors,
titles, money premiums, and other benefits. The principles of
socialist competition, formulated by Lenin in 1917, include
publicity, comparison of results, the possibility of repeating
good results, and "comradely cooperation." Socialist competition is supposed to mean not hostile rivalry, but emulation and
mutual aid in achieving high production and disseminating
the best methods.

Although the claim has long been made that this is a mass
movement reflecting the workers' own initiative, the campaigns
in the earlier years to a large degree were organized from
above, by management. Yet, in total, they contributed to increasing efficiency. There was enthusiastic support from some
workers, but opposition from many others who saw it only as
another pressure for more intense work.[32] The enhanced role
of the union committees after 1956 provided more favorable
conditions for organizing competition, starting in the shops.
Current improvements in methods were discussed in a 1958
publication of the State Committee on Labor and Wages:

Nationwide socialist competition at the present time increasingly is being freed from sham ballyhoo (paradnoi shymikhi) and unreal obligations, from a front-office style of establishing obligations, which not seldom occurred in the past. Obligations now are adopted after all-sided discussion at meetings of workers . . . and are reinforced by great organizational work of party, trade union and administrative organs.[33]

Socialist competition takes many forms and new forms develop constantly. Within shops there is competition for the title of best brigade or section; within plants, for best shop; between individuals, for the title of the best turner, fitter, spinner, or "Master of Golden Hands"; within economic regions, for best enterprise; in recent years for the title of shop or enterprise of "High Culture of Production"; and for shock worker, brigade, shop, or enterprise of "Communist Labor." Large enterprises challenge related enterprises in other regions to compete and to cooperate in exchanging experience and improving methods. Challenges are issued in the name of the entire body of workers of a city to other cities, as Leningrad to Moscow, for early fulfillment of the seven-year plan; or obligations are adopted in honor of special events—congresses of the party or the unions, or the anniversary of the revolution.[34]

Socialist competitions are governed by directives from the CCTU and the government and by agreements between administrative and union organizations. A joint decree of the Council of Ministers and the CCTU in 1959 required that the quarterly reviews of the work of enterprises should consider not only overall results in fulfilling production plans, but also reduction of costs, production of the planned assortment of goods, introduction of new technology, increases in productivity of labor, and other measures. All such indicators of success were to be considered in awarding the traveling Red Banners of the Council of Ministers and the CCTU, and premiums, to winning plants. Premiums up to 20,000 rubles (2,000 new rubles)[35] could be used entirely for individual awards to outstanding workers, engineers, and others, by agreement of the administration and the union committee. Of larger sums, up to 60-70 per cent could be used for individual premiums and the rest for improvements in housing and cultural and everyday services. In 1963 a joint decree of the CCTU and the Council of Ministers of the RSFSR set the number of traveling Red Banners and premiums to be awarded by sovnarkhozy and sovprofs: 91 banners of the Council of Ministers and the CCTU, 207 of the sovnarkhozy and sovprofs, all with premiums, and 431 and 551 additional second and third premiums, all divided among the regions.[36]

As described at the Leningrad sovprof in 1962, competition is organized in the region by the sovprof and the sovnarkhoz, and in the enterprise by the factory committee and the director, with the help of the production-mass-work commissions of the union committees. Meetings of workers in the trade union groups, brigades, and shops discuss past results and plans for the next period and adopt obligations as to production, productivity of labor, spoilage reduction, economies, and other measures. Often the process begins with individual workers' pledges, which are consolidated into obligations adopted by brigades and shops and finally by the plant. Obligations are publicized on bulletin boards, with current records of accomplishments. Results are posted daily in some cases, and at least monthly and quarterly for the entire plant. Each quarter the sovprof and sovnarkhoz award first, second, and third places to winning enterprises, after recommendations from the regional union committees and the industry administrations. About eight enterprises get first place, perhaps thirty, second place, and fifty, third place. All winners receive premium funds, and those in first place get the traveling Red Banners of the Council of Ministers and the CCTU. These handsome red flags are displayed proudly by plants that hold them. Premiums, varying according to the place won and the number of workers, may go as high as 50,000 rubles for a big plant. The competition is open to all rather than applied by industries; textiles, for instance, won three places in one quarter, five in another.

Leningrad in 1962 was also emphasizing competition for the title of "Enterprise of High Culture of Production." This movement started on the initiative of leading plants that decided to try for exceptional records in introducing new mechanization and automation, improving working conditions, safety, labor discipline, cleanliness and attractiveness of the plant and grounds. Forty plants had won this title, the first step toward the highest honor, the title of Enterprise of Communist Labor.

A clothing plant, "Enterprise of High Culture of Production," had won first place in one quarter and second place in another, getting premiums of 14,000 and 10,000 rubles. Thirty per cent of the sums went for collective purposes, the amount of the second quarter prize being used for costumes for the folk-song chorus. The rest of the prize money was used for individual premiums which were received by more than half of all workers and ranged from 10 to 25 rubles. Places in the competition within the plant were awarded each month by the factory committee. When two shops were close in their production indexes, other factors were considered, such as evidence of workers' attitudes—their public work, club activities, and study. The winner of first place received a premium for distribution to the best workers by agreement of the shop committee and shop chief; individual premiums amounted to 10 to 15 rubles. The title of "Master of Golden Hands" had been won by 75 workers, who displayed at their work places the handsome red shields bearing the title.

In a textile mill visited, the signs of socialist competition were everywhere to be seen—slogans, statements of obligations adopted by individuals and groups of spinners and weavers, records of daily and monthly production, red pennants and banners won by the best brigades and shops. Posters proclaimed "Here works a department fighting for the title Department of Communist Labor," or "Here works a Brigadier of Communist Labor." In a big, many-windowed area, kept neat and clean and made attractive with the fresh greenery of growing plants, a large overhead banner proclaimed "Section of High Culture of Production." Pictures of the best workers were displayed on "Boards of Honor." The title "Shock Worker of Communist Labor" had been won by about 600 workers, whose names were posted in their departments, and 3,000 were said to be competing. Wall newspapers publicized the progress of the competition.

A big machine plant visited had won second place in the inter-plant competition in one quarter and was a candidate for first place in the current period. Awards to the most active workers had ranged from ten up to thirty or more rubles. In the monthly competition the winning shop received a premium, which the shop committee distributed to the best workers in amounts ranging from five to twenty rubles; shop administrators also received bonuses.

The visitor was permitted to attend a monthly plant committee meeting at this plant for appraising the quarter's work and awarding places for the month in socialist competition. The meeting, in a room in the plant, opened promptly at 3:40 P.M., after work. The twenty-five members of the committee, including several women, sat at a long green baize-covered table; fourteen were workers, the others engineers, specialists, office and administrative personnel. At one end of the room and along the sides sat a still larger number of non-members —workers, shop committee members, foremen, and shop chiefs. The wall was hung with pictures of Lenin and others, and with charts of production records. The meeting lasted an hour and a half. It was businesslike and was followed with the greatest attention.

First, the deputy director reported on production for the quarter. Good records had been made on production, productivity of labor, economies. Wage fund expenditure was satisfactory. However, there had been several accidents, eighteen absences without excuse in the month and thirty in the quarter, and also tardinesses. The deputy director gave details for each shop, criticizing several for failure to fulfill their plans, and concluded with an appeal to every brigade and shop "to work for fulfillment of tasks in this crucial period for completion of the year's plan."

Next, the chairman of the union's production-mass-work commission reported: 405 brigades were competing for the title of "Communist Labor"; 278 workers were working "without control"—that is, taking full responsibility for the quality of their output without check by the department of control; productivity of labor had increased 4.5 per cent in September; two shops were reprimanded for lagging in their work. Then he announced the shops the commission recommended for first, second, and third place awards, and another shop for a commendation for good work, and called for questions. After a little discussion, the committee voted separately for each place and accepted the recommendation unanimously. Suddenly a worker, not a committee member, protested that his shop, given third place, was entitled to first place. Others supported him. The deputy director attempted to justify the recommendation and was answered with some heat from the floor. Criticisms of the commission were voiced. Many spoke up, some in favor, some against the recommendation. It was pointed out that a violation of labor discipline in the shop in question had to be considered. The chairman of the plant com-

mittee insisted that the commission had given the matter careful, objective consideration. He said, "The collective took an
obligation and all must share responsibility." Others reminded
the group, "The decision of the union committee is final and
the committee must act responsibly." Then, since the original
worker was still unconvinced, the committee decided to vote
again. The earlier decision was confirmed, but this time in the
show of hands there were five votes in opposition.

The chairman of the union committee said, later, that
stormy meetings were not unusual, that no one hesitated to
criticize either management or union officers. It was clear to
the visitor that these workers were interested, participated
actively, and were not afraid to speak up.

Socialist competition is carried on under constant pressure
and propaganda from above in successive nationwide campaigns. At the same time, when obligations are adopted in
the work groups after discussion, there is strong incentive for
workers to try to improve results through individual initiative
and group efforts. Success for one month leads to setting
higher goals for the next. But goals are set for short periods,
results are measurable, team spirit comes into play, and successes are celebrated and rewarded as people mobilize for the
next effort. The game itself helps to maintain interest and
avoid the dull monotony of endless pressure for production.
When results are poor, there is incentive to analyze the reasons and try to remove them. Criticisms of the leadership of
socialist competition most often cite weaknesses in analyzing
failures, in providing conditions favorable for good work, and
in spreading use of the best methods. When these are lacking,
socialist competition becomes simply a method of drive and
speed-up, which may bring boredom and resistance. Evidence
of such attitudes turns up occasionally in the press.

A new form of competition, the "Movement for Communist
Labor," started late in 1958 under the slogan, "Learn to live

and work communistically." Individuals and groups competing
for the title of shock worker, brigade, shop, or enterprise of
Communist Labor, promised not only to achieve especially
high production records but also to complete secondary education and continue study further, to take part in cultural and
public activities, and "to live and work in the spirit of the
communist code." This meant setting good examples in individual and public life, taking on public assignments, aiding
others, and seeking to develop communist attitudes among
their associates.

The movement was initiated by a group of Young Communist workers in a Moscow locomotive station where, in the
early days of the revolution, the first "communist subbotniks"
—Saturday and weekend voluntary work in plants and the
community—had arisen. The new movement was adopted by
other young groups and spread rapidly. By January 1960,
nearly 5 million were reported taking part; by January 1962,
over 20 million.[37] In 1963 the CCTU reported that 26 million
were participating, and that the title of Communist Labor had
been won by about 2,600 enterprises, over 50,000 shops and
departments, 400,000 brigades with 4 million members, and
3 million individual workers. In 1965 nearly half of all wage
and salary workers were said to be involved in the movement.[38] The party and the unions gave strong support to the
development. It was considered "deeply revolutionary," bringing not only participation in perfecting the organization of
production, but also "changes in the consciousness of people,
in their inter-relationships. The first objective . . . is not only
increase of productivity of labor, but also formation of new
traits of character, training of the new man of communist
society."[39]

Award of the honorary title to individuals, brigades, and
shops was generally by agreement of the factory committee
with the Komsomol, the party committee, and the administra-

tion, after discussion at workers' meetings. Awards to enterprises were made by the regional economic and trade union councils, with agreement of the party and the Komsomol. Each award was expected to be made with ceremony, as a highly important event. In a clothing plant, for example, a handsome certificate in a red booklet, given each brigade and each of its members when they won the title, was signed by the director and the officers of the union, the party, and the Komsomol.

As the movement spread beyond the ranks of young enthusiasts, it stimulated innovations in technology and organization and the growth of volunteer groups collaborating on special problems. The Institute of Labor, studying the experience, concluded that it had led to a significant increase in creative activity.[40] There had been rapid growth in the work of rationalizers and inventors and in new forms of individual and group initiative; more economical organization and more effective wage systems had been developed in some enterprises; feeling of individual responsibility for attendance and punctuality had increased, and brigades felt more responsible for the attitudes and behavior of their members. In some plants expressions of mutual trust developed: "work without control"; buffets without a checker—people just left money for what they took; "pay without cashiers"—wage money for a group was put on a table, from which each worker took the proper amount and signed for it. Improvements were frequently found in working conditions, in services, in cleanliness and beauty of the plant and grounds. The influx of workers into evening and correspondence courses was furthered.[41]

On the other hand, this Communist Labor movement showed the usual preoccupation of the Soviets with numbers and their frequent excesses in great nationwide campaigns of propaganda and emulation of innovators. In many cases the high moral intensity of the first young initiators was diluted.

A serious discussion developed on the meaning, requirements, and problems of the movement. A survey by the Institute of Public Opinion of *Komsomolskaya Pravda*, late in 1961, found evidence of high idealism, but also of great concern among participants over distortions and deficiencies.[42] Similar opinions were expressed in extensive discussion in the press.[43]

A major defect was violation of the principle of voluntarism. Obligations were sometimes adopted without thorough discussion by workers. Some enterprises claimed to be competing for the title of Communist Labor even though relatively few individuals, brigades, or shops had adopted any communist obligations or had won the honor. A second problem was the tendency to show off, to seek publicity, sometimes with extravagant pledges and misleading reports of participation. Sometimes, to help brigades or individuals make ostentatious records, artificial conditions were set up temporarily; but later the former conditions were reverted to, and morale slumped. There were reports of envy and discontent on the part of workers outside these programs. The constant pressure from Communist Labor groups for better work was sometimes resented by other workers.[44]

The most frequently mentioned shortcoming was that too much had become routine. Obligations were sometimes vague. Check-up was inadequate. Sometimes only the production record was considered, not other tests of communist attitudes. Awards were given to people who had done nothing to deserve them, or were given without appropriate ceremony. After receiving the honor, the winners sometimes relaxed and there was no check-up as to whether they were maintaining high standards. Once the movement had spread over a large part of the entire work force, the enthusiasm and initiative of the earlier groups could not be counted on. In spite of fear that central control might be limiting, the opinion grew that the

CCTU should regulate the conditions under which the title of Communist Labor could be won and kept, and the "moral and material rewards" that went with the distinction.[45]

The excessive demands made by some of the widely publicized slogans were also criticized—for instance, the call to achieve seven hours' work in six and to provide added production in the last hour. The dean of economists, Academician Strumilin, pointed out that such a demand was entirely too high for most workers, and that overplan products were not always needed, or did not make for balance in the economy. He called for more realism, with consideration always of special conditions and possibilities, rather than trying to cut creativity to one pattern.[46] This was a needed warning against the excessive propaganda, conformity, and pressure in such nationwide campaigns, which tend to overpower and distort the genuine local initiatives.

INCENTIVES FOR COOPERATION

Both material and moral incentives are believed necessary for the fullest development of initiative in industry. The moral incentives include not only the titles and honors, publicity on good results, places on Boards of Honor and in Books of Honor, red pennants and banners won in competitions, but also, it is said, satisfaction in collective effort and contribution to the good of the whole. The material rewards include the wage and salary system, designed to promote "individual self-interest in the results of one's work," with almost universal incentive systems, and the funds distributed in socialist competition as individual premiums as well as for collective purposes. In the shops, also, awards are made to the best workers from special foremen's funds, in agreement with union committees. Financial rewards are given for successful inventions and rationalizations. These are the material incentives that play a major part in stimulating cooperation on production problems.

Many enterprises also have "enterprise funds," made up of assignments from planned and overplan profits or economies from lowering costs, and spent by agreement of the administration and the union committee. According to decrees of 1961 and 1963, the assignments ranged from 1 to 6 per cent of planned profits or the sum of economies, and from 20 to 60 per cent of overplan profits; industries of greatest national significance, such as metallurgy, fuel and chemical production, have the largest percentages. Total amounts were limited in general to 5.5 per cent of the year's wage fund, but for some industries could go as high as 7 per cent when the share of new products was large in their total production. Not less than 20 per cent was to be spent for modernizing equipment, new technology, or expanding production; not less than 40 per cent for house building and repair, or construction of cultural facilities; and up to 40 per cent for individual premiums, improving services for the people, providing passes to rest homes and sanitariums, and for aid to individual workers.[47] These funds are often criticized as too small to have great significance as incentives, although their amounts were increased under the later decrees. In 1963 in Leningrad, 72 per cent of all enterprises under the sovnarkhoz had enterprise funds, but these averaged only 2.5 per cent of the wage funds and reached the limit of 5.5 per cent for only a few enterprises. Many complaints are made of the use of the funds. Sums for building often go unused for lack of assignment of needed materials, or are diverted to other uses by the enterprise or by order of higher agencies. The CCTU protested and urged the government to make the enterprise funds more useful as stimuli.[48]

It is difficult or impossible to appraise the effectiveness of the incentives, pressures, and propaganda that impinge on workers of all levels in Soviet industry. That not all respond as desired is clear from the concern of authorities for "survivals of the past," for slackers, truants, "disorganizers." That the attitudes expected of the new Soviet man are not always present is shown by the constant exhortations to unions and to party groups to improve their educational work. There is indifference, boredom with the moralizing and propaganda, resistance to pressures. Workers and managers alike are tempted to seek plans that are not too tight, and to hold possible advances in reserve, since overfulfillment of plans leads to bonuses. When activists in the ranks press for innovations and improvements in methods, not all management people or workers welcome the initiative, since earnings and bonuses may be reduced during the time of change-over.[49] Nevertheless, in visiting plant after plant, talking with union and management people and with workers, and reading letters and reports in the trade union press, it is impossible not to sense the frequent presence of a collective spirit, a feeling of cooperation in joint projects, a pride in joint achievements. The talk is typically of "our plant." It is clear that many enjoy using their capacities in solving technical and organizational problems and in taking part in union activities.

Important motivations are present in the bonuses, the benefits in vacation facilities, housing, and other rewards. Advancement is likely to be affected by the records of innovators and leaders in production and other activities. There is value in social approval and recognition, for instance, for young workers applying for admission to institutes. Whatever the motivation of individuals, Soviet enterprises gain through tapping the inventiveness and energy in the ranks. They also get substantial free services from out-of-hours "public work" on production problems. The rapid growth of productivity of labor reflects this mobilization of creative human resources, as well as increased capital investment, improved technology, and greater intensification of work.

Two further points contribute to this result. One is that a manager gets no support from any theory of management prerogatives if he resists criticisms and suggestions from the rank and file. When a manager stands on his authority and fails to listen to his workers, he may and sometimes does get into trouble. The second point is that workers do not in general resist technological change. Improvements typically are to the advantage of workers, through better working conditions and substitution of mechanization for laborious handwork. In addition, shortage of labor precludes widespread fear of unemployment. All this provides a setting in which it is possible to enlist the aid of many workers in improving production processes.

Although the claims for these movements of cooperation are exaggerated, there can be little doubt that millions of people are, in fact, enlisted in efforts to increase the effectiveness of industry, and that they make substantial contributions to the growth of productivity.

CHAPTER X

Wages and Hours in Industrial Relations

$\mathbf{F}$ROM 1956 through 1962 a country-wide reduction of working hours and a massive revision of wage and hour standards and systems took place in Soviet industry. With the reduction of hours from eight to a standard of seven per day, and six for underground work in mines, the standard day for adults in industry was reduced from an average of 7.96 hours in 1956 to 6.93 in 1962.[1] Before the return to the eight-hour day in 1940, the standard had been seven hours, six days a week. Now, with a shorter day on Saturdays, the work week for factory workers became 41 hours. The wage reform was reported in 1963 to have covered 49 million wage and salary workers in manufacturing, mining, construction, transportation, communications, and agriculture, and to have generally increased earnings, especially for the lower- and middle-paid workers. In July 1964 the Supreme Soviet provided for completing the wage reform by extending it to all other fields.[2]

The general principles of the Soviet wage system have been described earlier.[3] Here the concern is with the allocation of responsibilities in planning and regulating hours, wages, salaries, and incentive systems, and with wage administration in the enterprises. Local managements and union committees make their decisions within the bounds of central regulations and plans, and of the wage fund and average wages provided in the enterprise production plans. Some of their decisions apply specific standards. On other questions, where there is more room for local discretion, central policies provide guidelines and recommended methods and standards, though these are not always followed.

DECISION MAKING: CENTRAL

The far-reaching changes in wages initiated by the Twentieth Congress of the CPSU had the stated aim of "the most rapid elimination of deficiencies in the organization of labor and wages and the strengthening of individual material self-interest of workers in the results of their work." Real wages were expected to rise on the average by 30 per cent, with special increases for low-paid workers.[4]

One of the first results was an increase in minimum wage rates by decree of the Central Committee of the CPSU, the Council of Ministers, and the CCTU, in September 1956.[5] Replacing the former minimum of 220-225 rubles per month, which had been the rule since 1946, minimum rates were set at 270 (in old rubles) in rural places and 300 in cities, with not less than 300-350 in industry, construction, transportation, and communications. Wages of the low-paid groups were to be raised by approximately one-third. Central ministries and the republic councils of ministers were authorized to set minimum rates for branches of industry, in agreement with the State Committee on Labor and Wages and the CCTU. In 1959 the Twenty-First Congress provided for an increase in the minimum to 400-450 rubles a month as a first step toward a promised minimum of 500-600 rubles.[6] These minimum rates were the basis for the whole wage system, but rates for different industries were set at levels varying with all the factors that determine differentials. In the wage reform of 1958-1962 the rates for the lowest wage grade—shown now in new rubles —were set at about 40-50 rubles per month in light and food industries, 50-60 rubles in fabricating industries, and 50-70 in mining.[7] Universal application of the new minimum rates, planned for 1962, was delayed until 1964-1965 by economic difficulties that slowed the introduction of the wage reform in branches outside the sphere of physical production.

These minima are rates, not guaranteed monthly earnings, and some workers earn less. In general, a piece worker is paid according to his output. If failure to fulfill the production standard is considered the worker's fault, he has no guarantee. If he is not at fault, the guarantee of earnings is two-thirds of the base rate, or, in case of stoppages, one-half or in some cases two-thirds of the base rate of time workers. A 1962 report from the RSFSR showed the number receiving less than 40 rubles for a full month's work to be as much as 0.15 per cent of full-time workers in the coal industry, 0.9 per cent in the oil industry, and 2.3 per cent in the lower-paid bread baking field.[8]

The reduction of hours was carried out industry by industry as new wage systems were introduced. It began in coal mines in 1956, continued in heavy industry, and by 1959 reached textiles and some other fields. In May 1960 the Supreme Soviet decreed the shift of all wage and salary workers to the shorter day by the end of the year.[9]

Introduction of the new wage conditions proceeded under strict control from the top. A decree of the Central Committee of the party and the Council of Ministers on October 8, 1956, provided new wage rates for the coal industry of the Ukraine, and authorized the State Committee on Labor and Wages, on recommendation of the Ministry of Coal and in agreement with the CCTU, to approve a new list of underground occupations with their distribution by wage grades, and a new job evaluation handbook. In 1957 and 1958 similar decrees authorized the shift in a number of branches of heavy industry.[10]

Basic instructions were provided by the State Committee and the CCTU for the working out in industries of new wage rates, scales of differentials, territorial supplements, and salary scales.[11] Following the 1957 shift of administration of most industries to regional economic councils—the sovnarkhozy—, proposals for an industry were ordinarily approved jointly by the State Committee on Labor and Wages and the CCTU. The State Committee, with the cooperation of the republic councils of ministers, the sovnarkhozy, and the unions, presented concrete proposals for approval of the Council of Ministers and the Central Committee of the Communist Party. Under a September 1959 tripartite decree of the party Central Committee, the Council of Ministers, and the CCTU, the wage reform was introduced in 1960 in the remaining branches of manufacturing and construction, and in 1961-1962 in transportation, communications, and state farms.[12]

In July 1964 Khrushchev reported that more than 50 million workers had been shifted to new wage and salary conditions in the branches of physical production, with increases in earnings that averaged 13 to 25 per cent in these industries. Some increases had been made in other branches, but those planned for 1962 had not been possible because greater expenditures had become necessary on investment, especially for the chemical industry and agriculture, and for defense. Now wages could be increased in the remaining branches, covering 18 million people, or about one-fourth of all wage and salary workers. Increases were to average 21 per cent for the entire group, 25 per cent in education, 23 per cent in health services, 18 per cent in trade and public catering, 15 per cent in housing and communal services. The wage and salary increases were to be put into effect late in 1964 in education and medical services, and in all service fields in the Far North, and in 1965 for all other service workers. This plan was incorporated in a law proposed by the party Central Committee, the Council of Ministers, and the CCTU and then adopted by the Supreme Soviet.[13]

Plans for the growth of money wages are made at the highest levels of the party and the government, as part of the national economic plans. Following party directives, the planning organs work out yearly and quarterly plans for the wage fund and average wages, for the country as a whole and for republics and ministries. After these plans are approved by the USSR Council of Ministers, the funds are distributed by ministries and republic councils of ministers, to regional economic councils, local soviets, and other agencies. Finally, wage funds of enterprises are authorized. The unions have the right to share in this process at every stage.

Participation of the CCTU, the union central committees and republic and regional councils of trade unions is said to be increasingly active and significant.[14] The CCTU joins in issuing major wage decrees and the decisions of the State Committee on Labor and Wages. How far the CCTU and other union bodies go in pushing for higher wage levels is not known. CCTU staff members, however, told how they kept in close contact with Gosplan at national and republic levels, and how the CCTU takes its recommendations to the Council of Ministers; but they added, "We know what is possible." Representatives of the Medical Workers' Union told an American that their central committee had been more active since 1958 in arguing with the Ministry of Health the case for better salaries for doctors, and that consequently the differentials between the pay of doctors and engineers had been reduced.[15] The CCTU is said to have joined in working out the plan for the increases in the service fields. At the December 1963 session of the Central Committee of the party, devoted to the development of the chemical industry, Chairman Grishin spoke strongly of the need to improve incentives by eliminating inequities in wages, improving production standards, and making better use of premiums, in the interest of increasing production.[16]

Detailed standards and regulations are established under the control of the State Committee of the Council of Ministers on Questions of Labor and Wages, set up in 1955. All decisions on wage and salary rates and on other central regulations are recommended to the Council of Ministers by the State Committee or are made by the State Committee, in agreement with the CCTU. The committee has a Scientific-Investigation Institute of Labor, and its subsidiary Central Bureau of Industrial Normatives on Labor, which work closely with research institutes of different branches of industry, regional economic councils and enterprises, and the central committees of the unions and the CCTU.

In a statement of the functions of the State Committee, published by the Institute of Labor in 1960,[17] it is said that the committee "coordinates" between branches of industry and economic regions all questions related to pay. It organizes the working out of job evaluation handbooks and of standards for output norms, and approves them jointly with the CCTU—in construction jointly also with the State Committee on Construction. It reviews proposals for regional supplements from the republic councils of ministers and from central ministries, and approves these jointly with the CCTU, with the participation of Gosplan and the Ministry of Finance. The State Committee checks the work of all administrative agencies and enterprises, and it works with the republic councils of ministers, and with the sovnarkhozy and the ministries and departments that direct the plants.

Establishment of the State Committee on Labor and Wages resulted in substantially strengthening and unifying central control over wages and salaries; but as this regulation of wages developed, questions arose over the authority of all the organs concerned in deciding particular issues—the State Committee, other committees and ministries at the national and republic levels, the sovnarkhozy and their branch administrations, and enterprise directors. One expert called for further definition by law of the competence of different organs.[18]

The State Committee, working closely with the CCTU and with administrative and governmental agencies, sought more uniform and effective application of the principles governing wages. After the Commissariat of Labor was abolished early in the 1930's, there was no central organ for regulating wages under the Council of Ministers. Transfer of some functions to the CCTU did not meet this problem; though the CCTU could make representations to Gosplan and the Council of Ministers, it lacked authority. The "departmental" system of wage regulation by the industrial ministries resulted in wide and inequitable differences in pay. Efforts to attract and hold workers led to complex and confusing wage and premium systems and other supplementary payments to increase earnings. Geographic supplements to wage rates aimed to promote labor force stability, but their lack of uniformity led to unnecessary turnover.

A major defect in the wage structure was the extremely low level of base rates, which had not been revised for years and bore little relation to the level of planned and actual wages. Earnings depended rather on piece-rate systems and a variety of other payments—long service payments, regional supplements, bonuses of various kinds. Base rates lost their effectiveness as a means of insuring proper relationships between earnings of different groups. Almost no workers were placed in the two lowest wage classes. Piece-rate systems were applied artificially in order to increase earnings, regardless of whether this method of pay was suitable. Progressive piece rates, which rose steeply when production standards were overfulfilled, were used to increase earnings. Norms were set low, to make possible the needed levels of earnings, and were overfulfilled up to 150-200 per cent by the majority of workers in industry. The share of base rates in total earnings of workers was 50 per cent or less in many industries.[19]

Another difficulty was excessive differentials. In some industries rates in the highest wage grade were as much as 3.6 times that of the lowest grade. Actual earnings showed a considerably greater gap. In a huge iron and steel mill in 1956 the highest-paid hourly workers earned 12 times as much as the lowest-paid.[20] However, with the increased level of education and industrial experience among workers, the need for extreme differentiation of earnings had decreased. Key industries no longer required such exceptionally high earnings to attract workers. The general increases in levels of earnings, made possible by the growth of production, could accordingly be planned especially to benefit lower- and middle-paid workers and industries.

In addition, the effectiveness of wages as incentives was limited by the complexity of wage systems resulting from the low level of base rates, low production standards, and departmental regulation. Production standards failed to provide the needed stimulus. Enterprises had a useful safety valve in their possibility of manipulations that increased earnings on an unplanned basis, but this caused inequities and was contrary to the spirit and policy of the planned wage system.

The wage reform aimed to eliminate these deficiences as far as possible. General instructions given by the Twentieth Congress and reiterated by the CCTU included, in an order that suggests priorities, the following:[21]

To ensure the introduction of technically based norms of output corresponding to the contemporary level of techniques and organization of production;

To raise base wage rates and increase their share in earnings, and to establish proper relationships between their levels in different branches and occupations, considering the qualifications of workers and work under arduous and hot conditions;

To eliminate the multiplicity of systems of wages and salaries and the lack of coordination in conditions; and to revise salary systems;

To increase the role of premiums as incentives for the introduction of new technology, growth of productivity of labor, and lowering of costs;

To increase real wages, especially for the lower-paid workers.

The major purposes of the drastic reorganization of wages and salaries were, accordingly: first, to make the systems of pay more effective as incentives for raising efficiency and productivity; second, to reduce illogical and unnecessary differentials, both within and between industries, in the interest of lessening turnover that resulted from inequities; and third, to pay an installment on the promises to increase real wages, by raising the earnings of the lower- and middle-paid workers and salaried employees and reducing differentials between their levels and those of higher-paid people.

Central decisions were necessary on major points, especially on the base rates and schedules of differentials, systems for grading work and workers, and central standards and methods for fixing production standards in the plants. Base rates, as described by a CCTU staff member, are determined by the Council of Ministers after recommendations by the State Committee and the CCTU and in consultation with Gosplan and the Ministry of Finance and, when necessary, with other ministries. Schedules of differentials are approved by the State Committee and the CCTU, or by the Council of Ministers in major cases or when there is difference of opinion between the State Committee and the CCTU.[22] They are worked out by the Institute of Labor or by research institutes of the industries, with active involvement of the unions, regional economic councils, and big enterprises. They are discussed at workers' meetings, suggestions are collected and studied, and final drafts are reviewed by union committees and enterprise administrations. The job evaluation handbooks similarly are worked out by research institutes, in close contact with unions, workers, and plant administrations, and are finally approved by the State Committee on Labor and Wages and the CCTU. On production standards, materials on methods of establishing norms and on typical and uniform standards are worked out by agencies under the State Committee and by other research organizations and are issued by the State Committee.

Whatever the degree of order and unity achieved in the centrally determined structure of wage rates, decentralized decisions on other aspects of the wage system influence substantially the actual earnings and wage costs. Accordingly, the State Committee and the CCTU issue a large volume of other regulations and materials. Model regulations are approved for piece-premium and time-premium wage systems and for premium systems for administrative and engineering personnel in different industries. Model lists are issued of occupations entitled to higher pay for work under hot, arduous, or harmful conditions. Regional coefficients for supplements to wages have been approved for different industries. Rules are set for grouping enterprises for salary scales of administrators and engineers. The State Committee issues much methodological material on the grading of jobs and workers and on production standards, in an effort to bring sound and uniform methods into use in the localities and the plants.[23]

Job evaluation systems worked out earlier under the industrial ministries were out of date, since the Tariff-Qualifications Handbooks had not been revised to take account of technological progress. Inequities in pay for similar work resulted from differences in evaluation of jobs that were found in many industries. Early in 1957 the State Committee and the CCTU authorized the Institute of Labor to work out a Uniform Tariff-Qualifications Handbook for Universal Occupations, common to many industries, and to prepare instructions for research institutes on working out handbooks for branches of industry. The uniform handbook, approved in 1960, reduced some thousands of jobs described in the old handbooks to a few hundred, and is said to cover about 60 per cent of all work in industry. The branch handbooks were developed, on assignment from the State Committee, by research institutes in the industries with the participation of the central committees of the unions, regional economic and trade union councils, enterprises and their local unions. Parts were assigned to certain enterprises, where job descriptions were gathered and analyzed. In the end, after much discussion by workers, administrators, and union representatives, the draft was agreed on by the institute, the central committee of the union, and administrative groups, and presented to the State Committee for final approval in agreement with the CCTU.[24]

The method of job analysis worked out by the Institute of Labor involved a point system for evaluating the complexity of different jobs. Work was assigned to different wage grades according to the number of points resulting from grading four functions: computations, preparing the workplace for work, performing the work, and servicing equipment, with added points for responsibility. Handbooks developed in some industries, however, were less strict than in others, or than the uniform handbook, with the result that work of similar difficulty was graded higher in those industries than elsewhere. Some economists argue for a more objective method of job evaluation, to include estimates of the time required in training and experience to achieve a given level of skill.[25] Revisions in the job evaluation handbooks continued to be made in an effort for uniformity between industries and for adjusting to changes in occupations as technology developed. A revision of the Uniform Handbook in May 1964 changed the rating of a number of key occupations, such as that of machine operators

in the machine-building industry, whose average wage grade
was substantially raised. The State Committee also issued a
unified list of occupations, for use in revising the handbooks
for different industries, in the hope of eliminating their existing inequities. In 1964 over 100 research organizations were
reportedly working out new Tariff-Qualifications Handbooks,
in preparation for a new stage in the wage reform.[26]

The starting point for wage differentials between industries
is the base rate for the lowest wage grade. This, supposedly,
is determined by consideration of the complexity of the work,
and also of working conditions and the national economic
significance of the industry. Then the schedule of differentials
for skill takes account of increasing complexity of work. All
these issues are under serious study in the Institute of Labor.[27]
An estimate of the influence of these factors in determining
the rates for different industries showed additions to minimum
rates in connection with working conditions to range up to
36.9 per cent in coal mining and metallurgy; and for economic
significance of the industry, up to 8.2 per cent in textiles and
other light industries, and up to 21.7 per cent in coal and
metallurgy.[28] One leading expert argues that in determining
differentials there is need for increasing weight for difficult
conditions, and for less weight to the significance of the industry, except for developing industries with a special labor
supply problem. He expects that periodic revisions of the base
rates should reduce the differences between industries, as the
wages of the lower-paid are raised, and as more uniformity
is achieved in the wage schedules of different industries.[29]

Production standards also have a large influence on earnings, since incentive systems are almost universal. Central
instructions and a growing volume of central standards and
normative materials seek uniformity in norm-setting in the
plants. Before the wage reform, production standards were
revised annually in a mass campaign directed from above,

which temporarily stimulated growth in the productivity of labor. Managements tended to set loose norms, in order to prevent wage decreases and to maintain planned and effective levels of earnings, in the interest of holding work forces. When wage rates were increased after 1956 it became possible to tighten production standards. The Council of Ministers decreed that from January 1, 1957, norms should be reviewed continuously when new technology or improved organization raised the productivity of labor, and that the widely used loose norms based on statistical experience should be replaced by technically based norms.[30] For some industries, notably construction, uniform output standards were worked out and adopted. More widespread are typical norms and standards for machine performance and other elements of production standards, developed by the Central Bureau of Industrial Normatives on Labor and other research institutes. Standards for time and output on typical operations and products are available for many industries, along with much material on methods of norm-setting.[31]

DECISION MAKING: THE ENTERPRISE

The director carries the chief responsibility in wage administration in the plant, though his most important decisions must be made in agreement with the union committee. The plants' departments of labor and wages have technicians on wage questions and production standards, as also do big shops. While the party committee has no administrative responsibility, concern for the success of the enterprise involves it in work on wage questions. The union committees and their wage commissions have important roles in working out all decisions on wage matters.[32] Trade union group organizers and their production-mass-work organizers explain policies, collect suggestions, help to work out details for their groups, and are expected to see that wage systems are properly applied and wages properly paid. The commissions on labor disputes take up individual complaints that have not been resolved in the shops. The union works under instructions from its central committee, regional committee and the sov-prof, and can turn to them for help.

Grading jobs and workers according to the Tariff-Qualifications Handbooks is a major step in wage administration. The Uniform Handbook for Universal Occupations and the industry handbook together provide the basis for evaluating all jobs. They specify for each wage grade of an occupation "what the worker should know" and "what the worker should be able to do" and give examples. Grading of jobs is done by shop managements in consultation with the wage commission and other union representatives, and with discussion at workers' meetings. Recommended practice is to post the list of jobs as classified. After verification by the administration and the union, formal approval is given by the director in agreement with the factory committee. Any dispute goes to the next higher union and administrative bodies for decision.[33]

For assignment of workers to wage grades, joint qualifications commissions are set up. Shop commissions, consisting of management and union representatives and leading workers, check the worker's theoretical knowledge and his ability to do the work, as required by the handbooks. Decisions of the shop commission go to the director for final approval in agreement with the factory committee. If a worker disagrees, he appeals to the plant qualifications commission or to the factory committee. When the new handbooks were introduced, reclassification of workers was carried out generally without individual tests, except where there was disagreement. In case a worker has improved his qualifications, or when a new worker comes to the shop, or a young worker completes a course of training, he may be given theoretical and work tests.[34] When effectively done, such joint work in classifying

jobs and workers serves as a means of discovering workers'
needs for further training, and of assuring that they are used
according to their levels of skill, as the law required.

In general, workers are paid the rate for the job rather
than that of their personal wage grade. If a worker is used
on work of a grade different from his own, because of conditions of production, he is paid the rate for the job, whether
higher or lower than his own rate; but in many cases a piece
worker used on work rated more than one grade below his
own grade is entitled to supplementary payments based on
the difference between the two rates. This is intended to prevent lowering the earnings of highly skilled workers and to
induce managements to use them in accordance with their
skills.[35]

Wage rates for the grades in an occupation are differentiated
for time and piece work, with higher rates for the latter, and
with higher rates for work under hot, arduous, or possibly
harmful conditions. Lists of jobs entitled to the rates for such
working conditions are determined by the director in agreement with the factory committee, based on the model lists.
If it is thought that a job not specifically covered by the list
should be included, the question can be taken to the sovnarkhoz and sovprof for decision.

The enterprise has authority to determine what combination of piece and time work, with premiums of various kinds,
provides the best incentives under its particular conditions.
Union committees and commissions work with management in
developing or changing the wage system, with much discussion in the shops. Piece work continues to be the most prevalent
system, since it is considered the best way to relate a worker's
earnings to his production when conditions are suitable. But
technical progress has decreased the feasibility of individual
incentive pay. The proportion of all workers in industry on
piece rates, which had risen from 64 per cent in 1932 to 77 per

cent in 1953, dropped in the wage reform to 61 per cent. In many industries the reduction was drastic, as in oil refining where it dropped from 63 to 12 per cent.[36] The former widely used systems of piece rates rising steeply with increased output were largely replaced by piece-premium systems, while time workers rose to 39 per cent of all in industry, and time-premium systems became more prevalent. Of all workers in industry, 94 per cent were reported to be covered by incentive systems, 66 per cent of them by piece or time rates plus premiums.[37] Collective piece work systems became increasingly numerous.

Premium systems are considered of great significance for stimulating the interest both of workers and of administrative personnel in improving production and lowering costs. The previous great variety of systems was reduced and central guidance provided by model regulations for different industries. Detailed regulations worked out in the enterprises establish the conditions and amounts of premiums for various groups and the lists of those covered. Premiums must not lead to overpayment of the established wage funds, but may amount to as much as 40 to 60 per cent of basic wage and salary scales.

For workers, five chief systems of premiums were established, the amounts varying according to the economic significance of the industry. The main form is a premium for fulfilling the production plan of the brigade, department or shop, in an amount of from 10 to 20 per cent of average wages or rates, plus from 0.5 to 2 per cent for each per cent of overfulfillment of the plan. In industries where quality is especially important there are premiums for improvements in quality, up to 30 per cent of wage rates. Premiums for economies of materials may amount to not more than 40 per cent of the saving. In the machine-tool and textile industries and some others, there are premiums for fulfilling or overfulfilling technically based production standards. Premiums for auxiliary and repair workers depend on the quality of work and its completion on schedule. In construction, the main form of premium is for completing the job on time.[38]

Premiums for directors and other administrative, engineering, technical, and office employees are controlled by model regulations. The sovnarkhozy and sovprofs set limits for the amounts of premiums in different industries, and the detailed system is agreed on in the enterprise. The main type of premium is that paid to personnel who contribute directly to achieving planned cost reduction in their shops or sections, generally 15 per cent of monthly salaries, plus 1.5 per cent for each 0.1 per cent of overfulfillment. In some industries there are additional premiums for improving quality, up to 10-15 per cent of salaries, and in major industries premiums for fulfilling production plans, limited to 3 to 5 per cent of salaries. Premiums for the administrative staff are based on the results of the work of the plant as a whole. A basic requirement for all premiums is fulfillment of the planned assortment of products, the plan for productivity of labor, and planned supply of products to other economic regions.[39]

The wage reform brought more uniformity between industries in their premium systems and met some of the earlier criticisms. A serious problem remained in that most premiums rested on fulfilling plans and accordingly were affected by the relative tightness of the enterprise's plan. Efforts to improve the effectiveness of premium systems continued. In March 1964 the State Committee and the CCTU decided to introduce a new system experimentally in a number of enterprises in six industries. This was to emphasize improvements in the achievements of the enterprise over its previous period, and also its work in comparison with that of leading enterprises or with approved standards.[40]

These premium systems, discussed above, are integral parts

of the wage and salary system and are paid from the wage funds. Supplementary to them are special premiums paid from sums won in socialist competition or from the "enterprise funds," and also premiums for developing and introducing new technological improvements, paid from special funds provided to enterprises and the higher administrative agencies. These funds, as others, are distributed by agreement of the administrative agency and the coordinate trade union body.

The establishment and revision of production standards is another major part of wage administration. "Experience-statistical" norms, which in 1963 were reported still to be about half of all, are based on experience and statistical study of actual expenditure of time on a process as a whole. For the approved "technically-based" norms, the elements of the work process are analyzed, based on advanced technology and organization, with measurement of the time necessary on the basis of the technical possibilities and the "normal average intensity of work." Such norm-setting uses central standards of time, output, and staffing, and local normatives developed in the region and in the enterprise itself. There are complaints, however, that some so-called technically based norms are in reality still the old statistically determined standards.[41]

Production standards are generally worked out by technicians using time study and other methods, in consultation with the union wage commissions and with experienced workers. Proposals are discussed in workers' meetings. Trade union group organizers help check proposed norms at the work places and take questions to the shop committees. New norms go into effect only after approval by the factory committee and two weeks' notice to workers. If management and the union disagree, the issue goes to the regional union committee and the industrial administration in the sovnarkhoz, and, if necessary, to the sovprof and the sovnarkhoz. In the wage department of one sovprof it was said that they never agreed to a change in norms if it would reduce wages. If workers object to the new norm, they can appeal to the union committee or to the commission on labor disputes.[42]

In a 1962 report to the Central Committee of the CPSU, Khrushchev spoke of the need to involve workers themselves in improving productivity and raising production standards. After giving homely examples from his own experience in a mine, he went on:

Go to the workers, talk openly with them and say that it is necessary to raise the productivity of labor to such and such a level, and how this can be done. The workers themselves will show us, since every worker has his reserves. I myself was a worker and know well that the worker does not live without reserves. Speak with the workers, say what it is necessary to do, and they will understand you properly. But to do this it is necessary to go to the worker not as some administrator bureaucrats do, but as a comrade of that worker; then the worker will open his heart and show the possibilities he has for raising the productivity of labor and lowering costs.[43]

In plants visited and in press reports, revision of norms with the participation of workers and the union was described. A typical comment was that "where the work of the wage commission is well organized, where the public is brought widely into decision of labor questions, there are almost no complaints on the part of workers of improper establishment of norms."[44] Emphasis was put on introducing improved methods as a basis for tighter standards. One frequently used device was for workers themselves to keep time records, which often showed substantial losses from lack of materials or tools, poor service for their machines, or other administrative shortcomings, and led to demands on management for improvements.[45] Individual workers were helped to improve their methods. Stimulated by the "movement for communist labor," volunteer groups in many plants sought better review of norms and reduction of inequalities in tightness of standards. Workers were even reported in many cases to have volunteered to have their own norms raised. Management was sometimes warned, on the other hand, that all this activity did not relieve the manager of his final responsibility for the quality of production standards.

Resistance to review and replacement of outmoded standards also was reported. Tightening of norms in general is not expected to reduce earnings, but in some cases it must do so. Since this is not wanted either by managers or workers, fear of reduced earnings or bonuses may hold back revisions. If unions think the new standards are incorrect, they can refuse to accept them. In 1955 when a factory committee chairman was asked in the presence of his chief engineer whether there was ever difficulty, he refused to answer, calling this an insulting question. An economist in 1959, troubled at this suggestion of tension over the issue, asked, "Why?" He went on to say that workers were not so naive as always to want higher norms, but that the essence of the worker's attitude, even on this question, was his knowledge that he was working for the whole people and his feeling that individual and social interests coincide in general. Though such attitudes were expressed in many plants, there is evidence also of resistance to tightening of standards.[46]

Occasional reports tell of union committees' reluctance to agree to revisions, until pushed by higher union bodies or the party. Sometimes there were misunderstandings when the norm-setters had not worked closely enough with workers in the shops or the union had not done a good job of explaining the need. Sometimes the necessary conditions had not been provided for fulfilling tighter norms. Improperly changed standards were sometimes set aside on the protest of workers, but occasionally refusal to agree to the new norms was criticized as without basis. In a textile mill in 1962 the management proposed an average increase in norms of 30 per cent, following technological changes, but the factory committee agreed only to 15 per cent. In a three months' trial, large over-fulfillment of the norms resulted in an unapproved increase in earnings. The union committee then had to agree to higher norms, but this "gave rise to unfavorable criticisms on the part of the workers"—whether of the union or the management was not specified.[47]

In a building materials plant visited, where most norms were all-industry standards, one change was put into effect without getting the union committee's agreement. The workers objected and got reconsideration. Actually the norm was kept as correct; the objection was said to have been based on failure to follow proper procedures. In a textile mill, seven workers protested a new standard agreed on by the union. The commission on labor disputes checked the calculations in the shop and found them correct and that the norm was being fulfilled by 106 to 108 per cent. The workers had to accept the fact that the norm was right; but then they were helped to improve their methods of work and before long succeeded in overfulfilling the standard by larger amounts.

It is clear that workers can protect themselves from excessive pressure through too tight standards. To what extent they and the unions fail to do so, with resulting dissatisfaction like that often reported earlier, it is impossible to know. The increasing participation of workers in setting standards and seeing that their application is proper may tend to improve the quality of the norm-setting; at least it provides more assurance that the results are acceptable to workers.

The proportion of industrial workers covered by norms based on central normative materials reportedly increased from 43.5 per cent in 1961 to 60.9 per cent in 1964.[48] Nevertheless there is dissatisfaction over the slow progress in tightening production standards as technology and organization improve. On the other hand, sometimes norms are changed arbitrarily, without involving workers and without the necessary basis in conditions of production and help to workers in mastering the new standards. As a result, large numbers are unable to meet the standards. This was reported in 1962 for 12 per cent of all piece workers in industries under the sovnarkhozy, 35 per cent in the coal industry, 20 per cent in oil, 16 per cent in the clothing industries.[49] In August 1964 the State Committee on Labor and Wages and the CCTU, in a decree on improving norm-setting in industry, gave detailed recommendations for the work in the enterprises, its planning, joint work by the administration and the union and volunteer groups, use of central, branch, and regional norms, and other questions.[50]

In some industries norms were set more loosely than in others, and different levels of fulfillment of norms were assumed in planning average wages and wage funds. In 1963 the average fulfillment of norms was reported as 106 per cent in the coal industry, 111 in textiles, 115 in metallurgy, 120 in the chemical industry, and 133 in machine-tool and metal fabrication.[51] Soft and easily met standards were still used—for example in the machine industries to assure higher levels of earnings than in textiles. In the interest of providing equal pay for equal work, efforts were made to promote uniformity between industries by increasing emphasis on the development and use of central normatives. There was also attention to the relative strictness of job evaluation, and revisions upgraded jobs in some industries, as machine-building, to raise average wage rates and permit tighter production standards.

Attention has turned, on the other hand, to the cost of this attempt to establish scientific bases for production standards for much of the work in every plant. In 1964 there were said to be more than a thousand organizations working on production standards, with over 6,000 workers, in addition to norm-setters in the plants.[52] Many of the agencies are extremely small. It is hoped that coordination in planning their work and improvements in methods and instruments will reduce costs in norm-setting and improve the quantity and quality of the central standards. In the enterprises also, costs could be reduced by more use of central standards and by better training of the norm-setters. As to whether such efforts to develop and use production standards are worth their cost, little doubt is shown.

Some relief from the problems and costs of individual piece rate systems is offered by the growing use of "complex brigades" including workers of different skills, with pay according to "the final result" of the work of the group. These brigades are widely used in coal mining, metallurgy, the chemical industry, construction, and to some extent in line production, as in the machine industries and in shoe and clothing plants.[53] The wage for the entire group depends on the collective net result, such as tonnage mined. In general, the total wage sum is divided among workers according to their wage grades and time worked. In some cases where this is feasible, individual piece rates are combined with a collective piece system. The main basis for this development is mechanization and automation that eliminate narrow specialization and require broader skills, interchangeability, and cooperative efforts on a highly mechanized aggregate or on line production. In addition, the shift to collective pay was influenced by efforts to win the title, "Brigade of Communist Labor." To these brigades collective pay seemed appropriate to the aim of "communist relations to work." Experience is reported to have shown substantial advantages. The collective incentive is said to increase the interest of every worker in the final results, to stimulate feelings of collective responsibility, exchange of experience and mutual aid, and to improve labor discipline. It also stimulated the combining of trades and learning wider ranges of skills. Many examples showed increased output and productivity of labor and lower costs, sometimes with a smaller number of workers. These systems are believed to be valuable for reducing the costs of calculating and recording wages and output, as well as of norm-setting. They are expected to become the basic method of pay in many fields, as both economic and appropriate to the developing attitudes in industry.

Problems are seen, on the other hand, in collective pay systems that hurt individual incentives. In some plants the enthusiasts of the movement for communist labor distributed wages equally among all members in the brigade. Any such equalitarian tendency is denounced by the authorities as contrary to the principle of pay according to the quantity and quality of labor. No "equalizing" should be permitted, they say, since under present conditions this hurts the growth of productivity of labor, the prime essential for building the base for communism. In addition, they want continued attention to the work of individuals, with methods agreed on in the brigade for penalizing slackers or poor workers and rewarding excellent work.[54]

Although the coverage of time work grows, Soviet experts continue to express great confidence in individual piece work as providing the best incentives, when conditions are suitable. Shifts to time work during the wage reform sometimes led to decreases in productivity and increases in the number of workers. As a result, some enterprises returned groups of workers to piece work. Time work is, in general, not covered by production standards, but efforts are being made to develop standards for such work.

Soviet experts call for more emphasis on the main purpose of production standards, to promote efficient planning and organization of production. Norms should serve as a stimulus to increase productivity, not as a major means to raise earnings. They are expected to lead in general only to low levels of overfulfillment; large overfulfillment is taken to mean that they are unduly low. Revision of standards is supposed to be based on improvements in technology and organization, not on increased skill or intensity; exceptional individual skill or intensity of work would properly lead to exceptionally high overfulfillment of norms and high earnings. The dilemma remains, and is pointed out by experts, that while norms determine wages, it is still true that wages—the wage rates and planned average levels of earnings—determine norms. Production standards continue to serve as the safety valve by which the enterprise can regulate the average level of earnings; accordingly, norms lose their value for the purpose of organizing production. Full use of premiums is recommended as the proper method of assuring the level of earnings appropriate to the base rates and the wage plans.[55]

THE SHIFT TO SHORTER HOURS AND NEW WAGE SYSTEMS

The drastic shake-up in all aspects of the wage system in Soviet industry from 1956 through 1962 was eased by the fact that a reduction of hours accompanied it, and that it was introduced gradually with time for preparation. Cooperation of workers was encouraged by the promise of an additional daily hour of leisure, once their plant or shop had made the necessary preparations and was permitted to shift to the new hours and wages. Experimental introduction of the new conditions in selected plants helped develop methods for use when the main body of enterprises made the shift.

Instructions from the party and the government emphasized that the reduction of hours from eight to seven was to occur without lowering wages, decreasing output or the productivity of labor, or overexpending established wage funds.[56] Enterprises were called on to find internal reserves for improving technology, organization of production, and productivity of labor, and for saving labor and shifting workers to more productive uses. At the same time, complex processes were involved on details of the new wage and hour conditions. Each enterprise was to make the shift only when its readiness had been checked by the sovnarkhoz or other administrative body and the sovprof. Within an enterprise, shops would shift when the factory committee and the director agreed they were ready. In general, enterprises were expected to manage without increasing the number of workers, but when necessary, increases in the work force and the wage funds were permitted.

In many plants visited in 1959, activities related to the impending shift of hours and wages were under way. Some big enterprises were helping to work out the new job evaluation handbooks or wage schedules, and had sent in recommendations to the central committee of the union and the sovnarkhoz. Many had sent representatives to regional or national conferences to discuss proposals. Some plants were already on the shorter hour schedules. Some others were preparing for the shift, and reclassifying jobs and workers, explaining to workers why their wage grades were being reduced, while their base rates were usually to be increased. Work was being done on introducing tighter and better-based production standards.

Detailed accounts of the experience in different industries, which filled the pages of *Sotsialisticheskii Trud* from 1958 to 1960, put great emphasis on the search for ways to improve production in preparation for the shift, with participation of party and union committees and wide involvement of workers themselves. When it was thought that additional workers would be needed, ways were sought to improve efficiency, especially in the auxiliary services, in order to release workers, retrain them, and shift them to shops needing them. Often the result was to reduce substantially the need for additional workers and wage funds. Careful estimates were made of the effects on earnings of different groups, since wages were not to be decreased except where the old system had left some clearly out of line with others. Average earnings were expected to increase, but party and state policy demanded that productivity of labor must rise faster than wages.

Among many reports of early experience under the changed conditions, one from a plant producing reinforced concrete parts for construction will serve as an example. It had been expected that an additional wage fund of 625,000 rubles would be needed (old rubles), but improved methods reduced this to 124,000. Base rates were increased for piece workers by 49 to 70 per cent, and for time workers by 65.8 per cent. Production standards increased 41.6 per cent, and the average overfulfillment of norms decreased from 165 per cent to 120-125 per cent. Base rates, which had amounted to only 47 per cent of earnings, increased to an average of 69.5 per cent. Time work rose from almost none to cover 36.8 per cent of all workers. Average monthly wages increased from 931 to 947 rubles, with considerably larger gains in most shops and a temporary decrease in one. The volume of output and the number of workers increased 10 per cent and the wage fund 5.5 per cent. Daily output per worker was unchanged, while hourly output rose 12 per cent.[57]

The State Committee on Labor and Wages and the CCTU kept watch and urged union and management leaders to study and profit from the experience of plants that had already shifted. Mistakes were many, according to reports. In some plants preparations were inadequate, there was little involvement of the workers, and the sovprof and sovnarkhoz did not check adequately on the state of readiness before permitting the shift, with the result that production and productivity decreased. There were mistakes in applying the new wage and salary schedules. Production standards were not adequately revised, especially where there was too little use of the central standards. Uneconomic shifts to time work had adverse effects on productivity. In some instances the number of workers was unnecessarily increased. Improper decreases in earnings were permitted in some plants. Poor planning sometimes failed to supply the additional funds needed. Further improvement of wage conditions in individual enterprises, as well as of planning at the center, continued to be sought.[58]

Soviet authorities considered that the wage reform in industry had accomplished much by 1963 toward eliminating the worst of the defects in the former wage structure and systems. Although no comprehensive wage statistics are available, the results can be summarized, as follows, from many scattered sources and from the most extensive of the reports published in 1963 or 1964 by Soviet experts.[59]

Progress had been made toward uniformity in production standards. In many basic industries the proportion of technically based norms was as high as 70-80 per cent, although in the machine tool industry it was only 40-50 per cent, and for all industry only 50 per cent. Average fulfillment of norms in industry, nevertheless, decreased from 169 per cent to 118 per cent.

Wage rates had been substantially increased—doubled or more in the lowest grades. The share of wage rates in total earnings had increased from 30-50 per cent to 70-80 per cent, while payments for overfulfilling norms had decreased. The role of the base rates as the regulator of wage differences had grown.

Progress had been made toward simplifying and unifying the wage structure, presumably providing more equity. The number of wage schedules was reduced from some 2,000 to 6 basic schedules. In most industries the number of wage grades was reduced from as many as 10 or 12 to 6. Base rates for the lowest grade were reduced in number from some thousands to 40-50. At least some degree of uniformity had been brought about in differentials between industries, with consideration of working conditions, and, to a lesser extent, of the national significance of the industry. A degree of order and

unity had been brought into differentials for skill, although no
one was satisfied that a completely objective basis had yet
been attained. The range of rates between the lowest and
highest wage grades in most industries had been reduced to
1:1.8 or 1:2 for work under ordinary conditions; but rates for
work under difficult conditions went as high as 3.75 times the
lowest rates, as for underground work in coal mines. Rates for
hot, arduous, or harmful conditions were usually set at 10-15
per cent above those for ordinary work, sometimes more. The
number of salary scales had been reduced from 700 to 35, with
an effort to reduce inequalities between industries and between occupations. The highest salary for directors of industrial enterprises in important and difficult industries was set
at 6.7 times the lowest salary for engineering or technical personnel, and 10 times the lowest rates of wage earners.

A "serious step toward uniformity" in job evaluation had
been taken by the development of the Uniform Tariff-Qualifications Handbook for Universal Occupations and 235 revised
branch handbooks, most of them using the methods of evaluation developed by the Institute of Labor. The distribution of
workers by wage grades had been markedly changed, increasing the number of industrial workers in the two lowest
grades from little more than 3 per cent to 33 per cent. But
there were still inequities between industries in the strictness
of the handbooks and in the classification of jobs and workers
for wage grades.

A beginning had been made toward uniformity in geograph-
ical supplements to wages for different industries.

The multiplicity of piece work, time work, and premium
systems had been somewhat reduced. Some artificial piece-rate
systems had been eliminated and the proportion of workers on
time work had increased in all industry from 27 to 39 per cent.
Central regulations on premium systems for manual workers
and for engineering, administrative, and office workers had

established basic standards with the aim of increasing incentives. There were still complaints, nevertheless, that in many plants the possibilities for effective use of premiums were not fully utilized and that the share of premiums in earnings was less than had been assumed in the plans.

A summary of the results of the reduction of hours and the wage reform in industry—including manufacturing and mining—from 1956 to 1960 showed a reduction of hours by 16 per cent, a growth of earnings of manual and non-manual workers by about 15 per cent, growth of yearly productivity of labor by 37 per cent and of hourly productivity by more than 60 per cent. Growth of production was reported as 62 per cent, and lowering of costs as about 12 per cent.[60]

As to changes in earnings of different groups, all reports state unequivocally that average earnings increased, especially for the low-paid, that the number of low-paid decreased, and that the gap between their earnings and those of higher-paid people was significantly reduced. Only scattered data are available, but a number of reports coming from the publishing house of Gosplan are presumably based on the official statistics used in planning. In the materials branches of heavy industry, average earnings of wage earners were reported to have increased 15 per cent from 1956 to 1959, while office workers gained 9 per cent and engineering and technical personnel 10 per cent. Increases for workers in the machine-tool industry were 4 per cent, in light industry and the food industry 10 and 15 per cent, in railroad and automobile transport 12-15 per cent.[61] In 1963 it was reported to the CCTU that earnings had increased during the wage reform by 37 per cent in the coal industry, 11 per cent in iron and steel, 16 per cent in chemical production, 13 per cent in railroad and construction work, and 21 per cent on state farms.[62] The number in industry receiving 40 rubles or less per month reportedly decreased to one-fourth of their former number, and those receiving from 40 to 60 rubles to one-half or less, while the number with wages from 100 to 160 rubles a month almost doubled. Some excessively high-paid manual workers and engineers received cuts, while the number of comparatively low-paid engineering, technical and office workers, with salaries of 100 rubles or less, decreased by 60 per cent.[63]

Further evidence of the relatively large rise in earnings of wage earners and the reduction of extreme differences in incomes comes from a comparison of earnings of manual workers and of office workers with those of engineering and technical workers. From 1940 to 1960 average earnings of the engineering-technical group and of office employees increased about 90 per cent, while those of manual workers increased 2.4 times. In 1955, before the wage reform, average monthly earnings of engineers and technicians were 65 per cent above those of wage earners, but the difference had decreased by 1960 to 48 per cent. Office workers lost in comparison with manual workers during the entire twenty years. In 1955 their earnings were only 88 per cent of those of the manual workers, and in 1959, 80 per cent. Only in 1960, as the wage reform reached more of them, did they make some gain, up to 82 per cent of average wages.[64]

A reduction of the gap between high and low earnings is shown also in a study of the distribution of earnings of industrial wage earners published by the Institute of Labor in 1961, but without full details.[65] It indicated a reversal early in the 1950's of the trend toward increased differentiation in earnings that had been seen during the period of rapid industrialization. From 1946 to 1956 earnings of low-paid manual and nonmanual workers reportedly increased 4.2 times faster than those of the high-paid groups. From 1956 to 1959 the growth for the lower group was greater than for either the high-paid or the middle-paid group. All reports of changes since 1959 point toward further reduction of the gap.

Much seems to have been accomplished in the wage reform that accompanied the reduction of hours in the industrial sectors of the economy. A substantial payment had been made on the promise to raise the wages of the lower-paid workers, although some groups waited until 1964 or 1965 for their increases. Strengthened central regulation had brought more uniformity and equity into the wage structure. Wage and incentive systems had been simplified and on balance probably were more effective. But many problems continued both from poor administration of the new wage system and from defects in the plans and regulations.

PROBLEMS

In a planned economy as in a market economy, wages serve a number of ends. As a minimum they need to provide the necessities of life. Differentials should help to supply labor forces to occupations, industries, and regions according to needs. They should stimulate workers to get further training and to increase their efforts and initiative. The wage system needs to be understandable to workers and to seem to them equitable, if their attitudes toward their jobs are to be positively affected. Reflection of all such needs is found in extensive published discussions of the Institute of Labor of the State Committee on Labor and Wages and in publications of other economists.

A major problem is that of determining standards, when neither the impersonal forces of the market nor pressures from the parties in collective bargaining are allowed to be decisive, although the planners are never free from market influences. The Soviet policy in more recent years, of raising minimum and average wages and decreasing differentials, reflected the changed character of the working class, its increased levels of education, skill, and industrial experience, the growth of industry and national product and of productivity of labor, as well as the promises of the party to increase the standard of living of the population.

It is thought possible, on the other hand, or at least an attempt is made, to develop objective, scientific bases for determining wage levels and differentials. Studies of the minimum necessities of life and their costs give support to the establishment of legal minima. Studies are made of differing physical needs for life in the Far North and other difficult regions, of their costs, and of varying public provision of services for the inhabitants, all of which should influence money wages. Attempts are made to estimate needs of workers who perform heavy physical labor or work under other difficult conditions. A method was developed for analyzing the complexity of jobs as a basis for grading work and workers. It is recognized, nevertheless, that neither in theory nor in practice have completely objective bases for wage levels been achieved. Actual standards set also reflect historically developed relationships that are difficult to change and pragmatic attempts to meet particular problems of the labor supply.

Policies of decreasing differentials run into the problem of maintaining incentives. Raising earnings at the lower levels is said not to be "leveling." Equalitarianism is denounced as harmful to incentives for individuals to increase their skills and efforts. There is no easy and objective answer to the question of how much preference in earnings is needed for higher-skilled groups, foremen, engineers, and others, and for difficult conditions of work and life. There are many problems also as to the best form of incentives.[66] Frequent changes in central regulations and models show that these problems have a prominent place in the thinking of those responsible for wage regulation. The policy of "pay according to the quantity and quality of work" sets the problem, but objective answers have only imperfectly been found. The result is a workable but certainly rough approximation of the ideal.

In addition to such theoretical issues, many problems persist in the attempts to administer wages with uniformity and efficiency in the thousands of enterprises under hundreds of administrative authorities, the sovnarkhozy, local soviets, central and republic ministries. Lack of uniformity in the strictness with which work and workers are graded results in differences in wages for workers of similar skills, even in the same area. Still more serious, from the standpoint of central authorities who want the wage rates to be the basic regulator of wage differentials, is the continuing inequality in the tightness of production standards. This lessens the effectiveness of piece-rate systems as a stimulus to improvements in technology and organization as well as to individual efforts, and leads to inequalities in pay and to wasteful shifts of jobs. Enterprises get needed flexibility through manipulation of job evaluation, production standards, and premium systems, though to some degree they thus frustrate the efforts for uniformity through central regulation.

Inequities arise also in the planning of wage funds for enterprises. Some plants get relatively more generous assignments than others from the sovnarkhoz or other superior administrative organ. It is complained that, in planning wage funds and average wages, adequate consideration is not always given to the special conditions of each enterprise as to prospective production, types of workers, wage systems, and the character of production standards. Planning often starts with existing levels of average earnings, different percentages of overfulfillment of norms are assumed, and plants in an advantageous situation as to workers' earnings in the previous year may keep this advantage, although the result is failure to eliminate unplanned differentials. Defects in planning wage funds thus are among the reasons for inequities in earnings between similar workers in different plants, which lead to instability of labor forces.[67]

An uneasy balance continues between central control of policy and local administration in the wage field. There are pleas for more authority for regional agencies and enterprises to make needed adjustments. Whether there will be any extensive increase in local authority will depend on developments as a whole as the Soviet Union continues to seek the most workable combination of centralization and decentralization in planning and managing its economy. Strong central control over basic standards will surely continue.

What level of working hours is best under given conditions is another problem. At any time, with existing production levels, choice must be made between added income and added leisure. The party program adopted in 1961 set the goal of a decrease in ten years to the six-hour day with one day off, or a five-day, 35 hour week, with further reductions in the longer future. Experience in the shift to the seven- and six-hour day showed general increases in hourly productivity, but not universally in total productivity. The gains came both from improvements in technology and organization and from increased intensity of work. It is believed that while there is still room for some gains from the latter source in many fields with low productivity, gains in technology offer more possibilities for the long run. The great need for increased production precludes any drastic further cuts in hours in the near future. Reduction of hours as an answer to problems that may arise from automation seems a far-off prospect, since such great need continues for workers in many industries and in all the services essential for a rising standard of living.

The effect of working hours on the welfare of the workers is also considered. The use of free time is thought to be a matter of significance both for society and for the individual.

Free time should be increased, it is recognized, not only by reducing work hours, but by improving all the everyday services. In addition, emphasis grows on the need for increased educational, cultural, and recreational facilities. Significantly, in a study of the use of leisure time in a group of plants in Krasnoyarsk, large increases were found from 1959 to 1963 in time spent in study and reading, as well as in other recreation.[68] Scattered reports from other plants on experience in the reduction of hours showed increases in the number of workers studying. Reduction of hours is thought to be one of the ways to raise the educational and cultural levels of workers, which, in turn, helps the growth of production. The contribution to morale by a reduction of hours is also a consideration.

A major problem and a source of dissatisfaction in 1963-1964 was still the existence of substantial groups with exceptionally low incomes. Many of these were helped by the extension to the service fields of the 40 ruble minimum rate and the wage reform in 1964 and 1965. Low-paid groups were helped also by the abolition of income taxes on all with monthly incomes up to 60 rubles, along with a decrease for those with incomes of 60-70 rubles.[69] Low income families also get a larger addition to their real incomes from the increasing amounts of public funds and services than do the higher income groups. These subsidies from "public consumption funds" include the cost of education, medical care, social security benefits, part of the cost of housing, of child care institutions, rest and recreational facilities, and others. Studies of family budgets by the Institute of Labor indicate that for families with incomes up to 60 rubles a month, these public sources added 48 per cent to their incomes. For families with over 120 rubles, the addition was 16 per cent. On the average, benefits from public funds are estimated to add about one-third to the real incomes of wage and salary workers.[70]

Indications of dissatisfaction with wages are rarely published in the Soviet press. An exception was a public opinion poll on living standards, made by questionnaires distributed in coaches of all trains leaving Moscow on one day in 1960.[71] More than a third of the 1,399 returns were from workers. Higher wages were said by 27 per cent to be the most urgent problem; many of these reports were from groups not yet reached by the wage reform. Nearly three-fourths said that their standard of living had increased in recent years. Of 7 per cent who reported a decrease, most had retired or left work for health reasons or for study, but 24 persons had smaller earnings. Some reductions were from exceptionally high pay before the reform, but a few people complained of unjust wage decreases. Dissatisfaction with wages accounted only for a fourth or fifth of the quits, or less, in several studies of why workers leave jobs. Work satisfaction, according to a study of 436 workers in Leningrad in 1961, seemed to be correlated with the level of skill, but more often with the character of the work itself than with the pay.[72] Inequalities in earnings, nevertheless, have adverse economic effects as well as injurious effects on morale. Regional trade union officers comment that the unions hear constantly from workers about the need for wage increases in some fields. The unions provide at least a channel for bringing to the attention of the authorities the most urgent wage problems, as shown by the expressed feelings of their members.

The general level of earnings and the standard of living remain low, in spite of marked increases since the war and in the past decade. No comprehensive wage statistics have been published since the 1930's, but an American estimate of average annual money earnings of wage workers in Soviet industry, based on scattered data and reports of percentage increases, showed in new rubles (official exchange rate 1 ruble to $1.11) a gain from 925 rubles in 1950 to 1,190 in 1960 and 1,240 in 1961, or a 34 per cent gain over the period.[73]

Real wages, which had declined during the rapid industrialization and the war, rose rapidly after 1948—over 100 per cent between 1948 and 1954, according to an American scholar.[74] Further gains were achieved after 1954. Soviet authorities claim that the gain in real income per working person has been 61 per cent in ten years and 20 per cent in the five years ending in 1963.[75]

The meaning of these figures for the level of living is difficult to estimate. According to a Soviet economist, the average real per capita income in the Soviet Union in 1960 was 45 per cent of the American level, and for the working population, 55 per cent. Dr. Janet Chapman, however, estimated the real income of the average Soviet citizen as only one-fourth to one-third that of the average American.[76] A partial indicator of comparative living levels is the purchasing power of average wages in terms of food. An estimate for 1951-1952 found that the relative amount of food that an average hourly wage could buy was far less in the Soviet Union than in any of the other industrial countries studied, and less than one-fifth that in the United States.[77] In 1962 the approximate number of hours of work required to buy a week's consumption of selected foods for a family of four had decreased from 38 in 1953 to 30. The work time required to buy selected foods and items of clothing in 1962 in Moscow was estimated as from 4 to 19 times that in New York.[78]

In evaluating such comparisons, it must be remembered that the Soviet consumer has free education and medical and other services, very low rent for his small quarters, relatively good levels of pensions and disability benefits, and usually there is more than one wage-earner in the family. These compensating factors contribute substantially to the level of living in the USSR, although the actual level remains low in comparison with Western countries.[79] The marked progress of the past decade or so is a source of satisfaction to the Soviet people.

Their desire for continuing improvement in their material conditions is one of the strong reasons for supporting the programs for increasing production.

The 1961 program of the CPSU held forth the optimistic plan to increase the volume of industrial production in ten years by about two and a half times and the productivity of labor by more than twice. The real income of wage earners and salaried workers, including their share from public funds, was forecast to nearly double on the average in ten years, and for the low-paid groups to increase about three times. The workday and workweek were to decrease further. It was boasted that thus the Soviet Union would have "the shortest workday in the world and at the same time the most productive and most highly paid."[80]

Achievement of such high hopes appears doubtful. Rates of growth in the economy have been slowed by difficulties in agriculture and other problems. The prospects for growth in real incomes will depend on the extent to which these difficulties are solved. Competing needs will continue to be weighed against the desire for higher wages and more consumers' goods and services. Both money wages and the contribution of public expenditures to the welfare of the population can be expected to continue to rise and, as the lower-paid groups make relative gains, income differentials will probably decrease further. The extent will depend on economic realities and on decisions in the Communist Party as to how much can be done to meet the increasingly articulate expressions from the workers and all citizens of their desire for a higher standard of living.

CHAPTER XI

The Industrial Relations System: Problems and Prospects

THE status of Soviet workers and their unions and the nature of their relations with management are conditioned by the industrial technology and organization and by the social and political system, as these had developed by the fifth decade of Soviet rule.[1] In the state-owned and centrally planned economy, large scale industry predominates, but there are also numerous small enterprises. Modern technology, mechanization, and automation are increasingly prevalent, but in many fields inefficient hand labor continues. Managers are agents of the state. Workers have the right to choose their fields of work and their jobs, though exercise of this right is limited by many circumstances. Increasingly workers have a common educational background of seven or eight years of schooling; more and more of them also have, or are getting, secondary general, vocational, or technical training, or higher education. The rates of growth achieved in industrial production since the war have been very high, but in recent years there is evidence of a substantial slowing down.

All aspects of labor relations are affected by the dominance of the Communist Party, its monopoly of major decision-making and its ideological leadership. The general purposes of the Communist Party and its program for the future seem to be widely accepted, in spite of criticism and dissatisfaction on details. The people have been conditioned by communist ideology in more than forty years of Soviet rule, and relationships in industry are colored by such concepts as collectivism, the dream of a society of abundance and opportunity for all, and broad participation of citizens in the work of preparing for communism. The feeling of common interests is supported by constant propaganda in the press and by "agitation" and educational efforts by communists at all levels of life. Party membership among leading workers and among technical and management people provides an effective transmission belt for party policies and promotes mutual understanding and an acceptance of common purposes.

The Communist Party is dominant but it is not omnipotent, to quote a perceptive student of the Soviet system.[2] Although no organized opposition could exist, implementation of party policies has been limited by recalcitrance of the peasants, by extra-legal methods of industrial managers seeking to fulfill production plans, by graft and corruption occurring in all levels of society, by unwillingness of many workers to stay permanently on jobs in new areas, by failure of some to accept the responsibilities demanded of them for "communist relations to work." The party is limited also by resources that are inadequate to meet the mounting demands of the population for improvements in living conditions at a time when large expenditures are thought necessary for investment in heavy industry, for defense, science, and other needs.

Although the memory of the years of coercion and terror still remains, and undoubtedly inhibits free expression, the Soviet people, with their growing educational and cultural level and rising expectations, show more and more articulateness in expressing their aspirations for legality, "socialist democracy," and protection of individual rights. The party necessarily recognizes this. Increasingly after Stalin's death it

invited and organized mass discussion of particular major policies before new legislation was adopted. Many millions participated. When the party puts out a question for such discussion, the proposed policies and differing opinions on them get
wide publicity. Conflicts of opinion and interests undoubtedly
are threshed out in the councils of the party before decisions
are made. The party has ample means both to assess the state
of public opinion and to develop and influence it. Public opinion, though not controlling, may, and in some instances
apparently does, influence what the party decides is necessary
or feasible.[3] Without accepting Soviet definitions of democracy, it is possible to see that an important role is played by
widespread participation of the public at times in discussing
proposed policies, and in carrying them out.

Increasingly open protests are made against conditions that
cause discontent. Every year hundreds of thousands of letters
with complaints and suggestions are received by the press and
by party, governmental, trade union, and other agencies. Public opinion polls and investigations of attitudes by questionnaires and interviews also begin to supply illuminating
evidence on Soviet life, though limited by ideological re-
straints and in some instances by methodology.[4] Awareness of
all these reactions from citizens must to some extent condition
party decisions.

The interplay between central control and local opinion and
action is seen also in industry. While higher authority hands
down the larger part of the web of rules under which managers and the managed operate, these central regulations and
standards must be applied locally. The necessary local decisions could conceivably be left to the manager, subject to check
by the party and other higher authorities. To a degree this was
done during the 1930's and 1940's, the low ebb of union influence and the years of most compulsion in the labor field.
Increasingly such an authoritarian system failed to meet the

needs of the developing modern industry. By 1957 the party had decreed enlarged rights for the unions in the plants, along with more scope for regional and local managements. It called on the workers "to take an active part in the administration of industry." The result was to inject new life into local union activity, though under party leadership as before.

Thus, the control by the Communist Party and the state over industry and labor relations is accepted or evaded, strengthened or modified, perhaps at times humanized, by activity at the grass roots. Since human beings make the local decisions in applying general policies, the results turn out to be varied. Despite monolithic policies, individual plants are well or badly run, and union committees function democratically or to a greater or less degree are tools of the manager or the party boss; union and party leaders range from those who reflect the current ideology of democratic practices to those who are old-style bureaucrats, some of them corrupt; workers get protection and believe in the union or are disillusioned; the plants and the union committees generally observe the standards of the Soviet industrial relations system or, in varying degrees, fail to do so.

In this context of modern industry, party domination, central controls, and of local discussion, initiative, and decentralized decision-making, the workers live and work, the unions function, and labor-management relations develop. Extensive popular participation and, within limits, democratic processes characterize industrial and social life.

The status of Soviet workers depends on the controls, pressures, protections, opportunities and limitations provided in the social environment dominated by the Communist Party, which assumes to know what is good for the society and to have the right to make the crucial decisions. Workers are expected to conform to the communist principles of hard work and devotion to the common cause. There are equalitarian ideals, however limited in practice, for educational opportunity, provision of the necessities of life and of cultural development for all, and the dignity of all labor. The state takes a paternal care of workers, for their "upbringing" in communist attitudes and for their welfare, and is helped in this by all levels of the party, the Komsomol, the trade unions and other organizations. Real incomes, though still low, rose substantially in the two postwar decades, especially for the lower income groups. Pride in accomplishments and hope and confidence for the future are widespread, in spite of the economic difficulties that slowed the gains.

The constitutional duty to work and right to work result in opportunity for individual development and protection of interests, but also in pressure for conformity and strict and sometimes harsh discipline. The duty to engage in "socially useful labor" makes deviants subject to pressure from the group or the authorities. Possibilities of abuse of individual rights are inherent in the system and of concern to Soviet jurists. There are abuses in the exile of "parasites" and in the application of criminal penalties to "speculators" and others. The duty to work also means strict discipline on the job, enforced by administrative penalties and social pressure, but this is alleviated by the right of appeal through the grievance system. Efforts of many union committees to indoctrinate people and aid them in becoming good workers may help to develop a cooperative spirit and an environment in which people can work happily, but these efforts can also lead to boredom, resentment, unhappiness. The public pressure for conformity and discipline is sometimes unreasonable or unjust. Harmless non-conformity is sometimes suppressed. Pressure is used to silence critics, and for spite and personal advantage. Individuals who oppose particular policies or are indifferent may be harassed. A non-conformist, a person with open religious convictions, or one who wants to do his work without engaging in other group activities may be badgered or discriminated against. How the system works depends largely on the individuals who operate it. The courts often give protection against extreme abuses. Nevertheless, the drive for conformity to the pattern of "communist man" may be harmful to initiative, creativity, and morale, in industry as in literature and the arts.

In their right to choose their jobs, Soviet workers have an important weapon for asserting dissatisfaction and for improving their lot by moving. Yet workers become strongly attached to their enterprises. The remark, "Workers love this plant," was often heard in plants visited. This feeling for the collective is characteristic of many enterprises.

Free education supports the right to choose the type of work. Educational facilities are far from adequate, and some subjects are inadequately covered, yet it is probably true, as Soviet citizens say, that in general any able and hard-working young person can achieve finally the education he wants. The cost is often a strenuous combining of work and study, or loss of earned income that may be important to the family. But in the long run financial inability does not rule out getting further education. To obtain the necessary recommendations for admittance to an institute or university, the young person is wise to demonstrate the approved attitudes as a member of his work group and not to be known as a non-conformist or individualist.

Choice of work is not hampered by any extensive unemployment. State programs assist young people in getting started and allow considerable free choice even at this point; the young specialists are free to shift jobs after their required periods of work where assigned. In finding work and conditions that satisfy them, young workers create turnover that puts pressure on planning and administrative authorities to meet their needs, though it causes concern over wasteful shifts.

Continuing expansion of the economy provides an abundance of jobs, though not always in the immediate locality or in the worker's particular skill. There is no unemployment insurance since it is held that jobs are always available. A variety of local sources of information help workers find jobs. For those wanting to shift to other areas where workers are needed, help can be had through organized channels.

The claim that there is no unemployment is in part semantic, since the Soviets do not give that term to the existing frictional and seasonal unemployment or the losses of time and income in shifting jobs or from irregular work in plants. However, when technical or organizational changes reduce the need for labor, a major protection against unemployment lies in the reluctance to displace workers without assuring them other jobs or needed retraining. Workers are also protected by the law that defines permissible bases for discharge and by the right of unions to refuse consent, although many violations of these protections occur. For the most part, technologically displaced workers are with little difficulty retrained and shifted to other work, often in the same enterprise. But sometimes surplus staffs are kept on payrolls. Inefficient use of unnecessarily large numbers of workers is among the reasons for low productivity and low levels of income. Workers do not in large numbers suffer from unemployment, yet they suffer the effects of what may be called the Soviet equivalent of unemployment, through low incomes resulting from uneconomic use of manpower and through temporary losses of work time and income.

In many well-run enterprises the status of the workers is one of dignity—as people with rights and as participants in a joint endeavor in which they can use their capacities for their own advancement and for the collective good. Material and non-material incentives support their individual and collective efforts. The individual with initiative and creativity often finds scope for inventiveness on production problems or in solving problems affecting workers' welfare. Many workers appear to get satisfaction in developing their capacities and using their initiative.

When workers are dissatisfied with conditions or managements or unions, they can, and often do, protest in a variety of ways. Protests take initiative and persistence, and sometimes courage. At times the needed support from higher union officers or the party is lacking. Critics may be persecuted as troublemakers. Workers may hesitate to take the risks, knowing that for years the unions did little to protect members, and aware of the reports of long delays during which critics suffered and bad conditions continued. Nevertheless, workers know that in many reported cases protests led finally to rectification of wrongs. If the problem arises from lack of resources to make needed improvements the solution may be more difficult. Yet, in the long run, publicity on discontent over lacks may influence decisions of planning authorities. Improvements that have followed open protests encourage the spirit of independence and the willingness of workers to protest when their rights and interests are violated.

The unions are massive organizations that include most of the working people—except for collective farmers. Led by the Communist Party and carrying out the policies of the party and the state, they provide a well-organized line of communication between the country's top leadership and the workers. Messages and instructions go down through union channels—as well as party channels—to workers in their brigades and shops. Channels for upward communication exist also and are used, though how effectively it is impossible to say.

The first function of the unions is "the upbringing of the working people," the effort to develop communist attitudes and to promote cooperation and participation in the program for preparing for communism. All union activities are colored, or are supposed to be colored, by this educational purpose. In fact, rank and file participation in administrative, welfare, and cultural programs inevitably trains thousands, or millions, of people in the spirit of collectivism and mutual aid for the good of society.

Promotion of production is an appropriate function of the unions, if, as the leadership constantly reiterates, success in this sphere is necessary for the desired gains in standards of living and in individual incomes, both now and in the future. It is clear that this belief is widely held, even if skepticism and resistance to the constant pressure are also present. Broad programs that encourage participation in planning and in efforts to increase output are in part organized from above, and in some places they exist only on paper; but there is also evidence of grass-roots initiative and cooperation.

For such mass cooperation it is essential for workers to feel that their interests are protected and to have confidence in their local unions, the organizers of participation in administration. Recognition of this was behind the grant to the unions of broader powers. The traditional functions of unions in protecting the rights and interests of workers on their jobs then came into more prominence in the plants.

All these functions are closely related—the leadership, "upbringing" and discipline of workers, protection of their interests and rights and promotion of their welfare, and cooperation on production. While it cannot be said how effectively in general these functions are carried out, the unions in the plants seem in growing numbers to be recognized by the workers as a means through which they can influence their own work and lives. This is suggested not only by the stories of successes, but also by the fact that workers protest against failures. The statements heard frequently that the unions now have the confidence of workers and are popular with them, though far from universally true, have considerable basis in fact.

In the work groups, shops, and plants, where workers have their closest relations with the unions, the emphasis is on democratic processes and leadership, and on widespread participation by members. In huge numbers they attend meetings, discuss and criticize, and take part in electing their committees and officers and in carrying union responsibilities. While party units, higher trade union organs, and sometimes managements, exert influence in recommending candidates, and at times higher union bodies abuse their right of control over the lower units, union members in many cases reject officers who fail them, and elect the leaders they want. Yet there are numerous complaints that local unions and regional committees and councils violate the standards of "trade union democracy," have a bureaucratic "style of work," and neglect workers' problems. In many plants union committees are weak and inactive, especially in smaller enterprises. This may reflect poor leadership by the party or higher union organs, or by management, or ignorance or apathy among workers themselves, but the rising level of education among workers and constant propaganda as to their rights and those of their unions act against long continuation of such conditions. The policy adopted by the party that new blood should be brought into these organizations by replacing large numbers at each election was aimed in part to replace old officers who did not or could not cope with present needs. New local officers, supposedly more trusted by members and more effective, were elected, but it is not known to what extent union leadership at the regional level was changed.

At higher levels in the union hierarchy the relationship of members to the union inevitably becomes less close. Control from above becomes more prominent than control from below,

when union officers are farther from the workplace and nearer
to Moscow. Choice of officers is strongly influenced, or directed, by party and higher union bodies; key positions are
filled by party members. Nevertheless, at regional and national
conferences and congresses, and at sessions of the committees
and councils, according to many press accounts, elected delegates and members hear and discuss reports, and criticism
from below is encouraged so long as it is thought constructive
and not anti-Soviet.

The regional union organs, working closely with management agencies, put high on their agendas their responsibilities
to promote production. In many instances their concern for
production overrides their obligation to represent and protect
the workers, but their feeling of responsibility to the local
members must be increased by growing rank and file participation on commissions and public councils. In varying degrees
these regional committees and councils seek to influence planning and administrative agencies for more use of resources to
satisfy workers' needs and for better observance of standards
for their protection. Their independent initiatives, of which
many examples are reported, are within the limits of the general policies set by the current directives of the Communist
Party and the CCTU.

At the top, the union central committees and the Central
Council of Trade Unions, led by trusted communists, function
as agents of the Communist Party and the state, more like sections in a governmental department of labor than as independent trade union centers. The national union bodies are not
independent organizations expressing the will of their members. Their rights were given them by the party, not derived
from the power of the working class. At any time their work
is oriented to the current instructions from the party. But they
also have the duty and right to speak in the name of workers

before government bodies. National officers of the unions are communists first and union leaders second. Nevertheless, the interests of the party and the state require attention to the conditions of the work force. Top union leaders, as communists, have strong reasons for seeking the gains in living and working conditions that affect morale and confidence in the system. The CCTU functions as a watchdog over the unions, to see that they work along approved lines; but also to a degree it acts as a watchdog for the workers, seeking better protection of their interests.

The national union organs share formal responsibility in major decisions on wages and other legislation affecting workers. Union spokesmen assert that the unions press for further protection of workers' interests, but concrete evidence is limited. It is not impossible that, before decisions are made, the top leaders engage in negotiations approaching collective bargaining as they try to get as much for workers as they can in the whole complex of economic and political considerations. They have significant roles in analyzing issues important to workers, developing programs, and seeing that workers' needs and feelings are considered. Through union channels, leaders are aware of problems and discontents. They can keep before the policy makers the need for increased wages and more and better consumer goods and services. Although they have no power to change the distribution of national product to the workers' advantage, their efforts may lead at times to more concessions than had been contemplated. Whether union leaders have access to the full data on wages in the hands of the Central Statistical Administration and the State Committee on Labor and Wages, we do not know. The lack of regularly published wage statistics must limit the ability of unions at all levels to represent their members effectively on wage matters. Nevertheless, vigorous statements in recent years from the party and the CCTU indicate that the representing and guarding of workers' interests has a more prominent place in the programs of the national union organs than before the Twentieth Congress of the Communist Party.

It may turn out that the unions are in stronger position to work for their members' interests now that a central government agency on labor has been established with the particular duty to represent state interests—the State Committee of the Council of Ministers on Questions of Labor and Wages— though it also is expected to protect the rights of workers. While the CCTU is expected to consider the interests of society, as defined in party policy, it has the particular duty to protect workers, as well as to lead them. Though the responsibilities overlap, this division of functions gives the CCTU a better basis than earlier for speaking as advocate, not as neutral, on questions affecting workers. If, as some experts urge, the powers of the State Committee are further defined and increased, the position of the CCTU as representative of the workers may correspondingly be enhanced.[5]

Soviet unions thus are both like and unlike the traditional unions that developed in the West. Soviet unions are not responsible only to their members; they have explicit duties to the society as a whole, as defined by party policies. Nevertheless the unions are recognized as representing and protecting the interests of workers. Their public statements on workers' needs often seem cautious and lacking in independence, but their pressures may be stronger in the unpublished consultations and working out of joint decisions. Channels are available for more expression of workers' demands when more independence develops from below, as there are some signs of its doing. In the local unions, workers can more directly choose officers and press for effective use of the broad powers of their committees. Yet, to a degree, local unions fail to use their possibilities, and weak and subservient union leadership continues.

In labor-management relations, basic central rules result in a large degree of uniformity in structure and formal programs, and also in relationships. Nevertheless, there is a wide range of practice in individual plants, industries, and localities in the extent to which the established standards are followed. Local labor-management relations are sometimes in serious violation of the central rules. There can be little doubt, however, that the trend is toward more observance of labor laws and of the right of union committees to share in important decisions in the enterprises.

How the industrial relations system works, or is supposed to work, is frequently described in the Soviet press and in union books and pamphlets. Effective operation of the system was also seen in many plants that were open to the foreign visitor, presumably as good examples of Soviet industry. In these well-run plants the directors appeared to appreciate the need for good working and living conditions and good relations with workers and the union, and to recognize that workers could contribute through their initiative to the success of the enterprise and the welfare of the group. Union committees and officers in these plants cooperated with management in efforts to improve technology and organization, labor discipline, and the interest of workers in the results. Many union leaders interviewed also emphasized their duty and power to represent and protect the members who elected them. They talked like trade unionists as well as people with responsibilities for production. Many union committees used their powers with considerable effectiveness in seeing that workers' established rights were protected and in promoting both the welfare of their members and success in production. Frequently, also, the union took seriously its obligation to inculcate the spirit of responsibility, cooperation, and discipline. Pressures for conformity were strong.

In most of these plants it was evident that the increased rights of the union committees were actually used; the rights were not only doctrine but reality. Although managers had final authority and responsibility, management prerogatives did not prevent wide consultation and cooperation between workers, unions, and managers. Administrative authority was limited at important points by the necessity of getting agreement from the union. Relationships in many cases seemed to be in harmony with the standards of democratic procedures, joint consultation and decision, and observance of labor laws. There were signs of mutual respect and cooperation, recognition of human dignity and individual capacity, and encouragement of initiative.

On the other hand, according to reports in the press and in official statements, many plants and shops violate the approved standards of labor relations. There are arbitrary and tyrannical managers. There are working conditions far from established standards, crude violations of rules for protecting individuals, long persecution of critics. Although occasionally managers or other administrators on union demand lose their jobs or are otherwise penalized for persistent violations of obligations to workers, sometimes there is failure of union leaders in the plants and in regional and republic union organs to protest these violations. In many cases the desire to have "peace and quiet" and to "avoid spoiling relations" still prevents the militance and "demandingness" that union leaders are told they should show in protecting workers. Party committees also sometimes support managers who get out the production at the cost of violation of workers' rights.

The remedies available through many channels of individual and group protest, while often effective, do not always work promptly enough to satisfy workers. In extreme cases protests may develop into strikes or riots, although these are never reported in the Soviet press. Soviet spokesmen insist that there is no law banning strikes, but that stoppages are not needed, since so many other channels exist for settling disputes. In the early 1960's there was apparently an increased number of overt expressions of dissatisfaction. Some strikes, riots, and demonstrations were reportedly put down by force, but, significantly, ameliorative measures were taken also. Decrees of the party and the government, court decisions, and decisions of the CCTU called for improvements in provision of services for the people and for better observance of labor laws.

The range in the extent to which labor relations in Soviet plants meet the standards set for them is no doubt as great as that between Western plants with good local unions and good labor-management relationships and those where the opposite prevails. In seeking the reasons for such variations in local unions and labor relations in a totalitarian society, it may be doubted whether party policy-makers always want full enforcement of the standards, of labor legislation, or of protection of individual rights, or of democratic practices. An authoritarian system, it might be assumed, could achieve more complete observance of its published policies than has been done.

One problem, whatever the intention of the party, is in attempting to make standards universal in observance in a huge country. Until most recently there were over 100 economic regions, each with its economic and trade union councils. There are some 120,000 local unions in industrial plants, mines, construction, and transportation, and more than that number in other fields. Economic difficulties vary, as do abilities and attitudes among party, management, and union leaders. These affect results, in spite of strong central controls and efforts at education and enforcement by public pressures and by administrative action.

When Soviet lawyers or union or administrative leaders were asked about the many reported failures to follow approved standards, they answered in terms of people. "People differ, there are good and bad members of any family," and "It takes a long time to educate people, to develop in them changed attitudes." These experts insisted that the bad cases are exceptions, that increasingly workers are learning to demand their rights, and managements are learning to live with these demands and obey the laws. Undoubtedly personal differences among the hundreds of thousands of management people and union and party leaders help to explain the lags in acceptance of the standards. Some of these people are inefficient, unable to cope with their jobs. Some find it easier to operate on old dictatorial, "Stalinist" rules. In small enterprises, with less efficient managers and less experience with effective union committees, such attitudes are especially likely to be found; perhaps also in more recently developed areas and in non-Russian regions where the revolutionary tradition or trade union tradition is less strong.

Much of the continued violation of labor laws is accounted for by contradictions between pressures for production and pressures for observance of labor standards. There are still severe economic and technical difficulties. During the drive for industrialization and under war conditions, human rights and needs were subordinated to production, in the interest of "building socialism." Now, in the period of "construction of communism," production still has first place, in the interest of the strategic position of the Soviet Union and the ultimate aim of a communist society. Heavy industry still gets priority, although in word, and to a lesser extent in practice, increased attention is now given to the material needs and rights of the

people. Scarcity of capital and other resources limits the extent
to which demands can be met for better working and living
conditions.

Thus, it is easy for planners, administrative agencies, and
plant managers to put more stress on fulfilling production
plans than on the need to observe the labor laws. A manager
who is a good specialist and production man, but poor in human relations and observance of democratic processes, may be
allowed to operate in his own way without interference. Party
and administrative agencies in the regions, and even trade
union officers, may feel more strongly the pressures for production than the pressures from below, or from above, to observe the rules. Especially in industries and enterprises where
management finds difficulty in meeting production plans, the
plea that "production demands it" is frequently made an excuse for violating workers' rights. Officially, such an attempt at
justification is never acceptable. In practice, nevertheless, it is
sometimes accepted by regional economic councils and party
and union officials.

Although high authority in the party and the state apparently wants both the production and the protection of workers,
ambivalence on the priority to be given these needs is apparent throughout Soviet society, from the highest levels down to
the local managements and union and party leadership. In the
resolving of these dilemmas, both in particular cases and in
general policy, the human needs have not infrequently given
way to "production necessity." In all likelihood, there may be
doubt among many managers, workers, and local leaders of
the unions, party committees, and administrations that the
party really means its high sounding phrases, if the interests of
production appear to be at stake.

A shift of attention toward more satisfaction of workers' demands seems to have been influenced by attitudes in the working class itself. Workers have long been told of communist

ideals, and their increasing knowledge of their rights makes them more demanding. Growing willingness to risk standing up against wrongs is indicated by open mass protests and demonstrations and by the continuing individual protests against violations of rights. The authorities cannot now, without peril to morale and harm to the production effort, ignore the desire of workers for more democratic rights and protection and the better working and living conditions for which they have waited and worked. Many policy statements of the party show recognition of these aspirations and may be credited as expressions of the party's intentions, even though the policies are not fully enforced. The party must be aware that an increasingly educated and sophisticated working class would not long be fooled by policy statements not meant to be taken at face value and enforced.

A highly discreditable picture of Soviet labor relations can be, and sometimes is, drawn from the many reported cases of bad conditions and of violations of the code of labor relations, on the assumption that these are typical. Analysis must, however, include the fact that in many reported cases the final outcome was restoration of rights and, sometimes at least, punishment of those responsible; also, that these reports serve the purpose of education and pressure for reform, as well as providing a safety valve. The examples of good conditions must also be considered.

It is impossible to draw up an average or typical picture of Soviet labor relations. Clearly there is a wide range of conditions, but also pressure and movement toward observance of official policies. The many official statements of intention to increase the protection of workers and to give larger roles to the unions cannot be disregarded.

In brief, the industrial relations system in the Soviet Union, however imperfect in application, tends toward a constitutional system with large elements of worker-participation. At best the result is union-management cooperation within the framework of central planning and a common communist ideology. The system is characterized by initiative and creative use of energies in all levels of the work force. When standards are violated, management and unions are open to pressure from workers, the party, administrative and union agencies, public criticism in the press, and action in the courts. Human inefficiency and recalcitrance, old authoritarian methods, fears, pressures for production, all interfere, especially when economic conditions are difficult. Workers can make themselves heard, nevertheless, if they have courage and determination. The trend is toward an industrial relations system combining strong feelings of collective responsibility and common interests with opportunity for individuals to develop their capacities. At the same time, within the limits permitted by available resources and central policies, unions and their members participate in efforts to protect and expand the welfare of workers. It is understandable that in such a system strikes are not considered appropriate or necessary for settling disputes; but the lack of official approval of this weapon limits the possibilities for workers and unions in pressing for support of their interests and rights in extreme cases.

For the years immediately ahead, decisions as to the status of workers and the role of the unions will depend largely on economic and political developments, both domestic and international. Barring more serious difficulties, it seems probable that relaxations in control over labor will be continued or extended, and that protection of workers will grow and the rights and powers of the unions will be expanded. Trade unions, in all probability, will have increasingly important roles in Soviet society. How far the party will allow the unions to develop as representatives of workers' interests, remains a question. The unions in a communist society will continue to be led by communists and to follow the policies of the party. At the same time, since a modern industrial society needs a mechanism to insure that workers' interests are carefully considered, it is conceivable that as workers become more educated and experienced, the Soviet unions may be allowed more independently than now to express and defend the special interests of their members.

Soviet experience throws light on the question of whether there is a place for independent organization of workers under a planned economy, and especially in a modern industrial society that is centrally planned and under one-party control. Such a society needs managers who will carry out instructions and policies of the central planners and controllers, and who will exert initiative to further technical progress and to solve other issues left to their discretion. It also needs well-trained, industrious, enterprising, and cooperative workers at all levels. Labor organizations can serve both of these needs. An effective union in the plant can check on the administration's observance of labor standards and on its performance in planning and organizing production. It can stimulate and organize its members for participation in solving technical and organizational problems. For the workers, the union can serve as a means of education and indoctrination and also of protection and service.

To function effectively in these respects, unions must have the confidence and support of their members. As workers become more educated, they become more critical of unkept promises and violation of stated rights, and more independent in their attitudes. Accordingly, if unions are to fill the role expected of them, they must, in part at least, be agencies speaking for their members and responsive to opinion from below. The grant of broader powers to the unions in Soviet plants and localities has begun to meet this imperative. At the top level also, unions need to be able to speak freely for their members, even going beyond established party policies, since the successful working of the economy is vitally affected by the provision for workers' needs and by workers' feelings as to the equity of the use of resources, distribution of income, and protection of their interests. If unions are independent representatives of their members they can argue more effectively for the gains most needed. We cannot be sure, however, to what extent, if at all, Soviet unions at the republic and national levels can at present independently press for further gains for workers.

In a developing modern industrial society with an increasingly educated labor force, one essential need is for an organization to speak effectively for the working people, both as producers and as consumers. In the Soviet Union, and in other societies that combine a large degree of central planning and control with scope for local initiative and decision-making in the management of industry and community life, this role of spokesmen for the workers' interests is likely to be played by labor organizations with many of the traditional functions of trade unions and also with broader functions appropriate to a planned economy. These organizations will probably manage to blend, in some viable form, responsibility to their members and responsibility to the society as a whole, as defined in the predominant ideology and by the dominating political force. Their powers will be limited when one party has a monopoly of crucial decisions. Nonetheless, on major policy they will exert influence as consultants. In the enforcement and application of central policy and in decision-making in the plants and localities, they may have substantial power to promote the interests of the workers.

Bibliographical Note

Notes

Index

Bibliographical Note

Sources used in this study are primarily in Russian. Detailed references given in the footnotes will not be repeated here. This note supplements the "Note on Methods of Investigation and Sources" in Chapter I by indicating some of the most important documents and studies used on labor laws, trade unions, and labor relations in the past decade, which is the main interest in this book.

Works in English

Up to 1965 relatively little had been published on Soviet unions and labor legislation. Three indispensable studies of earlier policies and practices are Margaret Dewar, *Labour Policy in the USSR 1917-1928* (London, 1956); Isaac Deutscher, *Soviet Trade Unions* (London, 1950); and Solomon M. Schwarz, *Labor in the Soviet Union* (New York, 1952). A brief description of trade union structure and functions is provided by the International Labor Office, *The Trade Union Situation in the USSR* (Geneva, 1960). Detailed study of management, including material on unions and labor relations, is given by Joseph S. Berliner, *Factory and Manager in the USSR* (Cambridge, Mass., 1957), and David Granick, *Management of the Industrial Firm in the USSR* (New York, 1954), and *The Red Executive* (Garden City, 1960). For the position of unions and workers in the political system the best analysis is Merle Fainsod, *How Russia is Ruled* (Cambridge, Mass., 1963).

The United States Bureau of Labor Statistics has provided a useful collection of documents in *Principal Current Soviet Labor Legislation* (Washington, 1962); also *Labor Law and Practice in the USSR* (Washington, 1964). Studies of economic developments, including material on labor and wages, are reported by the Joint Economic Committee of the United States Congress, especially *Dimensions of Soviet Economic Power* (87th Congress, 2d session, 1962) and *Annual Economic Indicators for the USSR* (88th Congress, 2d session, 1964).

Two studies provide important evidence on the position of labor as to income distribution and real incomes: Abram Bergson, *The Real National Income of Soviet Russia since 1928* (Cambridge,

Mass., 1961) and Janet G. Chapman, *Real Wages in Soviet Russia since 1928* (Cambridge, Mass., 1963).

Soviet Documents

Statistical handbooks published regularly by the Central Statistical Administration since 1956 provide a large amount of data on the economy, but (until 1964) give no data on wages or distribution of income. They include *Narodnoe khozyaistvo SSSR v—gody* (National Economy of the USSR in the year—); and *SSSR v tsifrakh v—gody* (The USSR in Figures in the Year—).

The most convenient sources for labor laws, regulations and instructions issued by government agencies and the Central Council of Trade Unions are the collections *Sbornik zakonodatelnykh aktov o trude* (Collection of Legislative Acts on Labor; Moscow, Gosyurizdat, 1956, 1959, 1961) and *Spravochnik profsoyuznovo rabotnika* (Handbook of the Trade Union Worker; Moscow, Profizdat, 1949, 1958, 1960, 1962, 1964). These are selective and are said to give the most important documents, but they omit some significant decrees or orders not generally published. The same is true of the collections of decisions of the plenary sessions and of the secretariat and presidium of the CCTU, *Sbornik postanovlenii VTsSPS* (Collection of Decisions of the CCTU; Moscow, Profizdat, published quarterly) and *Postanovlenia plenumov VTsSPS 1954-1958* (Decisions of Plenums of CCTU 1954-1958; Moscow, Profizdat, 1961).

An encyclopedic dictionary published by the Bolshaya Sovetskaya Entsiklopedia, *Trudovoe pravo* (Labor Law; Moscow, 1959, 1963), is useful for definitions and descriptions.

The basic textbook on labor law for law students, N. G. Aleksandrov, *Sovetskoe trudovoe pravo* (Soviet Labor Law; Moscow, Gosyurizdat, 1954, 1959, 1963), in its successive editions outlines current law on the legal position of workers and unions, but is generally without explanation of changes or discussion of problems in practice. The textbook for students of technical institutes, Ya. L. Kiselev, *Osnovy trudovovo zakonodatelstva SSSR* (Bases of Labor Legislation, USSR; Moscow, Izdatelstv "Vysshaya shkola," 1964) is less theoretical and includes useful discussion of problems. The textbook on labor economics issued by the Central Council of Trade Unions, A. S. Kudryavtsev, ed., *Ekonomika truda v SSSR* (Labor Economics in the USSR; Moscow, Profizdat, 1957 and 1961) in addition to describing structure and policies gives considerable attention to actual practice and problems.

Trade Union Publications

Among the great number of works issued by the publishing house of the Central Council of Trade Unions (Profizdat) are the documents mentioned above and other collections of official material, a number of histories of particular unions, some valuable general descriptions of trade union work, and large numbers of pamphlets addressed to local trade union workers.

P. S. Petrov, ed., *Organizatsionno-massovaya rabota professional-nykh soyuzov* (Organizational-Mass-Work of Trade Unions; Moscow, 1961) gives a useful general description of union structure and functions. *Voprosy profsoyuznoi raboty, konsultatsii, kommentarii, otvety na voprosy* (Questions of Trade Union Work, Consultations, Commentaries, Answers to Questions; Moscow, 1961, 1963) provides detailed discussion of major aspects of union work, emphasizing official policies and also considerable data on operations and problems at local levels. A. Fastykovskii, *Profsoyuznomu aktivistu o trudovom zakonodatelstve* (For the Trade Union Activist on Labor Legislation; Moscow, 1962) is a detailed summary of major legislation and its application.

Pamphlets for training and help of local union officers and members since 1961 for the most part are included in the *Bibliotechka profsoyuznovo aktivista* (Little Library of the Trade Union Activist), issued twice a month. Many of them are listed in the footnotes. They include discussions of official policy and approved practices, written by staff members of the CCTU and other experts and union officers. There are also many accounts of particular problems in union organization and activity, written by local officers. These give much detail on methods of work and problems met, and in spite of the tendency to emphasize successes and give a glowing picture of activity, they provide much evidence on the operation of well-run unions.

All such union publications can make no claim of objectivity and they include no discussion of the basic problem of the character and position of unions in a system dominated by the Communist Party, or of the reasons for serious deficiencies of many unions in protecting the interests of workers. Nevertheless, their discussion of problems and lacks in the work, as well as of successes, gives much evidence useful for objective appraisal.

Collections of Studies by Economists and Legal Experts

Institutes of the USSR Academy of Sciences, other institutes, and universities publish many such collections, and also books in which chapters are written by different experts. These never question the basic assumptions and theory of their communist society, but within this framework many studies are made of theory and problems, with analyses of particular current issues and details on difficulties and efforts to solve them. Some of these studies are invaluable for data on policy and on problems.

From the Institute of Economics of the Academy of Sciences comes Ya. A. Kronrad, ed., *Problemy politicheskoi ekonomii sotsializma* (Problems of the Political Economy of Socialism; Moscow, 1959, 1961). From the Institute of State and Law of the Academy of Sciences: N. G. Aleksandrov, ed., *Trudovoe pravo v svete reshenii XXI syezda KPSS* (Labor Law in the Light of the XXI Congress of CPSU; Moscow, 1960) and L. Ya. Gintsburg, ed., *Uluchshenie uslovii truda rabochikh i sluzhashchikh* (Improvement of Conditions of Labor of Wage and Salary Workers; Moscow, 1963). From the Scientific-Investigation Institute of Labor of the State Committee of the USSR Council of Ministers on Questions of Labor and Wages are collections such as G. A. Prudenskii, ed., *Voprosy truda v SSSR* (Questions of Labor in the USSR; Moscow, 1958, and later editions).

Moscow University has published N. G. Aleksandrov, ed., *Novoe v razvitii trudovovo prava v period mezhdy XX i XXII syezdami KPSS* (New in the Development of Labor Law in the Period between XX and XXII Congresses CPSU; Moscow, 1961) and his *Sovetskoe gosudarstvo i obshchestvennost v usloviakh razvernutovo stroitelstva kommunizma* (The Soviet State and the Public under Conditions of Full-Scale Construction of Communism; Moscow, 1962). From Leningrad University comes F. M. Leviant and A. S. Pashkov, ed., *Pravovoe polozhenie professionalnykh soyuzov SSSR* (Legal Position of USSR Trade Unions; Leningrad, 1962).

Other Special Studies

Among the most valuable studies by Soviet scholars on questions of labor and labor relations are the following: On questions of the rights of workers, A. E. Pasherstnik, *Pravo na trud* (The Right to Work; Moscow, Academy of Sciences, 1951) and Ya. L. Kiselev, *Okhrana truda po sovetskomu trudovomu pravu* (Protection of Labor in Soviet Labor Law; Moscow, Gosyurizdat, 1962); on trade unions, A. V. Pyatakov, *Profsoyuzy i sovetskoe gosudarstvo* (Trade Unions and the Soviet State; Moscow, Gosyurizdat, 1960); on labor disputes, A. E. Pasherstnik, *Rassmotrenie trudovykh sporov* (Examination of Labor Disputes; Moscow, Gosyurizdat, 1958) and A. I. Stavtseva, *Poryadok rassmotrenia trudovykh sporov* (The System of Examination of Labor Disputes; Moscow, Gosyurizdat, 1960); on socialist competition, Institute of Labor of the State Committee on Questions of Labor and Wages, *Dvizhenie za kommunisticheskii trud v promyshlennosti SSSR* (The Movement for Communist Labor in USSR Industry; Moscow, Sotsekgiz, 1962).

Several studies provide valuable analyses of policy and practice on wages, with considerable statistical data. The most important are A. G. Aganbegian and V. F. Maier, *Zarabotnaya plata v SSSR* (Wages in the USSR; Moscow, Gosplanizdat, 1959); V. F. Maier, *Zarabotnaya plata v period perekhoda k kommunizmu* (Wages in the Period of Transition to Communism; Moscow, Ekonomizdat, 1963); studies from the Institute of Labor, E. I. Kapustin, ed., *Zarabotnaya plata v promyshlennosti SSSR i ee sovershenstvovanie* (Wages in USSR Industry and their Improvement; Moscow, Sotsekgiz, 1961), and S. I. Shkurko, ed., *Sovershenstvovanie organizatsii zarabotnoi platy* (Improving the Organization of Wages; Moscow, Ekonomizdat, 1961); E. I. Kapustin, *Kachestvo truda i zarabotnaya plata* (Quality of Labor and Wages; Moscow, Mysl, 1964); R. A. Batkaev and V. I. Markov, *Differentsiatsia zarabotnoi platy v promyshlennosti SSSR* (Differentiation of Wages in Industry USSR; Moscow, Ekonomika, 1964); also S. S. Karinskii, *Pravovoe regulirovanie zarabotnoi platy* (Legal Regulation of Wages; Moscow, Gosyurizdat, 1963).

Newspapers and Periodicals

The daily newspaper of the Central Council of Trade Unions, *Trud* (Labor) gives news of official policies, statements of the leaders, and accounts of life and problems in different enterprises and areas, although strikes or demonstrations are never mentioned. The union magazine *Sovetskie profsoyuzy* (Soviet Trade Unions) is useful for accounts of trade union life, although the most serious

difficulties get little or no attention. Two publications of the State
Committee on Questions of Labor and Wages and its Institute of
Labor, *Sotsialisticheskii Trud* (Socialist Labor) and *Trud i Zarabotnaya Plata* (Labor and Wages) include much technical discussion
of experience in administration of wages, production standards and
other questions, with an occasional valuable article on broad questions of policy and practice. The monthly *Byulleten* of the State
Committee gives the text of important current decisions.

Notes

(For abbreviations, see list facing page 1.)

CHAPTER I, THE POLITICAL AND ECONOMIC SETTING

1. *Pravda*, May 8, 1957, translated in *CDSP*, 9.18:16 (June 12, 1957).

2. *Trud*, October 29, 1963; *Voprosy profsoyuznoi raboty, konsultatsii, kommentarii, otvety na voprosy* (Questions of Trade Union Work, Consultations, Commentaries, Answers to Questions; Moscow, 1963), p. 29.

3. Sidney and Beatrice Webb, *The History of Trade Unionism* (London, 1920), p. 1.

4. *Trud*, November 20, 1962; *SSSR v tsifrakh v 1961 godu* (USSR in Figures in the Year 1961; Moscow, 1962), p. 32.

5. Many changes have been made over the years in structure and titles of the planning agencies. "Gosplan" is used here as the general term for the top planning agency.

6. For good descriptions of the system of economic planning and recent problems and reorganizations see A. Nove, *The Soviet Economy* (New York, 1961), pp. 73-95; idem, "Revamping the Economy," *Problems of Communism*, January-February 1963, pp. 10-16; Rush V. Greenslade, "Khrushchev and the Economists," *Problems of Communism*, May-June 1963, pp. 27-32.

7. Changes adopted in October 1965 provided for all-union and union-republic ministries to direct most industries, and for ultimate abolition of the regional economic councils, with an increase in decision-making authority of the enterprises. *CDSP*, 17.40:4-10 (October 27, 1965); 17.41:12-13 (November 3, 1965); and 17.42: 3-10 (November 10, 1965). Resulting changes in planning and administration cannot be covered in this book.

8. *SSSR v tsifrakh*, 1963, pp. 10, 141, 148.

9. Abram Bergson, *The Real National Income of Soviet Russia since 1928* (Cambridge, Mass., 1961); *SSSR v tsifrakh*, 1963, p. 73. For "A Note on the Availability and Reliability of Soviet Statistics" see Nove, *The Soviet Economy*, pp. 307-314.

10. Janet G. Chapman, *Real Wages in Soviet Russia since 1928* (Cambridge, Mass., 1963), pp. 145, 171; idem, "The Consumer in the Soviet Union and the United States," *Monthly Labor Review*, 86:11-13 (January 1963); *Trud*, January 24, 1964.

11. *Materialy XXII syezda KPSS* (Materials of the XXII Congress of the CPSU; Moscow, 1962), pp. 320-428, translated in *CDSP*, 13.45:3-16 (December 6, 1961) and 13.46:3-21 (December 13, 1961).

12. For example, A. I. Lukyanov and B. M. Lazarev, *Sovetskoe gosudarstvo i obshchestvennye organizatsii* (The Soviet State and Public Organizations; Moscow, 1961).
13. See the Bibliographical Note, pp. 333-338.

CHAPTER II, THE LABOR MARKET

1. An earlier form of this chapter was published in *Industrial and Labor Relations Review*, 10:179-200 (January 1957); also "A Note on Employment and Unemployment in the Soviet Union in the Light of Technical Progress," *Soviet Studies*, 12:231-240 (January 1961).
2. The 1962 conference had representatives from ninety statistical, scientific, and educational organizations. *TZP*, April 1962, pp. 34-39.
3. Murray S. Weitzman, Murray Feshbach, and Lydia Kulchycka, "Employment in the USSR," in Joint Economic Committee, Congress of the United States, *Dimensions of Soviet Economic Power*, 87th Cong., 2d sess., 1962, pp. 628-629.
4. N. Zabelin, in *ST*, February 1962, p. 26; F. I. Kotov, *Voprosy truda v semiletnem plane* (Questions of Labor in the Seven Year Plan; Moscow, 1960), pp. 94, 112-114.
5. The proportion of hand labor was still very high. In 1959 in all industry 40.7 per cent of workers in basic production were reported to be engaged in hand labor, compared with 61.3 per cent in 1925. In auxiliary work, transport, maintenance, and the like, 68.1 per cent was hand labor in 1959, and 91.4 per cent in 1925. *TZP*, October 1961, pp. 9-10.
6. Zabelin, p. 32; Kotov, pp. 114-115.
7. P. Podyachikh, "Trudovye resursy SSSR" (Labor Resources of the USSR), *ST*, February 1961, pp. 12-14. Another source was the able-bodied pensioners. Incentive to return to the labor force was given in a March 1964 decree liberalizing pension laws. In a broad list of fields and occupations pensions would be paid in addition to wages, up to 75 per cent of the pension in the Urals, Siberia and the Far East, 50 per cent in other regions; for agricultural work and underground work in mines, 100 per cent. *Trud*, March 6 and April 1, 1964. A million persons were expected to return to work.
8. Among many such discussions, Kotov, pp. 106-112; Zabelin, pp. 27, 33.
9. *TZP*, April 1962, p. 36.
10. *Ibid.* A similar report from the Kazakhstan Gosplan ap-

peared in *Izvestia*, November 14, 1964, p. 3, translated in *CDSP*, 16.46:25 (December 9, 1964). The Central Statistical Administration collects detailed reports on employment and makes them available to all government and economic agencies, but these are limited to the occupied population. Apparently there is no regular system of studying the extent and make-up of any people not currently employed but available for work. Cf. Ya. D. Katz, *Ocherki statistiki truda* (Essays in the Statistics of Labor; Moscow, 1960), p. 17; *TZP*, October 1962, pp. 43-44; Murray Feshbach, *The Soviet Statistical System: Labor Force Recordkeeping and Reporting since 1957* (Bureau of the Census, Washington, D. C., 1962), esp. pp. 13-32.

11. *Politicheskaya ekonomia* (Political Economy; Moscow, 1960), pp. 493, 525, 528.

12. The sentence of exile is given by public meetings of citizens or in some republics only by the People's Courts or the executive committees of local soviets. There is concern among jurists over abuses in practice. Many problems are reported in handling the exiles in places to which they have been sent. R. Beerman, "The Parasites' Law," *Soviet Studies*, 13:191-205 (October 1961), also 15:420-429 (April 1964); Harold J. Berman, *Justice in the USSR* (Cambridge, Mass., 1963), pp. 291-298. For the text of the law in the RSFSR see United States Bureau of Labor Statistics, *Principal Current Soviet Labor Legislation* (Washington, 1962), pp. 125-127. It has been reported that in 1961 in Moscow 2,000 persons were exiled as parasites and 8,000 were sent to work in Moscow. George Feifer, *Justice in Moscow* (New York, 1964), pp. 196-197.

13. A. S. Pashkov, *Pravovye formy obespechenia proizvodstva kadrami v SSSR* (Legal Forms of Providing Personnel to Production in the USSR; Moscow, 1961), p. 25.

14. *TZP*, April 1962, p. 36; V. Nemchinov, "Theoretical Problems of the Rational Distribution of Productive Forces," *Problems of Economics*, December 1961, p. 7, from *VE*, June 1961; M. Ya. Sonin, *Aktualnye problemy ispolzovania rabochei sily v SSSR* (Urgent Problems of the Utilization of Labor Forces in the USSR; Moscow, 1965), pp. 98-101.

15. M. Ya. Sonin, *Vosproizvodstvo rabochei sily v SSSR i balans truda* (Development of the Labor Force in the USSR and the Balance of Labor; Moscow, 1959), pp. 156-157; idem, *Aktualnye problemy . . .*, p. 246.

16. The text of the Labor Code of the Russian Soviet Federated Socialist Republic, which became the basic standard of labor law for the entire Soviet Union, is available in *Principal Current Soviet*

Labor Legislation, pp. 1-34. For the 1928 regulation on reduction of staffs, *Sbornik zakonodatelnykh aktov o trude* (Collection of Legislative Acts on Labor; Moscow, 1959), p. 64.

17. *Trud,* November 30, 1962. The collegium on civil affairs of the RSFSR Supreme Court issued a formal statement that "the administration is obligated to take active measures for placement" of a worker discharged in reduction of staff. *ST,* February 1964, p. 150.

18. *Trudovoe pravo, entsiklopedicheskii slovar* (Labor Law, Encyclopedic Dictionary; Moscow, 1959), pp. 450-451.

19. *Sbornik zakonodatelnykh aktov o trude,* 1959, pp. 65-66, 319-320; Pashkov, pp. 28-31. Notably for those displaced in the abolition of central ministries in 1957, for women removed from underground work in mines, workers who lost jobs in the reorganization of the machine-tractor stations, released members of the armed forces, and amnestied persons.

20. Sonin, *Aktualnye problemy . . . ,* p. 111.

21. A. E. Pasherstnik, *Pravo na trud* (The Right to Work; Moscow, 1951), p. 165.

Penal labor is not included in the scope of the present study. The largest use of such labor is believed to have been in the late 1930's. The number of forced laborers is not known, but a recent estimate concludes that there may have been 3 million in 1937 and 3.5 million in 1940 and perhaps in 1950, and 2 million in 1955. Amnesties after Stalin's death released large numbers. Abram Bergson, *The Real National Income of Soviet Russia Since 1928* (Cambridge, Mass., 1961), pp. 96, 447.

22. Solomon M. Schwarz, *Labor in the Soviet Union* (New York, 1952), pp. 98-103. For the early history see also Margaret Dewar, *Labor Policy in the USSR 1917-1928* (London, 1956).

23. The law of June 26, 1940 (*Vedomosti verkhovnovo soveta SSSR,* Records of the Supreme Soviet, 1940, No. 20) provided penalties of imprisonment for two to four months for leaving jobs without permission, and lesser penalties for absenteeism or lateness without adequate excuse. For experience under the law see Schwarz, pp. 106-155, and Jerzy G. Gliksman, "Recent Trends in Soviet Labor Policy," *Monthly Labor Review,* 79:767-775 (July 1956). For the text of the repeal see *Principal Current Soviet Labor Legislation,* pp. 63-65. The draft of youth for the Labor Reserve schools had been repealed in March 1955, *ibid.,* p. 58.

24. N. G. Aleksandrov, *Sovetskoe trudovoe pravo* (Soviet Labor Law; Moscow, 1959), pp. 50, 52, 169.

25. Pashkov, pp. 10-21.

26. A. S. Kudryavtsev, ed., *Ekonomika truda v SSSR* (Economics

of Labor in the USSR; Moscow, 1961), pp. 392-395, 550-558; N. N. Zabelin, G. N. Zelenskii, F. I. Kotov, V. T. Roshchin, *Planirovanie podgotovki i raspredelenia rabochikh kadrov v SSSR* (Planning the Preparation and Distribution of Labor in the USSR; Moscow, 1960), ch. ii.

27. Zabelin, Zelenskii, *et al.*, esp. pp. 47-50. This Gosplan publication gives forms for a number of these accounts. For every branch of activity the total balance for an area should give the planned numbers of workers by sex and occupation, the sources for new workers, and the deficit or surplus of workers in the various fields. Also Kudryavtsev, pp. 411-413, 550-570.

28. Zabelin, Zelenskii, *et al.*, p. 28.

29. Sonin, *Aktualnye problemy* . . . , pp. 244-251.

30. For a rather idyllic account see "When the Coal Mines Closed Down," *USSR Illustrated Monthly*, August 1962, pp. 57-59.

31. *Trud*, November 30, 1962.

32. The chairman of the Moscow regional trade union council held that mechanization of such operations in Moscow in 1963-1964 could free 45,000 people for other work. *Trud*, December 25, 1962.

33. Sonin, *Aktualnye problemy* . . . , pp. 105-106, 111-112, 246.

34. A. Orlov, "Some Problems of the Rational Use of the Labor Resources of an Economic Administrative Area," *Problems of Economics*, November 1962, pp. 43-46.

35. United States Department of Health, Education and Welfare, *A Report on Social Security Programs in the Soviet Union* (Washington, D. C., 1960), pp. 8-9.

36. *ST*, July 1962, pp. 23-24, 26-27, February 1963, pp. 131-132; *Izvestia*, August 13, 1964, p. 3.

37. *Narodnoe khozyaistvo SSSR v 1962* (National Economy of the USSR in 1962; Moscow, 1963), p. 460; Podyachikh, pp. 13-14.

38. Sonin, *Aktualnye problemy* . . . , pp. 207-212, also ch. iv; *TZP*, October 1962, pp. 40-45; *ST*, July 1962, pp. 19-21, 26-27, September 1964, pp. 138-144.

39. Sonin's 1965 book, *Aktualnye problemy ispolzovania rabochei sily* is a careful, realistic analysis of these problems.

40. For the English text, Nicholas DeWitt, *Education and Professional Employment in the USSR* (Washington, 1961), pp. 556-574. For later discussion see his "Education and the Development of Human Resources: Soviet and American Effort," *Dimensions of Soviet Economic Power*, pp. 235-268.

41. Zabelin, Zelenskii, *et al.*, chs. iii and iv; Kudryavtsev, pp. 493-517.

42. "Polytechnical" is a term used for basic instruction in math-

ematics, science and technology and in production techniques, with specific training in some specialized occupational skill.

43. The earlier system of vocational education included full-time factory schools, which until 1940 were the basic form of preparation of young skilled workers for mass production and which continued to serve the needs of light industry; and from 1940 the Labor Reserve Schools for skilled trades in heavy industry, mining, construction, and railroads, and later in agriculture. For details see DeWitt, *Education and Professional Employment,* chs. ii, iii. The Labor Reserve system, established in 1940 as one of the measures that tightened control over labor before the war, provided for a draft of urban and rural youth for two-year trade schools and six-month factory schools. Desertion was a criminal offense. Graduates were required to work for four years where sent.

To what extent the quotas given collective farms and cities in early years were filled by volunteers is not known, though officials later described the compulsion as having applied to villages, rather than to individuals. Later, the enrollments were said to have been entirely from volunteers. The draft was repealed in 1955. The schools served as a route by which rural children and others could get a start toward industrial jobs and opportunity for further education. In the middle 1950's increasing mechanization and the rising level of general education led to two-year mining schools and full-year schools for operators of agricultural machinery. Technical schools for secondary school graduates were established to prepare highly qualified personnel and junior technicians for industry.

44. In the Ukraine in 1961 more than two-thirds are reported to have continued study. In Moscow, in 1960, of all eighth-grade graduates, 75 per cent entered the ninth grade. In Leningrad in 1962 two school directors interviewed said that 15 per cent or less went to work, most of the rest to eleven-year schools, and a few to vocational schools, while the most able went to specialized technical schools. *Rost tvorcheskoi aktivnosti rabochevo klassa SSSR* (Growth of Creative Activeness of the USSR Working Class; Moscow, 1963), p. 228; *Uchitelskaya Gazeta,* July 10, 1960, quoted in Klaus Mehnert, *Soviet Man and His World* (New York, 1962), p. 135. *The New York Times,* August 13, 1964, stated that 40-50 per cent of eighth grade graduates have been taking full-time jobs.

45. *Trud,* January 24, 1964; *Narodnoe khozyaistvo,* 1962, pp. 551-554, 562.

46. N. G. Aleksandrov, ed., *Trudovoe pravo v svete reshenii XXI syezda KPSS* (Labor Law in the Light of Decisions of the XXI Congress of the CPSU; Moscow, 1960), pp. 163-193; Pash-

kov, pp. 100-105, 117-118; *ST*, April 1962, pp. 142-145; DeWitt, *Education and Professional Employment*, pp. 239-241.

47. Among many discussions, Sonin, *Aktualnye problemy . . . ,* pp. 258-265; G. Zelenko, "Podgotovka rabochikh kadrov na sovremenom etape" (Preparation of Workers in the Contemporary Stage), *ST*, January 1962, pp. 11-23; *Trud*, September 1, 1963.

48. R. A. Medvedev, "On Selecting an Occupation in Secondary School," *Soviet Education*, February 1963, pp. 35-41, from *Shkola i Proizvodstvo* (School and Production), April 1962; DeWitt, *Education and Professional Employment*, pp. 17, 86-88.

49. Pashkov, pp. 113-117; Kotov, pp. 135-137; DeWitt, *Education and Professional Employment*, pp. 169, 242-246, 254-256.

50. For a summary of discussions see Frederick Lilge, "The Soviet School Today," *Survey*, July 1963, pp. 92-104. For the changes in policy, *Pravda*, August 13 and 15, September 1, 1964; *Trud*, July 14, August 13, 1964, March 20, 1965.

51. Pashkov, pp. 80-99; Zabelin, Zelenskii, *et al.*, pp. 100-117.

52. *Narodnoe khozyaistvo*, 1962, p. 15; *SSSR v tsifrakh v 1963 godu* (USSR in Figures in 1963; Moscow, 1964), pp. 18-19, 149.

53. E. I. Kapustin, *Kachestvo truda i zarabotnaya plata* (The Quality of Labor and Wages; Moscow, 1964), p. 124.

54. Zelenko, in *ST*, January 1962, pp. 21-22. The 11 regions included 6 in Russia, 3 in the Ukraine, and Uzbekistan and Armenia. The percentages expected from each source were as follows:

Released from other enterprises	48.1
Individual and group training in enterprises	31.2
Vocational schools	10.4
Secondary schools with production training	3.0
Specialized technical schools	2.1
Prepared in other enterprises and sovnarkhozy	2.5
From organized recruitment systems	2.0
Other	0.7

55. K. Urzhinskii, "Trudoustroistvo molodezhi v SSSR" (Labor Placement of Youth in the USSR), *ST*, October 1963, pp. 108-114; also April 1963, pp. 150-151; *Trud*, March 12, 1964; Zabelin, Zelenskii, *et al.*, pp. 86-90. A similar system of quotas was used in the 1920's to assure jobs for youths in a time of unemployment. L. Ya. Gintsburg, ed., *Uluchshenie uslovii truda rabochikh i sluzhashchikh* (Improvement of the Conditions of Labor of Wage and Salary Workers; Moscow, 1963), pp. 236-241.

56. *Pravda*, December 26, 1964, from *CDSP*, 16.52:24-25 (January 20, 1965); Sonin, *Aktualnye problemy . . . ,* p. 267.

57. Pashkov, pp. 16-18, 26-30, 120-135; DeWitt, *Education and Professional Employment*, pp. 204, 360-363. The system of

directing graduates to work with a term of obligatory work for three years where sent was established in 1928. The 1940 adoption of the Labor Reserve System provided for placement and an obligatory four-year term of work for graduates of the Labor Reserve Schools. Before the repeal of the 1940 laws these young graduates, like all other workers, were liable to harsh criminal penalties if they left jobs without permission or failed to take the jobs assigned. We have no evidence of the extent to which such penalties were used. In later years they were replaced by moral pressure. The obligatory term of work for vocational school graduates seems to have been dropped. Ya. L. Kiselev, *Osnovy trudovovo zakonodatelstva SSSR* (Bases of USSR Labor Legislation; Moscow, 1964), pp. 76-79.

58. *ST*, August 1963, pp. 153-154, January 1964, pp. 147-148, March 1964, pp. 145-146; *Izvestia*, March 15, 1964.

59. Schwarz, pp. 51-53.

60. Kudryavtsev, p. 539.

61. Sonin, *Aktualnye problemy* . . . , pp. 254-255.

62. *Literaturnaya Gazeta*, September 10, 1957, translated in *CDSP*, 9.42:7 (November 27, 1957).

63. Sonin, *Vosproizvodstvo rabochei sily* . . . , pp. 229-230, 358; *TZP*, January 1960, p. 52; *SGP*, August 1961, pp. 7-8; *ST*, October 1963, pp. 112-113.

64. Sonin, *Aktualnye problemy* . . . , pp. 247, 255-257. See also articles by V. N. Shubkin in *Voprosy Filosofii*, May 1965, pp. 57-70, translated in *CDSP*, 17.30:3-9 (August 18, 1965); E. Manevich, *VE*, June 1965, pp. 23-30; V. Yagodkin and I. Maslova, *VE*, June 1965, pp. 31-39 and *Trud*, August 12, 1965; V. Nemchenko, *VE*, September 1965, pp. 54-61.

65. Schwarz, pp. 53-64; V. Moskalenko, "Voprosy organizovannovo nabora rabochikh" (Questions of the Organized Recruitment of Workers), *ST*, April 1960, pp. 72-78.

66. V. S. Andreev, P. A. Gureev, *Organizovanny nabor rabochikh v SSSR* (Organized Recruitment of Workers in the USSR; Moscow, 1960); Zabelin, Zelenskii, *et al.*, ch. v.

67. Sonin, *Vosproizvodstvo rabochei sily* . . . , pp. 177, 186-189, 207; Zabelin, Zelenskii, *et al.*, p. 135.

68. Sonin, *Vosproizvodstvo rabochei sily* . . . , ch. x.

69. *ST*, June 1961, p. 23.

70. For critical discussion see Sonin, *Vosproizvodstvo rabochei sily* . . . , pp. 214-220, 358; Moskalenko, pp. 75-78; *Izvestia*, Sept. 15, 1962; Weitzman, Feshbach, and Kulchycka, pp. 638-641.

71. Pashkov, pp. 143-148. See also J. R. Azrael, "Is Coercion

Withering Away?" *Problems of Communism,* November-December, 1962, pp. 13-14.

72. Sonin, *Vosproizvodstvo rabochei sily* . . . , pp. 231-249; Gintsburg, pp. 247-251; *Pravda,* November 6, 1959, June 26, 1962.

73. For an excellent study see R. Fakiolas, "Problems of Labor Mobility in the USSR," *Soviet Studies,* 14:16-40 (July 1962); also Mary Harris, "Social Aspects of Labour Turnover in the USSR," *British Journal of Industrial Relations,* November 1964, pp. 398-417.

74. I. Kaplan, "Anketnoe obsledovanie prichin tekuchesti kadrov v promyshlennosti sovnarkhozov" (Questionnaire Study of the Causes of Labor Turnover in Industry of the Regional Economic Councils), *TZP,* April 1961, pp. 33-39, translated in *Problems of Economics,* December 1961, pp. 42-47.

75. I. Kaplan, "Tekuchest kadrov na predpriatiakh i puti ee ustranenia" (Labor Turnover in Enterprises and Methods of its Elimination), *VE,* October 1963, pp. 47-48.

76. Fakiolas, pp. 18-21.

77. Kaplan in *VE,* pp. 47-48; in *TZP,* pp. 38-39; Podyachikh, p. 26.

78. V. Perevedentsev, "Voprosy territorialnovo pereraspredelenia trudovykh resursov" (Problems of Territorial Redistribution of Labor Resources), *VE,* May 1962, pp. 50, 52-55, translated in *CDSP,* 14.26:3-6 (July 25, 1962); *Pravda,* March 1, 1963.

79. Perevedentsev, p. 51.

80. Kaplan, in *VE,* pp. 45-47.

81. Kaplan, in *TZP,* April 1961, pp. 33-39; in *VE,* October 1963, pp. 45-54; and in *Ekonomicheskaya Gazeta,* February 23, 1963, pp. 32-33.

82. Perevedentsev, pp. 52-54.

83. *Trud,* December 2, 1964, p. 3.

84. Feshbach, pp. 14, 33-34.

85. *ST,* September 1961, pp. 52-55.

86. *Principal Current Soviet Labor Legislation,* pp. 63-65, 120.

87. Among many such discussions of causes and remedies, Kaplan in *VE,* pp. 48-54; Perevedentsev, pp. 55-56; *Partinaya Zhizn* (Party Life), no. 17 (September 1963), pp. 22-27, 36-37; *ST,* December 1963, pp. 45-50, August 1964, pp. 125-130; *Sbornik postanovlenii VTsSPS, April-June 1962* (Collection of Decisions of CCTU; Moscow, 1962), pp. 44-48.

88. *Trud,* August 1 and September 8, 1963, April 21 and July 19, 1964; *SP,* no. 2 (1965), p. 43.

89. *Politicheskaya ekonomia,* 1960, pp. 523-528.

90. S. S. Karinskii, in *SGP*, January 1962, p. 46.

91. V. F. Maier, *Zarabotnaya plata v period perekhoda k kommunizmu* (Wages in the Period of Transition to Communism; Moscow, 1963), ch. vi.

92. Cf. Murray Yanowitch, "Trends in Soviet Occupational Wage Differentials," *Industrial and Labor Relations Review*, 13: 166-191 (January 1960).

93. Kotov, p. 161; Kudryavtsev, pp. 308-311; Maier, pp. 148-150.

94. M. Mozhina, "Changes in the Distribution of USSR Industrial Workers according to Wages," *Problems of Economics*, April 1962, pp. 21-26, from *TZP*, October 1961, pp. 18-25.

95. G. Gendler, "Tekhnicheskii progress i tarifnaya sistema" (Technical Progress and the Tariff System), *ST*, February 1962, p. 56; E. I. Kapustin, ed., *Zarabotnaya plata v promyshlennosti SSSR i ee sovershenstvovanie* (Wages in Industry in the USSR and their Improvement; Moscow, 1961), pp. 59-65.

96. D. N. Karpukhin, *Sootnoshenie rosta proizvoditelnosti truda i zarabotnoi platy* (Correlation of Growth of Productivity of Labor and Wages; Moscow, 1963), p. 64.

97. I. A. Orlovskii and G. N. Sergeeva, *Sootnoshenie rosta proizvoditelnosti truda i zarabotnoi platy v promyshlennosti SSSR* (Correlation of Growth of Productivity of Labor and of Wages in USSR Industry; Moscow, 1961), pp. 50-52.

The relationship of average wages in 1959 was as follows:

All industry	100	Chemical	92.7
Coal	182.7	Woodworking	85.7
Iron and steel	128.9	Leather, fur and	
Oil	103.9	footwear	82.9
Paper	102.7	Textile	78.8
Machine tool and		Food	73.8
metal fabrication	99.8	Sewing	65.8

A report published in 1964 gave average wages for a few industries, compared with the food industry as 100: for textiles 107; machine tools 135; iron and steel 166; coal 230. This indicates a little narrowing of the gap, as the 1959 level for iron and steel and coal, according to the data above, was respectively 175 and 247, in comparison with the food industry. *Ekonomicheskaya Gazeta*, January 25, 1964, supplement, p. 4.

98. A. G. Aganbegian and V. F. Maier, *Zarabotnaya plata v SSSR* (Wages in the USSR; Moscow, 1959), pp. 184-186; Maier, pp. 248-251; Kapustin, ed., *Zarabotnaya plata . . .*, pp. 55-95.

99. Kapustin, ed., *Zarabotnaya plata . . .*, p. 93; also Kapustin, *Kachestvo truda i zarabotnaya plata*, pp. 293-295.

100. Aganbegian and Maier, pp. 191-198; Maier, pp. 256-270.
101. *ST*, August 1960, pp. 136-140; December 1962, pp. 133-134.
102. Kapustin, ed., *Zarabotnaya plata* . . . , pp. 94-95; Maier, pp. 268-270. See also for a later discussion, Kapustin, *Kachestvo truda i zarabotnaya plata*, ch. vi.
103. I am indebted for this phrase to Dr. Robert J. Myers of the United States Bureau of Labor Statistics.

CHAPTER III, TRADE UNIONS—DEVELOPMENT, PRINCIPLES AND STRUCTURE

1. N. Antropov, *The Role of Trade Unions in the State and Economic Life of the USSR* (Moscow, 1961), p. 23; *Trud*, October 29, 1963.
2. *Ustav professionalnykh soyuzov SSSR*, 1963 (Statute of the Trade Unions of the USSR).
3. This summary history relies largely on the definitive history of trade unions in the first decade by Margaret Dewar, *Labour Policy in the USSR, 1917-1928* (London, 1956); and for this period and later, Isaac Deutscher, *Soviet Trade Unions* (London, 1950), Solomon M. Schwarz, *Labor in the Soviet Union* (New York, 1952) and his unpublished study, *Trade Unions in the USSR* (Processed, 1953). Also useful are a number of publications since 1957 from the Central Council of Trade Unions, including a series of brief studies of the congresses of the trade unions.
4. Z. A. Astapovich, *Pervye meropriatia sovetskoi vlasti v oblasti truda* (First Measures of Soviet Power in the Field of Labor; Moscow, 1958); L. I. Petrova, *Sovetskie profsoyuzy v vosstanovitelny period 1921-1925* (Soviet Trade Unions in Reconstruction Period 1921-1925; Moscow, 1962).
5. *Proizvodstvenno-massovaya rabota professionalnykh soyuzov* (Production-Mass-Work of Trade Unions; Moscow, 1958), pp. 136-141; Petrova, pp. 59-68; Dewar, pp. 126-129.
6. E. Oparkina, *VII syezd sovetskikh profsoyuzov* (VII Congress of Soviet Trade Unions; Moscow, 1958), p. 37.
7. A. V. Pyatakov, *Profsoyuzy i sovetskoe gosudarstvo* (Trade Unions and the Soviet State; Moscow, 1960), pp. 83-86; R. Dadykin, *VIII syezd sovetskikh profsoyuzov* (VIII Congress of Soviet Trade Unions; Moscow, 1957), pp. 62-67. For the purge, Merle Fainsod, *How Russia is Ruled* (Cambridge, Mass., 1963), pp. 157-158, 310-311.
8. G. A. Prudenskii, ed., *Voprosy truda v SSSR* (Questions of

Labor in the USSR; Moscow, 1958), pp. 163-181. For a vivid account of life in industry at this time see John Scott, *Behind the Urals* (Cambridge, Mass., 1942), esp. pp. 34-36, 150-156. For the Stakhanovite movement see Maurice Dobb, *Soviet Economic Development since 1917* (New York, 1948), pp. 429-442; David Granick, *Management of the Industrial Firm in the USSR* (New York, 1954), pp. 243-252.

9. Schwarz, *Labor in the Soviet Union,* pp. 100-106.

10. *Ibid.,* pp. 303-307.

11. Fainsod, pp. 439-444. Rather detailed Soviet accounts of trade union life at this time are given in *Profsoyuz stroitelei* (Trade Union of Builders; Moscow, 1959), pp. 79-112; A. Slutskin, V. Sidorenko, *Profsoyuzy Ukrainy posle pobedy velikovo Oktyabrya* (Trade Unions of the Ukraine after the Great October Victory; Moscow, 1961), pp. 111-152; *Profsoyuz tekstilshchikov* (Trade Union of Textile Workers; Moscow, 1963), pp. 80-134.

12. Pyatakov, pp. 87-88, 117-119; *Profsoyuz stroitelei,* pp. 118-124; *Profsoyuz tekstilshchikov,* pp. 139-160.

13. *Spravochnik profsoyuznovo rabotnika* (Handbook of the Trade Union Worker; Moscow, 1949), pp. 451-468.

14. *Profsoyuz tekstilshchikov,* pp. 185-186.

15. Deutscher, pp. 128-129; I. Markov, *X syezd sovetskikh profsoyuzov,* 1949, pp. 12-18, 29-30.

16. *Ustav professionalnykh soyuzov SSSR,* 1949, 1954.

17. Reports of the congress appear in *CDSP,* 6.23:22-28 (July 21, 1954) and 6.24:20-22 (July 28, 1954).

18. *Postanovlenia plenumov VTsSPS, 1954-1958* (Decisions of Plenary Sessions of CCTU, 1954-1958; Moscow, 1961), p. 33; also decisions of August 10, 1955; June 30, 1956; June 11, 1957.

19. *Sbornik zakonodatelnykh aktov o trude,* 1961 (Collection of Legislative Acts on Labor; Moscow, 1961), pp. 24-32.

20. *Ibid.,* pp. 530-534.

21. Decree of January 31, 1957. *Ibid.,* pp. 454-462. The English text is available in the United States Bureau of Labor Statistics, *Principal Current Soviet Labor Legislation* (Washington, 1962), pp. 92-100.

22. Decree of July 15, 1958, *Sbornik zakonodatelnykh aktov o trude,* pp. 37-40; *Principal Current Soviet Labor Legislation,* pp. 107-111.

23. Decree of July 9, 1958, *Sbornik zakonodatelnykh aktov o trude,* pp. 41-43; *Principal Current Soviet Labor Legislation,* pp. 103-106.

24. *Materialy XXII syezda KPSS* (Materials of the XXII Con-

gress of CPSU; Moscow, 1962), pp. 107-108, 320-428, esp. 401-402. The English text of the Program is available in *CDSP*, 13.45:3-16 (December 6, 1961), and 13.46:3-21 (December 13, 1961).

25. I. Dvornikov, V. Dzhelomanov, A. Shtylko, *Professionalnye soyuzy SSSR* (Trade Unions, USSR; Moscow, *BPA*, no. 13, 1961), p. 3.

26. *Ustav kommunisticheskoi partii Sovetskovo Soyuza* (Statute of the Communist Party of the Soviet Union), 1958, sec. 67-68.

27. The concept is discussed in detail in an authoritative publication of the CCTU, P. S. Petrov, ed., *Organizatsionno–massovaya rabota professionalnykh soyuzov* (Organizational-Mass-Work of Trade Unions; Moscow, 1961), pp. 18-27.

28. *Ibid.*, p. 32.

29. In sections 151 and 158. *Sbornik zakonodatelnykh aktov o trude*, 1959, pp. 420-421; *Principal Current Soviet Labor Legislation*, pp. 24-26.

30. *Ustav professionalnykh soyuzov*, 1949, 1954, preamble and sec. 2.

31. *Postanovlenia plenumov VTsSPS 1954-1958*, p. 92.

32. *Ustav*, 1959, preamble, sec. 44.

33. *Materialy XXII syezda KPSS*, p. 401. "Employees" always means white collar, salaried employees, as against manual workers.

34. *Ustav*, 1963, preamble.

35. In 1964, however, union committees began to be set up on collective farms. It was reported early in 1965 that about 40,000 such committees had been organized, including over two million chairmen of collective farms, specialists, and machine operators, salaried employees, but apparently not the rank and file collective farmers. *SP*, no. 5 (March 1965), p. 3; *Trud*, April 16, 1965, p. 2.

36. A detailed description is given by P. S. Petrov in the CCTU textbook for schools of the trade union movement, *Organizatsionno-massovaya rabota professionalnykh soyuzov*. See also *Ustav*, 1959, 1963.

37. International Labor Office, *The Trade Union Situation in the USSR* (Geneva, 1960), pp. 69-70; *Sputnik Profgruporga* (Guide for the Group Organizer; Moscow, 1960), p. 24. Other publications of the CCTU also give the number of unions as twenty-two, e.g. *Voprosy profsoyuznoi raboty* (Questions of Trade Union Work; Moscow, 1963), p. 23. A number of publications, on the other hand, indicate twenty-three unions; e.g. S. Boriskin, *Trade Unions in the USSR, Organizational Structure, Forms and Methods of Work* (Moscow, 1960), p. 4; A. I. Lukyanov, B. M. Lazarev, *Sovetskoe gosudarstvo i obshchestvennye organizatsii* (The Soviet State and

Public Organizations; Moscow, 1961), p. 80. It has been said that the twenty-third union is the latest formed, and covers "medium machine building," or atomic energy operations.

38. Petrov, p. 78.

39. Report of Chairman Grishin to Thirteenth Congress of the trade unions, *Trud,* October 29, 1963; also December 25, 1962. At a later CCTU session Grishin suggested the possibility of further changes in union structure in view of the establishment of the larger sovnarkhozy and other larger administrative agencies, including state committees on certain industries. *Trud,* June 27, November 29, 1964.

40. *Trud,* November 22, 1962, October 29, 1963.

41. *Sbornik postanovlenii VTsSPS,* April-June 1962 (Collection of Decisions of CCTU; Moscow, 1962), p. 20.

42. Petrov, pp. 41-49; *Ustav,* sec. 4.

43. Decision of CCTU of August 4, 1960, *Sbornik postanovlenii presidiuma i secretariata VTsSPS January-September 1960* (Collection of Decisions of Presidium and Secretariat of CCTU; Moscow, 1961), p. 386.

44. Reports of Chairman Grishin and of auditing commission of CCTU, *Trud,* October 29, 1963. For each union organization the number of its paid workers, their salaries, and the wage fund are approved by a superior union organ. *Financy professionalnykh soyuzov SSSR* (Finances of the USSR Trade Unions; Moscow, 1961), pp. 88-90, also 4-6, 26-27.

45. *Ustav,* 1959, 1963, secs. 2 and 3.

CHAPTER IV, THE TRADE UNION CENTERS

1. *Ustav professionalnykh soyuzov SSSR,* 1959, 1963 (Statute of Trade Unions of the USSR). The 1959 statute appears in *Spravochnik profsoyuznovo rabotnika* (Handbook of the Trade Union Worker; Moscow, 1962), pp. 134-150. The 1963 statute was published in *Trud,* November 13, 1963.

2. The congresses are reported in considerable detail in *Trud,* March 24-April 2, 1959, October 29-November 3, 6, 13, 1963. Cf. also S. Schwarz, "Chto zhe dalshe? Profsoyuzy na svoem XIII syezde" (What Further? Trade Unions at their XIII Congress), *Sotsialisticheskii Vestnik,* November-December 1963, pp. 141-148, 151-152.

3. *Trud,* March 24, 1959, October 29, 1963.

4. *Ibid.,* March 26, 1959.

5. *Ibid.,* October 31, 1963.

6. *Ibid.*, March 24, 1959, October 29, 1963, translated in *CDSP*, 11.12:3-11 (April 22, 1959), and 15.44:5-10 (November 27, 1963).
7. *Trud,* November 1, 1963.
8. *Postanovlenia plenumov VTsSPS 1954-1958* (Decisions of Plenums of CCTU; Moscow, 1961), pp. 120-122.
9. *Trud,* March 28, 1959.
10. Published in *Trud,* April 2, 1959.
11. *Ibid.*, November 2, 1963. The statute was not published until November 13, 1963, apparently giving time for further editorial changes.
12. *Trud,* November 2, 1963.
13. *Ibid.*, November 3, 1963.
14. Lists of the membership of the CCTU appear in *Trud,* March 28, 1959 and November 3, 1963. For the list of delegates to the XXI Congress of the Communist Party, *Vneocherednoi XXI syezd kommunisticheskoi partii Sovetskovo Soyuza, stenograficheskii otchet* (Special XXI Congress of the Communist Party of the Soviet Union, Stenographic Report; Moscow, 1959), vol. II, pp. 553-602. The list of members of the Central Committee of the Communist Party elected in 1961 is in *Materialy XXII syezda KPSS* (Materials of the XXII Congress, CPSU; Moscow, 1962), pp. 454-457.
15. *Ustav,* 1963, sec. 29, d. The fullest description of the structure and work of the unions is in P. S. Petrov, ed., *Organizatsionno-massovaya rabota professionalnykh soyuzov* (Organizational-Mass-Work of Trade Unions; Moscow, 1961). For a detailed analysis of the personnel and operations of the CCTU presidium, secretariat, and staff, see Ph.D. thesis of Edwin B. Morrell, "Communist Unionism: Organized Labor and the Soviet State" (Department of Government, Harvard University, September 1965), chs. v-vii.
16. *Trud,* October 29, 1963; *SP,* no. 4 (February 1964), p. 18.
17. *Trud,* October 14, 1962.
18. *Ibid.*, July 22, 1961, November 26, 1964.
19. F. M. Leviant and A. S. Pashkov, eds., *Pravovoe polozhenie professionalnykh soyuzov SSSR* (Legal Situation of Trade Unions in the USSR; Leningrad, 1962), pp. 67-74; A. A. Abramova in N. G. Aleksandrov, ed., *Sovetskoe gosudarstvo i obshchestvennost v usloviakh razvernutovo stroitelstva kommunizma* (The Soviet State and the Public under Conditions of Full-Scale Construction of Communism; Moscow, 1962), pp. 195-203; *Trud,* February 22, 1962.
A similar function is played by the republic councils of trade unions for their areas. A. I. Lukyanov and B. M. Lazarev, *Sovetskoe gosudarstvo i obshchestvennye organizatsii* (The Soviet State and Public Organizations; Moscow, 1961), pp. 110-111. For a summary by a Soviet legal expert see A. Piatakov, "Labor Administration by

the State and the Trade Unions in the USSR," *International Labor Review,* 85:558-572 (June 1962).

20. Many decisions of the State Committee are published in its monthly *Byulleten* (Bulletin).

21. *Materialy XXII syezda KPSS,* pp. 320-428.

22. Leviant and Pashkov, pp. 72-74; *SGP,* August 1961, pp. 5-7.

23. Lukyanov and Lazarev, p. 107.

24. *Ibid.,* p. 111. The draft was published in *ST,* October 1959, pp. 3-16, translated in *CDSP,* 11.42:5-10 (November 18, 1959). Among many discussions, *ST,* February 1960, pp. 41-47; Ya. L. Kiselev, in N. G. Aleksandrov, ed., *Novoe v razvitii trudovovo prava v period mezhdu XX i XXII syezdami KPSS* (New in the Development of Labor Law in the Period between XX and XXII Congresses of the CPSU; Moscow, 1961), pp. 202-208.

The 1922 labor code of the RSFSR, with amendments to 1958, is available in United States Bureau of Labor Statistics, *Principal Current Soviet Labor Legislation* (Washington, 1962), pp. 1-34.

25. Abramova, pp. 198-203; Lukyanov and Lazarev, pp. 98-99.

26. I. Dvornikov, V. Dzhelomanov, A. Shtylko, *Professionalnye soyuzy SSSR* (Trade Unions of the USSR; Moscow, BPA, no. 13, 1961), pp. 52-53.

27. Abramova, p. 199. See also Gaston V. Rimlinger, "The Trade Union in Soviet Social Insurance; Historical Development and Present Functions," *Industrial and Labor Relations Review,* 14:397-419 (April 1961); Leviant and Pashkov, pp. 75-81. The social insurance fund is used partly for payments made directly by the enterprises for benefits to workers; the rest is transmitted to the local union, which keeps part for passes for workers for sanitaria and rest homes, cultural activities, and others, and transmits a planned amount to the CCTU; the CCTU uses part for social purposes and sends the rest to the Ministry of Social Security of each republic. U.S. Department of Health, Education and Welfare, *A Report on Social Security Programs in the Soviet Union* (Washington, 1960), pp. 76-77.

28. A fund made up of allocations from planned and over-plan profits, and used by agreement of the director and the plant committee for individual bonuses and improvement of services, housing, cultural, and production facilities.

29. *Sbornik postanovlenii presidiuma i secretariata VTsSPS* (Collection of Decisions of the Presidium and Secretariat of the CCTU; Moscow), vols. from 1960 through September 1962.

30. Ya. L. Kiselev, *Okhrana truda po sovetskomu trudovomu pravu* (Protection of Labor in Soviet Labor Law; Moscow, 1962),

pp. 170-171; Abramova, pp. 191-195; Lukyanov and Lazarev, pp. 102-104.

31. *Trud,* October 29, 1963.

32. Many of these instructions are included in *Spravochnik profsoyuznovo rabotnika,* issued every two years or so, and in *Sbornik postanovlenii VTsSPS.*

33. *Spravochnik profsoyuznovo rabotnika,* 1960, pp. 20, 22.

34. *Materialy XXII syezda KPSS,* pp. 226-227, 314-315, 401-402.

35. *Trud,* November 25, 1961; June 21, 1962; *Sbornik postanovlenii VTsSPS,* October-December 1961, pp. 20-21.

36. *Trud,* November 2, 1963.

37. Merle Fainsod, *How Russia is Ruled* (Cambridge, Mass., 1963), pp. 212-213, interprets the new party rules as a "form of permanent purge."

38. For instructions approved by the CCTU presidium on July 20, 1962, *Sbornik postanovlenii VTsSPS,* July-September 1962, pp. 57-67; and on January 17, 1964, *ibid.,* January-March 1964, pp. 40-50.

39. A further detail, from instructions of the party congress, was that in electing committees by secret ballot all who received a majority of the votes cast were considered elected, even if this resulted in electing a different number than had been planned. It was explained that in some cases "experienced, valuable workers" had been defeated because there were some votes against them, although they had a majority of all votes. *Trud,* June 21, 1962. This would apparently reduce the danger of rejection by a marginal vote of a candidate recommended or approved by the party or higher union authority.

40. For example, resolution of the CCTU presidium, July 1, 1960, on the results of reports and elections, *Spravochnik profsoyuznovo rabotnika,* 1960, pp. 256-259. For another analysis see Morrell, pp. 161-173, 271-272, 338-339, 369-376.

41. Petrov, pp. 156-157.

42. *Organizatsionno-massovaya rabota profsoyuzov, sbornik rukovodyashchikh materialov* (Organizational-Mass-Work of Trade Unions, Collection of Leading Materials; Moscow, 1962), pp. 209, 228-229.

43. See Jerry F. Hough, "The Technical Elite vs. the Party," *Problems of Communism,* September-October 1959, pp. 56-59; Nicholas DeWitt, *Educational and Professional Employment in the USSR* (Washington, 1961), pp. 463-466.

44. I am indebted to Edwin B. Morrell for the opportunity to read a document, "Nomenklatura of positions of directing officials

who are confirmed and released by decrees of the presidium and secretariat of CCTU," decree of presidium of CCTU, October 31, 1959. See Morrell, pp. 173-190, 380.

45. *Trud,* March 30, 1961.

46. *SP,* no. 24 (December 1964), pp. 2-3.

47. Professor Merle Fainsod reports that "trade union elections serve merely to ratify decisions which the party has already reached. At the lowest level, however, in the shops, factories and similar units, union members exercise some choice. . . . Ordinarily, however, an approved slate is prepared in advance by the party organization, and the party caucus operates to make sure that 'democracy' does not get out of hand." *How Russia is Ruled,* pp. 518-519.

48. *Trud,* March 6, 1963.

49. Petrov, pp. 155-157.

50. *SP,* no. 20 (October 1960), p. 10.

51. *Trud,* November 2, 1963; *Ustav,* 1963, sec. 20.

52. International Labor Office, *Trade Union Rights in the USSR* (Geneva, 1959), pp. 77, 136, 142.

53. Fainsod, pp. 322, 326-327, 333.

54. The CCTU puts out its daily newspaper *Trud* in an edition of more than a million and a half copies. Nine newspapers are published by central committees, many of them in cooperation with a ministry or state committee. Newspapers are published by unions in about two hundred large enterprises. There are twenty-three weekly, twice a month or monthly magazines published by the CCTU, central committees and other union organizations, in addition to forty-three technical journals published jointly by central committees and government agencies for different industries. The CCTU journals include a general trade union magazine, one on protection of labor and social insurance, one directed to women, one to club workers, and another on amateur art activities. The CCTU publishing house puts out a large number of books and brochures, over three hundred in 1961, in huge editions. The *Handbook of the Trade Union Worker* for 1962 had an edition of 350,000 copies. A series of popular pamphlets, detailed discussions of practical problems and experience, comes out twice a month with editions ranging up towards 200,000. Dvornikov, *et al.,* pp. 96-102.

55. *Trud,* February 16, 1963, October 29, 1963.

56. Petrov, pp. 72-77.

57. *Trud,* June 21, 1962.

58. *Ibid.,* April 4-29, 1962, June 21, 1962, August 30-October 16, 1963, November 2, 1963.

59. Petrov, p. 76; *Ustav professionalnykh soyuzov SSSR,* 1963, sec. 35. After the 1965 decision on reorganization of planning and

industrial management, Chairman Grishin of the CCTU announced that it would be necessary to increase the role of the central committees for participation with the industrial ministries on planning, wages, improvement of working conditions, etc. The CCTU, with the central committees and the regional trade union councils, were authorized to make the necessary decisions. The sovprofs were to continue to have important roles in relation to the local unions of their areas. *Trud,* November 2 and 5, 1965.

60. *Trud,* March 26, 1959.

61. *Ibid.,* October 29, 1963; Piatakov, pp. 568-570.

62. Kiselev, *Okhrana truda,* pp. 54-66, 166-167, 170-175; Abramova, pp. 203-204.

63. Petrov, p. 75.

64. *Trud,* March 25, 1959, December 22, 1962.

65. *Ibid.,* October 29, 1963.

66. *Sbornik postanovlenii VTsSPS,* January-March 1961, pp. 3-13; July-September 1962, pp. 39-45. Such sharp criticisms did not always lead to replacement of officers. At the 1962 congresses the food workers elected a new chairman, but the chairman of the construction workers was re-elected.

67. *Trud,* September 28, 1962, September 21, 1963.

68. *Ibid.,* September 22 and 28, October 9, 1963.

69. *Ibid.,* September 11, 1963.

70. *Ibid.,* April 18, 1962. A month later the CCTU issued a strong statement directed both to the ministry and to the central committee of the union on how they should improve working and living conditions and promote stability of work forces. *Sbornik postanovlenii VTsSPS,* April-June 1962, pp. 49-57.

CHAPTER V, REGIONAL TRADE UNION COUNCILS

1. The responsibilities and powers are listed in the *Ustav profes-sionalnykh soyuzov SSSR, 1963* (Statute of the Trade Unions of the USSR), and in the regulation on republic, territorial and regional trade union councils, approved by the presidium of the Central Council of Trade Unions, August 17, 1957. *Spravochnik prof-soyuznovo rabotnika,* 1962 (Handbook of the Trade Union Worker; Moscow, 1962), pp. 150-154.

2. P. S. Petrov, ed., *Organizatsionno-massovaya rabota profes-sionalnykh soyuzov* (Organizational-Mass-Work of Trade Unions; Moscow, 1961), p. 88.

3. *Narodnoe khozyaistvo SSSR v 1962 godu* (National Economy of the USSR in the Year 1962; Moscow, 1963), p. 21.

4. *Spravochnik profsoyuznovo rabotnika*, 1962, pp. 167-168.
5. *Trud*, April 18, 1963.
6. Petrov, p. 88.
7. *Trud*, February 27, August 24, 1962.
8. Petrov, ch. v, esp. pp. 83, 91.
9. *Ibid.*, pp. 86, 89. This was argued also in an editorial in *SP*, no. 24 (December 1964), pp. 1-3.
10. For sources, see supra, ch. iv, fn. 14.
11. *Sbornik postanovlenii VTsSPS*, October-December 1960 (Collection of Decisions of CCTU; Moscow, 1961), pp. 26-31, 38-42; *Trud*, July 28, 1962, March 6, October 29, 1963.
12. *Sbornik postanovlenii VTsSPS*, April-June 1961, pp. 7-13; July-September 1961, pp. 35-43; April-June 1962, pp. 19-24; July-September 1962, pp. 17-26.
13. *Trud*, July 28, 1962, October 29, 1963.
14. *Ibid.*, June 20, 27, 1962; *SP*, no. 3 (February 1963), pp. 15-16.
15. *Trud*, August 30, 1962.
16. *Sbornik postanovlenii VTsSPS*, July-September 1962, pp. 198-199; *Petrov*, pp. 160-164; *Trud*, April 24, 1964. For an appraisal of the volunteer movement in Soviet community life see Robert G. Wesson, "Volunteers and Soviets," *Soviet Studies*, 15: 231-249 (January 1964).
17. *Trud*, November 20, 1962. In 1963 about 56 per cent of all industrial enterprises had two hundred workers or less, and employed nearly 10 per cent of all industrial workers. The nearly 10 per cent of enterprises with over one thousand workers had about 58 per cent of all workers. *Narodnoe khozyaistvo SSSR*, 1963, p. 129.
18. *SP*, no. 1 (January 1963), pp. 15-16.
19. *Trud*, December 22, 1963.
20. For example, an agreement in Rostov for 1958; also *Sovnarkhoz i zhizn* (Sovnarkhoz and Life; Kharkov, 1959), pp. 83-84; *Trud*, June 18, July 11, 1964.
21. Cf. Chairman Grishin's report to Thirteenth Congress, *Trud*, October 29, 1963.
22. Report to Twelfth Congress, *Trud*, March 24, 1959; to Thirteenth Congress, *Trud*, October 29, 1963.
23. A. A. Abramova, in N. G. Aleksandrov, ed., *Sovetskoe gosudarstvo i obshchestvennost v usloviakh razvernutovo stroitelstva kommunisma* (The Soviet State and the Public under Conditions of Full-scale Construction of Communism; Moscow, 1962), pp. 205-207.
24. For example, resolutions on the work in Leningrad and

Sverdlovsk, Saratov, and Tadzhikestan, *Sbornik postanovlenii VTsSPS*, January-March 1961, pp. 51-55; July-September 1961, pp. 79-84; January-March 1962, pp. 56-59.

25. Ya. L. Kiselev, *Okhrana truda po Sovetskomu trudovomu pravy* (Protection of Labor in Soviet Labor Law; Moscow, 1962), pp. 176-188. Regulations of the Central Council of Trade Unions on technical inspectors, August 17, 1957, January 17, 1958, *Spravochnik profsoyuznovo rabotnika*, 1962, pp. 212-216; Criminal Code of RSFSR, secs. 138, 140, *ibid.*, p. 226.

26. *Pravda*, May 7, 1960, in *CDSP*, 12.20:17 (June 15, 1960); *Trud*, July 22, 1961, October 29, 1963. There is no general publication of accident rates, but they are believed to be very high.

27. *SP*, no. 24 (December 1962), p. 34.

28. *Kiselev*, pp. 196-204.

29. *Sbornik postanovlenii VTsSPS*, January-September 1960, pp. 276-279.

30. *Trud*, March 23, April 5, May 11, 1961.

31. *Ibid.*, October 29, 1963.

32. *Ibid.*, December 4, 1963, January 14, March 18, 1964.

33. *Ibid.*, February 22, 1962; L. Ya. Gintsburg, ed., *Uluchshenie uslovii truda rabochikh i sluzhashchikh* (Improving Working Conditions of Workers and Employees; Moscow, 1963), pp. 181-184, 186-187, 192-195.

34. *Sbornik postanovlenii VTsSPS*, April-June 1962, pp. 124-129.

35. Kiselev, pp. 181-184; *SP*, no. 4 (February 1963), p. 2; *Trud*, January 7, 1964.

36. *Sbornik postanovlenii VTsSPS*, April-June 1962, pp. 129-132.

37. *Trud*, December 21, 1962, January 26, 1963.

38. *Ibid.*, February 6, 1964.

39. For more detail see the excellent study by Gaston V. Rimlinger, "The Trade Union in Soviet Social Insurance: Historical Development and Present Functions," *Industrial and Labor Relations Review*, 14:397-418 (April 1961).

40. *Sbornik postanovlenii VTsSPS*, January 1960 to September 1962.

41. *Ibid.*, October-December 1961, pp. 64-70; July-September 1962, pp. 122-126.

42. *Voprosy profsoyuznoi raboty, konsultatsii, kommentarii, otvety na voprosy* (Questions of Trade Union Work, Consultations, Commentaries, Answers to Questions; Moscow, 1963), pp. 320-358.

43. Resolution of CCTU, February 12, 1960, *Sbornik postanovlenii VTsSPS*, January-September 1960, p. 287. Rules agreed on with the CCTU to govern local soviets and enterprises in distribution of housing were adopted in February 1964 by the Ministry of

360   Notes to Pages 130–139

Communal Economy of the RSFSR. *SP*, no. 11 (May 1964), pp. 44-46.

44. *Sbornik postanovlenii VTsSPS*, April-June 1962, pp. 136-139; *Trud*, June 18, 1961, June 15, 1962; *SP*, no. 18 (September 1963), p. 20.

45. *Sbornik postanovlenii VTsSPS*, January-September 1960, pp. 300-306; October-December 1961, pp. 105-108; July-September 1962, pp. 137-148.

46. *Spravochnik profsoyuznovo rabotnika*, 1962, pp. 405-441.

47. *Sbornik postanovlenii VTsSPS*, January-September 1960, pp. 358-362.

48. *Ibid.*, October-December 1961, pp. 121-124.

49. *Trud*, June 28, 1963.

50. *Sbornik postanovlenii VTsSPS*, January-March 1961, pp. 117-121. Impressive evidence of these activities in groups in many different cities comes in a book of pictures of many workers in their ordinary occupations as well as in their roles in dance, opera, drama, or music, *Narodnye talanty* (People's Talents; Moscow, 1958).

51. *Voprosy profsoyuznoi raboty*, pp. 455-460; *Trud*, February 16, 1963.

52. *SP*, no. 23 (December 1962), p. 27; no. 12 (June 1963), p. 25.

53. *Sbornik postanovlenii VTsSPS*, January-September 1960, pp. 316-319.

54. *Ibid.*, January-March 1962, pp. 104-119; July-September 1962, pp. 156-160.

55. *Trud*, June 28, July 2, 1963.

56. *Sbornik postanovlenii VTsSPS*, 1960 through 1962.

57. *Trud*, June 4, August 20, 1961.

58. *Sbornik postanovlenii VTsSPS*, January-September 1960, pp. 55-59; *Trud*, June 9, September 15, 1960.

59. *Sbornik postanovlenii VTsSPS*, October-December 1960, pp. 14-22; *Trud*, March 26, 1961.

60. *SP*, no. 24 (December 1962), pp. 25-26.

61. A. I. Lukyanov and B. M. Lazarev, *Sovetskoe gosudarstvo i obshchestvennye organizatsii* (The Soviet State and Public Organizations; Moscow, 1961), pp. 114-115; also Petrov, pp. 96-97.

CHAPTER VI, LOCAL UNIONS AND THEIR MEMBERS

1. Useful descriptions are given in the textbook on trade union work, P. S. Petrov, ed., *Organizatsionno-massovaya rabota profsionalnykh soyuzov* (Organizational-Mass-Work of Trade Unions;

Moscow, 1961), and in the series of pamphlets published by the Central Council of Trade Unions to help the local unions, *Bibliotechka profsoyuznovo aktivista* (Little Library of the Trade Union Activist), for example, V. Nikitinskii and A. Stavtseva, *Prava fabrichnykh, zavodskikh, i mestnykh komitetov profsoyuzov* (Rights of Factory, Plant, and Local Committees of the Trade Unions; Moscow, BPA, no. 13, 1961), and V. P. Lyutikov, *Organizatsia raboty komiteta profsoyuza na predpriatii* (Organization of Work of Trade Union Committee in the Enterprise; Moscow, BPA, no. 20, 1961).

2. Decree of Presidium of Supreme Soviet, *Sbornik zakonodatelnykh aktov o trude* (Collection of Legislative Acts on Labor; Moscow, 1961), pp. 37-40. For the English text, United States Bureau of Labor Statistics, *Principal Current Soviet Labor Legislation* (Washington, 1962), pp. 107-111. For the party's 1957 statement, *Sbornik zakonodatelnykh aktov o trude*, 1961, p. 31.

3. The much used Russian word "control" does not mean control, but has perhaps been best defined by Gregory Grossman as "a combination of supervision, surveillance, checking and administrative prophylaxis." *American Economic Review*, 49:51 (May 1959).

4. *Ustav professionalnykh soyuzov SSSR* (Statute of the Trade Unions of the USSR; Moscow, 1963), sec. v.

5. *Organizatsionno-massovaya rabota profsoyuzov* (Organizational-Mass-Work of Trade Unions; Moscow, 1962), pp. 185, 205.

6. *Trud*, October 29, 1963.

7. *Spravochnik profsoyuznovo rabotnika* (Handbook of the Trade Union Worker; Moscow, 1962), pp. 162-165.

8. I. S. Dvornikov, in *SP*, no. 8 (April 1960), p. 61; F. M. Leviant and A. S. Pashkov, eds., *Pravovoe polozhenie professionalnykh soyuzov SSSR* (Legal Position of the Trade Unions of the USSR; Leningrad, 1962), p. 61.

9. *Trud*, November 15, 1962. Detailed instructions for conducting elections are provided periodically by the CCTU, as in the January 1964 decision, replacing those of 1962. *Sbornik postanovlenii VTsSPS*, January-March 1964 (Collection of Decisions of CCTU; Moscow, 1964), pp. 40-50.

10. *Trud*, October 3, 1959; October 22, 1960; November 16, 1961; *SP*, no. 23 (December 1960), p. 42.

11. *Sbornik postanovlenii VTsSPS*, January-March 1964, pp. 58-61.

12. For examples, *Trud*, October 18, 1959; November 26, 1960; October 12, 1961; January 31, 1963; *SP*, no. 2 (January 1962), pp. 21-22.

13. *Trud*, March 14 and May 18, 1961; September 5, 1963; *SP*, no. 5 (March 1961), pp. 33-34.

14. *Supra,* ch. iv, pp. 90-92.

15. *Trud,* June 2, 1963.

16. *Sbornik postanovlenii VTsSPS,* July-September 1962, pp. 83-89; also Petrov, pp. 159-160.

17. *SP,* no. 20 (October 1963), p. 5.

18. *Ibid.,* p. 4.

19. *USSR Illustrated Monthly,* November 1963, p. 54.

20. International Labor Office, *The Trade Union Situation in the USSR* (Geneva, 1960), p. 85.

21. *Sbornik postanovlenii VTsSPS,* January-March 1964, pp. 59-60.

22. The figure presumably includes "incomplete secondary education" of seventh or eighth grade. *Sbornik postanovlenii VTsSPS,* January-March, 1964, p. 60.

23. Cf. also the union pamphlet, Lyutikov, *Organizatsia raboty komiteta profsoyuza na predpriatii,* esp. pp. 56-58, and a report in *SP,* no. 2 (January 1962), pp. 23-24.

24. *Trud,* February 20, 1965.

25. Examples of such programs are found in K. Isaev, *Kak organizovat rabotu profgruppy na predpriatii* (How to Organize the Work of the Trade Union Group in the Enterprise; Moscow, *BPA,* no. 9, 1961); I. Shlemis, *Komissia po kulturno-massovoi rabote FZMK* (Commission on Cultural-Mass-Work of the Factory, Plant or Local Committee; Moscow, *BPA,* no. 26, 1962); *SP,* no. 3 (February 1964), pp. 20-21.

26. *Spravochnik profsoyuznovo rabotnika,* 1962, pp. 80-84. For the English text, *Principal Current Soviet Labor Legislation,* pp. 87-91.

27. For example, A. Trutnev, *FZMK v borbe za soznatelnuyu distsiplinu truda* (The Factory, Plant and Local Committee in the Struggle for Conscious Discipline of Labor; Moscow, *BPA,* no. 65, 1963); R. Livshits, "Otvetstvennost rabochikh i sluzhashchikh za narushenie trudovoi distsipliny" (Responsibility of Workers and Employees for Violation of Labor Discipline), *ST,* February 1964, pp. 136-143.

28. *Trud,* October 29, 1963, also December 25 and 28, 1965; *Sbornik postanovlenii VTsSPS,* April-June 1962, pp. 44-48; July-September 1961, pp. 10-14.

29. *Trud,* August 1, September 8 and 22, 1963, April 21, 1964.

30. Leviant and Pashkov, pp. 108-111. For the 1961 decree on comradely courts, *Sbornik postanovlenii VTsSPS,* July-September 1961, pp. 20-30. Also G. A. Linenburg, N. N. Leonova, *Tovarishcheskii sud na predpriatii* (The Comradely Court in the Enterprise; Moscow, 1961).

31. *Spravochnik profsoyuznovo rabotnika,* 1962, pp. 254-340; K. Batygin, *Rabota FZMK po sotsialnomu strakhovaniyu* (The Work of Factory, Plant or Local Committee on Social Insurance; Moscow, *BPA,* no. 31, 1962); *V pomoshch strakhovomy delegatu i chlenu komissii po sotsialnomu strakhovaniyu* (For the Help of the Insurance Delegate and Member of the Commission on Social Insurance; Moscow, *BPA,* no. 10, 1961).

32. On this and other aspects of the administration of benefits see Gaston V. Rimlinger, "The Trade Union in Soviet Social Insurance," *Industrial and Labor Relations Review,* 14:397-418 (April 1961).

33. The right to benefits and the amounts are governed by a decree of the Council of Ministers and regulations of the Central Council of Trade Unions, issued in 1955 and modified in January 1962. Payments start with the first day of disability and continue until the return to work, or, in the case of permanent disability, until the worker goes on disability pension under the social security laws. For injury or illness related to work, benefits are 100 per cent of wages, without regard to the length of service or union membership. For non-occupational disability they range from 50 per cent of wages for those with less than three years of service, up to 90 per cent for those with over twelve years of uninterrupted work. Workers who are not union members, however, get only one-half of the usual amount for non-occupational disability. Youths under 18 get 60 per cent of wages, war invalids 90 per cent. A minimum is set of thirty rubles per month in cities and twenty-seven rubles in rural areas. The maximum, except for occupational disability, is ten rubles per day.

Maternity leave extends for fifty-six days before and fifty-six days after the birth, with additional days in case of multiple or abnormal births. Women who are union members receive from two-thirds up to 100 per cent of their wages, depending on their length of service and such factors as war experience, receipt of honors, or recognition as an innovator or leader of production. Non-members get two-thirds of their wages.

Complicated rules determine the record of uninterrupted service, even in case of changes of jobs. In most cases the uninterrupted record is kept if the worker takes another job within 30 days. Workers discharged for violations of discipline or because of imprisonment, however, must work 6 months on the new job before they have a right to non-occupational disability payments. Benefits may be decreased or lost also in case of failure of a worker to follow the regime set up for him by the doctor. *Spravochnik profsoyuznovo rabotnika,* 1962, pp. 272-301.

For old age pensions, in general, men are eligible for full pensions at age 60 after 25 years of work and women at 55 after 20 years work. Pensions range from 100 per cent of low earnings to 50 per cent of monthly earnings of 100 rubles or more, with additions for especially long service, and advantages in eligibility rules and rates for miners and others with dangerous or difficult conditions. *Sbornik zakonodatelnykh aktov o trude*, 1961, pp. 613-659.

34. Enterprises are also required to compensate workers or their survivors for losses of income resulting from injuries or damage to health related to their work, when it results from failure to observe the regulations on safety and working conditions, under a decree of the Presidium of the Supreme Soviet of October 2, 1961 and detailed rules issued jointly by the State Committee on Questions of Labor and Wages and the Central Council of Trade Unions, on December 22, 1961. Disputes over compensation are settled by the factory committees, subject to appeal to the People's Courts. This system supplements the general provision on temporary disability benefits and disability pensions. *Spravochnik profsoyuznovo rabotnika*, 1962, pp. 227-240; *ST*, October 1963, pp. 129-139.

35. *SP*, no. 8 (April 1963), p. 25.

36. *Spravochnik profsoyuznovo rabotnika*, 1962, pp. 346-361; *Voprosy profsoyuznoi raboty*, 1962, pp. 331-343.

37. *Trud*, October 3, 1959.

38. *Sbornik postanovlenii VTsSPS*, April-June 1962, pp. 136-139.

39. *Trud*, February 2, 1961.

40. *SP*, no. 3 (February 1965), pp. 6-7.

41. *Organizatsionno-massovaya rabota profsoyuzov*, pp. 131-134; *Trud*, January 22, 1965.

CHAPTER VII, LABOR-MANAGEMENT RELATIONS AND
PROTECTION OF WORKERS

1. E. L. Manevich, in *VE*, May 1961, p. 76.

2. Basic legislation and regulations are found in *Sbornik zakonodatelnykh aktov o trude* (Collection of Legislative Acts on Labor; Moscow, 1961); *Spravochnik profsoyuznovo rabotnika* (Handbook of the Trade Union Worker; Moscow, 1962); for English translations, United States Bureau of Labor Statistics, *Principal Current Soviet Labor Legislation* (Washington, 1962). The 1922 Code of Labor Law of the Russian Soviet Federated Socialist Republic is still the basic document on labor law, modified and supplemented by later decrees and regulations. For the English text, as amended to 1958, see *Principal Current Soviet Labor Legislation*, pp. 1-34.

3. Cf. Frederick Harbison and Charles A. Myers, *Management in the Industrial World* (New York, 1959), pp. 342-349.

4. *Sbornik zakonodatelnykh aktov o trude*, 1961, pp. 37-40; for the English text, *Principal Current Soviet Labor Legislation*, pp. 107-111.

5. *Spravochnik profsoyuznovo rabotnika*, 1949, pp. 139-149.

6. *Trud*, October 19, 1951, in *CDSP*, 3.43:34 (December 8, 1951); *Trud*, February 1, 1952, reported in *International Labor Review*, 66:481 (November-December 1952).

7. *Pravda*, February 15, 1956, translated in *CDSP*, 8.6:6 (March 21, 1956).

8. *Postanovlenia plenumov VTsSPS 1954-1958* (Resolutions of Plenums of CCTU; Moscow, 1961), pp. 64-78.

9. *ST*, April 1958, p. 146; N. G. Aleksandrov, in *ibid.*, May 1958, pp. 29-30.

10. *Sbornik postanovlenii VTsSPS* January-March 1962 (Collection of Decisions of CCTU; Moscow, 1962), pp. 39-44; *Trud*, December 22, 1963, December 12, 1965.

11. *Voprosy profsoyuznoi raboty* (Questions of Trade Union Work; Moscow, 1963), pp. 215-224; M. Kozlov, M. Panarin, and V. Solovev, *Kollektivny dogovor na predpriatii* (The Collective Contract in the Enterprise; Moscow, BPA, no. 24, 1961), pp. 13-40.

12. Kozlov, et al., pp. 58-59.

13. Analyzed in the author's "Labor Relations in Soviet Factories," *Industrial and Labor Relations Review*, 11:183-191 (January 1958).

14. G. Moskalenko, "Uluchshit soderzhanie kollektivnykh dogovorov" (To Improve the Contents of Collective Contracts), *ST*, February 1958, pp. 11-19.

15. *SP*, no. 20 (October 1960), pp. 35-38.

16. *Trud*, August 24, 1962.

17. Agreement of Rostov regional economic council and regional trade union council, 1958; *Sovnarkhoz i zhizn* (Sovnarkhoz and Life; Kharkov, 1959), pp. 83-85; *Trud*, December 27, 1961, December 22, 1963, June 18 and July 19, 1964. From Gorky came a report of a two-year agreement for 1964-1965 signed by the new sovnarkhoz of Volgo-Vyatka with five sovprofs, Gorky, Kirov, and others then covered by the larger economic region. It provided for thirty million rubles for two hundred large projects of improvements in ventilation, sanitary provisions, mechanization, and working conditions. *Trud*, July 11, 1964.

18. F. M. Leviant and A. S. Pashkov, eds., *Pravovoe polozhenie professionalnykh soyuzov SSSR* (Legal Position of Trade Unions of the USSR; Leningrad, 1962), p. 37.

366 Notes to Pages 193–199

19. G. K. Moskalenko, in N. G. Aleksandrov, ed., *Novoe v razvitii trudovovo prava v period mezhdy XX i XXII syezdami KPSS* (New in the Development of Labor Law in the Period between the XX and XXII Congresses of CPSU; Moscow, 1961), pp. 249-263; Ya. L. Kiselev, in N. G. Aleksandrov, ed., *Sovetskoe gosudarstvo i obshchestvennost v usloviakh razvernutovo stroitelstva kommunizma* (The Soviet State and the Public in Conditions of Full-Scale Construction of Communism; Moscow, 1962), pp. 148-153.

20. V. Nikitinskii and A. Stavtseva, *Prava fabrichnykh zavodskikh i mestnykh komitetov profsoyuzov* (Rights of Factory, Plant, and Local Committees of the Trade Unions; Moscow, *BPA*, no. 5-6, 1961), esp. pp. 31-85; A. A. Abramova, in Aleksandrov, ed., *Sovetskoe gosudarstvo i obshchestvennost*, pp. 191-262.

21. Ya. L. Kiselev, *Okhrana truda po sovetskomu trudovomy pravy* (Protection of Labor in Soviet Labor Law; Moscow, 1962), pp. 166-172, 191-196; K. Isaev, *Kak organizovat rabotu profgruppy na predpriatii* (How to Organize the Work of the Trade Union Group in the Enterprise; Moscow, *BPA*, no. 9, 1961), pp. 61-66; P. Baibarin and S. Putyaev, *Komissia FZMK po okhrane truda* (The Commission of the Factory, Plant and Local Committee on Protection of Labor; Moscow, *BPA*, no. 60, 1963).

Regulations of the CCTU on technical inspectors, public inspectors, and commissions on protection of labor are given in *Spravochnik profsoyuznovo rabotnika*, 1962, pp. 212-226; *Sbornik postanovlenii VTsSPS*, October-December 1963, pp. 49-51.

22. *Sbornik postanovlenii VTsSPS*, October-December 1963, pp. 52-53; *Trud*, May 29, 1964.

23. *SGP*, January 1961, p. 121.

24. Kiselev, *Okhrana truda*, pp. 110-138; *Trud*, January 10, 1963.

25. Kiselev, *Okhrana truda*, pp. 144-145. In some industries a five-day week was being introduced, and this was promised for all in the future.

26. Nikitinskii and Stavtseva, pp. 65-68; Y. Orlovskii, "O sverkhurochnykh rabotakh" (On Overtime Work), *ST*, May 1961, pp. 137-141.

27. Leviant and Pashkov, pp. 58-59.

28. Labor code of the RSFSR, 1922, secs. 47, 49, 88-90, in *Sbornik zakonodatelnykh aktov o trude*, 1961, pp. 102-104, 113.

29. Abramova, pp. 229-238; Nikitinskii and Stavtseva, pp. 58-65; A. I. Stavtseva, in N. G. Aleksandrov, ed., *Novoe v razvitii trudovovo prava*, pp. 209-221.

30. *ST*, February 1964, p. 150.

31. Decision of Supreme Court of the USSR on court practice in

labor cases, September 13, 1957, points 20, 23, *Sbornik zakonodatelnykh aktov o trude*, 1961, pp. 467-468; also a June 30, 1964 decision, *ST*, November 1964, pp. 151-152.
   32. Criminal Code of the RSFSR, secs. 137-140, in *Spravochnik profsoyuznovo rabotnika*, 1962, p. 226; *ST*, March 1961, p. 149.

CHAPTER VIII, LABOR DISPUTES

   1. A. E. Pasherstnik, *Rassmotrenie trudovykh sporov* (Examination of Labor Disputes; Moscow, 1958), pp. 23-26.
   2. *Ibid.*, pp. 3-9; N. G. Aleksandrov, *Sovetskoe trudovoe pravo* (Soviet Labor Law; Moscow, 1963), pp. 344-349; A. I. Stavtseva, *Poryadok rassmotrenia trudovykh sporov* (System of Examination of Labor Disputes; Moscow, 1960), pp. 3-12.
   3. Aleksandrov, pp. 345-346.
   4. Described by J. K. Zawodny, "Grievance Procedures in Soviet Factories," *Industrial and Labor Relations Review*, 10:532-553 (July 1957) and "Grievances and Sources of Tension during Stalin's Regime as Reported by Soviet Industrial Workers," *Soviet Studies*, 14:158-178 (October 1962).
   5. Decree of January 31, 1957, approving "Regulation on system of examination of labor disputes," *Sbornik zakonodatelnykh aktov o trude* (Collection of Legislative Acts on Labor; Moscow, 1961), pp. 454-462. For the English text, U.S. Bureau of Labor Statistics, *Principal Current Soviet Labor Legislation* (Washington, 1962), pp. 92-100. For major recent Soviet discussions see V. V. Karavaev, A. M. Kaftanovskaya, and R. Z. Lifshits, *Razreshenie trudovykh sporov, kommentarii* (Settlement of Labor Disputes, Commentary; Moscow, 1960); A. Lapai and A. Klyuev, *Kak reshayutsya trudovye spory* (How Labor Disputes are Settled; Moscow, 1960); V. Kamyshev, *Poryadok razreshenia trudovykh sporov* (System of Settlement of Labor Disputes; Moscow, *BPA*, no. 4, 1961 and no. 57, 1963); and Stavtseva.
   6. Karavaev, et al., p. 154.
   7. *SGP*, January 1961, p. 122.
   8. Kamyshev, 1961, p. 59.
   9. *SGP*, August 1961, pp. 13-14.
   10. *Soviet Studies*, 12:152, 165 (October 1960); *Trud*, January 9, 1963.
   11. V. E. Panyugin, *Trud*, February 11, 1965.
   12. Stavtseva, p. 66.
   13. A resolution of the CCTU on the work in the Moscow region, *ST*, July 1958, p. 137.

14. *SP*, no. 6 (March 1961), p. 47.

15. *Sbornik postanovlenii VTsSPS*, July-September 1962 (Collection of Decisions of CCTU; Moscow, 1962), pp. 77-81.

16. *Ibid.*, pp. 94-98.

17. *SP*, no. 15 (August 1963), p. 23; *Sbornik postanovlenii VTsSPS*, April-June 1963, pp. 59-62.

18. *SP*, no. 13 (July 1963), p. 36.

19. Cf. Zawodny, "Grievance Procedures," pp. 551-553.

20. Harold J. Berman, *Justice in the USSR* (Cambridge, Mass., 1963), p. 361.

21. Cf. Panyugin, *Trud*, February 11, 1965.

22. A. I. Stavtseva, in N. G. Aleksandrov, ed., *Novoe v razvitii trudovovo prava v period mezhdu XX i XXII syezdami KPSS* (New in the Development of Labor Law in the Period between the XX and XXII Congresses of CPSU; Moscow, 1961), p. 220.

23. *Trud*, March 22, 1960.

24. *Ibid.*, January 12, 1964.

25. *Ibid.*, January 30, 1962; *SP*, no. 10 (May 1963), pp. 18-19.

26. *Trud*, January 30, 1962.

27. *SP*, no. 5 (March 1964), p. 36.

28. *Trud*, September 24, October 23, December 1, 1963.
There is no unemployment insurance, but a variety of welfare services are provided under the republic Ministries of Health, Education, and Social Security, with programs for child care, family allowances, care for invalids, pensions, assistance to invalids or old people not on pension. According to an American report, welfare workers said the laws were interpreted broadly, and if a person was not entitled to one kind of help, it was usually possible to get him some other kind. Bernice Madison, "Welfare Personnel in the Soviet Union," *Social Work*, July 1962, pp. 57-68; United States Department of Health, Education, and Welfare, *A Report on Social Security in the Soviet Union* (Washington, 1960), pp. 91-100. Workers in financial difficulty may in some cases get aid from trade union funds, or if they are members of the mutual assistance fund or credit union of their enterprise, they may be able to borrow. *Spravochnik profsoyuznovo rabotnika* (Handbook of the Trade Union Worker; Moscow, 1962), pp. 475-484.

29. *Trud*, January 29, 1961, January 30, 1962, January 12, 1963, February 28, 1965; *SP*, no. 10 (May 1963), pp. 18-19.

30. *SP*, no. 4 (February 1965), pp. 30-31; *ST*, April 1965, pp. 145-146.

31. *Trud*, February 22, 1962.

32. *ST*, October 1963, pp. 115-120.

33. *Ibid.*, November 1964, pp. 151-152.

34. Panyugin, *Trud,* February 11, 1965; *SGP,* December 1964, pp. 20-28; *ST,* April 1965, pp. 145-146.

35. A legal expert states that Enterprises of Communist Labor or those seeking the title have no discharges. The union committee and the manager try to retrain and shift workers in case of mechanization or of incapacity to do the work, and to re-educate workers in cases of violation of discipline. A. I. Stavtseva, *Vosstanovlenie na rabote nepravilno uvolennykh rabochikh i sluzhashchikh* (Reinstatement of Illegally Discharged Wage and Salary Workers; Moscow, 1962), pp. 3-4.

36. *SP,* no. 14 (July 1961), pp. 18-19; no. 16 (August 1960), p. 13.

37. Aleksandrov, *Sovetskoe trudovoe pravo,* 1959, pp. 331-332, also 1963 edition, pp. 350-351. One legal authority in 1961 stated that the State Committee on Questions of Labor and Wages had competence to consider any disagreements between government organs and the CCTU on labor questions, and to make decisions within the limits of existing laws. On questions demanding the issuance of new or change in old laws and decisions, the State Committee takes appropriate proposals to the Council of Ministers of the USSR. A. I. Lukyanov and B. M. Lazarev, *Sovetskoe gosudarstvo i obshchestvennye organizatsii* (The Soviet State and Public Organizations; Moscow, 1961), p. 100.

38. *Sovnarkhoz i zhizn* (The Sovnarkhoz and Life; Kharkov, 1959), pp. 78-79.

39. Joseph S. Berliner, *Factory and Manager in the USSR* (Cambridge, Mass., 1957), pp. 272-273; Merle Fainsod, *How Russia is Ruled* (Cambridge, Mass., 1954), pp. 432-434, 440.

40. *Trud,* March 24, 1959.

41. *Ibid.,* June 22, 1963; see also July 22, 1961, July 28, 1962.

42. *Ibid.,* July 14, 1963.

43. *Ibid.,* June 27, 1964.

44. For examples, *ibid.,* May 14, June 4, August 26, 1961, December 29, 1962, May 31, 1964; *SP,* no. 13 (July 1961), pp. 16-17; no. 8 (April 1963), pp. 27-28; no. 8 (April 1964), p. 13.

45. *SP,* no. 17 (September 1962), pp. 31-32; *Trud,* February 24, 1963, June 6, 1963.

46. *Trud,* October 29, 1963, March 11, 1965; *SGP,* August 1963, pp. 56-57.

47. *Trud,* March 2, 1961.

48. *Ibid.,* October 29, 1963, January 1, 1964.

49. *SP,* no. 22 (November 1963), pp. 14-15.

50. *Izvestia,* February 8 and 14, 1963, in *CDSP,* 15.6:34-35 (March 6, 1963); 15.7:36 (March 13, 1963).

51. Yudif Grinfeld, "Proizvol rabotodatelei v SSSR" (Arbitrariness of Employers in the USSR), *Novy Zhurnal,* no. 73 (1963), pp. 259-277.

52. S. Schwarz, in *Sotsialisticheskii Vestnik,* November-December 1963, pp. 142-143.

53. *Trud,* June 23, 1961; for other examples, *ibid.,* October 3, 1961; *SP,* no. 8 (April 1963), pp. 27-28, no. 18 (September 1963), p. 17.

54. *SGP,* August 1958, pp. 109-112; V. Nikitinskii and A. Stavtseva, *Prava fabrichnykh, zavodskikh i mestnykh komitetov profsoyuzov* (Rights of Factory, Plant, and Local Committees of the Trade Unions; Moscow, BPA, no. 5-6, 1961), pp. 83-85.

55. *Trud,* September 8, 1961; for other instances, *ibid.,* July 18, 1961, June 6, 1962.

56. *Ibid.,* January 10, May 31, 1964; *SP,* no. 4 (February 1963), pp. 1-2; *SGP,* August 1963, pp. 53-60.

57. International Labor Office, *Trade Union Rights in the USSR* (Geneva, 1959), p. 74.

58. Quoted by Isaac Deutscher, *Soviet Trade Unions* (London, 1950), p. 61.

59. Margaret Dewar, *Labour Policy in the USSR 1917-1928* (London, 1956), pp. 102-105, 143-147.

60. Merle Fainsod, *Smolensk under Soviet Rule* (Cambridge, Mass., 1958), pp. 317-318.

61. *Ibid.,* p. 312.

62. Jacob Miller, *Soviet Russia* (London, 1955), pp. 148-149.

63. *The Dispatcher,* February 26, 1960.

64. Marvin L. Kalb, *Eastern Exposure* (New York, 1958), pp. 258-259, 263-264.

65. *New York Times,* October 15, December 8 and 30, 1959, April 24, 1960, June 25, 1961, October 8, 1962.

66. *USSR Illustrated Monthly,* December 1963, p. 14.

67. The most detailed account is by Albert Boiter, "When the Kettle Boils over . . . ," *Problems of Communism,* January-February 1964, pp. 33-43. There have been unconfirmed reports also of strikes late in 1964, which were forcefully suppressed, in the Donbas over increases in production standards, and in a Moscow auto plant over increases in prices at the canteen. *Communist Affairs,* November-December 1964, p. 13.

68. Boiter, pp. 40-41.

69. *New York Times,* March 31, 1964.

70. For the phrase and an analysis see Arthur M. Ross, "Changing Patterns of Industrial Conflict," *Proceedings of Twelfth Annual Meeting of Industrial Relations Research Association,* December 1959, pp. 146-169.

CHAPTER IX, COOPERATION IN PRODUCTION

1. *Trud,* October 29, 1963; *Sbornik postanovlenii VTsSPS,* April-June 1962 (Collection of Decisions of CCTU; Moscow, 1962), pp. 9-15; A. F. Garmashev, ed., *Izobretatelstvo i ratsionalizatsia v SSSR* (Invention and Rationalization in the USSR; Moscow, 1962), pp. 210-225.

2. *Trud,* June 27, July 2, 1964.

3. A. Sergeev, "Dvizhenie za kommunisticheskii trud i ispol-zovanie reservov proizvodstva" (Movement for Communist Labor and Utilization of Reserves of Production), *ST,* February 1963, pp. 1-11; also *ST,* July 1963, pp. 22-29; Institute of Labor, State Committee on Labor and Wages, *Dvizhenie za kommunisticheskii trud v promyshlennosti SSSR* (Movement for Communist Labor in Industry, USSR; Moscow, 1962), pp. 42-61.

4. A. Kornoukhov, *Obshchestvennoe byuro ekonomicheskovo analiza* (Public Bureau of Economic Analysis; Moscow, 1963).

5. *ST,* June 1963, p. 6.

6. V. Gritsai and V. Frolov, *Obshchestvenny nauchno-issledo-vatelskii institut na zavode* (Public Scientific-Investigation Institute in the Plant; Moscow, 1962).

7. A. Slepukhin, *Obshchestvenny smotr rezervov proizvodstva* (Public Review of Reserves of Production; Moscow, BPA, 1961).

8. See for example *Voprosy profsoyuznoi raboty* (Questions of Trade Union Work; Moscow, 1963), pp. 143-165.

9. Sergeev, p. 6; *Trud,* October 23, 1963; *SP,* no. 12 (June 1963), pp. 1-3.

10. *Voprosy profsoyuznoi raboty,* pp. 151-153, 179-182; P. Petrov, *Profaktivu o rezervakh povyshenia proizvoditelnosti truda* (For the Trade Union Activist on Reserves for Increasing Productivity of Labor; Moscow, BPA, no. 33, 1962), pp. 42-56; I. Leonov, "Estafeta trudovoi doblesti" (Relay Race of Labor Valor), *ST,* July 1963, pp. 13-21.

11. See for instance decisions of the Central Council of Trade Unions, *Sbornik postanovlenii VTsSPS,* July-September 1962, pp. 3-17, 111-115; *SP,* no. 12 (June 1963), pp. 1-3. On inducements to Soviet managers to hide productive capacity and not to innovate see Gregory Grossman, "Soviet Growth: Routine, Inertia and Pressure," *American Economic Review,* 50:62-72 (May 1960), and Harry G. Shaffer, "What Price Economic Reforms? Ills and Remedies," *Problems of Communism,* May-June 1963, pp. 19-20.

12. *Trud,* October 29, 1963; *Pravda,* February 7, 1964; *Sbornik postanovlenii VTsSPS,* January-March 1964, pp. 57-58.

13. Cf. F. M. Leviant and A. S. Pashkov, eds., *Pravovoe polozh-enie professionalnykh soyuzov SSSR* (Legal Position of Trade

Unions of the USSR; Leningrad, 1962), pp. 26-29; *SP*, no. 15 (August 1963), p. 23. A joint decree of the Central Committee of the Communist Party and the Council of Ministers, of May 19, 1961, held that to increase state discipline it was necessary to increase control by the unions over progress of fulfillment of plans, and to have regular reports by administrations to workers' meetings. The CCTU obligated the union committees to develop a feeling of responsibility against any deception. Leviant and Pashkov, pp. 132-133; *ST*, September 1961, p. 141.

14. I. Batulin, L. Geller, P. Troitskii, *Profsoyuznomy aktivy o planirovanii proizvodstva* (For the Trade Union Activist on Planning Production; Moscow, *BPA*, no. 51, 1963).

15. Cf. a description of planning in a Magnitogorsk steel mill, *USSR Illustrated Monthly*, September 1963, pp. 10-11.

16. *Voprosy profsoyuznoi raboty*, p. 69; I. Dvornikov, et al., *Professionalnye soyuzy SSSR* (Trade Unions USSR; Moscow, *BPA*, no. 13, 1961), pp. 36-37; Secretary V. I. Prokhorov of CCTU, *Trud*, August 7, 1963.

17. *Trud*, December 25, 1962, June 9, and August 7, 1963.

18. Ya. L. Kiselev, in N. G. Aleksandrov, ed., *Sovetskoe gosudarstvo i obshchestvennost v usloviakh razvernutovo stroitelstva kommunizma* (The Soviet State and the Public under Conditions of Full-Scale Construction of Communism; Moscow, 1962), pp. 154-155.

19. *Trud*, February 24, 1960, September 1 and 14, 1961, January 9 and December 26, 1964; *Soviet Studies*, 10:187-188 (October 1958); *SP*, no. 8 (April 1963), p. 32.

20. *Spravochnik profsoyuznovo rabotnika*, 1949 (Handbook of the Trade Union Worker; Moscow, 1949), pp. 451-461.

21. Cf. Joseph S. Berliner, *Factory and Manager in the USSR* (Cambridge, Mass., 1957), pp. 273-276; David Granick, *The Red Executive* (Garden City, N. Y., 1960), pp. 228-231.

22. *Proizvodstvenno-massovaya rabota professionalnykh soyuzov* (Production-Mass-Work of Trade Unions; Moscow, 1958), pp. 145-146; *Postanovlenia plenumov VTsSPS, 1954-1958* (Decisions of Plenums of CCTU; Moscow, 1961), pp. 17, 23-24, 79-85, 96-120.

23. *Spravochnik profsoyuznovo rabotnika*, 1962, pp. 91-94. For the English text, United States Bureau of Labor Statistics, *Principal Current Soviet Labor Legislation* (Washington, 1962), pp. 103-106.

24. I. I. Belonosov, ed., *Postoyanno deistvuyushchie proizvodstvennye soveshchania, dokumenty* (Permanently Functioning Production Conferences, Documents; Moscow, 1959). Among the best descriptions are V. Zagorulkin, *Postoyanno deistvuyushchie proizvodstvennye soveshchania* (Permanently Functioning Production

Conferences; Moscow, *BPA*, no. 69, 1963; *Voprosy profsoyuznoi raboty*, 1961, pp. 128-147; Kiselev, pp. 156-166.
25. *Trud*, October 29, 1963.
26. For examples, A. A. Shtylko, ed., *Postoyanno deistvuyushchie proizvodstvennye soveshchania na predpriatiakh* (Permanently Functioning Production Conferences at Enterprises; Moscow, 1960); *SP*, no. 7 (April 1960), pp. 45-46; no. 8 (April 1960), pp. 42-43; no. 1 (January 1962), p. 17; *Trud*, December 20, 1961, January 5, 1962, August 14, 1963.
27. Barry M. Richman, "Increasing Worker Productivity: How the Soviets Do It," *Personnel*, 41:8-21 (January-February 1964).
28. *SP*, no. 20 (October 1961), p. 6.
29. *Sbornik postanovlenii VTsSPS*, July-September 1963, pp. 59-64; also January-March, 1962, pp. 52-56, July-September 1962, pp. 3-17; *Trud*, July 26, December 26, 27, 1962, October 29, 1963; *SP*, no. 18 (September 1961), p. 14.
30. Kiselev, pp. 164-165; Leviant and Pashkov, p. 48; *Trud*, November 6, 1963.
31. *Trud*, October 29, 1963.
32. Cf. David Granick, *Management of the Industrial Firm in the USSR* (New York, 1954), pp. 243-252.
33. G. A. Prudenskii, ed., *Voprosy truda v SSSR* (Questions of Labor in the USSR; Moscow, 1958), p. 189.
34. N. Blagoveshchenskaya and V. Segalov, *Organizatsia sotsialisticheskovo sorevnovania na predpriatii* (Organization of Socialist Competition in the Enterprise; Moscow, *BPA*, no. 63, 1963); Kiselev, pp. 166-182; E. F. Borisov and R. L. Zaitsev, *Sotsialisticheskoe sorevnovanie i ekonomika predpriatii* (Socialist Competition and the Economics of Enterprises; Moscow, 1962), pp. 16-35.
35. The new "heavy ruble" introduced on January 1, 1961, replaced the old ruble on the basis of 1 to 10. The new ruble has an official exchange rate of 1 ruble to $1.11.
36. *Spravochnik profsoyuznovo rabotnika*, 1962, pp. 24-36; *Sbornik postanovlenii VTsSPS*, April-June 1963, p. 39. The CCTU in March 1964 approved a regulation on the work of the production-mass-work commissions, which organize the work in the plants. *Sbornik postanovlenii VTsSPS*, January-March 1964, pp. 81-85.
37. *TZP*, November 1962, p. 14; Blagoveshchenskaya and Segalov, pp. 15-24.
38. *Trud*, November 6, 1963, March 9, 1965. These figures are inflated by inclusion of whole groups in departments or plants that claim to be competing for the title, although relatively small numbers of individuals may have taken upon themselves the necessary obligations.
39. *TZP*, November 1962, p. 14.

40. *Ibid.*, April 1962, pp. 8-13; November 1962, pp. 14-19; Institute of Labor, *Dvizhenie za kommunisticheskii trud v promyshlennosti SSSR;* also Borisov and Zaitsev, pp. 36-76.

41. In six Moscow plants a study found that among all competing for the title of Communist Labor, 87 per cent were involved in some form of study; of those outside the movement only 41 per cent were studying. *ST,* August 1963, p. 150.

42. B. A. Grushin and V. V. Chikin, "Problems of the Movement for Communist Labor," *Soviet Review,* Fall 1963, pp. 10-31, from *Istoriia SSSR,* May 1962. The survey, based on a questionnaire published in the paper and another sent to communist labor groups, included replies from 1,295 individuals and from 367 groups with 44,000 members, from all areas of the country and different branches of industry.

43. Cf. *Trud,* September 5, 1963, October 8, 1963, February 20, March 9, 1965; *ST,* February 1963, pp. 3-11, June 1963, pp. 3-9; *Dvizhenie za kommunisticheskii trud v promyshlennosti,* pp. 129-145; *Sbornik postanovlenii VTsSPS,* April-June 1963, pp. 16-21.

44. For example, *Izvestia,* July 19, 1963 and January 11, 1964, in *CDSP,* 15.30:29-30 (August 21, 1963), and 16.2:27 (February 5, 1964); Irina Chymanovsky, "Closer to the Ground," *Survey,* October 1963, pp. 157-165.

45. *Trud,* February 20, 27, 28, and March 9, 1965.

46. S. Strumilin, "Za kommunisticheskii trud" (For Communist Labor), *ST,* August 1963, pp. 29-33.

47. *Voprosy profsoyuznoi raboty,* pp. 225-230; *SP,* no. 1 (January 1964), pp. 44-45.

48. *ST,* October 1963, pp. 76-79; September 1963, pp. 47-54; Chairman Grishin of CCTU in report to Thirteenth Congress of Unions, *Trud,* October 29, 1963. See also Alec Nove, *The Soviet Economy* (New York, 1961), pp. 33-36, 166-170.

49. Cf. Richman, pp. 12-20.

CHAPTER X, WAGES AND HOURS IN INDUSTRIAL RELATIONS

1. *SSSR v tsifrakh v 1962 godu* (USSR in Figures in the Year 1962; Moscow, 1963), pp. 305-306.

2. *Trud,* October 29, 1963, July 14 and 16, 1964.

3. Ch. ii, pp. 39-45.

4. *Sbornik zakonodatelnykh aktov o trude* (Collection of Legislative Acts on Labor; Moscow, 1956), pp. 3-5.

5. *Ibid.*, pp. 157-158, translated in United States Bureau of

Labor Statistics, *Principal Current Soviet Labor Legislation* (Washington, 1962), pp. 84-85.

6. V. F. Maier, *Zarabotnaya plata v period perekhoda k kommunizmu* (Wages in the Period of Transition to Communism; Moscow, 1963), pp. 108-111; *Vneocherednoi XXI Syezd Kommunisticheskoi Partii Sovetskovo Soyuza, stenograficheskii otchet* (Extraordinary XXI Congress of the Communist Party of the Soviet Union, Stenographic Report; Moscow, 1959), vol. II, p. 525.

7. I. M. Levin, *Planirovanie i analiz truda i zarabotnoi platy na promyshlennom predpriatii* (Planning and Analysis of Labor and Wages in the Industrial Enterprise; Moscow, 1961), p. 156; Maier, pp. 141-144.

The new "heavy" ruble introduced on January 1, 1961, replaced the old ruble on the basis of 10 to 1.

8. See Janet Chapman, "The Minimum Wage in the USSR," *Problems of Communism*, September-October 1964, pp. 76-79; Maier, pp. 110-111, 168.

9. Maier, p. 136; *Spravochnik profsoyuznovo rabotnika* (Handbook of the Trade Union Worker; Moscow, 1960), pp. 279-280.

10. *Direktivy KPSS i Sovetskovo Pravitelstva po khozyaistvennym voprosam* (Directives of the Communist Party of the Soviet Union and the Soviet Government on Economic Questions; Moscow, 1958), vol. IV, pp. 649-668, 703-710.

11. G. A. Prudenskii, ed., *Voprosy truda v SSSR* (Questions of Labor in the USSR; Moscow, 1958), pp. 313-315; *ST*, May 1957, pp. 144-146.

12. Maier, pp. 136-138; *ST*, September 1958, pp. 141-142; *Pravda*, September 20, 1959.

13. *Trud*, July 14 and 16, 1964. The CCTU presidium then issued detailed instructions to the central committees, sovprofs, and local union committees on their participation with the State Committee on Labor and Wages and administrative agencies in working out necessary standards and materials and in preparing for the shift. *Ibid.*, July 25 and 26, 1964.

14. S. S. Karinskii, *Pravovoe regulirovanie zarabotnoi platy* (Legal Regulation of Wages; Moscow, 1963), pp. 62-63.

15. Letter of Dr. William A. Glaser, July 21, 1963.

16. *Trud*, November 1 and December 12, 1963. A long resolution adopted at the following plenary session of the CCTU spoke of the need to improve the wage system in this industry, along with many measures to increase production, including improvement of working and living conditions. *Sbornik postanovlenii VTsSPS*, October-December 1963 (Collection of Decisions of CCTU; Moscow, 1964), pp. 3-17.

17. E. I. Kapustin, ed., *Spravochnye materialy po trudu i zara-botnoi plate* (Handbook Materials on Labor and Wages; Moscow, 1960), pp. 72-73.

18. Karinskii, pp. 156-158.

19. V. A. Kuznetsov, *Zarabotnaya plata pri sotsializme i sover-shenstvovanie ee organizatsii na sovremennom etape* (Wages under Socialism and Perfection of their Organization in the Contemporary Stage; Saratov, 1961), pp. 47-48; *ST*, February 1961, pp. 29-30.

20. Maier, p. 148; M. Gardner Clark, "Comparative Wage Structures in the Steel Industry of the Soviet Union and Western Countries," *Proceedings of Thirteenth Annual Meeting of the Industrial Relations Research Association*, 1960, p. 268.

21. *Sbornik zakonodatelnykh aktov o trude*, 1956, pp. 3-4; *Postanovlenia plenumov VTsSPS*, 1954-1958 (Decisions of Plenums of CCTU; Moscow, 1961), pp. 40-41. For a detailed study of many of these questions see Walter Galenson, *Wage Structure and Administration in Soviet Industry*, Reprint no. 221, Institute of Industrial Relations, University of California, Berkeley, 1964, from *Internal Wage Structure*, Amsterdam, the Netherlands.

22. In some cases republic councils of ministers or sovnarkhozy have the right to set rates for enterprises or occupations where central rates have not been established, or to decide other details of wage and salary systems, in agreement with the State Committee on Labor and Wages and the unions. A decree of September 14, 1963, of the USSR Council of Ministers defined further the right of the State Committee to decide such questions on application of republic councils of ministers, sovnarkhozy, and ministries of the USSR. *ST*, December 1963, p. 143; Karinskii, pp. 144-146.

23. Many of the regulations and decisions are published or summarized in the publications of the State Committee on Labor and Wages: *Sotsialisticheskii Trud* and the monthly *Byulletin*.

24. *ST*, May 1957, pp. 144-146; A. G. Aganbegian and V. F. Maier, *Zarabotnaya plata v SSSR* (Wages in the USSR; Moscow, 1959), pp. 136-141; N. N. Makarov, *Tarifno-kvalifikatsionny spra-vochnik* (Tariff-Qualifications Handbook; Moscow, 1958).

25. Makarov, pp. 60-68; Maier, pp. 67-90, 192-194; E. I. Kapustin, ed., *Zarabotnaya plata v promyshlennosti SSSR i ee sovershen-stvovanie* (Wages in USSR Industry and their Improvement; Moscow, 1961), pp. 55-70. Important later discussions are found in E. I. Kapustin, *Kachestvo truda i zarabotnaya plata* (The Quality of Labor and Wages; Moscow, 1964), ch. iii, and R. A. Batkaev and V. I. Markov, *Differentsiatsia zarabotnoi platy v promyshlen-nosti SSSR* (Differentiation of Wages in USSR Industry; Moscow, 1964), ch. ii.

26. *ST*, September 1964, pp. 133-137; December 1964, pp. 51-55.

27. Kapustin, *Kachestvo truda*, pp. 289-295; Batkaev and Markov, pp. 91-118, 228.

28. Batkaev and Markov, p. 116.

29. Kapustin, *Kachestvo truda*, pp. 289-295.

30. Aganbegian and Maier, pp. 105-108; Kapustin, *Zarabotnaya plata*, p. 34.

31. The Central Bureau had issued by 1964 more than 300 collections of uniform and model norms of output or time, and normatives on machine servicing, numbers of workers, etc., for production and auxiliary workers in different industries. *ST*, May 1964, pp. 81-86. For typical lists of materials available, see *ST*, April 1964, pp. 156-157.

32. A regulation detailing the wide responsibilities of the commissions on wages and norm-setting of the factory, plant, and local and shop committees of the unions was issued by the CCTU on December 4, 1963. *Sbornik postanovlenii VTsSPS*, October-December 1963, pp. 37-41. A useful description of wage administration was published as a supplement to *Ekonomicheskaya Gazeta*, January 25, 1964, cited below as *Ekon. Gazeta*.

33. Makarov, pp. 84-89.

34. *ST*, October 1962, pp. 134-142; Karinskii, pp. 165-169. Contrary to general practice, in one big plant with a strong trade union the qualifications commissions were considered administrative agencies, without union representation. Control by the plant committee in giving its agreement was considered adequate check on the correctness of decisions.

35. A. Fastykovskii, *Profsoyuznomu aktivistu o trudovom zakonodatelstve* (For the Trade Union Activist on Labor Legislation; Moscow, 1962), pp. 184-185, 192-193.

36. Aganbegian and Maier, p. 154; Maier, pp. 160-161; *Ekon. Gazeta*, pp. 5-7. The reduction in coal mining was from 57 to 49 per cent, in chemical production from 59 to 36 per cent, in nonferrous metallurgy from 63 to 42 per cent. Others, where the amount was reduced but remained relatively high, were iron and steel, from 70 to 66 per cent, machine tool and metal fabrication, 68 to 57 per cent, and cotton textiles, 87 to 68 per cent.

37. *Ekon. Gazeta*, p. 5. Changes in the structure of the wage fund under the regional economic councils from 1957 to 1960 reflected these shifts in methods of pay. Of the total yearly wage funds, pay of piece workers, including premiums, decreased from 66 per cent to 55 per cent; time pay, including premiums, increased from 18 per cent to 28 per cent of the total. The rest covered vaca-

tion pay, overtime pay, and other special sums. D. N. Karpukhin, *Sootnoshenie rosta proizvoditelnosti truda i zarabotnoi platy* (Correlation of the Growth of Productivity of Labor and Wages; Moscow, 1963), p. 61.

38. Maier, pp. 162-163.

39. *Ibid.*, pp. 164-166, 228-233; *Ekon. Gazeta*, pp. 9-10.

40. S. Shkurko, "Vazhny eksperiment v premirovanii rabotnikov promyshlennosti" (Important Experiment in Premiums for Workers of Industry), *ST*, April 1964, pp. 47-55.

41. Kapustin, *Spravochnye materialy*, pp. 45-49; A. Galtsov, *Profsoyuznomu aktivu o tekhnicheskom normirovanii* (For the Trade Union Activist on Technical Norm-setting; Moscow, *BPA*, no. 40, 1962); *Sbornik postanovlenii presidiuma i sekretariata VTsSPS*, January-March 1961 (Collection of Decisions of Presidium and Secretariat of CCTU; Moscow, 1961), pp. 51-55.

42. An example of pamphlets on these questions put out by the CCTU to help local unions is L. Pogrebnoi, *Komissia zarabotnoi platy* (The Wage Commission; Moscow, *BPA*, no. 23, 1961); also Galtsov, esp. pp. 45-62.

43. *Trud*, November 20, 1962.

44. *ST*, February 1963, p. 72.

45. Galtsov, pp. 26-31.

46. Cf. Barry M. Richman, "Increasing Worker Productivity; How the Soviets Do It," *Personnel*, January-February 1964, pp. 11-14.

47. *ST*, February 1963, pp. 82-83, also pp. 68-72; March 1958, pp. 76, 80; April 1959, pp. 151-152.

48. *Ibid.*, May 1964, p. 82.

49. *Trud*, December 25, 1962.

50. *ST*, December 1964, pp. 121-125.

51. Batkaev and Markov, p. 198.

52. *ST*, May 1964, p. 86. Many journal articles call for strengthening of the departments of labor and wages and their personnel. *ST*, October 1962, pp. 107-117; November 1962, pp. 45-58; January 1963, pp. 17-42.

53. Kapustin, *Zarabotnaya plata*, pp. 116-134; *TZP*, September 1961, pp. 33-39; *ST*, March 1963, pp. 73-81.

54. Kapustin, *Zarabotnaya plata*, p. 134; *SP*, no. 24 (December 1962), pp. 9-11; *Sbornik postanovlenii VTsSPS*, April-June 1962, pp. 35-38.

55. Aganbegian and Maier, pp. 113, 117-123; Maier, p. 197.

56. *ST*, September 1958, pp. 141-143; May 1959, pp. 8-13; November 1959, pp. 130-131.

57. *TZP*, October 1959, pp. 40-44. Cf. also M. D. Gorshunov, ed., *Iz opyta perekhoda predpriatii na sokrashchenny rabochii den* (From the Experience of the Shift of Enterprises to the Shortened Work Day; Moscow, 1959).

58. Cf. criticisms by the CCTU of the Saratov unions' work, *Sbornik postanovlenii VTsSPS*, July-September 1961, pp. 79-84.

59. Maier, pp. 140-173; *Voprosy profsoyuznoi raboty* (Questions of Trade Union Work; Moscow, 1963), pp. 238-239; *Ekon. Gazeta*, January 25, 1964, supplement.

60. Maier, p. 173.

61. *Ibid.*, pp. 166-167.

62. *Trud*, October 29, 1963.

63. Maier, p. 168.

64. Karpukhin, p. 62. The relationships of average earnings compared with those of manual workers as 100, were as follows:

	1940	1950	1955	1959	1960
Engineering and Technical Workers	210	175	165	151	148
Office Employees	109	92	88	80	82

65. M. Mozhina, "Changes in the Distribution of USSR Industrial Workers by Amount of Wages," *Problems of Economics*, April 1962, pp. 21-26, from *TZP*, October 1961, pp. 18-25. See also Murray Yanowitch, "The Soviet Income Revolution," *Slavic Review*, 22:683-697 (December 1963).

66. Cf. Maier, pp. 215-237; E. Manevich, "Printsip lichnoi materialnoi zainteresovannosti i nekotorye voprosy zarabotnoi platy v SSSR" (The Principle of Individual Material Self Interest and Some Questions of Wages in the USSR), *VE*, January 1959, pp. 35-47.

67. I. Orlovskii, "Puti sovershenstvovania planirovania zarabotnoi platy v promyshlennosti SSSR" (Ways of Improvement of Wage Planning in Industry, USSR), *TZP*, June 1962, pp. 24-30; Maier, p. 243; *ST*, November 1962, pp. 128-132.

68. G. Prudenskii, "Work and Leisure," *USSR Illustrated Monthly*, January 1964, p. 2; "On the Rational Use of Off-Work Time of the Working People," *CDSP*, 15.33:3-7 (September 11, 1963), from *VE*, June 1963; A. Aganbegian, "The Working Day and Communism," *Problems of Economics*, October 1961, pp. 25-31, from *VE*, July 1961.

69. Maier, pp. 113-114. The further reductions promised for 1962 had been indefinitely postponed. The income tax, which is only mildly progressive, with a maximum rate of 13 per cent, has been only a minor source of government revenue. More important

is the transfer of profits from state enterprises, and most important, the "turnover tax," a sales tax levied chiefly on consumers' goods and materials used in them. In 1958 turnover taxes amounted to 42 per cent of the retail price, including tax, of goods sold to households in state and cooperative shops. Rates vary, with high rates on certain luxuries, but also on bread. Soviet theory holds that this levy is not a tax on consumers but a transfer to the state of income from state enterprises. Accordingly, the regressive tendency of sales taxes is not considered. See Abram Bergson, *The Economics of Soviet Planning* (New Haven, 1964), pp. 118-126; F. D. Holzman, *Soviet Taxation* (Cambridge, Mass., 1955).

70. Maier, p. 115; *Trud,* July 14, 1964. Such estimates include vacation pay as supplementary benefits, not wages. An American estimate from study of Soviet data found supplements to money income to amount to 30 per cent in 1954. Janet G. Chapman, *Real Wages in Soviet Russia since 1928* (Cambridge, Mass., 1963), pp. 140-141.

71. *CDSP,* 12.41:9-18 (November 9, 1960), from *Komsomolskaya Pravda,* October 7, 1960.

72. *USSR Illustrated Monthly,* May 1963, p. 46.

73. United States Congress, Joint Economic Committee, *Annual Economic Indicators for the USSR,* 88th Cong., 2d sess. (Washington, 1964), p. 66. At last, *Narodnoe khozyaistvo SSSR v 1964g.* (National Economy of the USSR in the Year 1964; Moscow, 1965), pp. 554-555, includes data on average earnings in major branches of the economy. Average annual money earnings of all wage and salary workers increased from 767 rubles in 1950 to 1082 in 1964. Earnings of wage workers in industry (mainly manufacturing and mining) were 1184 rubles in 1964.

74. Chapman, *Real Wages in Soviet Russia,* pp. 145, 171.

75. *Trud,* January 24, July 14, 1964.

76. A. Aganbegian, "Living Standards of the Working People in the USSR and the USA," *Problems of Economics,* March 1962, pp. 10-24, from *Mirovaya Ekonomia,* October 1961; Janet G. Chapman, "The Consumer in the Soviet Union and the United States," *Monthly Labor Review,* 86:11-13 (January 1963).

77. Chapman, *Real Wages in Soviet Russia,* p. 176.

78. Edmund Nash, in United States Congress, Joint Economic Committee, *Dimensions of Soviet Economic Power,* 87th Cong., 2d sess. (Washington, 1962), pp. 405-407.

79. For the most thorough discussion of these questions see Chapman, *Real Wages in Soviet Russia,* esp. ch. x; also her "Levels and Patterns of Consumption in the Soviet Union and the United

States," in Abram Bergson and Simon Kuznets, *Economic Trends in the Soviet Union* (Cambridge, Mass., 1963), pp. 249-270.

80. *Programma Kommunisticheskoi Partii Sovetskovo Soyuza* (Moscow, 1961), pp. 68, 92, 95.

CHAPTER XI, THE INDUSTRIAL RELATIONS SYSTEM:
PROBLEMS AND PROSPECTS

1. For some of the concepts and terminology used here I am indebted to the Inter-University Study of Labor Problems in Economic Development. See especially Clark Kerr, John T. Dunlop, Frederick H. Harbison, and Charles A. Myers, *Industrialism and Industrial Man* (Cambridge, Mass., 1960), and John T. Dunlop, *Industrial Relations Systems* (New York, 1958).

2. Alec Nove, "The Uses and Abuses of Kremlinology," *Survey*, January 1964, pp. 181-182.

3. Cf. Harold J. Berman, *Justice in the USSR* (Cambridge, Mass., 1963), pp. 374-375.

4. For example, A. G. Zdravomyslov and V. A. Yadov, "An Experiment in Concrete Research on Attitudes toward Labor," *CDSP*, 16.24:12-17 (July 8, 1964), from *Voprosy Filosofii*, April 1964. Several studies were summarized in *USSR Illustrated Monthly*, April 1963, pp. 4-5; May 1963, pp. 46-47; June 1963, pp. 48-49. See Lewis S. Feuer, "Problems and Unproblems in Soviet Social Theory," *Slavic Review*, 23:117-124 (March 1964); also *Survey*, July 1963, pp. 57-65, 123-127.

5. For proposals as to the State Committee cf. S. S. Karinskii, *Pravovoe regulirovanie zarabotnoi platy* (Legal Regulation of Wages; Moscow, 1963), p. 190.

Index

Accident rates, 119-120, 122, 127, 195

Administration, industrial, *see* Economic councils, regional; Management

Aid: financial, 70, 125, 164, 190, 368 n.; legal, 70, 205, 212

Aleksandrov, N. G., quoted, 16, 203; cited, 220

All-Union Central Council of Trade Unions, *see* Central Council of Trade Unions

All-Union Congress of Trade Unions, *see* Congress of Trade Unions

Anti-parasite laws, 5, 13, 313, 341 n.

Appeals, *see* Letters

Apprenticeship, 22

Arbitration, 53, 220, 230

Assignments, public, 112, 114. *See also* Volunteer

Attitudes, workers', 39, 155, 229, 268-269, 289, 301, 311, 313, 316, 321, 326-327, 329-330; toward unions, 1-2, 7, 56, 103-104, 139, 141-142, 155, 166, 168-172, 213, 223, 229, 312, 317-318, 329; effect of past on, 5, 152, 170, 221, 310, 316. *See also*; Trade unions, complaints against; Worker

Authoritarianism, 58-59, 149, 223-224, 227, 311, 312, 323, 325-326, 328

Automation, *see* Mechanization

Back pay, *see* Discharge

Berman, Harold J., quoted, 213

Boiter, Albert, cited, 370 n.

Budget, family, 305

Central Bureau of Industrial Normatives on Labor, 275, 282, 377 n.

Central Council of Trade Unions (CCTU), 8, 9, 40, 49, 58, 60, 65, 66, 72, 80-96; governmental functions, 50-52, 55-56, 57, 81, 84-86, 276; share of in governmental decrees, 55, 57, 58, 82-83, 139, 179, 182, 203, 217-218, 248, 257-258, 271, 273-274; criticisms of, 60-61, 95, 225; relations with government, 78, 80-86, 96, 220, 274-276, 278-279, 286, 291, 296, 319-321, 369 n.; election of council and officers, 78-79, 81, 93-94; make-up, 79, 110; functions, 80-81, 96, 320-321; plenary sessions, 81, 94-95; supervision of unions, 87-92, 95-96, 100-101, 118, 127-128, 135-138, 142, 143-144, 149, 165, 167, 182-183, 212, 222-223, 228, 244, 245, 254-255, 296, 320

Chapman, Janet G., cited, 4, 307

Children: institutions for, 19, 36, 101, 108, 115, 128, 131-132, 185, 191; post-educational provisions for, 20-21, 23, 24, 344 n.

Civil codes, 5

Class interests, 179, 328-330. *See also* Worker

Classless society, 4

Club houses, 132-134, 159

Collective contracts, 50, 52, 53, 55, 58, 87, 180, 182-194; negotiation of, 111, 184-186, 191, 193, 220; regional, 115, 192, 365 n.; contents of, 128, 132, 186-191, 193; enforcement, 140, 183, 191-192, 195-196, 199-200, 219

Collective farms, *see* Farms

Collective gardens, *see* Gardens

Communication, lines of, 80, 99, 103-104, 306, 310, 316

Communism, 4, 62, 73, 76, 177, 310, 317, 325